FREEDOM

was the cause that was championed by Menachem Begin and the men of the Irgun—freedom from the mighty British forces in Palestine. It was a cause so clear and compelling that it galvanized a dispossessed people to regain a homeland.

From the grim terror of a Soviet camp in Siberia, where Begin was imprisoned in 1940, to the dawn of the reclaimed Israel, the Irgun's own story of what happened, why, and how, is told by a man who played a dominant role in the shocking events of this era, a man whose passion for the truth has become legendary among his opponents as well as his followers.

THE REVOLT

THE REVOLT

MENACHEM BEGIN

Revised Edition

A DELL BOOK

Published by
DELL PUBLISHING CO., INC.
1 Dag Hammarskjold Plaza
New York, N.Y. 10017

Dell ® TM 681510, Dell Publishing Co., Inc.

ISBN: 0-440-17598-4

Reprinted by arrangement with
Nash Publishing Corporation /Steimatzky's Agency, Ltd.

Printed in the United States of America

First Dell printing—May 1978

Contents

AUTHOR'S ACKNOWLEDGMENT

I wish to express my gratitude to Mr. Ivan M. Greenberg, former editor of the London "Jewish Chronicle," who generously placed at my disposal his experience and wisdom and rendered invaluable help in the preparation of the English Edition—M.B.

Editor's Preface

This book has been written by the man who, probably more than any single one of his contemporaries, was responsible for the emergence of the sovereign Jewish State of Israel. It is a document of considerable historical and political importance. Amongst several profound truths which it teaches are lessons derived from that noblest process in the story of Man, the triumph of spirit and mind over seemingly hopeless odds.

Mr. Begin has been at pains to stress that this book is NOT a history of the Hebrew revolt. He has deliberately confined himself to matters with which he personally was intimately concerned. It is a book of *personal* memoirs. His deductions and his opinions he makes clearly as such; his recorded facts have been so faithfully and fairly set down that despite the critical light which some of them shed upon influential groups in the reborn State of Israel, not one of his facts has been successfully disputed since the book was published some time ago in Israel in the original Hebrew.

The appearance of an edition in English affords the serious-minded citizens of this country the first opportunity they have had to acquaint themselves with the truth about the Hebrew revolt against British Mandatory rule in Palestine. Clearly, if democracy is to work, the people of a nation upon whom rests ultimate responsibility must at least have the opportunity of studying both sides of any controversy in which their nation becomes involved. Yet, this is precisely what did *not* happen in the case of the Hebrew revolt, more especially during those later critical years from the summer of 1946 to the survival of the State of Israel in the face of Arab military aggression in 1948-49.

A kind of conspiracy of silence, inspired by diverse and often irrelevant motives, barred all effective publication in the United Kingdom of the case of the Jewish "rebels," who were nevertheless so serious a challenge to British authority that they were able in a short while to create conditions which compelled Britain to withdraw her regime from Palestine. Nor was ignorance concerning the "rebels" and their case confined to the general British public; the debates in Parliament at the time bore melancholy witness to its prevalence even in high political circles. The withholding of such knowledge from a democratic nation points to a very dangerous breach in the always insecure defences of democratic liberty.

Political leaders have complained that a special responsibility rested upon those Jews in Britain who had opportunities for knowing about these things and whose duty it was to disseminate this knowledge so far as lay in their power. It is not fair, however, entirely to blame even those Jews who had the means to correct the public's ignorance, at least to a limited extent, and who shrank from this more difficult exercise in patriotism. They were profoundly embarrassed; and to sustain them they had neither the vision nor the courage of their brothers in Palestine who were actually fighting for the future of Jews everywhere.

This book was originally written in Hebrew, a highly inflected and compact language. To bring the English version within the compass of a single manageable volume, considerable condensation has been required. In the actual translation, Mr. Samuel Katz, working with the author, cut out a good deal of matter of a more limited and local interest. It may be that the result has caused local politics to seem even more complex and peculiar than they are. In the editing, further reductions have had to be made; but the endeavour has been to do this so as not to unbalance the message or the emphasis or in any way to impair the book's essential value.

Menachem Begin is probably one of the best known personalities in Israel, amongst his political opponents no less than amongst his followers in the Freedom Party which he leads in the Israel Parliament. Politically, he is best described as a patriotic Jew with a taste for practical, common-sense policy. Passionately devoted to the liberal ideas of individual freedom and justice, Mr. Begin is repelled by "the new idolatry," by political systems of both Right and Left which, in spite of their sugary promises, inevitably lead to the crushing of the individual beneath the ruthless, and in practice irresponsible, machinery of the deified State.

The author's modesty conceals in these Memoirs the decisive part which he himself played in the success of the struggle he led, the unfailing courage with which he accepted and endured almost unbearable responsibility, and the vital importance of the absolute trust which his fortitude, wisdom, and high moral principles inspired throughout the Irgun ranks and amongst all its supporters.

Historical irony chose one of the gentlest, kindest, most selfless of men to lead a rebellion against stupendous odds, and to dominate the forces which he led by the sheer strength of his moral influence. That he should have been cast by his opponents in the role of an ogre of all iniquities is merely another example of human stupidity, "with which," as Schiller so truly wrote, "the gods themselves struggle in vain."

Ivan M. Greenberg,
London
March, 1951

Preface to the Revised Edition

Early in the morning of the 18th of May 1977, 29 years after the renewal of our independence, it became clear that the party that had ruled uninterruptedly in Israel was now relegated to the opposition benches by the decision of the people. The Likud finally won a mandate from the people to form a new Coalition Government.

This was a momentous change for Israel. It took place 29 years after the liberation of our people and 46 years after the Seventeenth Zionist Congress (when Mapai—the Labour party—won the status of the first party). It is enough to note the passage of time—two generations—in order to understand the significance of the change brought about by the democratic decision of hundreds of thousands of free citizens of Israel. It is in this context that, as Prime Minister of Israel, I am writing a Preface to the Revised Edition of *The Revolt*.

A well-known journalist recently asked me the following question: "How does it feel to be in power?" I answered him in accordance with the facts: "I don't use power; in this task there is only one instrument I am using: moral influence." But there is great responsibility, and I can even add, grave responsibility. And I will continue to do my best, limited as it is, to bear it.

My colleagues and I are called upon to care for the future of the Jewish people, for the safety of the Jewish State, and for the security and the lives and the liberty of our children. How great and grave is such responsibility!

During the years of my long service in Parliamentary opposition and the three years of my participation in the Government of National Unity (1967-1970), I would say, to friend and opponent alike, that whatever position I may hold, it will never be comparable to the national and human importance of what my friends and I did in the underground during our fight for the liberation of our people. Some observers interpreted this statement as a form of self-consolation. "He has given up hope," they used to say, "that one day he may be elected as a member of the Government or as the Minister to head it; and that is why he contends that what was done in the past is more important than what may be done in the future." Those observers were wrong. My comments were correct. For the best proof is that I expressed that belief while serving as a Minister, not without some influence in the Cabinet.

Now my task is that of Prime Minister. When these lines appear in print I shall have been in office for some months. Now I am really in a position to make the comparison between the time when I was commander of the Irgun Zvai Leumi, fighting for the liberty and independence (and indeed the survival) of our people, with the period in which I now head the Government of Israel.

In the full recognition of the facts I say unhesitatingly: with all the grave responsibility that goes with this post in the State of Israel, it was a higher task to lead the fighting patriots in that unequal struggle, under the heaviest odds possible, of the few against the many.

Why do I still feel this way? The answer is clear. When a man fights for freedom with an incessant risk of his life, he identifies himself completely with the very essence of liberty. Such identification seldom comes more than once in a lifetime.

It is in a spirit of continued dedication to such a meaning of liberty that I present to the reader, whether Jew or Gentile, the new edition of *The Revolt*.

M. Begin

October 1977   Office of the Prime Minister

From the
Perspective of a Generation

A new generation has arisen since the events described in this book took place. The men of this generation, who were born in the forties, took part in the Six-Day War, finished their studies or their military service, established families, and even provided us with grandchildren. Certainly, there were historical deeds and events in the era of the sons as well. Have they confirmed or contradicted the assumptions and aspirations of the fathers? Let us examine. In comparative study we shall find the answer.

The book begins with a description of the author's experience in Stalin's Russia. The chapter was published in the days when Lavrenti Beria was the right-hand, or left-hand man of Joseph Vissarionovich. Not all the readers accepted the concise story as truthful. Communists said it was not at all possible that there should be such treatment of men in the Soviet Union. They expressed their absolute belief in socialist justice and its humane ways. With a measure of forgiveness, the admirers of the Soviet regime claimed that perhaps personal suffering had motivated me to lend a hand to anti-Soviet propaganda.

Stalin died. Beria was executed. Khrushchev spoke at the 20th Congress of the Soviet Communist Party. Solzhenitzin described one day, of the many, in the life of Denisovitch. After 23 years, there is no longer anyone, not even a Communist, who will doubt the truth of the tale about nights of interrogation and concentration camps in the Communist state. Of course truth is an absolute value. It needs not the confirmation of those who rebel against it. However, if those who deny it come to admit it, there is proof that its total triumph is inevitable.

The first chapter ends with the tale about Garin. This man was a Communist since his youth. He took part in the civil war and still remembered Lenin and Trotsky. Through loyal service to the Soviet regime, he reached a high position. He was assistant editor of "Pravda." When I met him, however, he was a broken man, a tormented prisoner, an enemy of the people, a degraded and beaten Jew. His spiritual agonies were immeasurable; they were certainly more acute than his bodily pains. When we were together below the deck of the prison, or slave ship, he asked me to sing for him "To Return"; that is the song Hatikvah, which he had heard in his youth, in Odessa. How interesting that he did not recall the name of the song. He knew nothing of its composer. Nevertheless, embedded in his memory for more than thirty years were the first words of the line: "To return to the land of our forefathers."

Another thirty years have passed. Garin is no longer alone in his hope and prayer. Tens of thousands of Jews in the Soviet Union sing and call out: "To return to the land of our fathers." This is a mighty, a wondrous historical phenomenon. A great miracle has taken place. Communism has been defeated not by force but by an ideal. Zionism is the idea which triumphed over Communist education. Since I came, or returned, to Eretz Israel, I have not ceased to express hope, or faith, that there would be a return to Zion from Russia as well. It has come.

In the chapter entitled: "We Fight, Therefore We Are," we find the following: "One cannot say that those who shaped British Middle Eastern Policy at that time didn't want to save the Jews. It would be more correct to say that they eagerly wanted the Jews not to be saved." I wrote these harsh words on the basis of study and analysis of the facts. In the forties and fifties we had no documents to confirm our serious accusation. The day came, however, when the truth, even the most awful truth, was vindicated with the aid of historical documents. My generation read these shocking papers by chance. It is likely that many of them would never have even been heard of, had Britain not changed its custom in regard to classified documents. It had been the custom in London that after fifty years, the government archives, locked away from the public, would be opened. A few years ago, the British government decided to shorten the period of secrecy. At the beginning of 1972, the minutes of cabinet meetings in the early forties were made public. Now we know.

The International Red Cross had planned, according to one of these documents, to transfer forty thousand Jews from Hungary to Turkey, with one clear intention that they would continue on to Eretz Israel. This intention gave the British no rest. They contacted Red Cross headquarters and protested against this plan, with the argument that the humanitarian organization had no right to implement it without the permission of the British government. The Red Cross plan dropped. Another forty thousand Hungarian Jews were sent to the gas chambers, because Britain opposed their transfer to Turkey lest they come to the Land of Israel from there.

Another document, revealed a number of years ago, tells of the Jews of France and Rumania. I discovered it in a book which I feel should be in every Jewish home, and in the home of every man of good will. I refer to Arthur Morse's study, "White Six Million Died." I am certain that the author, a Christian of good will, will not object to my quoting this one document exactly as it was written: "We have received the views of the Foreign Office on the proposal of the U.S. Treasury to license the remittance to Switzerland of 25,000 dollars as a preliminary installment, to be expended on the rescue of Jews from France and Rumania. The Foreign Office is concerned with the difficulties of disposing of a considerable number of Jews, should they be rescued." (December, 1943.)

There is no doubt to the meaning of this order, nor are there two ways of interpreting it. The British Foreign Office is not concerned with the problem of what to do in order to save a substantial number of Jews, but what to do with them should they be rescued.

It is possible to present additional documents discovered in the generation of the sons. But there is no need to do so. The two official documents—of whose existence we were unaware twenty, thirty years ago, are sufficient to demonstrate that the fathers did not err in their assumptions, nor in their conclusions. An entire nation, six million men, women and children, sank into an abyss, in a planned campaign of annihilation which lasted five whole years, because the Germans decided to destroy it, and the British—and others —decided not to rescue it.

From the holocaust to redemption.

The book describes the battles for Jerusalem, the Old and the New. When the City Between the Walls fell, in Iyar 5708 (1948), the Irgun Zvai Leumi broadcast this message:

". . . There was no surrender in the Old City, but a battle waged with supreme courage which returns us to the days of yore of our people, when its sons stood on the Temple Mount, and together with it went up heavenwards in flames. This fight and this courage strengthen our hearts on this bitter day; they give us the confidence that the liberators of Judea and the redeemers of Israel shall yet return to the Temple Mount, and shall yet raise our banner atop the Tower of David."

Nineteen years later, in Iyar 5727 (June 1967), they did return and raise the banner. This time we were careful that there should be no repetition of an outside decision of cease-fire, which prevented the liberation of the captured city. As dawn broke on Wednesday, 28 Iyar (June 7th, 1967), I first grasped the news of the Security Council's resolution to call upon both sides to immediately cease fire. The resolution contained a clause which forbade, upon the cease-fire taking effect, any movement of military forces. In the evening of the preceding day it had been summed up, despite conflicting opinions, that our troops would capture the

hills surrounding Jerusalem, encircle it from every
side, and wait for the besieged enemy to surrender and
hoist a white flag. The news from New York made the
heart tremble. Would a cease-fire once again take effect, and would we be left outside the wall, as in the
summer of 1948?

I got in touch with my colleague, the Defense Minister, Moshe Dayan, relayed to him the Security Council resolution, and suggested that we undertake steps
towards altering the decision of the previous night, so
that our soldiers could be ordered to break into the Old
City without delay. We agreed that I would immediately turn to the Prime Minister, Levi Eshkol, blessed be
his memory, and seek his consent to this change. I
awoke the Prime Minister and reported the developments to him. He agreed that we mustn't wait any
longer, and that orders should be given to advance
units on the Jerusalem front to storm into the Old
City. The order was given. The decisive battle was
brief. Between nine and ten in the morning our para-
troopers ascended the Temple Mount.

The wall of the Old City is not the boundary of
Jerusalem. This we claimed again and again for many
years. After the Six-Day War the entire nation of Israel
claimed the same. True has been our faith.

The campaign for Jerusalem in 1948 involved the
battle at Dir Yassin. How many lies have been published about this battle, from then until today, by Jews
and non-Jews?

But the truth cannot be suppressed. On March 16th
1969, the Foreign Ministry of the State of Israel published a booklet, "Background Pages," dedicated to
the capture of Dir Yassin. We quote the principal par-
agraphs:

The aim of the Arab onslaught was bluntly proclaimed by Azzam Pasha, Secretary-General of the
Arab League. When the full-scale invasion of Israel's
territory by the armies of the Arab States began on
15 May, 1948, he did not hesitate to declare: "This
will be a war of extermination and a momentous mas-

sacre, which will be spoken of like the Mongolian massacres and the Crusades."

It was no mere fantasy, no impetuously expressed but evanescent ambition. Azzam Pasha and the Arabs meant it. They have meant it ever since. The attack on Jerusalem, where a hundred and fifty thousand Jewish civilians were fighting for their lives, assumed many forms. Frontally, four-fifths of the part of the city where the Jews lived was being battered by the artillery and armoured cars of the British-led Arab Legion of Jordan, and bitter street fighting was in progress. Units of the same force were attempting to cut the only highway linking Jerusalem with Tel Aviv and the outside world. It had cut the pipeline upon which the defenders depended for water. Palestinian Arab contingents, stiffened by men of the regular Iraqi army, had seized vantage points overlooking the Jerusalem road, and from them were firing on trucks that tried to reach the beleaguered city with vital foodstuffs and supplies. Dir Yassin, like the strategic hill and village of Castel, was one of these vantage points.

In fact, the two villages were interconnected militarily, reinforcements passing from Dir Yassin to Castel during the fierce engagement for that hill. Hagana, the Jewish defence formation, after heavy uphill fighting in which it lost many men, took the strongly fortified height. Dir Yassin had been similarly fortified, its stone dwellings transformed into bastions. As its share in the battle for Jerusalem's approaches, the second—and smaller—Jewish paramilitary force, the Irgun Zvai Leumi (known as "Etzel" or "Irgun") decided to assault Dir Yassin. It detailed one hundred of its number for the purpose.

In those days, before Israel became a State, the Jewish defenders had no national army of unified command. They were poorly equipped, with light weapons, sparse medical supplies, and practically no communications equipment. The company that assaulted Dir Yassin was typical. Some of its men had rifles, some had pistols, a few had Sten guns, and the heaviest weapon in their possession was a Bren light machinegun. For close fighting, they had hand-grenades; for the injured, two sulphur tablets per man and a personal bandage. Some of them had never been in battle before; this was their first experience under fire.

A small open truck accompanied them, fitted with a loud-speaker. In the early dawn-light of 10th April, 1948, it was driven close to the village entrance, and a warning was broadcast in Arabic to civilian, non-combatant inhabitants, to withdraw from the danger zone, as an attack was imminent. Everyone who was left would be guaranteed safe passage—if not, it would be his or her own responsibility. Some two hundred villagers did come out, and took shelter on the lower slopes of the hill on which Dir Yassin was perched. None of them, during or after the fighting, were hurt or molested in the slightest, and all were afterwards transported to the fringe of the Arab-held quarter of East Jerusalem, and there released.

The actual battle of Dir Yassin began with a typical Arab subterfuge which has been often rehearsed since. The Palestinian Arab and Iraqi garrison hung out white flags from houses nearest the village entrance. When the advance party of the Irgun unit advanced towards the entrance, it was met by a hail of fire. One of the first to be hit was its commander. Fierce house-to-house fighting followed. Midway, the Irgunists ran out of ammunition, but went on as best they could, with the weapons and equipment found in the first houses to fall into their hands. Most of the stone buildings were defended hotly, and were captured only after grenades were lobbed through their windows. Some of the garrison, as the battle neared its close, attempted to escape in women's dress. When approached, they opened fire. They were discovered to be wearing Iraqi military uniforms under the disguise.

When the fighting ended, the Irgun unit found that it had sustained forty-one casualties, four of them fatal. In the captured houses they were horror-stricken to find that, side by side with those combatant Palestinians and Iraqis, were the bodies of women and children.

21

e luckless villagers had trusted the Arab
beat off the attack, or had been prevented
fro   ving the village with the others when the opportunity was given, before the fighting began, or perhaps had been afraid to go; whatever the reason, they
were the innocent victims of a cruel war, and the responsibility for their deaths rests squarely upon the
Arab soldiers, whose duty it was—under any rule of
war—to evacuate them the moment that they turned
Dir Yassin into a fortress, long before the battle for the
village began. Total Arab casualties, including soldiers
and civilians, were counted after the fighting at two
hundred. The Irgun unit, with its limited medical supplies, did what it could to tend its own and the village's wounded, before taking them to hospitals in
Jerusalem.

This is the statement of Yunes Ahmad Assad, a
prominent inhabitant of Dir Yassin who survived the
battle:

"The Jews never intended to hurt the population of
the village, but were forced to do so, after they met
enemy fire from the population which killed the Irgun
commander."

It was published in the Jordanian daily "Al Urdun"
of 9 April, 1955. Its only inaccuracy is in respect of
the Irgun commander: Assad undoubtedly saw him
fall in the attack, but he survived.

That the attackers, even at the cost of losing the surprise effect, and, as is evident at the risk of avoidable
casualties, had warned the inhabitants before the attack, is admitted in a pamphlet issued by the Secretar-
iat-General of the Arab League, entitled "Israel's Aggression." On page 10 we find this:

On the night of 9 April, 1948, the peaceful Arab
village of Dir Yassin, in the suburbs of Jerusalem, was
surprised by loud-speakers calling upon the inhabitants
of the village to evacuate it immediately."

In the chapter "Civil War—Never," the "Altalena"
affair is related. About twenty years after the tragedy,
one of the people closest to Mr. Ben Gurion came to

me and told me, on his own initiative, the following words: "We have arrived at the conclusion that in the Altalena matter Ben Gurion was misled."

In the summer of 1971, the internal debate on dissidence, the "season" and Altalena, broke out, or was renewed. It has, of course, not yet ended. It demonstrated beyond all doubt that there is a contradiction which cannot be bridged between the public statements of Mr. Ben Gurion and Mr. Galili. Mr. Galili writes: "I reported to the Prime Minister and Defence Minister, at every stage, both orally and in writing, fully, on the meetings with the heads of the Irgun Zvai Leumi, including the night meeting, the conversation on the morrow, and subsequent meetings."

"The night meeting" is the discussion at Irgun headquarters, on June 14, 1948, in which we relayed to the representatives of the Provisional Government, Mr. Galili and Mr. Eshkol, *all* the details of the ship, its means, and its arms. That night, four days before the Altalena approached the shores of Eretz Israel, we announced that the arrival of the ship depended on the decision of the government. The next morning, at ten o'clock, Mr. Galili, the authorized representative of the Defence Minister, relayed to me the following announcement: "We have decided that the Altalena is to come, and with all possible speed." Thus was it confirmed for the first time that the Irgun, which had been accused for an entire generation of bringing the Altalena, in order to seize control of the government, had prepared its rebellion with the knowledge, consent, and even the command, of the Provisional Government. . . .

Counter to Mr. Galili, Mr. Ben Gurion, who was then Prime Minister and Defence Minister, reasserts that he knew nothing of the Altalena's arrival until June 19, 1948. What happened then during those four fateful days? In whose name did the authorized representative of the Defence Minister make the positive statement following that night meeting? But if he had been empowered by the Prime Minister to relay to me this decision, for the Altalena to come with all possible speed, how can Mr. Ben Gurion claim that he heard of the arms ship only four whole day later?

The required replies have not yet been given to these questions. It should be remembered, however, that I could not present the questions themselves when this book was written. The two statements, whose contradiction is obvious to all, had not yet been made. Thus does the truth march on towards its complete vindication and triumph.

On Motzoei Shabat, May 15, 1948, I broadcast, directly for the first time, to the small, courageous, liberated fighting nation. These are some of the words I spoke:

"The homeland is historically and geographically an entity. Whoever fails to recognize our right to the entire homeland, does not recognize our right to any of its territories. We shall never yield our natural and eternal right. We shall bear the vision of a full liberation. We shall bear the vision of ultimate redemption, and we shall bring it into realisation. When the day arrives, we shall materialize it. This is an historical rule: a line passing through, or drawn by, someone, as a separation between a Nation's state and a People's country—such an artificial line must disappear."

So it happened between June 5th and June 11th, 1967. Since then, it is our duty, fathers and sons, to see to it that the artificial line which disappeared never returns. We must not yield our natural and eternal right.

1972   M. Begin

Introduction

I have written this book primarily for my own people, lest the Jew forget again—as he so disastrously forgot in the past—this simple truth: that there are things more precious than life, and more horrible than death.

But I have written this book also for Gentiles, lest they be unwilling to realise, or all too ready to overlook, the fact that out of blood and fire and tears and ashes a new specimen of human being was born, a specimen completely unknown to the world for over eighteen hundred years, "the Fighting Jew." That Jew, whom the world considered dead and buried never to rise again, has arisen. For he has learned that "simple truth" of life and death, and he will never again go down to the sides of the pit and vanish from the earth.

Amongst my Gentile readers I wish to address a special message to the British reader. He will read in the following pages some harsh words about some of his rulers, their policies, their agents; and he may feel that some of these strictures fall gratuitously upon himself as citizen voter in a democratic State. It would not be surprising, therefore, if he should feel himself prejudiced both against the author and the book. After all, for years the author fought against the British authorities. He was described by British newspapers, by members of both Houses of Parliament, by Ministers of State, by generals, admirals, bishops, lawyers, and all the other *dramatis personae* who "give the cues for cheers and boos" to the ordinary citizen—as "Terrorist Number One" in Eretz Israel, then called Palestine and ruled by the British government.

I will not offend my British readers' ears with a repetition of all the other offensive names which were used by way of enlightening him concerning the author of this book, during the years of the struggle. He can, if he so desires, take his pick from the rich international vocabulary of name-calling. It is only natural, therefore, that many English readers will ask quite sincerely: What can such a man have to tell us; what message can come from him except a message of hate?

Let us try, without fear, favour, or prejudice, to understand the meaning of the awful word "hate" in this connection. You may ask me: Was there hate in our actions, in our revolt against British rule of our country; and is that emotion expressed in this book written by the man who bore the burden of responsibility and subsequently wrote about the facts of the revolt?

To such a question the sincere answer is "Yes."

But was it hatred of the British people as such? The sincere answer is "No."

It is axiomatic that those who fight have to hate—something or somebody. And we fought. We had to hate first and foremost, the horrifying, age-old, inexcusable utter *defencelessness* of our Jewish people, wandering through millennia, through a cruel world, to the majority of whose inhabitants the defencelessness of the Jews was a standing invitation to massacre them. We had to hate the humiliating disgrace of the homelessness of our people. We had to hate—as any nation worthy of the name must and always will hate—the rule of the foreigner, rule, unjust and unjustifiable *per se*, foreign rule in the land of our ancestors, in our own country. We had to hate the barring of the gates of our own country to our own brethren, trampled and bleeding and crying out for help in a world morally deaf.

And, naturally, we had to hate all those who, equipped with modern arms and with the ancient machinery of the gallows, barred the way of our people to physical salvation, denied them the means of individual defence, frustrated their efforts for national independence, and ruthlessly withstood their attempts to regain their national honour and restore their self-respect.

Who will condemn the hatred of evil that springs

from the love of what is good and just? Such hatred has been the driving force of progress in the world's history—"not peace but a sword" in the cause of mankind's advancement. And in our case, such hate has been nothing more and nothing less than a manifestation of that highest human feeling: love. For if you love Freedom, you must hate Slavery; if you love your people, you cannot but hate the enemies that compass their destruction; if you love your country, you cannot but hate those who seek to annex it. Simply put: if you love your mother, would you not hate the man who sought to kill her: would you not hate him and fight him at the cost, if needs be, of your own life?

This is a fundamental human question in the violent and stormy world of today. Let every decent man search his soul and decently answer. Because ultimately the hope of every people lies in the readiness of its sons to stake their lives "for their mothers,"—for freedom which man loves, against serfdom which man hates and should hate in the name of his love.

The author has not written these preliminary lines in order to make harsh words less galling and bitter truths more palatable. He has written them, as he has written the whole of this book, for the sake of truth. And truth compels him to ask himself in the presence of his readers, Gentile readers and hostile readers, this testing question: If ever again your people should find themselves in a position like that in which they were when you had to "go underground," to fight, to become a hunted "rebel"—in such circumstances would you again do what you did then?

The answer is definitely: "Yes."

M.B.

Chapter 1

The Gateway to Freedom

The night of the First of April, 1941. In the old building called "Lukishki" in Wilno, the stillness peculiar to the institutions of human suffering—hospitals and prisons—was broken. The doors of the cells opened, amid a squeaking and groaning of locks and bolts and hinges. Two by two, the inmates, shaven-headed and pallid, came out, and were directed to a small table in the centre of the long dark corridor. Behind the table sat two silent men, and on it lay a pile of scraps of paper which could have been laundry-chits or demands from the municipal tax department.

That night I was among the people called out to the table in the corridor of Lukishki. I was one of many, of thousands and scores of thousands engulfed in the sea of destruction and sorrow which had drenched Europe, from west to east, when the Nazis let loose their drive towards world-domination and the destruction of the Jewish people. I approached the table together with my cell-comrades—a variety of strange people whom only the fantastic acrobatics of events could have brought together under one roof. When my turn came I proclaimed for the hundredth time that my name was Menahem Wolfovitch Begin. The men behind the table did not look at me. One of them searched through the pile of papers, found what he was after and passed it to his colleague, who read out aloud:

"The Special Advisory Commission to the People's Commissariat for Internal Affairs finds Menahem Wolfovitch Begin to be a dangerous element in society and decrees that he be imprisoned in a correctional labour-camp for a period of eight years."

Involuntarily I jerked out "April First." The man holding the paper shot a look at me, but said politely: "Please sign."

I signed as many others did, apathetically. Eight years? A concentration camp somewhere in the distant north? It was all so distant, so vague. Meanwhile you had to sign the "receipt." And you signed. As you would the laundryman's chit or the demand from the municipal tax department.

This then was the climax of a period of short days and long nights during which I had been accused, with absolute solemnity, of being one of the important helpers, practically an agent, of Great Britain.

The days had been spent in excursions—twofold excursions: marching to and fro from wall to wall or from window to door; and mental excursions into the past and into the unknown future. Such excursions make the prisoner forget his physical surroundings and help him formulate the nebulous reality of his desires. They shorten his days of imprisonment to a far greater degree than can be imagined by those who have never experienced the joys of the prison-cell. Prison days are like a passing dream. They are probably the most ordered days imaginable. They are filled with expectation. From the morning hooter at daybreak to the setting of the sun the prisoner is forever waiting for something. The feeling of expectation is powerful, overwhelming, just because it is directed towards the simplest, the most primitive things in a man's life, beginning with an unsatisfying meal and ending with the removal of the sanitary pail from the cell. Of unsatisfying meals we had three every day. And, the less satisfying they were, the stronger was the longing for them. The pail was removed twice a day, and even that was an event. If you add the mental excursions, which only those incapable of thinking could not enjoy, you have a complete picture of the daylight hours in prison. No, they are not the days you picture to yourself when you are free: days without beginning or end. They are very brief days: like a passing dream.

The nights are completely different. They are long, very long. I do not mean the nights when they let you sleep: sleep in prison, whether on a narrow iron bed or a broad stone floor, is deep and very peaceful. But there are also sleepless nights in prison. The sleepless nights in Lukishki lengthened the imprisonment of some, and shortened the "days" of others. . . . They were the nights of debate between interrogators and interrogated. They always began an hour or two after the prisoner had fallen asleep. But he never knew when or how they would end . . .

In the course of these endless nights of interrogation I took part in wide-ranging debates on the Russian Revolution, on Britain and Zionism, on Herzl[1] and Jabotinsky,[2] on Weizmann's[3] meetings with Mussolini, on the Russian commune and the Jewish kibbutz, on Zionist Youth movements, on Marx and Engels, Bukharin and Stalin, on capitalism, socialism, and communism, on the mystery of life and of death, on theism and science, on the Spanish Civil War and the French Popular Front, on idealistic theory, and materialistic philosophy. At times it was much more of a free discussion than an interrogation.

My interrogator was young, tall and handsome, and almost polite in his manner. He no more doubted my "guilt" than I that his accusations were nonsense. Hence there was no need for proofs or witnesses. The facts, which I did not dream of denying, were enough. From my early youth I had been taught by my father— who, as I was later told, went to his death at Nazi hands voicing the liturgic declaration of faith in God and singing the Hebrew national anthem, "Hatikvah"

[1] Dr. Theodor Herzl (1860-1904), founder of the modern Jewish National Movement called Zionism.
[2] Vladimir Jabotinsky (1880-1940), the Jewish nationalist leader whose teachings founded the Irgun Zvai Leumi.
[3] Dr. Chaim Weizmann, President of the Zionist Organisation almost continuously from 1919 to 1946, and first President of the State of Israel.

—that we Jews were to return to Eretz Israel.[1] Not to
"go" or "travel" or "come"—but to *return*. That was
the great difference, and it was all-embracing.

When I grew up I became, as a student, active in
Betar. Betar was the popular pioneering youth movement, into which Vladimir Jabotinsky, the greatest
Jewish personality of our era after Herzl, had poured
his love and intellectual genius. In the year before the
outbreak of war I had become the head of the movement in Poland, a country with millions of poverty-
stricken Jews, persecuted, dreaming of Zion. My friends
and I laboured to educate a generation which should be
prepared not only to toil for the rebuilding of a Jewish
State, but also to fight for it, suffer for it and, if needs
be, die for it. While we were engaged in educating the
youth and organizing their repatriation to Eretz Israel
—without British permits—there arose in Eretz Israel,
as a herald of Jewish national re-birth, the first beginning of Hebrew power: the Irgun Zvai Leumi,[2] with its
great and mysterious commander, David Raziel, and his
lieutenant, Abraham Stern, serious, quiet and convincing.

Here began the first counter-attacks against those
who sought our destruction, and, for that purpose, the
production of the first Jewish arms. Gathering weapons,

[1] "Eretz Israel," literally the "Land of Israel," has been regarded since Biblical times as the motherland of the Children
of Israel. It has always comprised what came subsequently to
be called Palestine on both sides of the river Jordan, that is
to say not only Western Palestine, but also the territory formerly occupied by three of the twelve Hebrew tribes, Manas-
seh, Gad, and Reuben.

[2] The three Hebrew words, Irgun Zvai Leumi, mean National Military Organisation. The Irgun was called into existence by Vladimir Jabotinsky—statesman, orator, poet, and
soldier—after Herzl, the greatest Jewish political leader of
modern times. With prophetic accuracy he foretold that the
Jewish people would never achieve national independence
unless they were prepared to fight for it. Unable to convince
the Zionist leadership in the inter-war period of the vital
necessity for a Jewish army, Jabotinsky was compelled to
tackle the job himself, and so created the Irgun Zvai Leumi.

training instructors, breaking the policy of 'self-restraint', which timid Jewish leaders had adopted in the face of Arab attacks, forcing the barred gates of the country—to me and to many thousands of young people all this was a work of sublime justice. To help in these undertakings was a great privilege and a solemn duty—a duty to our country of which others threatened to rob us; a duty to our people which, as we felt and proclaimed, was on the very edge of the abyss of destruction. We tried to do our duty.

My genial questioner at Lukishki saw our work in an entirely different light. His basic assumption was astounding nonsense, but the dialectic super-structure he built up on this foundation was nearly perfect. During those long nights of interrogation the young officer told me:

"Zionism in all its forms is a farce and a deception, a puppet show. It's not true that you aim to set up a Jewish State in Palestine, or that you intend to bring millions of Jews there. Both these aims are utterly impracticable and the Zionist leaders are perfectly well aware of it. This talk of a 'State' conceals the true purpose of Zionism—which is to divert the Jewish youth from the ranks of the revolution in Europe and put them at the disposal of British Imperialism in the Middle East. That's the kernel of Zionism. All the rest is an artificial shell, deliberately made to deceive. As for you, Menahem Wolfovitch, either you know the truth and are one of the deliberate deceivers serving Great Britain and the international bourgeoisie—or you're one of the dupes helping to divert the masses from their duty of fighting here—yes, here—against exploitation. In either case your guilt is heavy indeed."

I tried to show the error of his contentions, to explain that the Jewish urge to return to Eretz Israel was very deep and very real. How could it be a mere camouflage if it had been maintained by Jews for almost two thousand years, from generation to generation, going back centuries before capitalism and socialism had been dreamt of? How could Zionism be nothing but a farce when its foundations lay in the spiritual connection between the Jew and Eretz Israel, and had expressed itself in the prayers and individual self-sacrifice of millions? In our own times had not thousands given up wealth and comfort, university studies, brilliant careers, in order to become common labourers in Eretz Israel?

My efforts were in vain. My arguments not only failed to convince him, but even recoiled on me. He would reply:

"What you say only supports our view. Of course there was a sentiment for Palestine among the Jews, the product of a certain kind of education, itself the result of a certain historical development. That feeling is precisely what Herzl exploited in order to carry out the task given him by the international bourgeoisie—to divert the attention of the Jews from their revolutionary duty by this wild phantasy of a State. What's the use of denying it? As for abandoning university studies— that's only another proof of the reactionary character of your Movement. An engineer should remain an engineer, a doctor should stick to medicine. What do you do? You take intellectuals and push their brains into the earth. Incidentally, one prisoner here who belongs to the political party Hashomer Hatzair[1] boasts that Zionism has set up communes in Palestine. The idiot! How have they done it—with the money of American millionaires! No, Begin, rhetoric won't change the facts. All these stories are hollow mockeries. Zionism is a farce, a puppet show."

One night our discussion centred on revolution as

_____

[1] Hashomer Hatzair was the extreme left-wing party in Zionism whose members sought to avail themselves of the solid advantages of Jewish Nationalism while professing the political ideology of pure Marxism. To-day, they form the principal element in the "Mapam" party of Israel, where they continue to preach the ideals of Communism from which they deem the present-day U.S.S.R. woefully to have lapsed. They are a wealthy group, influential disproportionately to their numbers, fanatically anti-religious, rigidly disciplined, shrewdly organised, and politically flexible to the point of opportunism.

the solution to the Jewish problem, on Birobidjan[1] and anti-Semitism. My questioner insisted that only the victory of the revolution would solve the problem of nationalism, of which the Jewish problem was a part. "But the revolution," he declared heatedly, "needs fighters, and not deserters who run away to a non-existent State. Why didn't you join the Popular Front, which would have dammed the flood of reaction?"

I tried to explain our attitude with an allegory:

"Imagine, citizen-judge, that you are walking in the street and see a house on fire. What do you do? Obviously you call the fire brigade. But if you suddenly hear the cry of a woman or of a child coming from the house, do you wait for the firemen? Surely not. You rush in and try to save them. That's our situation. Assuming, for a moment, that the Revolution is the final solution for the homeless Jewish people—though the Birobidjan experiment shows that even the Soviet Union realises that we Jews need a territory of our own—can't you too see that *we* are like men and women trapped in a burning house? You know what militant anti-Semitism has done to us. You know what the Germans are doing to us. Not only are our houses burning; our families are in flames. Could we—can we wait till the fire brigade arrives? And what if they're late? No, our people must be saved now. We have been trying to get them out of the flames, into our Homeland. Is that such a bad thing?"

At moments like these I am afraid I tended to become rather rhetorical. My circumstances were forbidding: a small, bare room at night, my head shaven, my beard overgrown. I sat, helpless, facing the representative of an all-powerful State and—what was more important—of a theory which permits no shadow of doubt. Of what use arguments and proofs? Yet at such moments my surroundings seemed to recede and I felt within me that I was fulfilling a mission not for myself

[1] The autonomous Jewish Republic established years ago in the Soviet Union.

but in defence of my people and their national rebirth.

But my interrogator would remain quite calm, dismissing my vehement argument with a single epithet: "Hair splitting!"

Our "debate" would go on night after night. The questioner usually maintained his calm and his politeness. Sometimes he would even introduce a note of condescending "humour." He would say, for example:

"You are just like all the other prisoners. Instead of sitting on their backsides and thinking with their heads, they do the opposite."

On a few occasions he warmed up even to the extent of losing his temper. He beat the table with his fist and used language which, as I reminded him, the Soviet law expressly forbade. One of these occasions is worth recalling.

One night I had quoted a clause in the Constitution of the Soviet Union. I reminded him that Paragraph 129 of Stalin's Constitution lays down clearly that the Soviet Union will give refuge to citizens of foreign States persecuted for fighting for national liberation. As I was later able to confirm, the text runs: "The Soviet Union affords refuge to foreign citizens persecuted for their defence of the interests of the workers, or in connection with their scientific work, or because of their struggle for national liberation."

"You have no right," I asserted, rather naïvely it is true, "to keep me in gaol. On the contrary you ought to give me and people like me shelter and help. Over the border we are hounded to death merely because we are Jews, only because we fight, directly or indirectly, for our national rights in Eretz Israel. Finding ourselves in the Soviet Union, we are entitled to ask for and to expect refuge."

At these words, the Russian's face went alternately red and white. No longer the polite officer, he clenched his fist and raised his voice: "Stop this nonsense, you stupid lawyer! You dare quote the Stalin Constitution? You're behaving just like that mad dog, that enemy of humanity, that international spy—(Whom can he mean? I wondered)—Bukharin," he thundered. "You

talk just like the traitor Bukharin, who used to quote
Marx and Engels to prove he was right. But it's no use.
Stalin has taught us that the teachings of Marx and
Engels are a unity and cannot be quoted out of their
context." He laughed derisively. "So, now a new genius has turned up in Wilno, it seems, who tries to convince me by a paragraph from the Constitution. . . ."

I was dumbfounded by this unusual outburst. He was,
of course, right in one respect. Quotations out of their
context are often calculated to deceive. But—I told
him—though a Constitution is a unity, there are clauses
which express a complete idea, unaffected by other
clauses. What I had quoted was not part of a paragraph,
but a whole paragraph. It referred to the right of refuge
in the Soviet Union and had nothing to do with anything
else, for example, with the mode of election to the Supreme Soviet.

My argument had not the slightest effect. He insisted
on the comparison with "the international spy Bukharin."

When I heard with what vehemence this disciple of
the Communist Revolution spoke of the famous author
of "The A.B.C. of Communism" I began to understand
many things which had puzzled me. I understood how
Bukharin and many others like him had been brought
to confess that they were spies and enemies of Soviet
society.

We have all read how the Russians are supposed to
have used mysterious drugs to hypnotize their prisoners
and make them act according to the will of their gaol-
ers. I have come to the conclusion that these are foolish fabrications. What then? How is it done? Physical
pressure? Beatings? I can only say that during all the
time I was questioned, not a finger was laid on me,
even though I was regarded as a serious "political
criminal" and our "sessions" were sometimes very
stormy. Of the hundreds of prisoners I met later, not
one complained of any physical maltreatment. A few
of them told me they had heard that others had been
beaten. But even if we assume that the Soviet police
sometimes use force, only those have a right to cast a

stone whose police forces, security agents, or officers have never resorted to that barbaric form of "convincing argument." We learnt something in Eretz Israel of the sadistic habits of the police of even the "democratic" British Mandatory. And if we are honest, we cannot acquit our own Jewish police of certain of these detestable habits! It is hard to have to admit it—but there is no doubt that police everywhere have much in common.

How is it then that the Soviet police, in their process of interrogation, have achieved results of which no other police force can boast? How, for example, did a young Soviet citizen, probably a diligent reader of the "A.B.C. of Communism," come to the definite conclusion that Bukharin was an unmitigated traitor? In answering this question we may look into the minds of Bukharin himself and many others who shared his fate. We shall then see a man whose whole world has suddenly tumbled about him and who finds himself in utter isolation—not only physical, but, what is worse, mental and political isolation. This double isolation is absolute. Such was the isolation of smaller fry like us in Lukishki, such the isolation of the big fry in the Lubishki Prison in Moscow. Solitude. Not a word of what you say will reach a single person in the world outside. Only what those, whose theory permits no doubting, want the outside world to learn will pierce the prison walls. In certain countries, at certain times, there exist illegal newspapers which publish news and views that never see the light of day in the legitimate press. Here there is no breach in the wall of silence. Nobody will hear, or read. Declarations made within these prison walls will give rise to no new revolutionary movement. No already existing movement will receive inspiration from this source. Thus the inspiration of a revolutionary's behaviour evaporates; the foundations are destroyed. The revolutionary holds his head high before his accusers, his judges, or his executioners only so long as he knows that behind him are many who are aware of his stand, whom his words will reach. He becomes identified with an idea, consumed by it. He is unafraid of torture or death because he believes that his idea will find other spokesmen, that it will spread and conquer.

But what if this belief is utterly destroyed; if he is forced to the realisation that his isolation is absolute, that not a single soul can see, or hear, or will ever see or hear. Then his readiness to sacrifice himself for the idea dies within him—and the foremost element in the make-up of a revolutionary, which gives him wings and steels his heart, has been destroyed. Then the most exalted revolutionary becomes a pitiful suppliant, asking for his own life instead of fighting for his idea. Then, and only then, is he given his chance to speak to the world. And if, in addition, he is promised, explicitly or implicitly, the chance of a new life after he has served the punishment for his past sins, or is given the hint that he might be forgiven right away and not be punished at all—you will see that the 'secret' of the Russian method of securing these public confessions and self-accusations is really no secret at all. Chemistry has nothing to do with it; and physical violence little or nothing. What is decisive is the psychological factor, whose effect is very clear, certainly on those who come from the innermost circles of the ruling Soviet group and who, for one reason or another, have quarrelled with its leaders.

Of these things I thought much in Lukishki; especially as, soon after my argument about the Soviet Constitution, I was given an excellent opportunity for thinking. I was given seven days' solitary confinement. The punishment had nothing to do with my interrogator. Indeed, the reason was irrelevant and stupid. The guard overheard me telling a salty Yiddish joke with a pun in it about an idiot. He thought I was talking about him, reported me—and there I was in "solitary." Having only three and a half paces within which to move my body in that triangular, windowless, smelly cell, I had to make up for it by mental exercise.

Those 170 hours were not very pleasant. I was given nothing to eat but dry bread and water. But there were worse things. There was dirt in very large quantities.

The sanitary pail was never taken out. There was a bare stone floor. For a pillow I had to use my arm—a rather small, hard and painful pillow. By day it was too hot, and at night freezing cold. In addition I was entertained by a thriving colony of rats.

But, I survived it. My fellow prisoners were anxious about me. Seven days in "solitary" is a long time. One of the prisoners, a young thief who for some unknown reason had been housed together with the "politicals," demanded his share of my belongings. He was certain, he said, that a weakling like myself would not come back after seven days "there." The poor fellow was disappointed. (Later on, however, other members of his profession did share out my personal belongings but this was on another occasion.)

My stay in the solitary cell taught me a lesson in values which will probably last me all my life. How few are man's needs, even a cultured man's. During the days I spent in the solitary cell my mental exercises were ceaseless. But whenever the foul reality of my surroundings forced itself on me I dreamt—not of the free world, not of a decent house, or a warm bath, or a walk in the woods, or of any of the boons given by freedom to a civilized human being. No! I dreamt of the cell in the prison, the barred cell, where there was company and my meagre mattress on the stone floor. It may be that happiness has no degrees—but there are certainly gradations of suffering. If you subject a man to the first degree of suffering, he will strive to return to his starting point. But if you push him further down the ladder—he will no longer dream of returning to a state of non-suffering; he will dream of getting back to the immediately previous stage. He will almost have forgotten what goes on outside and beyond this last stage of suffering. And the lesson is one that throws much light on many of the phenomena of the grim and evil age in which we live.

When I returned to my cell my companions were very kind. Even the thief smiled at me—though whether to conceal his disappointment or not I do not know. The dirt I had accumulated in "solitary" was in inverse proportion to the strength that was left me, and my friends had to help me to wash.

A few weeks after my seven days in solitary came the "First of April" announcement, referred to at the beginning of this Chapter, which "provided" for the next eight years of my life. Two more months passed quickly, and then once again there was unusual activity in Lukishki. We were called from our cells—but this time it was daylight—and told to collect our things.

We bundled up our belongings, went through various questionings and registrations, and were then packed into a small, black car. There was room for three, perhaps four in the car. We were over a dozen. One man started shouting that he could not breathe. What exaggeration! The human animal is one of the strongest of creatures: he is not easily smothered. The drive in the car was uncomfortable, it is true, but it did not last long. From the prison to the railway station, perhaps fifteen minutes.

And when the gates of the prison were opened and the car slid out into the deserted street, somebody whispered: "This is the beginning of the journey to Eretz Israel."

Impracticable faith? Maybe. Yet faith is perhaps stronger than reality; faith itself creates reality.

Chapter II

Land of Our Fathers

The long train that took us north-eastward into the depths of Russia had no Pullman cars. It was a goods train, and there were fifty men to a truck. We set out early in June. The way was long, the train slow. When the news reached us of Hitler's attack on the Soviet Union—such news penetrates even the bars of a prison-truck—we had only gone half way. As we proceeded we passed trains carrying recruits to the front. Behind us came trainloads like ours. It was a real migration of peoples.

When we arrived at our destination it was, we were told, two o'clock in the morning; yet it was broad daylight. One could have read a book if there had been one to read. As it was we enjoyed the beauties of the "white nights" which lit up our darkened days. One autumn night as, overwhelmed and humbled, I watched the glorious northern dawn, which makes the earth glow as with a thousand lights, one of my companions, a legless cripple, sighed deeply and, pointing to the horizon, said "There are people crying there too. . . ."

I do not intend to write about people crying. This book is devoted not to tears but to revolt; not to unfortunates but to rebels; not to Russia and her labour camps but to Eretz Israel and the struggle for freedom from foreign rule. But if I mention the words of the cripple I do so in the faint hope that they may reach some who have the power to lighten suffering and wipe away tears. I know that those are not the only places in the world where man cries. I know, too, that great enterprises and buildings have been built by men who, like myself, were given eight years of "re-education." In the country to which I was sent a prisoner no man had set foot twenty-five years ago. Today you will find railways and bridges and a huge output of previously unexploited natural resources. But the price; good heavens, the *price*!

I write these words without personal feeling and without consideration of my own ideology, the be-all and end-all of which is Freedom—the freedom and happiness of the individual. My personal feelings, in this case, play no part. The suffering which was my portion was only a minute drop in the ocean of blood and tears in which six million Jews were drowned. What significance had my passing troubles in the face of the general catastrophe? After it was over it became for me an experience, certainly a fortifying and toughening experience, but nothing more. On the other hand, I cannot forget, and no Jew should forget, two fundamental facts. Thanks to the Soviet Union hundreds of thousands of Jews were saved from Nazi hands—though some of them suffered greatly and some of them died in prison, in exile or as refugees.

Secondly, when the Soviet Union concluded, if only temporarily, that our striving for Jewish independence in Palestine was not a comedy dictated by British imperialists, but a purpose as serious as death—the death of rebels and oppressors—it helped us to achieve the first stage of our independence. The world was astonished, both because of past memories, of which the 'debate' in Lukishki is illustrative, and also because Soviet help was given to us simultaneously with aid by the United States. I shall later try to explain these "surprises." But these are the facts. We shall not forget them—even though in the meantime a tragic change has taken place and the absurd theories of the Lukishki interrogator are again in the ascendant.

Nor can we forget that there is a permanent dilemma facing humanity: how to combine and reconcile the urge for individual freedom with the striving for social justice. The freedom of the individual requires that the State should not interfere with his life; yet elimination of unjust inequalities is impossible without some calcu-

lated intervention of organised society, or in other
words the State. I have no doubt that the solution is to
be found in the golden mean. But the baffling question
facing the wise men of the age is where is that happy
mean, and how can we discover it?

The task of the French revolutionaries was much
simpler. True, they asked in one breath for Liberty and
Equality. But the inequality against which they rose
was very gross and obvious and could have been cor-
rected virtually by a stroke of the pen. Inherited privileges can be eliminated together with noble titles and
their symbols. But life itself creates real differences
which are unconnected with inherited titles, or with any
other such political, social and economic privileges.
What about *these* differences?

Humanity continues to seek a solution. The Soviet
peoples too are searching—and have not found it yet.
As a result of practical experience in their country,
they have rejected the basic idea of Communism—the
idea of absolute equality. The principle "to every man
the same" has long ceased to operate. It has been replaced by the principle of "each according to his labour." But not all labour is equal. Hours alone do not
determine its value. Every form of labour in Soviet
Russia has its own quality. And its qualitative value is
fixed not by the workers but by their rulers "the State."
Thus, for example, a railway worker is paid much less
than a film star. True, a promise has been made that
one day the principle of "to each according to his
labour" will be replaced by "to each according to his
needs." But even that will not mean absolute equality
—for people's needs differ. And anyhow the question
remains: who is to determine what those needs are.
The individual himself? Or must we go back again to
that "superior power," the rulers, the State?

The cure-all for the ills of society has not yet been
found, though some may claim to have discovered it.
The Soviet peoples have made very heavy sacrifices in
their attempt to seek it out. They have sacrificed their
individual freedom. That is a fact which cannot be
denied. They have made other sacrifices too. After all,

if the State undertakes to supply all the people's needs, from heavy machines down to needles and threads, toothbrushes, soap and shoelaces, it is inevitable that it will first produce the heavy machine, while soap and shoelaces will have to wait. That is natural and logical. But logic and "law" are here in collision with the conditions which make life worth living. For millions of little people working conditions depend not on the great machine but precisely on these small things; a pair of shoes, or even a shoelace. One has to experience the lack of these trifles to appreciate what they mean in the daily life of the individual—not to mention the grim significance of the lack of such elementary needs as bread, a little sugar, a drop of milk.

In Russia one can learn the tragic meaning of general dearth. Yet one can also learn to respect and honour the people who have accepted this dearth— even if its acceptance has been compulsory—in their search for the longed-for panacea. The limits of human suffering, accepted in other parts of the world as final, as something beyond which life is unbearable, have in the Soviet Union been extended immeasurably. Stretching the limits of suffering is not a pleasant experience; but we should remember that it enabled Russia to survive the iron fist of the Nazis, to remain unbroken under its blows and then, finally, to smash it.

The lesson of life in a concentration camp is very enlightening. It becomes evident that what we call "civilised living" is not at all a necessity, is nothing more than a habit. One can rid oneself of the habits of "civilisation" just as one stops smoking; at first with difficulty, then more easily, and finally—who wants to smoke? There is a phrase in the camp, epitomizing a whole philosophy. "You'll get used to it." Or one may say: "You'll get used to doing without." And so it is. When you find the first louse on your body your whole being is revolted. But, no matter—you'll get used to it. Soon you will get used to doing without a clean shirt, and to the hundreds of lice which cover what used to be your clean underclothes. The first louse is a terrifying creature. The hundredth is an accepted neighbour.

It is no longer repulsive; it is part of your existence.
You find it hard to sleep without pyjamas? Nonsense.
In a matter of weeks you will not only have learnt to
sleep in the dirty rags of your shirt, you will have learnt
not to undress at all—to sleep in your stinking clothes
—and to sleep very well. You can't eat without first
washing your hands? You will only be too thankful for
anything to grab hold of with your dirty hands and put
in your mouth. You have to brush your teeth morning
and night? Rubbish. No brush will come anywhere
near your teeth and yet you'll live and want to continue
living. You need a bed to rest on? Nonsense. You will
lie on boards, on a floor, in the snow, on the earth, and
you will sleep.

No, civilisation is not essential. You shake it off
quickly if you are forced to. Yet, strangely enough, the
less civilisation in your life, the greater your desire to
live. Just to live, to live, to live. Man is a vigorous animal. Even when he is reduced to semi-bestial circumstances his will to live is elemental. He gets used to
everything, except death.

But—is it essential to create conditions in which
people will always be thinking of food though they
have absolutely forgotten what a decent meal tastes
like? Is it essential to turn man into half-beast? Must
the urge to live be strengthened at the cost of life's contents? One ought to press these questions wherever society, whatever its form of organization, either forces
man to "live" as if he were half a beast, or tolerates
his living in this way. It is impossible to avoid posing
these questions about places which one saw with one's
own eyes. Why, why do so many tears have to be shed
into the mighty Pechora River? Are those who decide
the fate of millions unable to ease the lot of the unfortunates on its banks?

The fate of one of those unfortunates is engraved
sharply on my memory. I doubt whether he is still
alive. His official name was Garin: his real, Jewish
name I do not know. At first he did not want to speak
in his mother-tongue, Yiddish, and did not even admit
he was a Jew. We spoke Russian, and we spoke a great

deal. He had once been an important figure in Soviet politics—General Secretary of the Communist Party in the Ukraine, and Assistant Editor of *Pravda*. From his early youth he had been a loyal member of the Communist Party. But his career was cut short in the fateful year 1937. Garin was arrested and charged with the most heinous of all crimes in the Soviet Union: Trotskyism. For four years he was under interrogation, but was never put on trial. In 1941 he was given the maximum administrative sentence: eight years in a "correctional labour camp," and was sent to the banks of the Pechora River. That was how destiny brought us together.

Garin assured me that he was *not* a Trotskyist. As a student in the "twenties" he had, it was true, tended to the Trotskyist side in the public debate that was going on in the Party. But that had been a free and recognised debate, and many other students who today occupy important posts in the State, had preached the same views. Afterwards—Garin told me—he had had no connection with what was called "Trotskyism." Indeed he had fought Trotsky. Several days before his arrest he had published in *Pravda* a long article against the Trotskyist ideology or "deviation," as it was called. The original name of the article was "Complete Retreat to Menshevism." Briefly, he accused Trotsky of abandoning Bolshevism for his earlier love, Menshevism. But his interrogator's immediate reply to the mention of this article in his defence was: "Trotskyist headquarters ordered you to publish it to cover up your work of undermining the Party and the State."

In spite of all his tribulations, Garin remained a Soviet patriot. In the July days of 1941 he was filled with concern at the persistently grave news from the front. And when another political prisoner, an embittered Communist, burst out with the wish that the Germans might continue to advance so that he might be saved, Garin rebuked him, called him a traitor and was himself favoured in reply with the epithets popular in the camp: "parasite," "vermin."

As a faithful Communist Garin continued to combat

my Zionist faith. He recalled his fight against Zionism
and particularly against the Zionist Socialists whom
he regarded as traitors to the working class. He had
fought against them in his youth in Odessa and had
not changed his opinions. During long talks which we
carried on while lying on our wooden bunks he tried
to convince me that Zionism was nothing but the coun-
ter-part of anti-Semitism. Both were nationalisms ir-
reconcilable with human progress. National solidarity
was an invention of the bourgeoisie. The only true solidarity was that of the workers of the various peoples.
He did not, of course, omit to pay me the usual compliments about my "service to British imperialism." Palestine, he urged, belongs to the Arabs. The Zionists
are merely tools employed by the British Imperialists to
subjugate the Arab proletariat, to oppress and exploit
them. Our debates were, understandably, often very
stormy. Prisoners are like children. Surrounded by
terrors, they play games with unusual concentration, or
lose themselves utterly in abstract arguments.

But one day something was destroyed in Garin's
spirit. We were unloading heavy rails from a boat when
he got into a quarrel with one of the criminal prisoners
who were known as "Urki" or "Zhuliki." The criminal
splenetically called Garin "Dirty Jew." Garin stood
petrified, as though the heavens had fallen. This, apparently, was the most terrible blow he had received.
He had long fallen from his high station, but to be so
degraded—he, he a "dirty Jew"!

Garin knew, as we all learnt, that the Soviet Government fought anti-Semitism with characteristic perti-
nacity. Only anti-Semitic agitators or deluded idiots will
argue that the Soviet Government is either "Jewish" or
"pro-Jewish." The truth is that the Soviet Government
is anti-antisemitic, regards anti-Semitism not only as a
manifestation of racial or nationalistic emotion but also
—and perhaps especially—as a dangerous weapon in
the hands of the enemies of the Soviet regime. But this
does not prevent anti-Semitism, which springs from
congenital hatred or consuming envy. At any rate, it is
almost, if not quite, impossible to fight against anti-

Semitic manifestations in a concentration camp. The camp is an enclosed world. The armed guards take you to your place of work and return you to your sleeping-quarters. They do not arbitrate in internal disputes. You do not go near them unless they call you. If you complain to them, it will not help, and may even harm you. Whether you are in the right or wrong, telling tales is forbidden. That is the basic morality of every prison, and certainly of a concentration camp.

Garin knew all this. He knew too, poor creature, that he was one of the most hated men in the camp. Not because he was a Jew—the "Urki" were on good terms with other Jews—but because he was an intellectual and a Communist. It is a universal law that criminal prisoners cannot tolerate the "intelligentsia" in their midst; and woe to the intellectual prisoner who looks down, or appears to look down, on his fellows. Garin did not put on airs, but he could never forget the barriers between himself and the Urki and Zhuliki in the labour "brigade" of which we were both members.

Ironically enough, they hated him perhaps even more because he was a Communist, and therefore symbolical of the Government. It did not matter what kind of Communist—a Commissar giving orders, or a hounded prisoner, a Stalinist or a Trotskyist. All that mattered to them was that he was a Communist and that now they had a chance to get a little of their own back on the regime responsible for their plight.

The hooligan's outburst could thus be explained logically. But of what avail are logical explanations in the face of an abysmal spiritual melancholy? Garin was utterly broken. He was no longer just an unfortunate; he was the most miserable of unfortunates. The backbone of his faith was shattered. He did not even try to conceal it. He complained and poured his heart out to me, his friendly antagonist. If this could happen—he asked me—what was the purpose of all his labours?

It is said that Herzl, then an assimilated and successful journalist, went through the spiritual crisis which led him to the idea of a Jewish State when he heard the hooligans cry "Death to the Jews" during the Dreyfus trial. Garin was no Herzl. When I met him he was completely crushed, with a weak heart and bewildered eyes. But that spiritual crisis which, after twenty years of denial, brought him back, if only for a while, to his own people, certainly began with the cry of "dirty Jew."

The crisis reached its climax during the "etape." This word, in its particular meaning, is unknown outside the Soviet Union. It is not particularly well-known inside except in the concentration camps. But there it is only too full of meaning.

"Etape" means the transfer of prisoners from one camp to another. This transfer is feared like death by every prisoner, from the man of "Dixie No. 1"—that is, the prisoner who has fulfilled less than half of his work-assignment and gets the smallest ration—to the "brigadiers," the group-leaders and the overseers. None of them wants to "go on etape"—for the simple reason that the transfer is always for the worse. Even more terrifying is the thought of the journey itself.

The transfers are carried out by land and water, and irrespective of weather conditions. The journey frequently takes many weeks. And in order to understand why the prisoner prefers to remain in his filthy hut, teeming with lice and fleas, rather than to take a change of air and try his luck elsewhere, it is enough to recall that in the region of which I am writing the winter lasts more than nine months. The winter night goes on for eighteen or twenty hours and the temperature goes down to 60 and 70 degrees below zero. The local inhabitants even joke about their climate. "Our winter," they say, "lasts only nine months. After that you have as much summer as you like." No wonder, then, that the word "etape" has a terrifying significance.

Transfers are frequent. One of the reasons is probably security; not to keep the same embittered people together for too long. But the main reason is that the Government's construction programme must go on. The work done in the camp is, in the circumstances, relatively slow. But every task, after all, must come to an end, and the constructional programme in the huge Eurasian continent is wide-spread and ever-increasing. No sooner is one undertaking completed than another is begun. Camps are emptied, others are filled. The movement between camps, like the work itself, is incessant.

I was thrown together with Garin in one of these transfers. My good friend Kroll, who had been promoted to "brigade leader" (he was not freed from the camps and is believed to have died in one of them some years later), made strenuous efforts to have my name erased from the list of "travellers." But in vain. Even the shirts with collars, highly-prized in the camps, even by group-leaders and overseers, did not help. The order was given for us to be sent further north. Garin did not even try to have his name removed from the list. His identity-card, marked with the three letters, C.R.T.—Counter-Revolutionary Trotskyist—closed all doors and all hearts to him. And he had no shirts with collars!

By good fortune our transfer took place a little while before the winter set in. Conditions, however, were hard enough. We travelled in a small river-boat, designed for carrying freight. On this journey seven or eight hundred souls were squeezed into it. There were three or four tiers of planks for bunks. We were forbidden to go on deck, except with the permission of the armed guard, and then only for pressing bodily needs. But even to satisfy these urgent needs there was always a queue. We numbered hundreds, and there were only two places where we could find relief. Stomachs were in constant revolt against the food, or the lack of it, and against the raw river-water we had to drink. The lice ate your flesh. The stench tore at your lungs. This was Etape.

But the people were even more difficult than the conditions. The "Urki" here are no longer "your" Urki whom you had pitied and who, after their fashion, had begun to like and respect you. Here the "Urki" are strangers, and you are nothing more to them than an "intellectual," a target for their all-comprehensive curses, and a prey for their thieving hands. Moreover, the Urki who, by virtue of their numbers, determine the life in the camps, are here, in the depths of the boat, absolute masters. Among the seven or eight hundred exiled prisoners there are only a few dozen "politicals." And the guard is up on deck, always on deck. He will not interfere in any trouble: he, too, knows the Urki.

In this atmosphere, Garin's crisis reached its climax. One night—or maybe it was day, who knows?—Garin woke up from a doze, with a cold sweat gleaming on his brow. His three hundred roubles had disappeared. Three hundred roubles is not a large sum; and in any case there was not much to be got for money in the camp. Still, a prisoner finds some kind of comfort in the little money he carries. Maybe he will be able to buy a little tobacco, or an unsweetened hard biscuit. Garin had nobody left in the world from whom he could hope to get anything. His wife, a university lecturer, had also been arrested as a Trotskyist. She had indeed succeeded for a time in clearing herself. After attempting suicide she had written to Stalin and by a miracle her letter had reached him. Stalin accepted her plea, ordered her transfer to hospital and the restoration of her party card. Garin himself was then still at liberty. These, said Garin, were the couple's happiest days. But soon, all was shattered. His wife was re-arrested. Maybe she wrote more letters to Stalin, but there was no result. Immediately afterwards Garin himself was arrested and they disappeared from each other's ken. Then war broke out. Three hundred roubles had been his only possession—and now he had nothing, except the filth on his body and the pain in his heart.

But the distress brought about by the theft of his last meagre money was not the cause of his final crisis. Garin was not at all angry with the thieves. On the contrary, he pleaded with them not to be angry with him. The "Urki" did not tolerate complaints being made against them to the guard, and we had heard rumours, even before setting sail on the Pechora River, that the Urki "fixed" any informers so that they would never inform again. We heard that from time to time the Urki played card games in which the stakes were 'heads' and the one who lost had to mete out his fate to a selected victim.

Garin was evidently much impressed with these stories. In his terror he persuaded himself that the Urki who had robbed him suspected him of having informed on them to the guard. He began to imagine things. Passing near a group of criminals who were playing cards—the prohibition of card-playing is successfully disregarded even in Russia, even in gaol and concentration camps—he decided that they were "playing for his head." For days and nights Garin clung to me like a frightened child. No, he did not go out of his mind. He remained the intelligent intellectual. When I succeeded in making him forget his terror, we talked of literature and philosophy, of Dostoievsky and Socrates. He was full of wit and wisdom. But something had evidently broken finally within him.

As we lay on our bunks, one of the Urki began slowly getting down from his bunk in an upper tier. Garin, who lay beside me, squeezed himself under my arm and called out, this time not in Russian but in Yiddish, "He's coming to kill me!" I looked where he was pointing. The scene was indeed sinister. The man was moving slowly, and made a big shadow in the semi-darkness that always reigned in the belly of the ship. Then he came nearer to us, and in his hand he held something—something, but we could not tell what it was. In that boat, in such an atmosphere, to the fevered imagination of a man shattered to the depths of his being, this was sufficient to make him believe his end was approaching, that the Urki was about to murder him. The Urki was in fact not even thinking of Garin. The "instrument" he carried was only a spoon. But Garin went through an agony of panic. I quietened him with difficulty, and then only for a while.

He continued to be convinced that the Urki would never forgive him, that his fate was sealed, that they would finish him sooner or later. And one night—again, maybe it was daytime—he turned to me with an astonishing request:

"Menahem, do you remember the song 'Loshuv'?"

He uttered the word, the first Hebrew word I had ever heard him use, with the Ashkenazic pronunciation,

and I did not at once understand to what song he was
referring.

He became somewhat angry.

"How come you don't remember? It's the song the
Zionists used to sing in Odessa when I was a young
man. 'Loshuv.' Sing it to me. These may be my last
days, maybe my last hours. We shall never meet again.
Go on, sing it."

There were several more Jews in the boat. They were
neither political nor criminal prisoners. They had been
caught crossing the frontier. Among them were two
young Betar[1] members, whose bunks were near mine.
We were still able to sing. We did as Garin asked. We
sang him "Loshuv"—that is Hatikvah—the Hebrew
national anthem 'lashuv le'eretz avotenu'—"Our hope
to return to the land of our fathers."

There was the boat, travelling northwards towards
the subpolar regions. Darkness. Filth. Stench. Fleas
and lice. Seven hundred half-bestial Urki. A few Jews.
A handful of dreamers of Zion. Why had they come
here? Where were they going? What help could they
hope for? And among them, a Jew, or rather a Russian
of Jewish origin, who had never dreamt of Zion, and
who had never believed in Zion, who had preached all
his life that Zion was "reactionary." All his life he had
served another idea, a universalist ideal—fighting for it
on the barricades, being captured and tortured for it by
the "White Russians." Faithfully serving, he had risen
and become the Secretary of the Central Committee of
the Party, and then Assistant Editor of the Party's
national daily paper. How far was he from Zion! And
how far from Zion was the place to which fate had
brought us! And *this* man, in what he thought might
be his last hours on earth, asked us to sing the song of
Zion!

---

[1] Betar is the short name for Brit Trumpeldor, the youth organisation founded by Vladimir Jabotinsky. Betar was the
fortress where Bar Kochba made his last heroic stand in the
revolt against Roman rule in Palestine in the Second Century. C. E.

We sang. Had the greenish Pechora River ever heard "Hatikvah" before? Had the dumbfounded Urki ever heard a Hebrew song before? From the belly of the boat the song burst forth:

"To return to the land of our fathers."

Chapter III

"Au Revoir in Freedom"

It was on this of all boats that my freedom was restored to me. We were still on the way to our destination on the Arctic Sea, when an order arrived to liberate all Polish citizens. Sikorski had signed his pact with Stalin.

Alphabetically, mine was the first name on the list of those about to be freed. One of the Urki shouted:

"He's a Jew, not a Pole!"

Poor Urki. His protest was natural. There is no deeper envy than that of the prisoner for the liberated. And could one expect an Urki to know the difference between citizenship and nationality?

We approached the shore. A small boat came up, the boat of freedom to take us off the prison ship. We stepped out onto the shore. We were free.

We spent several days in the transit camp. And then, by the same route as we had come northwards, we returned. We passed the camp where I had helped build the northern railway. The group-leader Makarov was on the shore.

"Hi, comrade Makarov, how are things? Where is Kroll?"

"Everything's all right. Kroll has been transferred to another camp. He'll probably soon be free. And you —are you being released?"

"Yes, comrade Makarov. I am free. Do you remember you didn't believe we would come back from the etape?"

"I remember, comrade Begin. You Poles have been lucky. But who knows? Maybe we shall also get out soon. The war's going on, and they're talking of a pardon."

"Good luck to you, comrade Makarov. I hope your pardon comes soon. Good luck. Au revoir in freedom."

We proceeded on our way to freedom. On foot, in goods trains, in passenger-trains, clinging to the sides. Southwards, southwards. And the wonders did not cease. I searched for my sister. She too had been exiled, though not imprisoned. How was she to be found? Russia is so huge, the refugees numbered millions. Yet by pure chance I found her. Then I found some of my friends. I sent my first telegram to Eretz Israel. I received my first telegram from Eretz Israel. Among the signatures was that of my wife. . . .

I recalled the last news I had had of her. Before I was sent northwards from Lukishki permission had been given for a single farewell visit by a relative. And in place of my wife there had come a young Betar girl, Paula Daiches. Paula later immortalized her name in the fight against the Nazis. She became one of the chief aides of my friend and colleague Joseph Glazman, the hero of the Wilno ghetto, and died, as he did, arms in hand, fighting to the last. She came to give me information. As we had to speak a language the guards could understand, we talked Polish. But this is how Paula spoke:

"Your aunt sends her love." Then she mumbled in Hebrew "letter in soap." The guards cut that soap down the middle, but the note had been squeezed into one half. Thus, even in a Russian prison, a message reached its destination. That note told me that my wife, as well as some other good friends, was on her was to Eretz Israel. It was a great comfort at the time. But what that child risked! If they had caught me with the letter in the soap I might have been given another seven days' solitary. But she . . .

After months of wandering I joined the Polish Army, and found an atmosphere of anti-Semitism, of insults and humiliation. But this period was not to last long. We moved ever southwards. The Caspian port of Krasnovodsk . . . the small Persian port of Pahlevi . . . the highway of the Persian conquerors. We crossed the mighty mountains. Babylon. Bagdad. Lake Habbaniyeh.

I did not know then that only a few steps away was the grave of the Commander of the Irgun Zvai Leumi— David Raziel killed while carrying out a mission for the British Army. I was still living in the hope of placing myself at his disposal and fighting under his command.

And here was Transjordan. Our heritage. Broad fields, broad as the sea. I realized then why the Romans had called this part of Eretz Israel *Palestina Salutaris*. In those days it was the granary of the Middle East. Now, despite neglect, bursting forth from underneath the stones covering the infinite fields, there is grass, green, tall and pleasant. The region is almost entirely empty. Here and there, in the wide expanse, you see a Bedouin hovel or a camel. Only as you approach the Jordan itself, do you see a few people and fields of welcome corn. The eastern bank of the Jordan—Eretz Israel. The military convoy stopped. We rested. I left the automobile, waded a little way into the grass, and drank in the odour of the fields of my Homeland.

"Good to be home, eh?" It was one of the soldiers, not a Jew, by my side.

As he spoke I recalled how in the transit camp on the banks of the Pechora, the official in the registry had told me: "You will be released on the 20th September, 1948."

The prospect of spending the years till 1948 in the "brigade" of Makarov or Yermenke was not attractive. Yet, what man can foretell his fate? Now it was summer 1942. "Only" 1942—yet here I was on the eastern bank of the Jordan.

And I remembered Garin. I recall him now. I wonder—is he still alive? Has he heard that meanwhile we *have* returned to the land of our fathers and become a free people in it? Has he heard that there was a revolt in Israel—his *Pravda* even wrote at times of the deeds of the rebels—and that the State of Israel has arisen? Has he heard that the mighty State he served, which combated the striving for a Jewish State, eventually helped, in the international arena, to have it established? Maybe at least these wonders gave him some comfort in his suffering.

One chapter ended, another began. Fate had played a peculiar joke upon me. In early June 1941 I had begun my journey northward from Lukishki. In early May 1942 I reached—Eretz Israel. I had been arrested, charged, sentenced and exiled as an "agent of British Imperialism." What became of this British agent? Arriving in Eretz Israel with the Polish Army he soon had on his head the largest of the rewards offered by the British police for the capture of those who were trying to smash British rule in Eretz Israel. (This is the only "record" I have ever achieved and I shall always be very proud of it.)

In this new chapter fate played another of its tricks on me. Conspiratorial work was to me quite unknown before I plunged perforce into its depths. I knew nothing of underground activities, beyond what I had read in an occasional book. I had never dreamt I would fight underground. In all things I always preferred the open to the secret, and yet . . .

Man proposes, God disposes. Up to September 1948 I did indeed serve in the brigade, but it was not the brigade of Makarov or Yermenke. It did not work on the banks of the Pechora. It did not build a railway for carrying coal. The brigade I served in was a brigade of Hebrew rebels. It operated on the banks of the Jordan, and built a road to freedom for Israel.

Chapter IV

We Fight, Therefore We Are

1

Two predominating facts determined the condition of
the Jewish people at the height of the Second World
War. Hitler was exterminating millions of Jews in
Europe, and—in spite of this—Britain continued to
keep the gates of the Jewish "National Home" tightly
shut against the Jews.

The reports on the campaign of extermination in
Europe were at first not very clear; and their publication was slow. The Red Cross institutions, the diplomatic representatives of the neutral countries, and,
above all, the British Intelligence—one of whose agents,
it appears, actually worked in German G.H.Q.—undoubtedly knew perfectly well to what end Hitler was
transporting the Jews of Holland and Belgium, of Warsaw and Lodz. But they remained silent. Why they were
silent is anybody's guess. The fact remains that it was
months after the extermination had begun that the first
reports came seeping through about the Nazi "special
platoons" dispatched with orders not to leave a Jew
alive anywhere in the whole of German-Occupied Territory.

Many Jews, too, treated these reports with scepticism
—and no wonder! It is difficult for a normal human
being to believe that his parents, or his children, or his
brothers and sisters have been wiped out "just like
that"—like sheep led to the slaughter. Man generally
believes what he *wants* to believe. The doomed families
themselves, even as they stood beside the graves which
the Nazis had ordered them to dig, did not want to
believe that these graves were for themselves. They
believed even up to the last that somehow they would

be saved. Little wonder, then, that the Jews in the rest of the world did not easily believe in the mass graves of Ponari, nor in the crematoria of Treblinki.[1] Was it possible, they asked themselves, to wipe out a whole people—and in the Twentieth Century? What would the world say?

How naïve they were! They did not realise that it was precisely the spirit and scientific advancement of the Twentieth Century that made the destruction of a whole people possible; and furthermore, that, as it was the Jewish people, "the world" would remain largely unmoved.

The angel of forgetfulness is a blessed creature. The touch of his wings goes far to heal our wounds. Our capacity to forget is every bit as important as our capacity to remember. That is why we should not be angry, nor even be surprised, that though only a few years have elapsed since this nation-wide massacre, un-exampled in human history, there are many among us who already almost forget. But we dare not resign our-selves to this forgetfulness. For the sake of our future, and possibly for that of the future of humanity, we dare not forget what happened to us in this century of mechanized civilisation, in the heart of "cultured" Europe.

The campaign of extermination did not come about suddenly. It was carefully prepared over years, sys-tematically, scientifically. Already in 1936 Hitler was declaring in the Reichstag: "Another war will mean the end of European Jewry." In 1939 the Germans began preparing an area of "Reservation" for Jews

---

[1] Treblinki, in Eastern Europe, was one of several vast hu-man slaughterhouses set up by the Germans during the war for the extermination of Jews. It has been estimated that nearly one million Jewish men, women and children were slaughtered and their bodies cremated by this plant alone. The clothes and possessions of the slaughtered were carefully sorted for use by the German economy; and when allied forces entered they found amongst other evidence of German careful management, some sixty thousand pairs of children's shoes which had been taken from Jewish kiddies prior to slaughter.

near Lublin; and German newspapers talked about a
plan to transfer all the Jews to a "State" in the heart
of Africa, or to Madagascar. Then came news of the
setting up of various ghettoes, accompanied by acts
of bloodshed, the "minor" massacres and the major
humiliations and degradations which were, in fact,
the preliminary experiments, carefully calculated and
checked. The experiments were directed to test the
reactions both of the Jews and of "the world." Only
after they had been "reduced to dust" in their lifetime
were Jews in their millions slaughtered and converted
into ashes.

Step by step, stage by stage, the German butcher had
turned our people into a panic-stricken, disunited mass
striving only to live and forgetting that sometimes the
only hope of living is to be ready to risk one's life. At
the same time he was testing the reactions of the world,
which he assumed, for the purpose of this experiment,
was largely indifferent to the shedding of Jewish blood.
He was not mistaken. Years after all these horrors had
been laid bare to the world, Mr. Paget, a British Socialist M.P. could assert in the Hamburg War Crimes Court
that the Army of the Nazi General Meinstein had fought
and behaved decently in Poland—in Poland, whose
rivers had run red with the blood of hundreds of thousands of Jews! And Mr. Paget was a respected and
well-known lawyer in Britain long before his professional appearance at that trial. Hitler did not start
wholesale killing at once. First, he imprisoned the Jews;
and noted the world's indifference. Then he starved
them; and still the world did not move. He dug his
claws in, bared his teeth; the world did not even raise
an eyebrow. So he went on, step by step, until he
reached the climax of the gas-chambers. Hitler had
originally prepared poison gas for use, if occasion favoured it, on the warfronts; but though his military position grew more desperate from year to year, the only
people on whom he dared use gas was on Jews in the
gas-chambers.

Indifference—that is the danger. Humanity might
claim that it was at least progressing when it could be

aroused on account of injustice to a single Dreyfus in Paris, to a Sacco and Vanzetti in America, to a Dimitrov in Berlin. Humanity will retrogress in the darkness of savagery if it remains unconcerned about the fate of millions of 'Dreyfuses' or if it fails to produce—as it has failed during these terrible years—a single Emile Zola. And if humanity at large is threatened by the enemy called indifference, how much greater is this threat to the Jewish people? That is why the most solemn warning for Jews as for Gentiles, speaks to us in Kipling's immortal words, "Lest we forget!"

This plea not to forget is nothing new. Actually I am merely repeating the call we issued after the reports we received of the deluge of Jewish blood had been fully confirmed. But the call went unheeded at the time. And those who most determinedly shut their ears to the cry of Jewish blood dyeing the rivers of Europe were fellow-countrymen of Mr. Paget, the governors of the "National Home for the Jewish People"—the British rulers of the Hebrew Homeland.

One cannot say that those who shaped British Middle East policy at that time did not want to save the Jews. It would be more correct to say that they very eagerly wanted the Jews not to be saved. The average Englishman was probably as indifferent to Jewish lives as any other non-Jew in the world. But those who ruled Palestine and the Middle East were not in the least "indifferent." They were highly interested in achieving the maximum reduction in the number of Jews liable to seek to enter the land of Israel. I write this not to make out a case, nor to define my attitude to the British Government, or its attitude to us. I am stating a fact, and I have no doubt that any honest British statesman who was really informed of the British Government's policy at that time, would admit that the purpose of British policy in Eretz Israel during the war years was to reduce to the minimum the number of Jews seeking to enter. Randolph Churchill once related that his father had avoided seeing Dr. Weizmann during the war. "Whenever I see him," Winston is supposed to have said, "I can't sleep at nights." Yet he could easily have seen Dr. Weizmann and still enjoyed his night's rest: he could have opened the gates of Eretz Israel to those who were about to be dragged off to the crematoria at Auschwitz, and for whom, or at least for some of whom, Weizmann had come to him to plead.

But he did not do so. He avoided seeing Weizmann. The Jews were slaughtered—in millions—men, women and children, according to the German plan. And by a grim and ghastly irony, the German plan helped to fulfil—by means unexpected and gruesome—the fundamental British plan for Eretz Israel.

British Middle Eastern policy had long wanted Palestine. Mr. Ivan Greenberg, the former editor of the *Jewish Chronicle* (a man who sacrificed his career for his beliefs) told me, in a long conversation we had when I was "underground," that his father, L. J. Greenberg, one of Herzl's leading helpers and his special envoy to Egypt to prepare for the El-Arish Enquiry Mission, had been told by Lord Cromer, Britain's great pro-consul in Egypt: "When the Ottoman Empire crumbles, as sooner or later it surely will, we must have Palestine."

That was early in the twentieth century. In fact direct British interest in the fate of Eretz Israel had already become apparent in the nineteenth century. This helps to explain why, among the early "Zionists" who preceded Herzl, there were so many Englishmen. It explains, too, why the British Government in those days were concerned with the protection of Jews persecuted by the Sultan.

The peculiar genius of British statesmanship is—or was—to give to British interests the outward form of a general ideal. Disraeli once said to Mr. Gladstone: "I do not object to my honourable friend's holding the fifth ace up his sleeve; but I do protest at his suggestion that it is the Lord who put it there." It is the peculiar genius of British statesmen to make that fifth ace appear not only legal and fair but positively holy. In the nineteenth century fortune favoured Britain. Metternich's Triple Alliance was certainly unholy. The Tsarist regime was undoubtedly reactionary; the rule of the

Sultan was unquestionably nefarious. Britain stood on the side of progress. The glove fitted the hand. The hand caressed and conquered. Britain went from strength to strength—hand in glove with humanitarian progress.

The revolt of the Greeks against their Turkish oppressors was one of the manifestations of the unconquerable spirit of freedom. It was fine to help a small people. But it was also *worth while*. To weaken the Sublime Port—not to destroy it while the Russians were strong, but merely to weaken and soften it—could do nothing but good to Progress and to Britain. Was it Britain's fault that helping Progress meant also helping Britain? Giving refuge to persecuted political exiles is a sacred humanitarian duty. The Russian revolutionaries were given refuge in Britain. This was noble. It was also sound policy. It helped weaken from within the Great Power which was casting eyes both at Constantinople and at India. Indeed it would clearly benefit human progress—and Britain's. And Britain could not be blamed if the two went hand-in-hand. What could be more humanitarian than extending protection to persecuted Jews—the People of the Bible—against the cruelties of Turkish *Kaimakams*? And if, as it turned out, this also paid Imperial dividends—what of it? All the Powers were anxious to interfere in the affairs of Turkey, the disintegrating "sick man of Europe." France intervened on behalf of the Catholics, Russia in the interests of the Greek Church. The Germans claimed Protestant interests, and were in any case friendly with the Sultan, and were busy planning the Berlin-Bagdad railway. What was left for Britain? The Jews! And, incidentally, to whom did Palestine belong? To the Jews of course. It said so in the Bible. (But— "Mr. Greenberg, Britain must have Palestine . . .")

I do not make this analysis in a critical spirit towards British policy. I do not deny that British policy often benefited humanity. But also at times the contrary happened. Moreover, it is only fair to ask: "Is it only British policy that works this way? Is the British Government the only Power that invokes the name of

progress and freedom and justice in the pursuance of
its policy?" Of course not!

In Eretz Israel, too, the same game was played. Only
here the game ended in tragedy. The British wanted
Eretz Israel because it lies at the Eastern end of the
Mediterranean, because it is at the crossroads of three
continents, because it dominates one bank of the Suez
Canal, because it lies athwart the road to India, because . . . there are many important reasons. Palestine
has been desired by all the world's rulers since Ne-
buchadnezzar. But if a great Power wants a country,
does it just take it, 'annex' it? Not if it is a clever Power!

British policy, therefore, was ready to back a great
ideal which would enable Britain to take over control
of Palestine without seeming to. The ideal was at hand:
the Jews to whom the Bible had promised Palestine,
were persecuted and needed a home. The ideal was
very appealing. Britain would promise the Jews a Home
—in Palestine. Not Palestine as a Home, but a Home
in Palestine. Britain would have Palestine, and the Jews
would have a Home in it. Such a policy would also
help British interests in America, for the Jews there
had influence.

But what if too many Jews should want to go to
their National Home? At first, this possibility was not
seriously entertained. After all, it was the general
opinion in the world that Jews preferred business to
manual work. They would not be willing to leave their
shops and offices for the hardships of life in the waste
lands of Palestine with its bare hills and stony soil.
Apart from a handful of idealists and a few paupers,
the mass of Jews would stay where they were. In any
case, in the event of over-abundance of Jews, there
were always Arabs available as trouble-makers. The
Jews might be good merchants, but soldiers, fighters?
The mere thought was enough to make the British administrators laugh. The Jews had not handled arms for
thousands of years. Those not yet in Palestine would
be easily frightened off, and those already there would
have to look to the British for protection. Thus the

blueprint was evolved; the Arabs, when required, would "rebel" against the "foreign invasion"; and the Jews would be forever a threatened minority. Each would have to be protected from the other—by British bayonets.

2

That, roughly, was the flavour of thought underlying the Balfour Declaration. That was how the British Mandate was hatched, and how British policy in Eretz Israel developed, reaching its climax during the Second World War. The plan was clear and consistent, both in purpose and content. To achieve its purpose the British were anxious for a limited number of Jews to enter Eretz Israel—but no more than that. What does one do in such a case? One "plays the ends against the middle." As for Jewish reactions—the Jews were good at business, but not at politics, as the British correctly foresaw. At any rate they were not clever enough to have learnt the importance of choosing their leaders.

Even this plan, however—what I term the British Master Plan—turned out to be inadequate to meet the situation in Europe between the wars, a continent soaked as it was in hatred and blood. In Poland there lived millions of Jews surrounded by violent anti-semitism. In the Baltic and Balkan countries there were hundreds of thousands of Jews, and anti-semitism was growing apace. Scores of thousands of young Jews who, despite their abilities, their university degrees and their diplomas, could find no place in the life of the countries they lived in, turned, naturally, to Eretz Israel. Masses of Jews were straining every nerve to get there.

What was to be done? The flood of Jewish repatriation was a potential threat to British domination. At the Cairo Conference in 1921, attended by Churchill and T. E. Lawrence, where the lines of British policy in the Middle East were clearly defined, Churchill had said that what the Arab princes and kings called themselves was not important "so long as they do what we want when we want it." But could the same be said of the Jews? There seemed a real danger here.

Arab riots and attacks could be easily brought about, but their fruits had to be harvested more carefully. Two highly respectable instruments were invoked. The first was the Commission of Inquiry—of which a whole series came and went. These Commissions had the added psychological advantage of appearing as impartial adjudicators emphasising and re-emphasising that there were two conflicting "rights" in Palestine, and thus underlining the need for the permanent presence in Palestine of the Mandatory Power as a third and deciding party. The other instrument was the White Paper—of which quite a number were published, proclaiming in judicial and measured language the various pretexts and justifications for the policy of keeping Jews out of Palestine, and restricting the development of those already there.

This cycle of events was repeated again and again. The Arabs were encouraged, sometimes quite openly, to organize attacks on the Jews. Then would come an Inquiry Commission with their reports. A White Paper would be published, and immigration stopped or reduced almost to nothing.

In January 1933 Hitler came to power. The Jewish communities in Europe were shaken to the core. A new wave of Jewish immigrants swept towards Palestine. No longer a stream, but a stampede. By now, however, the mechanism of British policy was well run in. In 1936, with Jewish pressure on the gates of Eretz Israel at its peak, bloody disturbances broke out, and continued and could not be stopped. "Broke out" to intimidate waverers, and "continued" in order to provide the excuse for shutting the gates. One Royal Commission. A Second Commission. And finally, in May 1939, a White Paper associated with the name of the none too clever son of the woolly-headed Ramsay MacDonald. This was to be the final White Paper, designed to destroy once and for all the hopes of the Jewish people so far as Palestine was concerned. Four months later, World War broke out. Millions of Jews were trapped, or were about to be trapped, by their pitiless hunters, at that time Hitler and Himmler. What next?

To the men of Whitehall this presented no really new problem. The solution to the Palestine question was by now cut-and dried. The White Paper provided for everything: it finally liquidated the Jewish "claim" to Palestine by promising to allow the last 75,000 to enter the country by 1944, including even 2,500 of the "unfortunate German Jews." Five years after that there was to come about "independence" based on Britain's "traditional friendship with the Arabs" and guaranteed by a treaty between H.M. Government and the new legal government of the country. In this, too, the Jews would not be forgotten. Britain, after all, could claim to have honoured all her obligations—and the Jews would get cultural autonomy, equal rights, and a strictly proportional share—about one-third—in the Government. They would be protected. The Arabs would "govern"—and the British "adviser" would see that they governed in the right direction. That was all clear. It only remained to ensure the application of the plan, which was henceforth to be called "the law."

The difficulty lay in the unfortunate desire of the Jews to save their lives and run away from Hitler. Soon any dormant belief that the sealed frontiers of Europe would prevent their escape was shattered. The Irgun Zvai Leumi, which in association with the Zionist-Revisionist Party and the Betar youth organisation, had brought many thousands of "illegal" immigrants into the country, never halted its activities. The British authorities exerted themselves to horrify the world by gruesome descriptions of the conditions aboard the refugee ships, the "coffin-ships," which, old and dilapidated, were crowded to the gunwales. The British Consul at Constanza, who visited one of the ships, had reported that no Englishman would be prepared to travel in such unhygienic and insanitary conditions. . . . But the transports continued.

No diplomatic effort had been spared in the countries

of Eastern Europe to put a stop to the assistance, overt
and unofficial, which the organizers of the exodus were
receiving from Government agencies or officials in
those countries. Two thousand Jews who had reached
the Rumanian frontier, bearing Rumanian transit visas
on passports containing Bolivian destination visas, had
been turned back following British pressure on Rumanian Foreign Minister Celinescu. This did not prevent some of them from crossing the frontier and joining other Jews from Czechoslovakia, Austria and Rumania in a new effort to get to Eretz Israel.[1]

Again news reached the British officials of a large
number of Italian ships lying idle at Trieste and the
presence in that port of many Jewish "tourists." It was
plain not only that the Jews had not given up, but that
they were planning a "large-scale invasion" of illegal
immigrants. By this time the Haganah[2], much more
wealthy than the Irgun, and backed by the resources
of the Jewish Agency,[3] had also become active in the
immigration field.

[1] They succeeded. They reached Eretz Israel in the famous
Sekariya expedition organized by Mr. Eri Jabotinsky, son of
the creator of the Irgun.
[2] The Haganah was an organisation under the control of
the Zionist Executive designed primarily to afford something
like police protection to the various Jewish colonies in Palestine. Its personnel was composed of colonists themselves plus
a small full-time staff. The official Zionist leaders, especially
those of the Left, were fanatically opposed to its developing a
military nature, something which in their minds could only be
associated with reaction and the Right. Hence, when Jabotinsky
called for a Jewish Army he was denounced by the Left as a
"militarist" and a "Fascist" for daring to utter such a naughty
thought. Many of these Zionist Leftists, of course, had had
bitter experience of East European democracy where the man
who controls the army always seems to poll a "democratic"
majority. Actually, the origins of the Haganah go back to the
old Jewish Watchmen (Shomerin) who guarded the Jewish
colonies, in days of Turkish rule, against Arab bandits and
such-like murderous and light-fingered gentry.
[3] For all practical purposes the reader may regard the term,
"the Jewish Agency" as being the British Government's func-
tional name for the Zionist Organisation. The tangle of organi-

The British Government's ingenuity, however, did not falter. Sympathy for the Jews fleeing from the gas-chambers was countered—by inspired questions in the British House of Commons worded something like this: "Is the Minister aware that the Germans are concentrating shipping at Trieste with the intention of transporting large numbers of Jews to Palestine illegally, in order to create difficulties for Great Britain in the Middle East? What preventive action does the Minister propose taking?"

And the government propaganda was ready to let loose floods of justification. After all, the British authorities told the world, we are not cruel, in fact we are very unhappy about these poor people. And they even insinuated that it was mainly for "these poor people" that the war was being fought. And when the war was over, the Government hoped that "these people" would be able to go back to their homes. But "German spies" could not be allowed to penetrate the Middle East and thus endanger British interests—identical with humanity's interests—in the war. The British High Commissioner in Jerusalem was told to use this argument—a new version of the old discount business in idealism—to justify the new policy of sending "illegal" Jewish immigrants back to Hitler's Europe.

3

The harvest of inevitable tragedy was not long in ripening. The *Struma* arrived off the coast of Eretz Israel carrying more than seven hundred immigrants who, inspite of blockade and warnings, were trying to enter the country. In accordance with instructions she was sent back to her point of departure in Rumania. Half-way there, the ship sank and all on board were drowned. The direct cause has never been discovered.

sations which were gathered under or associated closely with the Zionist Organisation, and more or less amenable to control by the Zionist Executive, are often referred to by the author as "the Jewish institutions."

That was the *Struma*. There were also the *Milos*, the *Pacific*, the *Patria*.

The British government now evolved a new humane means of dealing with the immigrants. Sir Harold McMichael, the High Commissioner, announced that they would not be sent back to Europe—propaganda had not succeeded in justifying that kind of treatment in the eyes of civilised men and women—but would be packed off to Mauritius. He added, however, that with the war's end they would be returned to their "homes" in Europe. To teach the "illegal" immigrants a lesson, the military forces carrying out the deportation used "a certain amount of force" before the ships were sent off on their way to Mauritius. The *Patria* never sailed. Jewish "terrorists" placed a bomb to prevent its departure. The bomb exploded and more than two hundred Jews were killed or drowned. The British authorities noted the fact that this was not an Irgun Zvai Leumi operation; it was the Haganah which had placed the bomb.

In this particular case, the echoes of the explosion were such that McMichael showed "clemency" to the survivors and allowed them to enter Eretz Israel. But the statement which accompanied the clemency unambiguously reaffirmed that it would not serve as a precedent and emphasized that "illegal immigration" would not be tolerated. "The law" would be enforced, and anybody caught entering illegally would be returned to the country of his origin.

Thus we reached the years 1942-43, during which Himmler's programme of mass-extermination got into its stride. All appeals to what the Jews hoped was a sensitive British conscience were fruitless. Vain was the appeal of the events themselves, vain the verbal appeals of Jewish leaders. British policy in Palestine was admirably consistent. The White Paper was the law. The law was the White Paper. The entry of Jews into Eretz Israel was forbidden. The Eretz Israel problem had been finally "solved" by the White Paper.

Dark night, the darkest of all nights, descended on

the Jewish people in Europe. One million five hundred thousand Jewish children were transported in the death trains to the gas-chambers. Millions of men and women were shot, or drowned, or burned, or gassed or buried alive. When man becomes a beast, the Jew ceases to be regarded as a human being. There is no room here for self-delusion. It was not only the Nazis and their friends who regarded the Jews as germs to be destroyed. The whole world which calls itself "enlightened" began to get used to the idea that perhaps the Jew is not as other human beings. Just as "the world" does not pity the thousands of cattle led to the slaughter-pens in the Chicago abattoirs, equally it did not pity—or else it got used to—the tens of thousands of human beings taken like sheep to the slaughter in Treblinki. The world does not pity the slaughtered. It only respects those who fight. For better or for worse, that is the truth.

All the peoples of the world knew this grim truth except the Jews. That is why our enemies were able to trap us and shed our blood at will.

Britain enforced an economic blockade against the territories occupied by the Germans: that was her war against Nazism. But she also enforced a political blockade against the Jews in German-Occupied territories, which was an aid to Nazism. It was not intended as such, but it did help achieve one of Nazism's purposes: the destruction of the masses of the Jewish people, or, in Foreign Office terms, the maximum reduction of the number of Jews likely to flood into Palestine. The maximum reduction of the number of Jews wanting to go to Palestine was essential for the fulfilment of the Master Plan. The essence of the plan, though its names were many and its form as flexible as current opinion, remained constant. The White Paper was one of its names. The partition slogan of the Peel Commission of 1937 was another. The Morrison Plan was a third name, the Bevin Plan a fourth. It appeared at different times as "federation" and "cantonisation," as "autonomy," and "independence." The aim was to maintain the British government's control over Eretz Israel with a number of "protected Jews" in the midst of an Arab sea, whose waves would be ruled by the traditional rulers of the waves.

Wave-rulers have wide horizons, and they are forever calculating the objectives and probable steps of their antagonists. A document compiled in this spirit by the well-known "Arab Bureau" in Cairo, and marked "Secret," fell into the hands of the Irgun Zvai Leumi in 1945. This "Bureau" which is under the Foreign Office, looked beyond the victory over Hitler. It assumed, not without satisfaction, that the number of Jews wanting to go to Eretz Israel after the war would be considerably reduced. But it also assumed that the Jews would try to resist—even by force—the execution of the British plan. A small increase in the number of Jews in Eretz Israel would be permitted in order to appease the noise-makers—but no more. This would make the Jews one-third of the population. In the language of democracy, as interpreted in Downing Street, this was "equal rights." In the language of Jewish realities, it was ghetto. In the inevitable language of the history of ghettoes, it was destruction.

The Cairo wirepullers themselves realised that it would not be easy to carry out the plan. The Irgun Zvai Leumi and the Stern Group, they wrote in their document, would carry out acts of terrorism. Later the Haganah would join them and possibly unite with the Irgun, "permitting" the Stern Group to remain outside and operate independently. Illegal immigration would be organized on a large scale, efforts would be made to cause trouble between the British authorities on the spot (in Jerusalem and Cairo) and the London Government, and Jewish influence would be exerted in the United States. That influence was a very serious factor. Nevertheless, the Cairo Bureau assumed that it would be possible to overcome Jewish resistance. For that it would be necessary, in the first place, to secure the acquiescence of the American Government in the British plan.

This was of great importance to the British Government. They regarded the Jews as depending to a great extent on American support. On the other hand, they knew that the five million Jews in the United States constituted a substantial factor at elections—a fact to be regretted but not to be changed. Consequently they thought it important to forestall the Jews and secure early American consent for their plan; and they designed a scheme of persuasion.

They did their utmost to impress upon the Americans that although the war with Germany, Italy and Japan was still in progress—Soviet Russia would certainly have to be dealt with later on. In that struggle, too, Britain would be in the front line of defence of democracy and freedom. Consequently the United States must not hinder British plans for the Middle East. This simple line of reasoning promised good results. With America backing the British, the Jews would simply not dare to oppose them. The Haganah, supervised by the official Jewish authorities, would certainly not be allowed to indulge in terrorism. As for the "terrorists," who ostensibly did not accept the discipline of the authorities—responsibility for their good behaviour would be placed upon the Jewish leaders who would be forced to collaborate in liquidating the "terror." The prospects looked good.

4

It was against this background that the Jewish revolt in Eretz Israel broke out. The two fundamental facts— the campaign of extermination of the Jews of Europe and the barred gates in the very days of that campaign —were the immediate causes of its outbreak. I stress the word "immediate," for in every war and in every revolution the fundamental causes which inevitably create wars or revolutions must be distinguished from those immediate causes which merely determine the time of their outbreak.

The famine in France at the end of the eighteenth century and the Salt Tax did not cause the great Revolution: they only accelerated its onset, just as the Tea Tax served to light the ready fuse of the American War of Independence. Similarly it was the Defenestration of Prague which brought on the Thirty Years' War, the assassination at Sarajevo which brought on the First World War, the Danzig issue in 1939 which converted the inevitable struggle between Germany and the rest of the world into an accomplished fact.

These historic laws operated, though on a far different scale, in the case of the Eretz Israel rising. The rising was inevitable. For many years Zionist leaders had decried the idea of Hebrew independence, and of Statehood. But Vladimir Jabotinsky warned them that nobody would believe their protestations, neither British nor Arabs nor the world in general. All of them, he said, had read the Bible and knew that once we Jews started *coming back* to Eretz Israel, our aim must be clear: that Eretz Israel should be our again. And that, after all, was our aim. It was in our blood. Our national anthem proclaimed it. The British did not notice the change of text introduced in the Eretz Israel version of the Jewish national anthem. In the Diaspora Jews sang of our ancient hope to return to the land of our fathers. In Eretz Israel the Jews sang of our ancient hope *to be free people in our own country*. A free people . . . in our own country. Such a people cannot be ruled by aliens. It must liberate itself from their yoke; and the effort at liberation can only be a matter of time.

There is no doubt that even had there been no extermination in Europe, even if the British had not been so consistent in their policy, a Jewish revolt in one form or another would have been launched against any foreign rule trying to impose itself for any length of time on our stiff-necked and freedom-loving people. But those two factors, coming simultaneously and in their very coincidence threatening to strangle the hopes of Israel and utterly to destroy the Jewish people— determined the moment for its outbreak.

On the other hand, it is no less clear that if, in spite of this combination of factors, there had not been found in a section of Jewry the strength and the spirit to rise in revolt, the sun would have set on our people. The "plan" would have been carried out. We should

not today have a Jewish State. We should have had a
ghetto with our enemies trying to turn it into a graveyard. The revolt, for a number of reasons not dependent
on the rebels, did not bring about complete redemption: the State was established in only a part of our
country. But it did prevent complete destruction.

The revolt sprang from the earth. The ancient Greek
story of Antaeus and the strength he drew from contact
with Mother Earth, is a legend. The renewed strength
which came to us, and especially to our youth, from
contact with the soil of our ancient land, is no legend
but a fact. The officials of the British Foreign Office
had no conception of this when they made their plans.
What could they foresee of those hidden forces which
Herzl used to speak of as the "imponderables"?[1] Their
error was not mathematical; they were not wrong about
the number of Jews wanting to come to Eretz Israel. It
was moral. They could not gauge the character of the
Jews who came to Eretz Israel. They assumed that in
Eretz Israel, too, the Jews would continue to be timid
suppliants for protection. The conduct of the Jews—
or rather the attitude of their official leaders, expressed
in the well-known policy of self-restraint (havlagah)[2]
—seemed to justify and confirm this assumption. But
those unseen forces, which have ever saved the Jewish
people from obliteration, demolished the British assumption. Vladimir Jabotinsky appeared, educating a
whole generation to resist, to be ready for sacrifice, for
revolt and for war. David Raziel appeared, the greatest
Jewish military mind of our generation, to carry out
the decisive act; the *first attack* by Jewish arms. The

---

[1] The term was previously so used by Bismarck.
[2] During the disturbances of 1936-39 the Haganah pursued
a policy known as *havlagah,* a Hebrew word meaning self-restraint. It prescribed non-retaliation except under direct attack.
As a result of this policy the Arabs were always sure of the
initiative and never suffered any counter-attack. Their risks
were reduced to what they were liable to suffer during attacks
timed to suit themselves and on a battlefield chosen by themselves. It was largely in negation of this policy that the I.Z.L.
came into being in 1937.

Jewish underground army, the Irgun Zvai Leumi, arose. Another underground organisation called the Fighters for the Freedom of Israel[1] arose. A new generation grew up which turned its back on fear. It began to fight instead of to plead. For nearly two thousand years, the Jews, as Jews, had not borne arms, and it was on this complete disarmament, as much psychological as physical, that our oppressors calculated. They did not realize that the two phenomena were interdependent: we gave up our arms when we were exiled from our country. With our return to the land of our fathers our strength was restored.

Blood too brought the revolt to life. The blood of our people cried out to us from the foreign soil on which it had been shed, fired revolt in our hearts and gave the rebels strength. When the gruesome reports from Europe were confirmed, we knew that we must fight not only for the freedom of our people but for its very existence. Had we anything to lose? This was no rhetorical question. There are certain famous slogans which are usually more exciting in their effect than serious in their content. "We shall fight to the last drop of blood" contains considerable exaggeration even when related to some of the most famous battles in history. "We have nothing to lose" is another example. Usually people do not fight till their last drop of blood. Normally they always have something to lose.

Our case, however, was unique. When we launched our revolt against the yoke of oppression and against the wanton shedding of Jewish blood we were convinced that our people truly had nothing to lose except the prospect of extermination. This was not a mere phrase or hyperbole. It was the truth; and it strengthened immeasurably the rebels' capacity for sacrifice. Capacity for sacrifice is the measure of revolt and the father of victory. Only when you are prepared to stand up to Zeus himself in order to bring fire to humanity can you achieve the fire-revolution. When you continue

[1] F.F.I. for short; frequently called the Stern Group after its leader Abraham Stern.

to assert, even when threatened by the stake, that the earth goes round the sun, not only are you unconquerable, but you ensure ultimate victory for your idea, the idea of truth. In short, in all history there is no greater force than the readiness for self-sacrifice, just as there is no greater love than the love of freedom. The soil of their country and the blood of their murdered people infused the Hebrew rebels with both that force and that love.

The change brought about in the Jewish soul by these two forces found expression both in deeds and in words, in battle and in the court-room. The rebels who were brought before the military courts never asked for pity or for mercy. Never once. Either they kept silent in order not to give away information, or they carried their fight into the court-room, attacking the judges who threatened them with the gallows, attacking instead of defending themselves, accusing instead of pleading. This is what one-armed Meir Feinstein, among the great heroes of our generation, said to the British judges in one of the sharpest and most eloquent of these declarations:

"A regime of gallows—that is the regime you want to establish in this country, whose destiny it is to serve as a lighthouse for humanity. In your stupid wickedness you assume that by this means you will succeed in breaking the spirit of our people, the people to whom the whole country has become a gallows. You are mistaken. You will learn that what you have come up against is steel, steel tempered by the fire of love and hatred—love of the Homeland and freedom, hatred for the oppressor and invader. It is burning steel. You will not break it. You will destroy your hands.

"How blind you are, British tyrants: Have you not learnt yet whom you are fighting in this struggle, unexampled in human history? Do you believe *we* are to be frightened by death—we who for years heard the rattle of the trucks that bore our brothers, our parents, the best of our people, to a slaughter which, too, had no precedent in history? We who asked and ask ourselves every day; how are we better than they, than

millions of our brothers? In what lies our virtue? For
we could have been among and with them in the days
of fear and in the moments that came before death.

"To these recurring questions our conscience makes
one reply: We were not spared in order to live in
slavery and oppression and to await some new Treblinki. We were spared in order to ensure life and freedom and honour for ourselves, for our people, for our
children and our children's children. We were spared
in order that there should be no repetition of what
happened there and of what has happened and is still
likely to happen here, under your rule, the rule of
treachery, the rule of blood.

"That is why we shall not be frightened. We have
learnt—and at what price in vain sacrifices!—that there
is a life that is worse than death and a death greater
than life."

These words, uttered on the very brink of death,
expressed the feeling that infused the rebels. The same
feeling permeated the public call to revolt published
by the Irgun Zvai Leumi throughout the length and
breadth of Eretz Israel early in 1944. That call, which
included a survey of the past, stated the political demands of the Jewish people at the close of the Second
World War and charted the road of uprising and
struggle. It said in conclusion:

"Four years have passed since the war began, and
all the hopes that beat in your hearts then have evaporated without a trace. We have not been accorded international status, no Jewish Army has been set up,
the gates of the country have not been opened. The
British regime has sealed its shameful betrayal of the
Jewish people and there is no moral basis whatsoever
for its presence in Eretz Israel.

"We shall fearlessly draw conclusions. There is no
longer any armistice between the Jewish people and
the British Administration in Eretz Israel which hands
our brothers over to Hitler. Our people is at war with
this regime—war to the end.

"This war will demand many and heavy sacrifices,
but we enter on it in the consciousness that we are

being faithful to the children of our people who have been and are being slaughtered. It is for their sake that we fight, to their dying testimony that we remain loyal.

"This, then is our demand: Immediate transfer of power in Eretz Israel to a Provisional Hebrew Government.

"We shall fight, every Jew in the Homeland will fight. The God of Israel, the Lord of Hosts, will aid us. There will be no retreat. Freedom—or death.

"Build a protecting wall around your fighting youth. Do not forsake them. . . .

"The fighting youth will not flinch from tribulation and sacrifice, from blood and suffering. They will not surrender until they have renewed our days as of old, until they have ensured for our people a Homeland, freedom, honour, bread and justice. And if you will give them your aid you will see in our days the Return to Zion and the restoration of Israel."

5

This call was due to appear not in January 1944, but in the first half of 1943. It was drafted when I was still a private—I was never more than that—in a foreign army. Because of indirect circumstances, inside and outside the Irgun, our Zero Hour was delayed. But it arrived. We went out to fight. We put on the whole armour of freedom. We uttered the specific demand: a Provisional Jewish Government. We undertook not to retreat. We opened a chapter whose end we could not foresee. Our present was bitter, the future vague. We could only have faith—and indeed we had faith—that our toil and our sacrifice, our blood and our suffering would bring us victory.

Before publishing the proclamation of revolt, the Command of the Irgun considered long and earnestly whether, in view of the postponement, it was desirable to publish it at all. Would it not be preferable to start at once with action rather than with explanations?

Some of my colleagues felt that external and internal reasons both dictated that we start with a military attack and not with a political dissertation. Their arguments were weighty. Our people are practical. They do not respect words unless they are backed by action. Consequently, these colleagues argued, they would not take our proclamation seriously. They would read it, nod their heads, say to themselves that they had read better and even more "explosive" stuff—and go on their way, unmoved. As for our own ranks, their will to fight was beyond question. But how many times had they already been told that the fight was beginning? The unfulfilled promises had been many—though there had been every intention of keeping them. Disappointment had been frequent and bitter. A new promise, one more proclamation, would not capture their hearts. They, too, would read it, nod their heads and say—they had heard it all before.

Despite the weight of these arguments, reinforced by the fact that "first" action would give us the military advantage of complete surprise, we decided to publish the proclamation. It was clear to us that, however matters developed, we were embarking on a prolonged struggle. No single operation, however wide its repercussions, could be decisive. We would have to carry out many operations. There would be suffering and we would be hounded incessantly. Consequently, it was our duty to elucidate the principles of the struggle and its aims. The world must know what we are fighting for. The people should know why they must be prepared, through our operations, to endure recurring troubles. The youth must know why they are risking their lives. We knew too that our fight would not be only military. The relative strength of the oppressor and the rebels was out of all proportion. We should clearly have to weight the scales with other factors. One of them would be the political factor. To be more precise, the fight would be a political one pursued by military means. Consequently political explanation, clear and persistent, would have to accompany the military operations. Thus was born and thus came to be published the long proclamation which in the underground —though not publicly—came to be called "palabra."

When I first heard the word "palabra" I did not know what it meant, and when on investigation I discovered that it was Spanish and meant "word" I did not grasp the connection. But my friends told me that it also bore the meaning "idle chatter," and that it had been applied to our proclamation by the printer. This man, a Sephardi, printed our underground literature with the help of his sons for several years, but at that early stage he was naturally somewhat nervous, and, wanting to get it out of his hands as quickly as possible, he complained at its excessive length—in short *palabra*.

While the printer had justifiable personal reasons of his own for his term of contempt, there were unfortunately many more who agreed with him, both friends and others. None of them treated our proclamation seriously. None of them believed that there would be any follow-up, or any follow-up to the follow-up. I heard of typical complimentary comments: "Begin is a public speaker, and now that he's gone underground and can't make speeches he's begun to write them on the walls." Just *Palabra*.

It seems that this was also the view of the British. Among the doubters was Wilkin, a well-known C.I.D. officer. Wilkin was as cunning as a fox and one of the few really capable members of the British detective force. He had risen from the ranks, knew Hebrew well and was a good psychologist. When he caught a suspect, he would put the astonishing question to him:

"To what organization do you belong, the Irgun or the Stern Group?"

And when the answer was "Neither," Wilkin would storm:

"What, a traitor? Hitler's killing the Jews in Europe, the White Paper is still in force, and you don't belong to the underground?"

True he did not often succeed, but some of his captives swallowed the bait.

With the intensification of the underground struggle, Wilkin was promoted and transferred to C.I.D. Headquarters in Jerusalem, where he was later killed.

When, with the publication of our long proclamation, Wilkin was told that great troubles were in the offing, that the Irgun Zvai Leumi had declared war on the British regime and had called for a general revolt, he remained calm.

"There's nothing to worry about," he remarked contemptuously.

That was the general reaction among both Jews and British. Considerable derision, little belief. *Palabra!* But we, who had gone down into the depths of the underground in order to raise up a struggle for liberation, knew that it was very serious indeed. Our decimated[1] people had only one way left: the way of revolutionary uprising. The only way is, in the nature of things, the right way. The two fateful words, which have changed history and made history, were flung into the arena of Eretz Israel. Freedom or death. Two great simple words.

Now there could be no retreat. A heavy burden was lifted from our hearts. True, our anxiety was infinite. It was indeed only just beginning. How long would the struggle last? What sacrifices would we have to make? Blood . . . bereaved families . . . forsaken children . . . fallen sons . . . widowed mothers. The responsibility was terrifying.

But in our minds there was the constant knowledge of what British policy was planning for us; in our ears echoed the rattle of the death-trucks of Europe. And we steeled our hearts against doubts, and against alternative "solutions."

What use was there in writing memoranda? What

[1] It is worth noting that the word "decimate" in its original meaning, viz. to kill a tenth, is here a considerable understatement. The Jewish people who numbered some sixteen and a half millions throughout the world in 1939, were reduced by six millions slaughtered by the Germans between that year and 1945. In less than six years more than a third of all the Jews in the world were deliberately murdered. The same proportions applied to the inhabitants of Great Britain would give a death-roll of some sixteen millions, or one in every three. These facts are accepted as platitudinous by many to-day. Their awful significance is grasped by very few.

value in speeches? If you are attacked by a wolf in the forest, do you try to persuade him that it is not fair to tear you to pieces, or that he is not a wolf at all but an innocent lamb? Do you send him a "memorandum"? No, there was no other way. If we did not fight we should be destroyed. To fight was the only way to salvation.

When Descartes said: "I think, therefore I am," he uttered a very profound thought. But there are times in the history of peoples when thought alone does not prove their existence. A people may "think" and yet its sons, with their thoughts and in spite of them, may be turned into a herd of slaves—or into soap. There are times when everything in you cries out: your very self-respect as a human being lies in your resistance to evil.

We fight, therefore we are!

Chapter V
Logic of the Revolt

It would be a grave error to conclude from what I have written in the previous chapter that the main source of the rebels' strength and endurance was their emotions. To assume that the revolt was merely the "heroic adventure" of "desperate" people which only by chance did not end in failure or disaster wiuld be more than a mistake: it would be foolish. Nevertheless, this was the assumption of Lord Samuel, one-time High Commissioner in Palestine. In a debate in the British House of Lords, in the summer of 1946 he invited his fellow-peers to compare what was happening in Eretz Israel under British rule in the Twentieth Century, with what had happened in the First Century when the Romans ruled there. Now, he said, there was a body called the Irgun Zvai Leumi. Centuries before there had been a group called the Zealots, who displayed great heroism and self-sacrifice in their brave stand against the might of the Roman Empire. But, asked Lord Samuel, what had been the outcome? The Zealots died to a man. In the historic siege of Massada the last survivors killed their wives and children and then killed each other, so that none was left alive to fall into the hands of the Romans when they entered the fortress. This had been a death-blow to the Jewish people, which had been exiled from its country and dispersed to the four winds. That great act of heroism, he reminded their Lordships, had achieved nothing; and the Jewish people must beware of treading the same path.

We all know that subsequent events proved that his lordship of Carmel was mistaken. The heroism of the Irgun was not inconsiderable—and something *was* achieved. The revolt against the British did not end as the revolt against the Romans had ended. It is not Massada but Modi'in[1] that symbolises the Hebrew revolt of our times. The reason is simple. The recent revolt was not only produced by natural emotions; it was guided by common-sense and political logic. Emotion gave birth to its heroism; logic brought about its strategy; and good strategy ensured victory.

Already in the early stages of the revolt we achieved an important strategic objective: we succeeded in nullifying the local Arab factor. For twenty years the Arabs had held the military and political initiative. To be more precise, the British administration throughout the whole Mandatory period had pressed the initiative upon the Arabs. This, on the one hand, had provided a pretext for not allowing too many Jews to enter the country, and, on the other hand suggested that British forces had to be in Eretz Israel to protect the Jews. The historical facts of the Arab attacks are known: the pogrom in the Old City of Jerusalem in 1920, the murderous attack in Jaffa in 1921, the blood-bath of 1929, the incessant campaign of violence from 1936 to 1939. The psychological consequences of these one-sided attacks were as disastrous as their political aftermath. The Arabs who, while they cannot be accused of undue cowardice, are not regarded as particularly courageous, began seriously to look upon the Jew as *walad-al-mawt*—a child of death—and to look forward to the great festival of "*tbah el-yahud*," of general slaughter. In the world at large the belief took root that the Jews in Eretz Israel, just as elsewhere, were merely a burden on Gentile security forces. Unfortunates? Certainly. In the right? Possibly. But woe to the justice that can be slaughtered by the knife of a son of the desert.

The Hebrew revolt put an end to this shameful and dangerous phase. The British, attacked by the Jewish rebels, could scarcely argue that they were in Palestine to protect the Jews. The Arabs soon forgot the "child

[1] Village in the Judean Hills where the successful Hasmonean revolt against the Greeks was launched in 165 B.C.E.

of death" and began to respect and even to admire the Jewish "jeddah." This last was an indirect result, but of great practical significance. The Arabs lost the military initiative. The Mandatory no longer succeeded in pressing the initiative upon them. Not that they did not try. On the contrary; throughout the revolt the Government spared no effort to turn back the tide, to convert the Anglo-Jewish struggle into an Arab-Jewish conflict. The Arab contacts of both the Haganah and the Irgun Zvai Leumi often told of the visits of government agents to Arab villages and of their inciting speeches to the Arabs. The incitement, however, bore no fruit. The Arabs listened and remained passive. At last, a high-ranking British officer, General D'Arcy, evolved a new theory concerning the British mission in Eretz Israel. He told the Anglo-American Committee of Inquiry that if the British left, the Jews would take control of the whole country. In other words, the British now had to protect the Arabs from the Jews. . . . The tune had certainly changed!

I had occasion, in the early days of the revolt, to see for myself the psychological effect among the Arabs of our surprise attacks. The day after our triple attack on the police headquarters in Jerusalem, Haifa and Jaffa, I went to Jerusalem from Tel Aviv. For safety's sake I travelled, together with a Sephardi comrade, in an Arab bus. On the road we were held up several times by British patrols. But while searches of Jewish vehicles were very thorough, the scrutiny of the "loyal" Arab vehicles was most perfunctory. Our papers were "in order" and we were passed through. My companion, Shimshon, who knows Arabic well, listened to the conversations among our Arab fellow-travellers. Their only subject of conversation was the attack on the headquarters of Authority. They were full of wonderment. Their excitable imagination was fired. "There are no more police," they said.

When we reached Jerusalem we saw a huge mass of Arabs, gathered in the area between Barclay's Bank and the Post Office, viewing from a more or less safe distance the destruction the Irgun had wrought at the

General Headquarters of the Police. We studied them closely. They were dumbfounded. Shimshon again overheard some of their conversation. Their talk was a confused mixture of amazement, fear and admiration. And so it was with all the later attacks the results of which they were able to see.

A new type of "pilgrimage" developed among the Arabs. From town and village they would stream to the places where we had "visited" the regime of oppression and blown up buildings—"laid them flat," as one British Member of Parliament put it. During that period we used to address the Arabs in their own language. Thousands of our leaflets were distributed in Arab towns and villages, either by some of our boys who resemble Arabs in appearance or by Arab friends. The Arabs, it is true, do not read much, but their curiosity to find out what the underground was saying was very marked. Often an educated Arab would read aloud to an eager audience which could not read.

We told the Arabs that we had no desire to fight or harm them; that we were anxious to see them as peaceful citizens of the Jewish State-to-be; we pointed to the undeniable fact that in our operations in Arab areas there had been not the slightest intrusion on Arab peace or security. We warned them that it was the object of the British officially to inflame them against us and to get us to fight each other. We hoped earnestly they would not heed propaganda of this kind. If they did, however, and raised a hand against the Jews, we would have no option but to move against them with all dispatch and severity.

But great as may have been the influence of our literature, it is certain that deeds had a greater effect. The fact that the mighty British Government not only failed to put an end to our struggle but, on the contrary, continued to be subjected to blows of ever-increasing severity, exercised a very healthy influence on the Arabs. Their imagination did the rest.

The Arabs not only refrained from hindering us in our attacks on the regime; some of them actively helped us. Their aid, it is true, was not given gratis, but it was

vital. Of the few arms we had, some were bought from
Arabs. Until we found our own means of manufacturing
substantial quantities of explosives—the main weapon
in the struggle for liberation—and apart from what we
"borrowed" from the British themselves, the major
part of our T.N.T. was acquired from Arab suppliers.

At a later stage of the revolt we were approached by
representatives of certain Arab tribes with the proposal
to set up a "common war front against the British." All
they wanted from us was money to finance war-propa-
ganda among their people. We were unable to fall in
with their proposal. What little money we had was
needed for buying explosives from the Arabs.

Only after the United Nations Organization had come
to its decision on the future of Eretz Israel (a decision
which was the direct result of the Jewish revolt), did
the Arabs raise their hand against us. They did so
because they were promised that the regular armies of
the Arab States would be thrown into the battle to van-
quish or destroy the Jews. They anticipated that Tel
Aviv, its buildings and its daughters would be delivered
up to the Palestine Arabs. But even during the period
of fighting which opened on the 30th November, 1947
and during the invasion which began on the 15th of
May, 1948, the attitude of respect mingled with fear,
which Jewish arms had evoked among all Arabs during
the revolt against the British, had its effects. In a head-
on battle it is strength that decides. But what is
strength? It is not the physical factor alone. Spiritual
and psychological factors are very important, sometimes decisive, elements in a fighting force. One of
them is the legend that goes before the fighting force,
e.g. that it is a "terror to its enemies," that it "always
wins," that it is "unconquerable" and so on. The legend
of Jewish strength was created by the underground; by
the Hebrew revolt. This legend, which grew up during
the years before the international political decision was
taken, played an important part in the repulse of the
invaders and in casting fear into their hearts—something which has not even yet been adequately evaluated.

The Haganah played a historical part in the struggle

against the Arab invaders before the Israel Army, uniting all the fighting forces, was set up. But it is childish to claim that it was the "very existence" of the Haganah that in 1944-8 prevented the repetition of the 1936-1939 Arab disturbances. The Arabs no doubt heard the story of the "scores of thousands of rifles" which the Haganah was alleged to possess. But they also remembered the Haganah from the days of *havlagah*. That memory could hardly have restrained them. What, if anything, gave them pause was the memory of the pre-war retaliatory operations of the Irgun Zvai Leumi under the command of David Raziel.

It is true that despite its inactivity for many years, the prestige of the Haganah among the Arabs was high. But it had gained this prestige because of the logical calculation the Arabs made when they viewed our successful surprise attacks against the British. They doubled, and trebled our strength and, with the aid of their imagination, multiplied it still more. If the Irgun "dissidents," they argued, are so strong, if this relatively small rebel force cannot be put down by the mighty British, what must be the strength of the "seventy thousand" of the Haganah? Thus each new attack on the forces of the oppressor fortified amongst the Arabs the legend of Jewish military might.

In this way the revolt brought about the neutralisation of the Arab factor. Before the British authority could bring it into operation against us as in the past, it had been paralyzed. And later when the Arabs, under British encouragement tried to measure their strength against us, it was too late. Their hand was "cut off" as we had warned them it would be. The first clash ended, albeit at a heavy cost in Jewish lives, in the victory of Jewish arms.

"Securing the flank" during the revolt against the Mandatory regime was a substantial strategic achievement, but it was achieved indirectly. The major strategy of the revolt was aimed against the government itself and was designed to achieve—and ultimately did achieve—direct objectives. It was not shaped in a day but was fashioned laboriously and hammered out in the heat of battle and in the light of experience. Our strategy was established on three sound bases: on a comprehensive study of the methods used by oppressor administrations in foreign countries; on an objective study of the international situation; and on searching examination of the position and condition of Great Britain at the end of the second World War.

British Government departments have vast experience of ruling over foreign—especially over backward —peoples. He studied and examined this experience. We learned that in general British officials avoid making their rule dependent on force, but rather on the power of prestige. They know that "you can do anything with bayonets except sit on them." It is much better to sit in their shadow. Consequently, when the British administrators are faced with violent opposition they tend to seek a way out, by foregoing direct rule and substituting indirect British rule. Thus, the Commander-in-Chief is replaced by an "Advisor," the High Commissioner by an "Ambassador." Leaving by the door, they come back through the window. The history of the Middle and Far East in the last two generations provides evidence of this system in its various phases.

History and our observation persuaded us that if we could succeed in destroying the government's prestige in Eretz Israel, the removal of its rule would follow automatically. Thenceforward we gave no peace to this weak spot. Throughout all the years of our uprising, we hit at the British Government's prestige, deliberately, tirelessly, unceasingly.

The very existence of an underground, which oppression, hangings, torture and deportations fail to crush or to weaken, must, in the end, undermine the prestige of a colonial regime that lives by the legend of its omnipotence. Every attack which it fails to prevent is a blow at its standing. Even if the attack does not succeed, it makes a dent in that prestige, and that dent widens into a crack which is extended with every succeeding attack.

Most of our attacks were successful, but there were some failures. We learnt how to avoid them. But we

knew too that they were failures only in the military
sense. Politically, every attack was an achievement. And
there were military attacks which had a specially disintegrating effect on the government's prestige. Foremost
among these was the storming of the Acre Prison, which
compelled the chief of the Occupation Government to
publish a bewildered apologia. It was an admission of
failure to destroy the underground or to prevent its
attacks.

But there were, as we shall yet tell, events and actions, great and small, not strictly speaking military,
which struck at the roots of the Government's prestige
perhaps even more than successful military operations.
The arrest of British officers in order to secure the
annulment of a death "sentence," the arrest of more
officers which did not prevent the murder of our captive comrades, but which did bring about the retreat of
Palestine officials into the famous "Ghettoes"; the frustration of martial law, the last attempt at mass oppression, the whipping of officers in retaliation for the whipping of our young soldiers; hangings in retaliation for
hangings—all these things not only shook the Government's prestige, but eventually destroyed it in Eretz
Israel.

We often encountered the argument that the British
Government if it so chose could take revenge by destroying us all and thus our operations were endangering
the whole Jewish population. This was indeed a very
serious question, perhaps the most serious we ever
faced. General Cunningham, the last High Commissioner, referred to it in his report on the storming of
Acre fortress. The General argued that there was no
means of destroying the Jewish underground except
by the application of the whole military might against
the entire population.

But, added the General, the British, unlike the Germans, could not do such a thing.

Reliance, or undue reliance, on the moral restraints
of an enemy, is no part of strategy. So, we did not depend on the Government's "humanity." We had witnessed the wanton behaviour of the Airborne troops

in our towns and villages and Kibbutzim. We had read
the internal literature distributed among the British
soldiers. Characteristic of the attitude of some of the
troops was the threat scribbled on a copy of our underground newspaper *Herut:* "Oh, Gee, oh Gee, Hitler
killed 6,000,000 Jews. The Sixth Airborne will kill
60,000,000 if you don't bloody well behave yourselves."

We had in front of us an official document, issued
in Eretz Israel by G.H.Q., British Forces in the Middle
East. It was the "Middle East Training Pamphlet No.
9, Part XIII," containing instructions on how to "deal
with" civilian demonstrations. This is what it said:

"Since the famous incident at Amritsar at the end
of the First World War, dispersing a crowd has been
regarded as a dangerous task, and it has been assumed
that any action that may be taken in carrying it out will
be regarded as unwarranted. This is an unjustified assumption.

This is how to act:

(*a*) Warn the crowd that you will open fire if they
do not disperse.

(*b*) Choose three men from your platoon. Look out
for the ringleaders, *who are not usually at the
front of the crowd but are inciting from behind.*
Show them to your men as their target. When
you think such action justified, order them to
shoot, and to shoot to kill."

It was in this spirit that the Occupation Army in
Eretz Israel was trained. The reference to Amritsar was
not accidental.

In spite of all this we were not afraid that the troops
would be turned on to destroy the Yishuv—the Jews in
Palestine—as some of the panic-stricken Jewish officials feared, or said they feared. We were convinced
that such procedure was out of the question; and our
conviction was the product of sober reflection.

A civilian population, even if it numbers only hundreds of thousands, cannot be destroyed all at once. A
prolonged campaign of destruction would be required.
The authorities knew, or would learn as time went on,
that this would not be a one-sided process. Not only

would much Jewish blood be shed, but considerable British blood as well, much more than in all the underground attacks put together. Colonel Patterson, Commander of the Jewish Legion (formed by Vladimir Jabotinsky in the First World War), a British officer of Irish extraction who went into exile and denounced the British Government's betrayal of the Jewish people, once said in a conversation with officers of the Irgun Zvai Leumi:

"Remember, the English don't like to be killed."

Of course, nobody likes being killed. Respect and concern for life are the measure of human civilisation. But Socrates was right when he said that life is not always the main thing. There are things in life more important than life itself. Maybe the British Government, or some of its officials, believed that British interests are precisely the things which are more important than life itself—at any rate than the lives of other people.

However, we remembered what Patterson had told us, and we found confirmation of what he had said in our own ever-increasing experience. The British authorities were, after all, intelligent and educated. They knew that if they attempted to destroy the civilian population they would launch a desperate war of vengeance in which they would pay dearly in manhood before they could achieve their purpose.

Moreover, Tel Aviv is not Amritsar, nor is Eretz Israel the Punjab. Eretz Israel was a centre of world interest. The revolt had made it so. It is a fact that no partisan struggle had been so publicized throughout the world as was ours. While our revolt was in progress, a number of battles of considerable magnitude were fought in the Greek mountains. They were accorded but a few lines in the world's press. The reports on our operations, under screaming headlines, covered the front pages of newspapers everywhere, particularly in the United States. There are some people who argued that it was merely to pander to sensationalism that the American newspapers gave so much space to our operations and even to our secret broadcasts and public statements.

Even if there is a grain of truth in this commercial evaluation, what does it matter? The interest of the newspapers is the measure of the interest of the public. And the public—not only Jews but non-Jews too—were manifestly interested in the blows we were striking in Eretz Israel.

It is characteristic that even the subsequent operations of the Israel Army were given much less publicity throughout the world than the earlier operations of the rebels. The reason is obvious. The operations of a regular Army, even if it achieves great victories, are less spectacular than the daring attacks of a handful of rebels against a mighty Government and army.

In this publicity, which was sometimes exaggerated but always spontaneous, we recognised the second factor which would preclude a deliberate "destruction of the Yishuv." We wanted more and more people to interest themselves in what was going on in Eretz Israel. This interest, which our struggle created, built a kind of invisible lifebelt round the Jewish population. The extensive campaign of enlightenment conducted by the Hebrew Committee of National Liberation in the United States played an important part in this field. The British Government were very susceptible to American opinion and could not ignore the feelings of their "rich Transatlantic uncle." True, there was always the danger of individual acts of vengeance by the troops, and we did all we could to prevent them. Whenever our military arrangements permitted, we published preliminary warnings to the civilian population involved, issuing an English translation for British civilians. Such a warning was published, for example, in the spring of 1945, when we planned to set off an electric mortar against British military G.H.Q. Another was published in the spring of 1947 before our contact mines were operated against the railway system.

This was a typical example of these warnings:

"(1) The Government of oppression is called on to evacuate without delay children, women, civilian persons and officials from all its offices, buildings, dwelling-houses, etc. throughout the country.

"(2) The civilian population, Jews, Arabs and others are asked, for their own sakes, to abstain henceforth and until this warning is recalled, from visiting or going near Government offices, etc.

"You Have Been Warned!"

No; we never believed that our struggle would cause the total destruction of our people. We knew that Eretz Israel, in consequence of the revolt, resembled a glass house. The world was looking into it with ever-increasing interest and could see most of what was happening inside. That is very largely why we were able to pursue our struggle until we brought it to its successful climax in 1946-47. Arms were our weapons of attack; the transparency of the "glass" was our shield of defence. Served by these two instruments we continued to deliver our blows at the structure of the Mandatory's prestige.

2

No less firm was the second pillar on which we built the strategy of the revolt. A study of the international situation during and immediately after the final phase of the last War convinced us that conditions would be in our favour. The War brought about a radical change in the relation of world forces. Mighty navies had been sunk. Great armies had been destroyed or dispersed. Great Powers had become second-rate. Medium-sized and smaller Powers were being swallowed up, in one way or another, by great blocs. There arose two mammoth State Powers encompassing areas, populations and economic and military resources of stupendous magnitude.

Whether the changes that have taken place in our time will last, and whether they will benefit humanity, only time will tell. But there is no doubt that they favoured the Jewish revolt against the Mandatory's rule. As a result of World War II the Power which was oppressing us was confronted with a hostile Power in

the east and a not very friendly Power in the west. And
as time went on her difficulties increased.

During the years of revolt, we met and talked with
official and unofficial representatives of the Soviet Union
and her friends. We learnt that as a result of our struggle for liberation, the attitude of Russia to our striving
for Jewish National independence was changing. Only
somebody who knew, as I did from personal experience,
what habits of thought have to be overcome before
Soviet policy changes can measure the magnitude of the
effect which the Jewish revolt in Palestine produced.
But the change of Russia's attitude certainly came. At
an international press conference in Prague in 1947,
David Zaslavsky, one of the chief political editors of
Pravda asked the Hebrew newspapermen why no representative of the Irgun's underground Press had come
to the conference with them. When he was given a
vague reply, he insisted that as the Irgun had its own
Press the Eretz Israel delegation should have included
one of its representatives. "They are brave people," he
said, "and are doing a great job."

Another Soviet representative, with considerable influence in a whole continent, explained to the Irgun
man he met that the struggle of the Irgun Zvai Leumi
was inherently progressive in that it was being waged
against a colonial regime, and the Irgun itself was a
progressive movement in that it sprang from the people.
The proof of that, he said, was the inability of the
British to liquidate the Irgun. The change of Russian
attitude was given complete and vivid expression in the
famous speech by Andrei Gromyko to the United Nations Assembly in the spring of 1947.

"The bloody occurrences in Palestine are known to
all," said the Soviet envoy. "They are becoming an ever
more frequent phenomenon and are consequently pressing themselves ever more insistently on the attention
of the peoples of the world and primarily of the United
Nations Organization. The bankruptcy of the Mandatory system in governing Palestine, which has brought
about the decided worsening of the situation and caused
the bloody disturbances, is the reason why the problem

has been brought for consideration before the General Assembly."

Maybe in those brief, pointed sentences there was also expressed the Soviet's own wishful thinking. The Soviet Union naturally desired the "bankruptcy" of the British colonial regime in Eretz Israel. The "bloody disturbances" not only resulted in the bankruptcy of British rule but paraded that bankruptcy before the eyes of the whole world. The conclusions drawn by realistic statesmen from the revolutionary situation that developed in Eretz Israel—and the inhabitants of the Kremlin are often very realistic statesmen—were inevitable. The Eretz Israel Communist newspaper *Kol Ha'am* and the pro-Soviet *Mishmar*[1] were completely nonplussed when the Soviet Union, in spite of the past, took its stand among the supporters of an independent Jewish State. The leading articles of these Jewish Communist papers were still "rebelling" against the idea of the Jewish State. The acrobatic feat of adjusting themselves to the momentous declaration of the Soviet Union was no light task. But only to such short-sighted observers did Soviet policy appear to have changed overnight. The historic truth is that the change had slowly been evolving during the long nights of the revolt.

On the heels of the revolt came also the United States' demand for an immediate solution to the Eretz Israel question. It is noteworthy that the American, Warren Austin, in supporting the demand for the replacement of British rule in Eretz Israel by a new regime, used language almost identical with that of the Russian, Gromyko.

[1] Organ of the Hashomer Hatzair Party of Communist Socialists, now merged in the Mapam Party in Israel.

Chapter VI
Army of the Underground

Our enemies called us terrorists. People who were neither friends nor enemies, like the correspondents of the *New York Herald-Tribune,* also used this Latin name, either under the influence of British propaganda or out of habit. Our friends, like the Irishman O'Reilly, preferred, as he wrote in his letter, to "get ahead of history" and called us by a simpler, though also a Latin name: patriots. General McMillan, who succeeded General Barker as G.O.C. of the Government's forces in Eretz Israel, thought that "terrorists" was too good for us. He claimed that it had acquired a certain aura of heroism; moreover, it implied that the terrorists aroused fear in the British troops. Therefore—the General ordered—they must not be called terrorists any longer, but "murderers," "thugs" and . . . McMillan added half-a-dozen more of the pleasant epithets from the vocabulary of the barrackroom. His order, however, did not make any difference. The British Press and the British troops continued to call us by the name which, in their General's opinion, suggested bravery on our part and fear on theirs. They called us "terrorists" to the end. No doubt there was a psychological explanation of this.

And yet, we were not terrorists. The original Latin word "terror" means fear. If I am not mistaken the term "terror" became current in political terminology during the French Revolution. The revolutionaries began cutting off heads with the guillotine in order to instil fear. Thenceforward the word "terror" came to define the acts of revolutionaries or counter-revolutionaries, of fighters for freedom and oppressors. It all de-

pends on who uses the term. It frequently happens that
it is used by both sides in their mutual exchange of
compliments.

The historical and linguistic origins of the political
term "terror" prove that it cannot be applied to a revolutionary war of liberation. A revolution may give birth
to what we call "terror," as happened in France. Terror
may at times be its herald, as happened in Russia. But
the revolution itself is not terror, and terror is not the
revolution. A revolution, or a revolutionary war, does
not aim at instilling fear. Its object is to overthrow a
regime and to set up a new regime in its place. In a
revolutionary war both sides use force. Tyranny is
armed. Otherwise it would be liquidated overnight.
Fighters for freedom must arm; otherwise they would
be crushed overnight. Certainly the use of force also
wakens fear. Tyrannous rulers begin to fear for their
positions, or their lives, or both. And consequently
they try to sow fear among those they rule. But the
instilling of fear is not an aim in itself. The sole aim
on the one side is the overthrow of armed tyranny; on
the other side it is the perpetuation of that tyranny.

The underground fighters of the Irgun arose to overthrow and replace a regime. We used physical force
because we were faced by physical force. But physical
force was neither our aim nor our creed. We believed
in the supremacy of moral forces. It was our enemy
who mocked at them. That is why, notwithstanding
the enemy's tremendous preponderance in physical
strength, he it was who was defeated, and not we. That
is the law of history. We rejoiced at the opportunity to
try to prove that this law operated not only in the
century of idealism, the Nineteenth Century, but also
in our own century of materialism and cruelty, not only
in the "springtime of the nations" but also in their Fall.
We were thankful that we were able to prove it, not
only for our own people, but for humanity as a whole.
But what has a struggle for the dignity of man, against
oppression and subjugation, to do with "terrorism"?
Our purpose, in fact, was precisely the reverse of "terrorism." The whole essence of our struggle was the

determination to free our people of its chief affliction—
fear. How could we continue to live in this hostile
world in which the Jew was attacked because he was a
Jew—how could we go on living without arms, without
a Homeland, without elementary means of defence? We
of the Irgun Zvai Leumi arose therefore to rebel and
fight, not in order to instil fear but to eradicate it. The
definition of that gallant Irishman, Paul O'Dwyer, was
perhaps accurate as far as the nerves of the government
officials were concerned. But historically we were not
"terrorists." We were strictly speaking anti-terrorists.

In building our organisation, too, we created no
group of assassins to lurk in wait for important victims.
From foundation to attic we set up our underground
as an army which planned attacks on the most vital
enemy targets, which shook the very foundations of the
enemy's military establishment and his civil rule,
which brought about enemy losses in the course of military attacks. We began, it is true, with a small underground army, numbering no more than several hundreds. But our strength increased *pari passu* with the
intensification of the struggle. In spite—perhaps because—of persecution we built up an underground
army, divided into many sections and units, and numbering many thousands. We were not a "terrorist"
group—neither in the structure of our organisation, in
our methods of warfare, nor in spirit.

2

The organisational structure of our little army was
simple enough. At its head stood a High Command advised by a General Staff, organised in departments
suited to underground requirements. The general body
was organised in divisions of a size suited to the requirements of the struggle. Our administrative "machine" was always very small. The British military and
secret service believed that we had at our disposal
thousands of professional soldiers engaged in nothing
but anti-British "terrorism." Enemy Intelligence were
utterly misled in this as in so many other respects and

it never occurred to us to disillusion them. In fact, until the British forces evacuated Palestine, we never had more than a few dozen (at times less than twenty, never more than 30-40) members on full-time service in the underground struggle. All the rest of the hundreds, and subsequently thousands, of our members carried on with their ordinary daily work, though they were at the disposal of the organisation whenever called upon. It was in very truth a People's Army.

The High Command controlled all the activities of the Irgun, both military and political. It considered general principles, strategy and tactics, information and training, relations with other bodies and negotiations with their representatives. The High Command took decisions. Orders were given in the Irgun as in all military organisations; but there were never any decisions by an individual. There was always discussion. Each member of the High Command tried to persuade his comrades. Decisions were usually unanimous. We did not put questions to a formal vote; there was usually a synthesis of the various opinions. When there were differences of opinion, the view of the majority prevailed. Consciousness of responsibility, mutual understanding, and a profound sense of fraternity were the factors which made this system work—probably the best possible system for taking practical decisions. Our meetings, which were frequent, were always strictly practical. I do not remember a single meeting which got bogged down in barren theory, or one at which all that was done was to call a second meeting. We decided and acted. The Government forces never learnt of our decisions until they had been carried out.

When I was first appointed to head the High Command its other members were Yaacov Meridor, Arieh Ben-Eliezer, Eliahu Lankin and Shlomo Levi.

Yaacov Meridor, one of the ablest Jewish military commanders, was at the head of the Irgun during the crisis years between the death of David Raziel and the beginning of the revolt. Yaacov kept the flame alive. His position was difficult, sometimes intolerable. He had intended to launch the revolt early in 1943, but his hands were tied. I understood his difficulties even before I took over the command. I was drawn to him from the moment I presented myself to him, on my arrival from Russia, to tell him what I had intended telling David Raziel—that I was entirely at his disposal. We talked in the small room, dimly lit by an oil-lamp, from which, in the guise of the owner of a transport company, "Mr. Honig," he conducted the affairs of the Irgun. We talked like old friends, we surveyed the situation. We were of one mind: that there was only one way—revolt.

Yaacov did his utmost to train men and prepare arms for the struggle. If we had the minimum necessary to launch our first attacks we have in the first place to thank Yaacov, his stubbornness and the brave smile with which he took blows and disappointments. When the time came he did not hesitate, great and modest man that he is, to hand over his command to one who had placed himself under his orders. To him, our personal position was of not the slightest importance; the Cause was everything. The opening of the revolt brought great satisfaction to Yaacov, who rejoiced like a true teacher at the good work of his pupils. But he did not remain for long with his comrades in the High Command. In the winter of 1944 agents of the Jewish Agency betrayed him to the British who, as a signal act of kindness, placed a special airplane at his disposal to transport him to prison and exile in Africa. In the dark continent, behind British barbed wire, he demonstrated that while it is possible to imprison a man, it is impossible to imprison his soul. Yaacov was of course not the only one of our fighters who tried to escape and return to the struggle. Our comrades hated imprisonment as much as they loved the freedom for which they fought. In captivity they were physically more or less safe; outside, danger lurked everywhere. But they preferred the dangers of action in the fight for freedom to the security of idleness. Where are the prisons from which the underground fighters did not escape? What means did they not use in order to burst their bonds and thus help destroy the shackles of their people? Yaacov Meridor served as a shining example to all of them. In concentration camps he was like a bird of freedom. Barbed wire fences could not hold him. Escaped once and recaptured, he escaped again. And when he was recaptured, he escaped yet again. And again and yet again, until he finally succeeded in returning to the front—late indeed, but still in time to place himself at the head of the "overground" regiments of the Irgun Zvai Leumi, to lead them in the defensive war against the Arab invasion forces, and then into the unified Israel Army. He has written the story of his daring escapes in his memorable book "Long is the Way to Freedom."

Arieh Ben-Eliezer passed the first years of World War II in the United States as a representative of the Irgun. He came to Eretz Israel in 1943 on behalf of the Hebrew Committee of National Liberation set up by Hillel Kook[1] and Shmuel Merlin. When he arrived, the Irgun was passing through a severe crisis. And the crisis was overcome primarily because of Arieh. He became my close friend from the very beginning of our common labours. It was in our never-ending conversations, before and after the declaration of the revolt, during night-time strolls, or at his sister's home, or in the Savoy Hotel in Tel Aviv, that the foundations of our revolutionary struggle were laid. Together we endured the spiritual crises inseparable from the launching of a revolt. They were crises of sorrow and pain; though sometimes also periods of joy at achievement. After the successful attack on the three headquarters of the C.I.D., we said to each other: "Now it does not matter if we die." We were certain that after these operations which aroused world-wide astonishment, the continuance of the revolt was assured even if we were captured or killed. That was the beginning; and though we looked forward to great things we could not then fore-

---

[1] Hillel Kook, nephew of the renowned Chief Rabbi Kook of Jerusalem, was widely known in the United States under the name of Peter Bergson, where his ingenuity in keeping a fierce light of publicity upon the Irgun's struggle was an important factor in the success of the revolt.

see that the day would come when we should breach "impenetrable strongholds" like Acre Fortress. On the other hand we saw before us tragic loss and suffering such as young Benjamin, one of our best boys, killed in the Jerusalem attack, and Shimon Amrani, another of our best young fighters, who fell into enemy captivity (Amrani was subjected to brutal grilling by police but gave no secrets away. We freed him in the attack on Acre Prison but, alas, he fell on the very threshold of freedom, in the battle that accompanied the withdrawal.)

The first shocks are the worst. Each of us sought strength in the words of his comrade—and found it. We knew there was no other way. We believed with perfect faith that these sacrifices would not be in vain. We believed with perfect faith in ultimate victory. And each of us strengthened the other.

With Arieh, too, I worked together for only a short time. He was arrested in the spring of 1944. Maybe his capture was also the result of denunciation; maybe it was caused indirectly by a cerain naïveté on our part, or by a mistake we made out of concern for the work of our comrades and friends abroad. We feared that if Arieh should disappear altogether this act of his would provide dangerous testimony against those who were well known to be his colleagues in the Hebrew Committee in the United States, and that the British might succeed, then, in persuading the Americans to clamp down on the Committee's invaluable work and maybe to deport its members. At the same time we assumed that if Arieh remained in a state of "semi-underground" we should be able to get the best of both worlds: he would probably avoid capture, and even if he were captured he would soon be released on account of his not having gone into hiding. Arieh, therefore, while doing his work secretly, lived openly in a hotel. We were mistaken. Arieh was arrested and was not released until he released himself. He too escaped from the concentration camp in Eritrea. His adventures are an epic in themselves.

Eliahu Lankin, who came from Harbin, became one

of the pillars of the struggle. Eliahu is a pure idealist, prepared to give his life for his friend, a truly altruistic spirit. I loved Eliahu with all my heart. It was always good to listen to his thoughtful words, whether they were in appreciation of things done or in criticism of things left undone. I was not alone in my feelings. The whole underground loved him. Eliahu who was a member of the High Command was at the same time the Jerusalem Regional Commander. In the operation against the Jerusalem C.I.D. Headquarters—whose ruins are still to be seen in Mamillah Road as a reminder of the revolt—he participated in the attack under the orders of the field commander, his subordinate. Not long after that attack Eliahu followed in the footsteps of so many others of my comrades. He too was betrayed to the British, in the heart of Jerusalem, and was exiled to Eritrea. He too escaped from the concentration camp. His odyssey, a tale of fact, is perhaps no less thrilling than that of which Homer sang. Eliahu was the first of the escapees to reach Europe, where he took over command of the Irgun organisation abroad and later commanded our men on board the *Altalena*.

The youngest member of the High Command was "Danny"—Shlomo Levi, son of a pioneer family, who came from Petah Tikva. A soldier and an officer through and through, utterly devoted to the Irgun, he served as Chief of Staff from the beginning of the revolt until his capture. I was deeply attached to him, and I looked upon him as a younger brother or a grown-up son. But he too fell into enemy captivity. On the capture of Eliahu Lankin, "Danny" was sent to take over in Jerusalem. On the way his car was stopped by a British patrol and from a second car that had been following him there stepped out an Agency official who pointed to Danny and exclaimed: "That is the man."

Danny was also one of the large group that escaped from the Eritrea detention-camp, but luck did not favour him. He was recaptured, and he returned to the Homeland only with the liquidation of British rule.

Several months after this Command was formed we added Yeruham Livni, known as Eitan, our first Chief

of Operations. Eitan, a man of unusual perception,
showed extraordinary ability in planning the military
attacks of the Irgun. But he was captured during the
withdrawal from a series of widespread operations in
the south. He thereupon became "Haim Luster" and
led another attack—the "counter-attack" in the trial of
thirty-one Irgun soldiers by the Military "Court" in
Jerusalem.

Eitan used to visit my home frequently in the course
of duty, by night as well as by day. When he found the
door locked he would go in through the window. It was
an unavoidable necessity, but had our neighbours noticed they might have called the police to protect me
from "burglars"! But our neighbours fortunately slept
well. My little son Benny was very attached to this
cheerful uncle who used to show him the funniest tricks.
He called him Uncle Moshe. Every "uncle" who visited
us had his special name for Benny's use. Children are
naturally the greatest enemies of conspiracy. But do
parents, even in the underground, always know what
their children's ears pick up? We were always careful,
but apparently the three-year-old child once overheard
something, for one day he asked me, with a mischievous smile on his lips:

"Father, where is Uncle Moshe who is called Yeruham?"

I was somewhat taken aback by this surprising and
dangerous question. On the other hand I could not help
a feeling of pleasure at the sharpness of the child.

"Uncle Moshe has gone to Haifa," I told him. "He'll
come back."

It is a bad thing for a son not to be able to tell his
father the truth. It is even worse when a father cannot
tell his son the truth. In addition to the great and obvious sacrifices inherent in an underground struggle, it
sometimes exacts unseen sacrifices, seemingly trivial,
but extremely painful to have to make.

And why "to Haifa"? May the parents forgive their
sons for the untruths they had to tell them for the sake
of the essential struggle. And may the sons forgive their
parents for the same transgression. Uncle Moshe, my

son, was really Yeruham. He did not go to Haifa but to Jerusalem, to the prison, and from there to Acre, again to prison. For fifteen years—so the British said. But Uncle Moshe returned to us—from Acre, not Haifa—fourteen years earlier than the British authorities intended.

3

From all that happened to the High Command of the Irgun and its evolution, an important conclusion may be drawn in the historico-philosophical argument between the "idealists" and the "materialists": Which is cause and which effect? Do men make events or do unavoidable events make the men? In our underground cellar we did not find the answer to this weighty question. But we did learn that an *idea*, after it has taken shape, mysteriously gives birth to the men who bring it to fruition. Recognizing this truth, I assert that if at any stage of the revolt all of us in the Irgun had been captured or killed, others would have taken our places and fought the oppressor until he was beaten. We learnt that the aim makes heroes of the weak, turns privates into officers, quite ordinary people into swayers of minds and hearts, theoreticians into men of action, students into strategists. I have read somewhere a denial of the old theory that nature abhors a vacuum. What is certain is that an idea will not tolerate a vacuum in the ranks of those who are to bring it to fruition. Nobody knows how or when but it will be filled. When Arieh Ben-Eliezer was captured everything seemed to go black. When Yaacov Meridor fell into enemy hands I thought the blow would be fatal. When Eliahu Lankin was betrayed I found neither rest nor comfort. When Shlomo Levi's little sister told me of his capture I was overwhelmed. When Eitan fell—with thirty others, including some of our best officers—it seemed all was lost. These people were veritably the pillars of the Irgun. Who would take their places? Who would do the work?

But the place of each was filled. The work was done, because it had to be done. The idea was stronger than all of us.

Avraham came. He had been one of the officers in Haifa. Soon he was the keystone of our organisation. Avraham is a perpetual fountain of energy. He knows neither weariness nor obstacles. Through the years of revolt Avraham was the busiest man in Eretz Israel. He worked eighteen hours a day. And there was always a smile on his lips, though not always in his heart. All the bad news came to him first, and he stood firm as a rock.

"Avraham, shall we recover from this blow?"

"What a question. It'll be O.K. Don't worry."

Amitzur came. He was not only one of our best organisers, but had one of the clearest minds I have ever encountered. I never remember his expressing an opinion which had not been thoroughly thought out. It was not only a joy to listen to him; I enjoyed taking his advice. Amitzur had particularly good fortune. He was never caught by the British. When he was arrested it was by his fellow-Jews!

Gideon came, our Giddy. He was young in years—still in his early twenties—when he succeeded Eitan as Chief of Operations. The deeds of this young man, whose abilities border on genius, will be remembered by his adversaries as long as they live. The biggest and most daring confiscations of arms were planned, or executed by Giddy. On one occasion he went out to enrich the Irgun with a huge store of machine-guns, rifles and ammunition. At first I opposed his leading the operation himself. Our officers always wanted to lead their men into action. And the senior officers were no exception. I knew of this desire. It was not only good to go with the boys; it was also much easier to go with them than to wait for their return. Underground officers are not "army officers" who count the losses among their men very much as statistics. Underground officers are fathers and brothers to the men; hence their days are days of sorrow, their nights—anguish. Hence that quiet, but deeply urgent, appeal: "Let me go out with the boys."

We had to struggle with each other to overcome this desire. No, there were no "dramatic" scenes, but there was much persuasion, indeed incessant persuasion. Gideon knew both the desire and the anxiety. He would usually ask for permission to go out with the boys, and would usually get a refusal. But sometimes he "rebelled," and argued convincingly enough to win his point. One of these occasions was the attack on the R.A.F. airfield at Akir, that is Ekron.

"There are tremendous stores of arms and ammunition there," said Gideon with the customary calm which concealed his fiery spirit. "This is an unusual opportunity and it's quite impossible for me to hand over the operation to anyone else."

"And Joshua and Arieh and Haim and . . . ?" I rolled off the names of a number of field officers whom I did not know personally but whom I knew by repute for their achievements and abilities.

"Yes, I shall probably have to take them along too. The operation is a most serious one. There are difficulties at every step. But I feel I must go myself. I really cannot give it a fair chance otherwise."

So the discussion went on, one of many in the underground, which knew little joy and much anxiety. This time Gideon won.

He worked fast. The party was organized. It looked absolutely like a British unit. The uniform, the caps, the arms, all were right. Even the accents, particularly the Scots accent of "Jackson" were just right. The necessary passes were found. These were essential. Our soldiers had already made many successful raids on military camps and taken away arms superfluous to them but very urgently needed by us. Special warnings had therefore been issued to all camps against Irgun attempts to appease its appetite for arms. One of these orders fell into our hands. "It seems"—said the order —"that the Irgun is short of automatic weapons" (they weren't wrong!) "which it is trying to acquire from British armouries." The author of the order admitted that the Irgun arms-raids were "carefully prepared and boldly carried out." Consequently—and there followed a list of instructions aimed at providing the utmost security for armouries and their approaches, laying down means of identification and so on. In the course of time these orders were elaborated. The less they helped, the more were issued. But right to the end of our fight we never ceased taking arms from government forces—in spite of all their precautions and notwithstanding the big notices stuck up in all the camps exhorting the soldiers: "Your uniform does not prove your identity." Every soldier therefore had to carry papers to prove to suspicious guards that he was truly a British soldier. This was most inconvenient. All the more so as sometimes it was the guard himself who was masquerading as a British soldier.

The papers required for the Akir camp were prepared. Gideon gave the customary detailed briefing. He inspected the party. They were all in order. The men inspected Giddy. He too was in order: a British captain.

"Everything O.K.? Let's go then, ' 'S-long-as-you-have-your-health'. To Akir."

" 'S-long-as-you-have-your-health (a literal translation of the much briefer Yiddish *Abi gezunt*) was the Irgun's soldier's traditional valediction before going into battle. It was an undramatic slogan, without any obvious meaning. But it was used by everybody, including the non-Yiddish speaking native-born Palestinians, and even by the Yemenites who, while they may not have known the meaning of the words, fully understood their significance. *Abi Gezunt* symbolized the inner calm of our fighters and their freedom from accepted prejudices. If you mention the possibility of a puncture to a driver about to set off on the road, he will be prepared to eat you alive. The airman, even when he has a thousand flying hours to his credit, looks for all kinds of signs in heaven and earth to assure his safe landing. Even students, before an examination which is certainly unlikely to be fatal, look for lucky signs. I remember the students of my generation always asked to be sent off with a parting "Break your neck!" A pe-culiar prejudice suggested to them that just the con-trary wish would act as a charm. And if you forgot to say the magic words and, instead, simply wished them luck, you might easily have all their books thrown at your head.

The underground fighters, with few exceptions, were free of these superstitions. They knew, when they went to a training lecture, or to a briefing, or to the op-eration itself, that they were heading straight for the danger of capture, of injury or of death. But they went with their eyes open. They were not afraid to speak of the future before they went into battle. They did not look for charms, but kept their good humour. No dra-matics. Simply *abi gezunt*. The military authorities would have paid heavily for the knowledge of these two words and of the places where they were uttered. But these words were an underground secret.

"Captain" Gideon's party arrived safely at Akir: a truckload of soldiers, their arms "at the ready" for re-pulsing terrorists; a jeep carrying the officer and his aides. Everything was natural, to the British they passed on the way as well as to the Arabs enjoying their nargillahs and leisurely watching the dust raised by the vehicles. It was not so natural in the Hatikvah Quarter.[1] A British officer, British soldiers—but the Hatikvah Quarter knew how to keep secrets. *Abi gezunt*.

When the party arrived at the camp-gate the men's papers were punctiliously examined. Everything was in order, especially "Jackson's" Scots accent. They drove into the camp. They found the big armoury. The truck was halted where it could not be seen from outside. Ex-cellent. Inside the store were many British soldiers and workers, mostly Arabs, a few Jews. The boys spread out and took up their positions. Their eyes were gleam-ing. Arms! Such huge quantities! Tense silence. When would Giddy begin? Giddy was waiting. The real Brit-

[1] The Tel Aviv suburb inhabited mainly by Jews from Yemen.

ish soldiers had saluted the tall captain. He returned the greeting . . .

Giddy put his hand on his revolver and said quietly: "Hands up, please."

The British soldiers thought the captain was drunk. "What's that?"

"Hands up!"

"Sir . . ."

"Hands up, quick. I'm not a bloody British officer, I'm a terrorist of the Irgun Zvai Leumi."

All the hands went up, quickly. The soldiers had learnt from experience that such Irgun requests had to be fulfilled. And they were obliged to help load the arms. The loading was consequently quick. There was no time to be lost. Our boys worked with redoubled energy. But the British worked hard enough too. The truck filled up. Machine-guns, sub-machine-guns, ammunition. "Perhaps that's enough." "No—not enough. Take some more."

Maybe they took too much. It was the rainy season. The road back was muddy. We always used paths and secondary roads as much as possible. It helped create the element of surprise in attack; it facilitated the withdrawal. But that road was very muddy. Quite near the camp, the truck sank into the mud and foundered. The efforts of the boys to move it may be imagined. Meanwhile the alarm had been given in the camp. Armoured cars were rushing hither and thither. Airplanes were taking off, all searching, hunting. The enemy's forces were strong, and though they would have suffered heavy casualties, it was hopeless to join battle with them. And the truck could not be moved. The treasure could not be saved. There was no choice. On to the Jeep! Each one took what he could off the truck. The jeep groaned under its too heavy load. But jeeps have extraordinary pulling power.

The boys returned. They brought a small quantity of arms. Most important: there were no casualties. Who can describe the dejection? The bitter irony of it! To our last day in the underground we never ceased regretting that lost truckload of arms.

We had a special liking for these operations, called "confiscations." They dealt a blow to the enemy and were a boon for us. They did not always end as well and as badly as the one at Akir. There were operations from which we brought back comparatively large quantities of modern arms. There were operations in which battles developed. The government's forces, though they were always vastly superior in numbers, never emerged the victors. There was the operation at Sarafand when Ashbel and Simchon were wounded and captured, opening a unique chapter in the revolt. There was the operation at Ramat Gan in which Dov Gruner was wounded. There were operations in which the combination of traditional Jewish brains and reborn Jewish heroism performed deeds which bordered on the miraculous.

The guiding spirit of all these operations, after Eitan had been captured, was Giddy. Giddy has an unusual combination of qualities. He has both an inventive brain and constructive hands. He is both a planner and an executor. He has innumerable technical and tactical inventions to his credit. He invented the heavy electrically-operated mortar which the British army, for some reason, called V3 and from which was later evolved the Israel Army's famous "Davidka." Giddy invented the contact-mine for railway sabotage, against which no counter-measures were of any avail. It could not be dismantled. Whoever tried paid with his life for disregarding our warnings. A pilot-engine would pass over the mined spot without mishap, but when the train followed, it was thrown into the air. The mine was constructed on a weight principle. A light weight would not set it off; a heavy weight would be destroyed on contact with it. A time-mechanism was also attached—allowing one day, two days, three days, even whole weeks. At one time we paralysed almost all railway traffic in the country by these mines. Giddy's brain continued to invent: special road-mines; flame-throwers; "milkcans"; the "barrel-bomb." Giddy planned the attack on Acre. Giddy, together with Shimson, the commander of the Acre operation, delivered tremendous blows at the government forces during the period of martial law. And after Simon the Hasmonean, Gideon is entitled to be called "Conqueror of Jaffa."

Such was our Giddy. Reserved, obstinate, universally loved. Modest, a man of action, he hated publicity. Never would you imagine from seeing him that this modest, lean young man had with his own hands written whole pages in the military history of our people.

Where did he come from? He was at one time in the Haganah. His brother, secretary to Israel Galili, was among the 23 missing in the operation in Syria during World War II. He was brought to us by the magnet of our ideal, and little Amihai became Gideon who did such great things for the realisation of that ideal and for the life of his people. . . .

In addition to Gideon, Amitzur and Avraham, the High Command was augmented, in the course of time, by Yoel, Reuven, Yitshak and Shmuel. Yoel was the head of our Intelligence. Taciturn as befitted his task, a man of action, he was one of the most cool and collected people I have encountered. In his appearance and dress he looked a typical Englishman. His own Intelligence Service warned us from time to time against his wife—herself a devoted fighter—because she had been seen in the company of an Englishman! When we were about to emerge from the underground into the field of open battle, Yoel, at his own request, went abroad to secure much-needed arms. He made a supreme effort and endured much suffering in carrying out his task.

Reuven was the man of practical, productive work. For many years he was commander of the large Tel-Aviv region. He organized the medical detachment, the underground radio service and the system of storing arms—a very ticklish problem. He was in charge of our own production of arms when, farsightedly, we began preparing for the clash with the Arab hirelings of Whitehall policy.

Yitshak, one of the oldest Irgun officers, dealt with our financial and organisational problems. His vast experience frequently stood us in good stead.

Shmuel, the latest addition to the High Command, came to us from South Africa and within a few months was entirely one of us, universally liked and respected. He is one of the wisest of men. He served as the Irgun spokesman to foreign correspondents and in the decisive period, was the officer responsible for Jerusalem, until the dissolution of the military regiments of the Irgun Zvai Leumi.

4

The story of the members of the High Command is the story of all the officers of the Irgun. Many were denounced, exiled, captured, killed. Those who took their places were young and inexperienced. Could they cope with their responsibilities? They did. Will-power made up for experience. Devotion established their prestige. Affection and loyalty bred affection and loyalty from their subordinates. The Irgun never faltered under the heavy blows it received. Three regional commanders were captured one after the other in Haifa. Four regional commanders were betrayed to the British Authorities, one after the other, in Jerusalem. Very young officers, Arieh, Amnon, Raanan, Alon, Tamir, Elitzur took their places and proved themselves worthy of the confidence placed in them.

All these people became my friends. More: we were all like brothers. And the mutual deep affection, the affection of fighters, than which there is no greater, was the source of our happiness, perhaps the only happiness in the darkness of the underground. In our small army of freedom there reigned a profound spirit of fraternity, the like of which it would be difficult to find. It was not by chance that one of the pseudonyms we used for the Irgun was "the fighting family." We *were* a family. There was mutual trust. Each was prepared to give his life for his comrade. Day after day almost the whole Press wrote the most repulsive things about the Irgun and particularly about us officers. The members knew very few of their comrades. They never saw their senior officers, nor in most cases did they even know who they were. Whence came this absolute confidence that those unknown men were not the evil beings described by the newspapers with pens dipped in vitriol? Why did they face death unflinchingly? Whence came their "incomprehensible" loyalty? We shall have to return to these questions. Here, in writing of the underground army, I shall mention one of the factors that made the Irgun, not in a phrase, but in reality, a "fighting family." It was *love*, love of the ideal, that infused the fighters with mutual fraternal affection. That was their strength.

These relations did not interfere with discipline; they strengthened it. Discipline was very strong in the Irgun. It did not originate in compulsion. The Irgun was one of the few underground organisations that permitted its members to resign from its ranks. Despite the risk of secrets being disclosed, we never attempted to force anybody to remain in the Irgun if he wished to leave. There were members who left; some returned, others never came back. I have no wish to create the impression that everything was perfect in the Irgun. Human weakness operates in every society. There are misunderstandings, disappointments. But it is the rule that counts, not the exception. The fact is that discipline flowed not from external compulsion, which did not exist, but from a deep inner consciousness. Faults? Mistakes? Failures? Of course we had them. We have no need of legends. The truth is finer than any myth. And the truth is that the family of rebels was free in its discipline, just as it was pure in its faith.

We retained the rank introduced by David Raziel. We had lance-corporals, corporals, sergeants, sergeant-majors, lieutenants, and one captain—Yaacov Meridor. These ranks bore no relation, except in a few instances, to the actual responsibility or task of the officer. A man who at one stage commanded thousands of men—as, for example, in the Tel-Aviv Region—was a "lieutenant." In a regular army a lieutenant commands at the most a few score of men. Our "sergeants" sometimes commanded several hundred men; in a regular army this is the responsibility of a captain or a major. There were never any conflicts about rank. They symbolized the measure of responsibility. They were very modest—like their bearers. The officer was no different from his men except in the weight of work and responsibilities. His rank gave him no privileges. An Irgun man who devoted his whole day to the underground and was obliged to obtain his minimum means of existence from the organisation, received a salary not according to his rank but according to his family circumstances. A bachelor, whether he were a ranker or a member of the High Command, got 25 pounds (then 100 dollars) a month. We had drivers who were fathers of families and received a higher "salary" than members of the High Command. I deliberately write "salaries" in quotation marks. Salaries in the Irgun barely sufficed for elementary needs. Our budget for expenses on personnel was never greater than 14, sometimes it was less than 12 per cent. The contributions made by Jews, and the money we occasionally took from the Mandatory authorities, were devoted, directly or indirectly, to the immediate needs of the struggle. Otherwise we could not have done what we did. If the word "austerity" has any meaning, it certainly was the law of the Irgun. And if the term "democratic army" has any meaning, the rebel family in Eretz Israel was one of the most democratic armies in the world.

We chose two days in the year for announcing promotions. They were the 14th November—the day on which David Raziel carried out the first Irgun attack against the enemies of our people, and the 29th of Tammuz, the day on which "the wonder-violin which was to have been the first in Israel, was shattered" as "Davar," one of the fiercest of his opponents, wrote of Vladimir Jabotinsky's death in distant New York on 3rd August, 1940. On the days of commemoration of the teacher, his pupil, and the first act of revolt we rewarded the officers and men who had distinguished themselves. On those days there was a holiday atmosphere in the Irgun. But the Irgun was fighting a life-and-death battle. The promotion ceremonies—which took place in many places at the same time—were therefore solemn. Though we gave it little thought, all of us knew we were constantly at no great distance from the gallows. There was an air of ceremonial solemnity. The parades were short, the orders of the day shorter still. No speeches, no talking. There was an unspoken oath in the air. Every officer knew his responsibility, and dedicated himself anew to the aim of liberation. There are few ceremonies in a fighting underground. But those few are very impressive. It was not easy to attain rank in the Irgun—in which Dov Gruner was a private. . . .

That it was not easy I knew from my personal experience. I had no rank. Not because of any excess of modesty, but by force of circumstances. In the Polish Army I had been a private. But even if I had been a colonel it would have brought me no credit in our fighting organisation. Men who had been officers in various armies were proud, after much toil, to attain the rank of sergeant in the Irgun. The essential condition for rank was the completion of a training course. As my ill luck would have it I never had the opportunity of completing such a course. Regulations are regulations. Without that essential first step, I could move no higher. This almost caused an "international misunderstanding." When I met the representatives of the United Nations Special Committee, the Chairman, Judge Sandstrom, asked me formally what was my authority for speaking in the name of the Irgun Zvai Leumi.

"Are you a general?" he asked with perfect gravity.

I had to laugh.

"No, I have no rank."

This preliminary exchange ended in general laughter. A smile hovered on the lips of the mirthless Swede, Mr. Sandstrom.

Nevertheless, I did have some kind of rank, but I could not tell Judge Sandstrom about it. It was not military—indeed it was essentially anti-military. In my presence my friends called me "the commander." But among themselves they called me "the old man." I admit I liked it. While my thinning hair hinted that soon the name would no longer be metaphorical, its use reflected good, heart-warming spontaneous affection.

These were the relations that were established in the years of revolt in the leadership and in the ranks—and between the two. Unshakeable loyalty. Unlimited preparedness for sacrifice. Unconditional devotion. Common dangers and common suffering. Above all a powerful will to victory. Thus all the soldiers of the Irgun fought. Thus all its units did their work.

5

At the launching of the revolt we divided the Irgun into a number of sections—in addition to the natural administrative and geographical divisions. We called these Sections:

1. A.R.—Army of the Revolution.
2. S.U.—Shock Units.
3. A.F.—Assault Force.
4. R.P.F.—Revolutionary Propaganda Force.

We intended, therefore, to have four sections. But reality is stronger than any decisions of a fighting Command. The A.R. existed only in theory. It was supposed to serve as a Reserve, embracing all the soldiers who were in none of the three remaining sections. But this arrangement never worked. Newcomers passed through it, and after their basic training were transferred to one of the other sections. It had neither officers nor men of its own. It had its day only when we emerged from the underground into the battle with the Arab invaders—when every man in the Irgun was drafted to a regular army unit: section, platoon, company, battalion.

The Shock Units were never actually set up. This was merely a new name given to a unit that had existed before the revolt. It was known—to those that knew of its existence—as the "Red Section" or the "Black Squad." The idea behind this unit was very interesting. It was Yaacov Meridor's idea. He assumed that the struggle for liberation would require men especially trained to operate in the Arab areas, both in Eretz Israel and in the Arab countries. The men chosen were, therefore, brave and dark-skinned. They were given a military training and lessons in Arabic. The composition of the "Red Section" was to be kept absolutely secret even from other members of the Irgun. This was the "underground within the underground" idea—which did not succeed. It was daring, but its execution caused a mixture of difficulties, some of them not unamusing. Suddenly the best men, and even officers, began leaving the Irgun. Loyal members who had gone with the Irgun through thick and thin wondered and could not understand. *He*—a deserter? And the deserter would add insult to injury. Not content with loud declarations that he had nothing more to do with the Irgun, he would curse and swear at it. This strange behaviour of formerly devoted men and important officers was bound to lower morale in the ranks. It was impossible to explain, or even hint at, the truth. Despite this, however, the deserters were not followed by real ones. Our boys were fortified by the principle we had succeeded in embedding in their hearts: that the ideal is the important thing and not the man. So-and-so had left, such-and-such a one had deserted? What matter? You, the soldier, had taken a historic mission upon yourself out of inner conviction. You had to fulfil it without regard to what anybody might say or do in negation of that mission, whether it were your antagonists or your friends of the day before, or your comrades or your officers. As a soldier of freedom—your supreme commander was the cause itself.

The affair of the "Red Section," though it opened in sorrow, ended in joy and gladness. When the revolt began, all the deserters reappeared in their regular units. There was renewed surprise, but this time it was accompanied by happy relief. Only yesterday that so-and-so had been cursing the Irgun up hill and down dale, and now he was an officer in the front line? They rubbed their eyes. Friendships were reformed. Much-lowered morale rose up once more.

In the "Red Section" there were many excellent fighters and all, or almost all, looked like Arabs. But it is not only people from the Arab countries who are

dark-skinned. There are many Ashkenazi Jews from
Europe who are no less dark—and are sometimes dark-
er—than the purest Sephardi. The only two members
of the unit I knew personally came from Lodz in Poland. It is true that many of the fighters in the Shock
Units sprang from the eastern communities. Hence the
story, disseminated particularly by the British Press
correspondents, of the "Black Squad" of the Irgun, allegedly composed only of Yemenites. This legend was
helped along to no small extent by certain Jewish politicians. Wishing to belittle us, these gentlemen whispered, or said aloud, that the *whole* of the Irgun consisted only of Yemenites. Our enemies, who disseminated tales about "black Yemenites" on the one hand and
"the scum of Eastern Europe" on the other, were trying
to besmirch us. It is a pity that our Jewish political opponents stooped to this nasty "racial" invective so beloved of anti-semitic propagandists between the wars.
The Nazis used to say: "Maybe not all Jews are Communists, but all the Communists are Jews." Similarly,
some Zionists said of us: "Not all Yemenites are Irgunists, but all the Irgun people are Yemenites."

Nothing of the sort. In the Shock Units and in all
the divisions of the Irgun we had members who came
from all Jewish communities and of all classes. We had
people from Tunis and Harbin, Poland and Persia,
France and Yemen, Belgium and Iraq, Czechoslovakia
and Syria; we had natives of the United States and Bok-
hara, of England, Scotland, Argentina and South
Africa, and most of all, of Eretz Israel itself. We were
the melting-pot of the Jewish nation in miniature. We
never asked about origins: we demanded only loyalty
and ability. Our comrades from the eastern communities felt happy and at home in the Irgun. Nobody ever
displayed any stupid airs of superiority toward them;
and they were thus helped to free themselves of any
unjustified sense of inferiority they may have har-
boured. They were fighting comrades and that was
enough. They could, and did, attain the highest positions of responsibility. Shlomo Levi, the first Chief of
Staff in the revolt, is a Sephardi. His brother, "Uzi," on

his return from the Eritrea prison-camp, became Regional Commander at Tel-Aviv and commanded thousands of men until he fell, fighting heroically, in the decisive battle for Jaffa. Shimshon, Regional Commander at Haifa until he was betrayed to the British military authorities, came from Persia. We had a Gideon in Jerusalem, who led the historic operation against the G.H.Q. of the Occupation Army and led it with consummate bravery and coolness. He was a Sephardi too. Two of the men who went to the gallows, Alkoshi and Kashani, were Sephardim. The "smear" with which our enemies and opponents tried to belittle us, was to us a source of pride. People who had been humiliated and degraded became proud fighters in our ranks, free and equal men and women, bearers of liberty and honour. Statistics? We never counted along these lines. But I believe I shall be very near the truth if I say that in the various sections of the Irgun there were no less than 25% and no more than 35% Sephardim and members of the Eastern Communities. In the Shock Units, in view of the special emphasis on dark skins, the proportion was probably greater; possible between 40 and 50%.

The members of the Shock Units carried out the early operations of the revolt, but their separate existence was not justified in practical tests. In the course of time and with the deepening of the struggle the Shock Units were united with the Assault Units and became the famous Assault Force of the Irgun, which delivered the heaviest blows against the oppressor and was directly responsible for the disintegration of the Mandatory rule in the Eretz Israel. Of the four sections we had planned there remained in practice only two: the Assault Force and the Revolutionary Propaganda Force. And between them there was permanent conflict: every R.P.F. man wanted a transfer to the A.F., and no A.F. man ever agreed to go over to the R.P.F.

This was not the only conflict inside the underground. A fighting underground is a veritable State in miniature: a State at war. It has its army, its policy, its own courts. It has at its disposal all the executive arms of a state. Above all, it bore the responsibility for life-and-death not only for individuals, but for whole generations. Nor is it only in this sense that an underground resembles a state. Just as in the ministries and departments of government, so too in the underground and its divisions and sections, there is co-operation and there are quarrels, arising from human nature itself. The Regional Commanders did not like the "autonomy" granted to the Shock Units and later to the Assault Force. "We," said the Regional Commanders, "handle all the work in the area under our command. We know what arms we have (or have not). We know our people. Why should we not be in charge of the preparations for battle operations and of the operations themselves?" This argument was quite logical. But the retort of the Assault Force Commanders was no less so. "Battle operations," they said, "have often to be prepared very speedily. The Regional Commander is like a father of many children. He is preoccupied with scores of organizational problems. We can only be sure of maximum efficiency if we have direct contact with the local operational officers."

It was not easy to judge between the two sides, particularly as both were seeking only the best means of carrying on the struggle. At times I felt like the judge who had decreed both parties in a dispute to be right and who, when asked by his wife how this could possibly be, replied gently, "You are right too, my love!"

This dispute over autonomy that had been granted in the case of the Assault Force went on at the same time as another discussion over autonomy which was not granted. Our Intelligence Service never ceased asking for a certain measure of autonomy. This Section did great work during the struggle. While the Assault Force belaboured the enemy with iron and lead, the Intelligence fought him with brains. Indeed, the victory over the government forces depended largely on our Intelligence, its revelations, its information and the security belt it built, laboriously and with unerring common sense, round the fighting underground. Its members, headed by Yoel's deputy and successor, Mi-

chael, were anxious for even greater achievements and
believed they could obtain them if they were given a
measure of freedom of action. Characteristically, they
quoted in support of their argument the custom in
many countries in which the Intelligence and counter-
espionage services are under the direct control of the
central government.

Thanks to the understanding and tolerance which
all our comrades displayed, we succeeded in overcoming these internecine difficulties, which flowed from the
necessary division of labour among many people and
their eager desire to succeed in their tasks. It is no exaggeration to say that in the underground we all gained
some experience of the machinery of State, with its
light and shadow, its virtues and its defects. Generally
we overcame the "inter-departmental" problems, but
we never succeeded in putting an end to the sacred dispute between the Assault Force and the Revolutionary
Propaganda Force.

6

The R.P.F. was given the task of disseminating the
message of revolt. We set great store by the work of
public information. Eretz Israel has not many natural
resources, but the Jewish people has one very valuable
natural asset: brains. And people who think are not
content either with empty words or with blind action.
They want to know why something was done and why
it was done when it was done. Our people expected explanations of our actions, and we had to give explanations in order to secure what we wished to secure: their
understanding and their sympathy.

There was another reason for the work of the R.P.F.
We were compelled to repulse verbal attacks as well as
physical ones. Enemy propaganda tried to paint us as
the lowest of the low. Abusive name-calling was of
course constant and unbridled. But enemy propaganda
used other means as well. Many will remember our attack on the government's "pay-roll-train," from which
we confiscated a large sum of money. Orders were

given, as in all similar operations which the exigencies
of war compelled us to carry out, to avoid hurting
anybody. The quantity of explosives employed for halt-
ing the train was so calculated as to force the train to
stop, albeit with an unpleasant jolt, but not to destroy
or seriously damage it. The boys rushed out of the
wood where they had been waiting, the guard surrendered and was disarmed. All the officials on the train—
which carried no civilian passengers—were placed in
custody. A few who had been scratched by broken
glass were bandaged—to their great surprise—by members of our First Aid detachment. The money—
£38,000—was seized. The boys returned to their base.
The British officials, knowing what we would do with
the money, made the most strenuous efforts to recover
it. Neighbouring Hadera was placed under curfew. Special patrols were sent out on the roads. Searches were
made in all vehicles. The vehicle carrying the money
was also searched thoroughly—but fruitlessly.

The operation was carried out during the short period of the united Resistance Movement when for a
while the Haganah fought with us against British rule.
At one of our regular meetings with the Haganah
chiefs, Moshe Sneh[1] told me that a high British Staff
Officer had expressed wry admiration of the plan and
its efficient execution. He had described the attack in
the Hadera wood as a "clean job." We were prepared
to forego the compliment, but it was hard to forgive
what was written about this "clean job" by a high officer on another British Staff, the Staff of a newspaper.
This lady, sent to Eretz Israel by one of the most
widely-circulated newspapers, told her millions of readers that the attack was led by "my fiancée, a blonde
young woman, who carried a Tommygun night and
day." And after a description of this vampire came a
hair-raising account of the behaviour of the "wild ter-

---

[1] This gentleman, who was a politician in a group working
with Mr. Ben Gurion's executive, subsequently joined what is
called "Mapam," the extreme Socialist-Communist Party in
Israel.

rorists" at Hadera. Maybe these stories helped us in the
long run, by creating an impression among the hundreds of thousands of people in Britain who had relatives serving in Eretz Israel, that their unfortunate boys
had been transported by the British government into an
inferno, thus adding to the growing demand in Britain
to bring back the British troops from Eretz Israel with
the least possible delay. So that even that journalist,
who gave me a blonde fiancée in place of my brunette
wife, even that hate-consumed scribbler helped, however unintentionally, to expedite the departure of the
Mandatory regime. She had been sent out to calumniate
us and what she wrote was calculated to make people
hate us. Regrettably, certain Jewish elements and or-
gans of information did their share, too, of this das-
tardly vilification.

We were compelled to defend ourselves. Public enlightenment was an inseparable part of our struggle.
One of our most important means was our radio station. We were not able at once to make regular and
effective use of the underground radio. We began with
a double failure. Our transmitter was captured, after
the first few broadcasts, at the home of Esther Raziel,
David's sister. Esther and her husband were arrested.
They left behind their two children and David's aged
parents, still mourning their beloved elder son. And the
sorrow at the capture of Esther and Yehuda was greater than at the capture of the "box." Esther spent a long
time in the Bethlehem Jail, and Yehuda remained for
years in the African concentration camps—but we soon
acquired another and better transmitter.

At first we broadcast for only five minutes at a time.
We had read in European underground literature that
the Germans, using special instruments, were able to
locate underground transmitters within six minutes. We
assumed that the British had such instruments. We
therefore allowed one minute for getting the transmitter
away. But we grew tired of this arrangement. The situation in the country was growing ever more serious, the
struggle more and more intense. It was necessary to
expand our broadcasts. We published a warning that

the station was under armed guard and that if the military forces tried to seize our transmitter they would pay for the attempt with their lives. The warning was effective. Thereafter we broadcast for ten, fifteen or twenty minutes. The authorities could probably have located the transmitter, but they never tried to send their detectors near it. Perhaps they reasoned that if they came they would suffer casualties and possibly not even succeed in removing the transmitter; and even if they did succeed the Irgun helped by their technicians—who were incidentally among the best in the country—would soon have another.

But they found other means of interfering with our broadcasts, which by now had attracted tens of thousands of listeners. Goebbels during the World War had made stupendous efforts to "jam" the B.B.C. broadcasts. The Mandatory government scraped and screeched on our wavelength just as the Germans had done to the B.B.C. Our technicians racked their brains for a way of overcoming the interference. They built a transmitter which made it possible to jump from one wavelength to another. And there followed a strange hide-and-seek in the air as well as on the ground. At the appointed hour the "illegal" broadcast would begin. A minute later the jamming machine would set up its whining and banshee wailing. The broadcaster would jump to another wave-length. Listeners feverishly twiddled the knobs of their receivers in pursuit of an American's voice. Sometimes they caught up with the second wavelength, sometimes not. Meanwhile the jamming machine was following in hot pursuit. There—it had cut the new wavelength. The broadcaster jumped to the third wavelength or retreated back to his first position, the listeners in his wake, the "jammers" closely behind them. It was an exhausting game.

We tried another strategem. We published a warning that if the British Authorities did not give up their efforts to silence us, we would silence them. This warning did not help. We worked out a plan for blowing up the British radio station in Jerusalem. Several times we were on the brink of carrying out the plan but each

time unexpected difficulties arose. We had to avoid injuring the civilians working in the broadcasting service,
among whom were many Jews and also women. In the
conditions created by the war, we never found a means
of overcoming this difficulty. We therefore postponed
the execution of the plan, though we never gave it up
entirely. But ultimately the British evacuated Sarona
where they kept their jamming apparatus, and henceforth we were able to broadcast without interference.
The warning about the radio was one of the very few
Irgun warnings to which we did not give effect.

We were never silenced. We translated our broadcasts into foreign languages and distributed them
among the foreign newspaper correspondents and foreign diplomatic representatives. Our broadcasts generally contained factual news, and political analysis. As
we learnt, they received very wide publicity in the
world's Press, from Sydney to San Francisco. This was
important in keeping the Eretz Israel problem in the
focus of international attention. The voice of revolt and
of freedom was carried far and wide despite the British
Government's jamming. If scores of thousands were
prevented from hearing it, millions heard it, and Eretz
Israel continued to hold the world's attention even
when the explosives were silent.

A mighty means of enlightenment in Eretz Israel was
the "wall." We disseminated the declaration of revolt
through the length and breadth of the country by post-
ing it up on the walls. We did the same with nearly
all our published material with the exception of pamphlets. We brought out a wall-newspaper *Herut* (Freedom), the first of its kind in Eretz Israel and possibly
the first anywhere. We published leaflets, appeals and
communiqués on military operations. At least once
every two or three days, at times every day or every
night, our message was proclaimed. We never tired of
explaining. The boys of the R.P.F. never tired of pasting up. The public grew more and more interested in
reading what the underground had to say. Long queues
would gather to read our posters, leaflets and sheets.
We addressed the public in the simple language of

truth. We never aimed at any particular class, we spoke
to the people as a whole. Bit by bit they learned to
believe us. Little by little they learned to trust us. For
we told them only the truth.

Indeed, the one sacred principle of our information
was to tell the truth and nothing but the truth. We
could not of course tell the whole truth. We were underground. Facing us was an enemy listening, searching
and taking notes: facing us were his aides and agents
who spied on us and aimed at harming us. We could
not publish everything, but whatever we published was
true.

On an August day in 1944 we attacked the police
stations on the Jaffa-Tel Aviv border, at Abu Kebir, at
Neve Shaanan and the C.I.D. Headquarters in Jaffa itself. On this occasion we did not, as in previous attacks,
have any "town planning" purpose. We simply wanted
to take a few arms from the British police. At that time
we were leaving military camps alone. We had decided
not to attack military installations so long as the war
with Nazi Germany was in progress. This decision, dictated by true political wisdom, was punctiliously
obeyed until May 1945, when the "as long as" ceased
to have effect. But the British police and their armouries were always a legitimate target for the Assault
Force, which now went to carry out the Irgun's first
confiscation operation. Had we had the time we would
have been quite prepared on this occasion, too, to "decorate" the C.I.D. Headquarters, which had been moved
to another building after our first "visit" in the spring;
but the other stations interested us only for their rifles
and machine-guns. Our main target was the old C.I.D.
building which we had blown up in the spring. Our information was that the undamaged portion contained a
large number of rifles and automatic weapons.

Only part of the operation was carried out. Our boys
did not reach the armoury. Their explosives were inadequate for smashing the iron door which guarded that
section. In a renewed attempt, a clash developed on
the Tel-Aviv-Jaffa border, but the way to the armoury
was by this time completely blocked and the men had

to withdraw. In the other places the tasks were fulfilled as planned. The booty was not great but the boys, who had gained experience both from the successes and the failure, were glad that they had not returned empty-handed. The A.F. had done its work. The R.P.F. at once got down to its part. Throughout the country a communiqué was pasted up, briefly describing the clashes with the enemy. As for arms, we wrote, fourteen rifles were confiscated in one of the stations.

This statement, or admission, angered some of our friends who argued that we were under no obligation to say how many weapons we had acquired. Why not let the public, which needed consolation and morale-building, think that the quantity was much greater? We did not disregard the psychological arguments of our friends. Of course we could have avoided mentioning details and said a "quantity of arms." But we stood our ground. We had acquired fourteen rifles in a certain place, and we would tell the public fourteen rifles. And the incident of these fourteen rifles gave a pointer to the policy we were to pursue. We did not soil our mouths or our pens with falsehood. We told the truth. Good or bad, pleasant or annoying, it was always the truth. This policy lost us temporary rewards, but in the long run it gained us the trust of the people and of the world. They all learnt that our statements were facts. They all learnt that our warnings were fulfilled. As time went on it became common to hear people in Eretz Israel offering as authority for their confident assertions: "Haven't you heard? The I.Z.L. said so."

A Jewish journalist, who served as local assistant to foreign correspondents, told us that when they were given a communiqué from the Haganah Command they would ask their Jewish assistants: "Have you checked?" Irgun statements on the other hand, were accepted without hesitation or further question.

The "14 rifles" policy which we pursued in our publicity gave us the trust of the people—the most valuable asset of a fighting underground surrounded by enemies and detractors.

How did we print our material? We used various

methods. At first we worked in the little printing shop near the Jaffa-Tel Aviv border which had printed the *palabra*. There was no choice; we had not enough money to acquire our own printing-press. But in the autumn of 1944 we managed to buy a small printing-press. Our boys, who went there as full-time workers, accepted commercial orders of all kinds, but between printing receipt-books and letter-heads they would do the work for which they had been mobilized. We loaded this press with work, perhaps too heavily. We were still in the early stages of the revolt; we had a good deal to say. Meanwhile the campaign of denunciations had begun. Our printing-press, too, fell victim to the informers, and we remained for a time without a press. Only occasionally were we able to print something with our old friend, the owner of the Mizrachi Press. But later, having learnt from experience, we managed to repair the situation. We decided to build a press literally underground. We found a suitable place. The essential camouflage was worked out. The boys toiled and dug. Everything was almost ready—when we learnt that somebody in the neighbourhood had found out. We did not want to rely on miracles. We left the building. As fate would have it, that building was later destroyed in one of the first Egyptian air-attacks on Tel-Aviv.

We did not despair. Necessity rules in the underground. We found another place, and burrowed out an underground compartment. Giddy solved the problem of ventilation by constructing a mechanical ventilator. A new anxiety arose. The porters—the famous Salonican stevedores—who brought the printing-machines to the place, got wind of something. Our Intelligence Service learnt that there was talk among them of a secret Irgun printing-press. This was disquieting. Innocent talk might spread; the enemy had many listening ears. But the anxiety passed. The good strong-armed Salonicans understood the necessity of absolute silence. The press was set going. The work there was truly hard labour. The air was suffocating, the heat terrible, sometimes putting the very machine out of action. But the Irgun workers knew no rest, often toiling round the

clock without a break. Above ground, too, our boys
worked, though in greater comfort. Above the printing-
press was a modest carpentry workshop which took orders for furniture. A big truck would arrive at the shop,
ostensibly to bring wood and take away furniture. But
no alien eye saw that among the wood and furniture
were packages of papers, the sacred packages for which
the whole workshop had been set up. This subterranean
press was never discovered by the British authorities.
Only with the establishment of the State did we reveal
the hidden location from which we had called upon the
people not to bow down under the shame of oppression.

From the press the material was taken to regional
distribution centres. Thence it was distributed to local
centres where the R.P.F. men went off to publish it on
the walls. It was our ambition to paste up our newspapers and leaflets on the same day throughout the
country. We therefore set up an inter-urban postal delivery. The transport of the material, like the transfer
of arms, was carried out under the very noses of the
police.

7

Generally speaking, the R.P.F. followed in the wake
of the Assault Force, to explain the reasons for military
attacks. Sometimes they would precede the Assault
Force in order to prepare the minds of the people for
coming operations. But there were also cases, though
they were few, when the R.P.F. operated *instead* of the
Assault Force. Leaflets instead of bullets. And they had
the effect of bullets. One of these occasions was connected with the Wailing Wall.

The dispute over the Wailing Wall and the Old City
is probably a reflection of the whole struggle for the
ownership of Eretz Israel. It must be said to the credit
of the British authorities that they understood very well
the political value of traditional symbols. It was in English, not in Hebrew, that Disraeli wrote that people
are led by force or by tradition. British policy therefore

directed its shafts at the heart of Jewish tradition. As elsewhere it used Arabs, or Moslems. As usual an Inquiry Commission was set up and published its "verdict"—this time in the form of the "Order-in-Council, 1929." There they wrote with superb impertinence that the Moslems had the sole right of ownership and possession of the Wailing Wall, as well as the right of ownership to the adjacent courtyard and the area overlooking the Wall. And there they decreed "Jews are forbidden to blow the Shofar at the Wailing Wall."

The British, famous for their observance of law, enforced this prohibition religiously. And if the law they decreed said that the very stones of the Western Wall of the Hebrew Temple belong to the Moslem mosque built on the ruins of that Temple—that of course was the law against which there could be no appeal. Sacred tradition? Living testimony to a glorious past? A charter of rights hewn in ancient stone? Precisely for these reasons must the stones of the wall be taken from the Jews. And how helpful it was for this purpose that among the Jews themselves there were unexpected allies who, in snobbish pretence of "progress," argued that a few pedigree cows were worth more than all these stones.

But the ancient stones themselves refute the nonsense of these pathetic "progressives" who try to impress foreigners with their "freedom from old fashioned prejudice." These stones are not silent. They do not cry out. They whisper. They speak softly of the house that once stood there, of kings who knelt here once in prayer, of prophets and seers who here declaimed their message, of heroes who fell here, dying; and of how the great flame, at once destructive and illuminating, was here kindled. This was the house, and this the country which, with its seers and kings and fighters, was ours before the British were a nation. The testimony of these stones, sending out their light across the generations.

Ever since the first years of their enslavement, the Wailing Wall has been the repository of the yearning of our people. And let not cynics prattle of "mysti-

cism." The voice of history is not mystic. It is a mighty
factor in reality. It was this voice the British Government tried to silence. They decreed that Jews were forbidden to blow the Shofar at the Wall. And when Jews
ignored the ban—as the young disciples of Jabotinsky
did for thirteen consecutive years—there followed an
ugly spectacle, humiliating and infuriating. I saw this
spectacle for myself on the Day of Atonement in 1943
when with a group of friends I prayed at the Wall.

The sun was setting. The congregation of sorrowing
Jews lifted their voices on high: it was the sacred Nei-
lah (closing) Prayer at the holy place, and the time
was that of the great catastrophe in Europe. . . . And
then, from both sides of the courtyard in streamed British police armed with rifles and batons. They stood
among the worshippers, threatening them with their
very presence. They had come "in the King's name" to
prevent an "illegal act": the blowing of the Shofar at
the close of the Sabbath of Sabbaths. As the end of the
prayer approached they squeezed further into the mass
of worshippers, some even elbowing their way up to
the Wall. And when in spite of them the Shofar was
heard, their fury was unrestrained. They set upon the
worshippers—while prayer was still in progress. They
hit out at heads; batons whistled through the air. Here
and there was heard the cry of somebody injured. A
song too burst forth, Hatikvah. Then the police struck
out in all directions and chaos reigned. Finally they
withdrew.

That night as, more heart-sore than injured, we stood
by the Wailing Wall, we said to each other: "This is the
real slavery. What the Roman proconsuls did not dare
do, Britain's Commissioners are doing. What our ancestors refused to tolerate from their ancient oppressors, even at the cost of their lives and freedom—is tolerated by the generation of Jews which describes itself
as the last of oppression and the first of redemption. A
people that does not defend its holy places—that does
not even try to defend them—is not free, however
much it may babble about freedom. People that permit
the holiest spot in their country and their most sacred

feelings to be trampled underfoot—are slaves in spirit.
And we determined there and then that when the time
came we would cleanse our people of this shame, and if
we should have the strength we would not permit the
oppressor's myrmidons to violate our Holy Place, disturb our prayers and desecrate our Festival.

On the following New Year[1] (ten days before the
Day of Atonement) we recalled the shame and our decision. We determined not to permit a repetition or, if
it occurred, not to let it go unpunished. We made a
complex plan, both psychological and practical. The
task was given to the R.P.F. We began warning the
British authorities. Night after night the "pasters-up"
went out to make known in varying texts our essential
warning. These repeated warnings were summed up in
a statement we published in English as well as Hebrew.

"1. On the Day of Atonement, at the Western Wall,
large numbers of the people will unite with the
spirit of the martyrs of Israel who fell victim to
German cruelty and British treachery.

"2. The principles of civilized humanity dictate that
the sacred prayer should not be disturbed, nor
the Holy Place violated.

"3. The British Government—ruling temporarily
against the will of the Jewish people in its Homeland—is required not to infringe these principles.

"4. Any British policeman who on the Day of
Atonement dares to burst into the area of the
Wailing Wall and to disturb the traditional service—will be regarded as a criminal and will be
punished accordingly."

As our warnings followed one another and the Day
of Atonement drew near, anxiety grew in Jerusalem
and the whole country. Nobody knew how we intended
defending the people's honour. Some feared there
would be terrible bloodshed at the Wall. Others argued
that we were only conducting a war of nerves against

[1] The Jewish year begins in the autumn during September-
October.

the British. Others again reported concentration of arms in the Old City. And there were some who, as usual, made jokes.

The official Jewish institutions, of course, did not remain passive. Articles on our "criminal lunacy" were witten in abundance. And articles were supplemented by actions. The Chief Rabbinate was asked to "undo" our work with a stroke of the pen. The Rabbinate responded. An appeal was published in its name claiming that the blowing of the Shofar at the close of the Day of Atonement was no more than a custom which was not obligatory and, in any case, "the law of the land is the law." . . .

We did not retreat. We were imbued with a consciousness of our mission perhaps more than at any other stage of the revolt. We continued with our plans. Our basic assumption was that we had placed the Government in an awkward position both psychologically and perhaps even more so, politically: and that they would consequently retreat. That the Wailing Wall is sacred is admitted on all hands, and it was no simple matter for a Government which wanted to appear "civilized" to be responsible for a bloody clash because they wished to ban the observance of religious tradition.

We, naturally, had no intention of bringing about such a clash. We planned this special campaign down to the last detail. To start with we launched the psychological attack, the practical value of which will be clear to anybody who knows anything about war. Complete victories can sometimes be won with the psychological weapon.

At times, however, that weapon proves ineffective. We took this possibility into account. And we knew that if, despite our warnings and his fears, the enemy nevertheless decided to send his men to the Wall, as he had done for thirteen years, we should be unable to retaliate on the spot. For old men, women and children would be hurt. And all the tactical advantages were with the enemy.

It was equally clear to us however that our intention

not to start a clash at the Wall must be kept a dead secret. The whole value of our warnings lay in letting the enemy believe that if he dared come near the Wall he would be fired on from every direction and suffer heavy casualties. We were therefore compelled to refrain from reassuring the anxious people—both those who cursed and abused us and those whose anxiety was sincere.

So we kept the truth to ourselves, and it was very simple. We decided to exploit the psychological weapon to the utmost. Should it fail and the enemy repeat his sacriligious operation—we would attack him, but not where he expected to be attacked. We would hit him elsewhere, but at the same time, and he would learn, and the world would learn, that the feelings of our people could not be desecrated without retribution. Thus was born the idea of an attack that night on the Tegart[1] police fortresses at Haifa, Beit-Dajan, Kalkiliah and Katara. Our series of warnings were not designed, therefore, as many people thought, merely to delude the enemy and to facilitate the attacks on the "unconquerable" fortresses. On the contrary, the attacks on the fortresses were planned as an immediate punishment for the Mandatory's desecration at the Wailing Wall.

The combination of psychological warfare and a practical plan did not fail. The Tegart fortresses were attacked that night, but not as a punishment for British action at the Wailing Wall. Our warning proved effective. The oppressor retreated. On the Day of Atonement in 1944—for the first time in fourteen years—the British police did not come near the Wailing Wall. They stood at a distance, and for greater security, took off their number tags. The prayer was not interrupted. The great blast of the Shofar was truly great. The sounder was no longer "illegal." He did not hide nor disguise himself. He stood up openly and let himself be heard through the Shofar—the trumpet of revolt.

[1] Fortress-like police stations set up all over the country by the British on the advice of Sir James Tegart during the Arab disturbances of 1936-39.

8

As the struggle grew in intensity, the work of the R.P.F. became more and more dangerous. The "pasters-up" were not armed. We kept our arms for military attacks. But the British detectives and police were armed. Many pasting-up operations were therefore accompanied by shooting. There were leaflet-stickers who sealed the message of revolt with their blood. One of them, Asher Tratner, a fine popular youngster, was not only wounded but subsequently murdered.

Asher Tratner was a pupil in the eighth class at the Haifa High School. He joined the Irgun at the beginning of the revolt, and worked in the R.P.F. One night, as he was pasting up a proclamation he was shot by a policeman and wounded in the hip. What does an allegedly civilized regime do with a wounded man, even a wounded enemy? I regret to record that some British officers did not treat our wounded men as we in the underground treated their wounded prisoners in our hands. Tratner was not seen by a doctor nor sent to hospital. He was dispatched, his wound open and bleeding, to the Acre Jail. The wound festered. His jailers tied him to the bed. The boy had to wipe the blood and pus from his wound with strips torn from his shirt. The guards continued to maltreat him. I was told by Rabbi Blum, whom the authorities had appointed prison chaplain, that he had drawn the attention of the British to the critical condition of the young prisoner. The reply was characteristic: "Rabbis should concern themselves with the souls of the prisoners, not with their bodies. Mind your own business."

Asher's spirit was not broken, but his body was destroyed. When at last the prison doctor was brought he diagnosed severe blood-poisoning and the boy was removed to hospital. But it was too late. Even amputation of his leg did not save Asher. After weeks of suffering in the Acre Jail and the Haifa hospital, he died.

Asher Tratner is one of the noble figures whose memory keeps coming back to me whenever I think of the Revolt and of the wonderful generation that suddenly sprang up like a forest of fresh saplings on the soil of the Homeland. Why did they maltreat him? Why did they force on him a slow and painful death? I mourned for Asher as for a son.

9

The chief bearer of the Irgun message was the Assault Force. To it, after its merger with the Shock Unit, was allocated the task of "hitting the enemy with new weapons in order to disintegrate alien rule." And the A.F. carried out its task. It gave the enemy no respite: it penetrated the heavily defended centres of government. The superior forces of the British army did not help. Their buildings and barracks were speedily reduced to rubble. The A.F. penetrated the fortresses of the enemy. The walls of the Tegart police stations did not stand up to its blows. The A.F. disrupted enemy transport; it destroyed bridges, tore up railway lines, demolished stations, blew up trains, mined roads, sent armoured cars flying. After the end of the war against Nazi Germany in May 1945 the A.F. directed its attentions to the Anglo-Iraqi oil pipeline and gave no rest to that artery of British economy in the Middle East. The A.F. penetrated Army camps. At times, as during martial law, it delivered tremendous blows against them. At other times it filled them with fear and took away their arms. The A.F. descended on airfields and reduced dozens of four-engined heavy bombers to smoking ruins. The A.F. pierced the heart of the British regime, the G.H.Q. of the Occupation Army. The A.F. burst through the "Bevingrads"—the ghettoes of the officials, ringed with kilometers of barbed wire massed in depth, fortified by concealed machine-gun nests and defended by whole regiments of heavily-armed troops. The Officers' Club at Goldschmidt House, the military barracks in the Schneller Quarter in Jerusalem, and the police headquarters at Haifa, even though they were in the heart of the "security zones," crumbled under the blows of the A.F.

The A.F. effected the collapse of martial law in March 1947. After our attack on Goldschmidt House, which was accompanied by other attacks and sabotage operations throughout the country, the authorities decreed a state of martial law in the areas populated by Jews. The big towns were occupied by troops. Every region was sealed off and isolated. The movement of all vehicles was banned. Postal communications were stopped. Wherever one turned there was a military strong-point. Martial law!

But the A.F. pierced the ring everywhere. Its men, led by Gideon and Shimshon, swept like a flame across the country. Nearly twenty operations were carried out during the period of martial law and in spite of it. Among them was an attack on military transport near Rishon Le Zion; an attack with machineguns and hand-grenades on a military camp near Hadera; an attack on a military patrol on the main road near Beit-Lidd; more attacks on military patrols near Beit-Lidd and military convoys in the south; an attack with machine-guns, hand-grenades and two-inch mortars, on a military camp near Kfar Yonah; an attack on a military patrol on the banks of the Yarkon River. A military camp at Hadera was attacked and blown up; a military patrol was attacked at the Rosh Ha'ayin-Lydda cross-roads; the oil pipeline was blown up at three places in Haifa and again in three places near Kfar Hassidim.

The list is by no means complete. The onslaught was crowned by the attack on the enemy fortress at Schneller House. There the boys had to blast a fortified wall under machine-gun crossfire; then cut their way through three barbed wire defences—all under enemy fire; place their explosives in position and set them off—and then withdraw from the area, which by this time was surrounded by British armoured cars and tanks. In spite of all these hazards the boys carried out the attack as planned—perhaps with the exception of the Acre operation, amongst the most daring attacks of the Hebrew underground and possibly of any underground. The barracks of the Occupation Army were flung into the air, and the boys returned safely to base. Tanks and

armoured cars were repulsed. They were stopped, partly
by our Bren-guns and partly by the fear aroused by
our luminous mines. What were these mines? They
were tin cans which carried, in luminous letters, the English inscription: "Mines!" In actual fact, as we happened to be suffering from a shortage of material at the
time, they contained not an ounce of explosives. But
the metal was real!

Even the enemy who did not know that we were
short of explosives was forced to acknowledge the bravery of our boys. The British Army Commander of the
Jerusalem District said to his subordinate officers:
"They struck just like commandos."

And Mr. Gershon Agronsky, the editor of the *Palestine Post*, said in my hearing, something like this: "If
there are boys in the Irgun who are prepared to get up
at two in the morning to carry out an attack, the Irgun
is no mean force."

The A.F. continued to attack, before and after midnight. It carried out scores of operations, big and small.
Some have been mentioned; of others I shall yet tell.
They are all part of the military history of the Jewish
people. The A.F. did not, except in specific cases, carry
out attacks on individuals. It launched battles face to
face with the enemy forces, the first partisan battles of
a Hebrew force against the oppressor and his occupation army since the Hasmonean Revolt. The A.F. fulfilled what we promised Churchill in 1944, in words
borrowed from his own: "We shall fight on the beaches
and on the roads; we shall fight in the hills and the
plains; we shall fight in the towns and in the villages;
we shall fight in the streets and in the houses; we shall
fight even if we are alone, even if the struggle goes on
for years."

The battle tactics of the A.F. were based on the maximum exploitation of the factor of surprise and the employment of small forces for big blows. Thanks to the
combination of these two factors the Military Power
truly sat on scorpions in Eretz Israel. The forces of oppression knew no respite by day or by night. It was
bad for them when operations were in progress; it was

not good for them when there were no operations—for then they waited expectantly for some surprise "visit." Their nervous system might be compared to a broken down piano: you press one note and the whole piano emits a cacophony of noise. We did not have to attack twenty British camps simultaneously in order to develop acute apprehension amongst all. It was enough to attack one in order that all should be afflicted with fear by night and with uneasy expectation by day.

The A.F. units attained a high degree of skill in exploiting the surprise attack, blasting a path with explosives, and blowing up their objective while continuously "covered" by machine-guns both during the advance and the withdrawal. General Cunningham complained that we had learnt this method from the Germans, and that it was practically impossible to withstand it if the break-through group were composed of men who were heedless of risk. If he was right in the second half of his statement he was mistaken in the first. We did not learn this from others. We taught ourselves, and experience improved the teaching. Readiness for sacrifice did wonders. But it is true that the armed forces hardly ever withstood the co-ordinated action of the break-through and covering groups. And if at times we failed, it was invariably due to a miscalculation on our part or to blind chance.

The A.F. attacked every day of the week—except on the Sabbath. The Irgun had observed the Jewish religious traditions, ever since the days of David Raziel, who was devoutly religious. We too were believers. We believed in the Almighty, we believed in our mission and in the justice of our cause. And though we knew that our struggle was obligatory and so permissible on the Sabbath, we generally preferred to give respite to our arms on that day. The British knew this, and consequently looked forward to the Jewish Sabbath more than to Sunday.

But there were a number of exceptional operations. One of them was the attack on the first "Security Zone" in Jerusalem. This was carried out at midday on the Sabbath because only at that time was the neighbourhood comparatively unfrequented by civilians. At the time of that completely unexpected attack, two very important British personalities were playing tennis in another "Security Zone." They were Gurney, Chief Secretary of the Palestine Government, and Fitzgerald, the British Chief Justice. Homer Bigart, the capable correspondent of the *New York Herald-Tribune*, wrote ironically that when the shattering explosion was heard those two gentlemen—in breach of the tradition established by Sir Francis Drake—*did* stop their game.

Chapter VII
Overt Underground

The British Secret Service is an institution enveloped in legend. Who has not heard of its achievements? The legend has been passed on from generation to generation, and from country to country, and from continent to continent—until some have come to believe that the British Intelligence is omniscient and infallible. Those who are interested in the dissemination of such stories know that in spying, as in war, the legend of success is in itself a success factor. The strength of British Intelligence however does not lie only in the legend. This Service was, and may still prove to be, a tremendous factor in international relations. It has at its disposal the accumulated experience of centuries.

But during the revolt in Eretz Israel neither great experience nor the vast resources of the British Intelligence Service were of much help. The Hebrew underground smote the Intelligence hip and thigh. We proved that the Secret Service was neither omniscient nor infallible. We scattered to the winds the legends woven around their secret agents. We proved that many of them were fools, too lazy even to think, and that it is not difficult to reduce them to the condition of blind men groping in the dark.

Why did the Intelligence fail in our little country? One of the reasons was its habit of thinking in a rut—Enemy Number One of all creative thought. The British Colonial Office was accustomed to ruling backward peoples. Amongst such peoples agents can easily be secured with money or with drink. Somebody needs—or likes—money. And "somebody," on the watch, proposes, out of friendship, "help" or a "loan." The open hand closes its grip. The first piece of information is passed on. Then comes more information for more money. And if the information does not come, a Damoclean sword is suspended over the victim's head. . . . The victim's head begins to turn. His tongue wags. Too late he struggles in the web. He tries hard to cut himself loose, to get out, to save himself—but in vain. The blackmail begins. "If you don't give us more information, we shall expose you to your friends." The victim is in a terrible dilemma. His downward slide continues. He has no longer any choice.

These methods, which Intelligence Services throughout the world have developed into an art, failed utterly in Eretz Israel. They found great difficulty in buying Jewish informers. There were, it is true, cases of treachery for money, but they were few and, on the whole, of little importance.

Nor did drink help British Intelligence in Eretz Israel. There is little or no drunkenness among Jews. Unlike Arthur Koestler, I believe that sobriety in this respect is one of the happy characteristics of our people. Koestler complained to me once of the undue sobriety of Jews. He argued that as the work of diplomacy is usually done over a drink, inability to drink is in some measure proof of political incapacity. That may be. But it must be borne in mind that whisky-diplomacy works both ways. One may be forced to admit that Jewish leaders have not up to now excelled at politics, but that is not because of their sobriety. There are other reasons. At any rate, while I believe that there are many things we ought to learn from other peoples, drinking is not one of them. Preferably, others should learn abstinence from us.

British rule-of-thumb thinking also did not take into account the fact that the Hebrew underground was very serious-minded. In other underground movements there were not a few who were drawn to participate more by their love of adventure than by the ideal. In our underground there were no "adventurers," or almost none. Our ranks were filled by idealists who risked their lives to save their people. Richard Mowrer, the well-known

American journalist and a friend of our people, once said to me, "I know that your boys fight with their eyes open."

This was a profound truth. Our eyes were open to the sufferings of our people, to the strength of the opposition, to the vital character of our fight, to the dangers that lurked everywhere.

Day and night we impressed on our officers, and ordered them to impress on the ranks, that the two main enemies of secrecy were—curiosity and boastfulness. Curiosity, they were taught, extorts the secret from those who know it; vain boastfulness reveals it to those who do not know it. Both are anathema. The rule is: Don't ask and don't tell. What has to be known is known only to those who have to know it; and they know only as much as they have to. More they do not know; and apart from them nobody knows. Unless you accept this you will bring down disaster not only on your own head but on your comrades, not only on the individual but on the whole fighting family.

Our education bore fruit. The British Intelligence inclined many listening ears. They heard nothing. We were girded around by a wall of silence. Occasionally, of course, it developed cracks, but they were few. The British Intelligence never succeeded in breaking through them into the underground.

The wall of silence, the most important defence line of an underground, also protected us from the consequences of provocation. As a rule conspiracy and provocation go together. There is no underground on earth which has escaped the plague of agents-provocateurs. There are few underground movements in history that have not been disintegrated from within by provocateurs introduced from outside. "B.O.," the terrorist underground of the Social-Revolutionaries in Tsarist Russia, was given its death-blow by the Okhrana—the Tsarist Secret Police—through the aid of agent-informers, the greatest and best known of whom was himself one of the leaders of the underground, the notorious Azeff. The Irish underground suffered heavily from leakages. The Communist Party in Poland, which worked underground before the Second World War, was in actual fact under the command of the Polish Government's Secret Police! The Comintern was ultimately forced to dissolve its Polish branch, which was rotten with treachery, not only in its ranks but especially in its headquarters.

The ugly shadow of the provocateur, of the agent who deliberately joins the rebels in order to betray their secrets, or the traitor who, for one reason or another, deserts his comrades and goes over to the enemy, was cast over our underground as well. The British Intelligence did its best to introduce informers into our ranks and to acquire agents from among our members. In all the years of the revolt there were only three cases of treachery and the enemy Intelligence never once succeeded in introducing their own agents into the underground without their being discovered almost immediately. They never succeeded—and this is most important—in getting agents into positions high up in the direction of the struggle.

Our security service worked energetically, devotedly and ably. Its anonymous helpers, among them Jewish police in the British service, succeeded in penetrating the enemy camp without letting the enemy into ours. Consequently, we generally knew in advance what the Government forces intended doing. The struggle was subterranean in the full sense of the term. The world outside saw the physical clash. Our blows, it is true, were planned underground but their execution was on the surface, often face to face with the armed enemy. What the world did not see was the clash of brains. This went on deep underground, and was perhaps the decisive battle in the struggle for liberation. The British were faced with the problem of disintegrating us from within in order to smash us. We were faced with the problem of smashing their rule in order to disintegrate it. The cunning of the Intelligence Service encountered Jewish brains; and cunning lost.

The most serious situation of this kind for us arose in the first stage of the revolt from the treachery of one Simon Tsorros. We became aware that somebody among us, or connected with us, was giving away information to the enemy. I have already told of the arrest of Esther Raziel and her husband and the discovery of the radio-transmitter in their home. That arrests should be made throughout the country after our first operations did not surprise us. The people seized were, on the whole, well-known for their views, lived openly and made no attempt to hide. What did surprise us was that the British should have found out our radio-transmitter in the Raziel house without undue effort and before we had time to move it. "That," we concluded, "was the result of inside information"; and we began ferreting out the servant of his people's enemies. It was not long before the tracks led us to Simon Tsorros.

But before I tell of Tsorros I must refer to the effect the mass arrests had, not on the public at large, but on the underground itself. The revolt having barely begun, the shock of that first blow was tremendous. I do not deny that in those nights I could not sleep. I could hardly work. I was constantly thinking of the disrupted families, especially of the children. I visited some of the families, and found sorrow and anguish. I saw Mrs. Raziel, the great mother of a great son, whose hair had turned white as snow but whose spirit remained firm as a rock. I did not try to comfort her. I asked how she was. She thanked me and added quietly, with the composure and dignity of one who believes that the Lord who had given, and had taken away, would also give back: "See, overnight, our home has been destroyed—again."

We began to be subjected to pressure. It came from various quarters. All asked us to try to secure the release of the prisoners and especially of Esther. With the pressure came mental conflict. Had we the right to bring suffering to people and families? Had we the right to jeopardize their freedom and their lives? How could we be certain that our fight would bear fruit? Whoever has not been subjected to these awful moral trials will never understand their full impact.

My friends helped me overcome my torturing doubts. They said aloud what the inner voice whispered: "Is not every one of us prepared to give up his freedom, or his life?" And they added: "Will not those who remain outside, in the underground, be prisoners too? Perhaps more so than those kept behind barbed wire? And what is the alternative? Shall we make peace with enslavement?"

This mental conflict, which began with the launching of the revolt, ended only on our leaving the underground. And naturally so. There is no need to create legends about "men of steel." Where there are no soulsearchings there is only insensate hard-heartedness. The atrophy of natural, deep human feelings is no proof of a strong character. If such a thing as a "heart of steel" exists, or evolves, it is acquired at a heavy cost in suffering.

Though the inner conflict arose afresh with every new victim and every new enemy decree, the issue was decided in those days after the first arrests. We did not submit to the pressure. We refused to try to secure the release of the prisoners. We told our friends:

"We shall engage a lawyer. We shall help the families to the utmost of our capacity. But we shall not agree to any approaches, official or semi-official, to the authorities. We shall make no effort even for Esther. There will be no negotiations for the release of prisoners. There is no war without suffering, no revolt without prisoners. There is no victory without sacrifices. We must all stand up to the test. Otherwise the enemy will discover our Achilles' heel, and will press, and promise, and extort, and seduce and so demoralize us."

From this attitude we did not budge. In the course of the revolt hundreds and thousands of prisoners were taken from our ranks. But we never had a "Twentyninth of June,"[1] or its consequences. . . .

Like every underground, however, we had a traitor.

[1] On June 29th, 1946, the British Authorities arrested a number of Zionist and Jewish Agency leaders and officials who subsequently bought their release by giving up the fight so far as they were concerned and agreeing to withdraw their forces—the Haganah—from the Struggle.

Tsorros was never a member of the Irgun. For a time he worked for the fund from which the Irgun received financial aid. This brought him in touch with a number of people active in the Irgun and a number of others whom he believed to be active. It is hard to say when exactly he established contact with the special police, and became their agent. Tsorros was a gambler and liked to dress well. He was short of money and, it seems, he was also a coward. Once he had begun to slip, he continued going downhill. When he denounced the radio-transmitter at the Raziel home he was already in the web of the Intelligence Service. Several weeks later he handed to Catling, the Head of the Jewish Department of the British C.I.D., a list of names, descriptions and addresses. Among them was that of Yaacov Meridor. He noted an identifying mark: a boil on the nose. The information was correct at the time, for Yaacov was suffering then from boils. But even this precise information did not result in the arrest of the Deputy-Commander of the Irgun Zvai Leumi. The police did indeed come to "Mr. Honig's" place of business but "Mr. Honig" had left in good time. For a long while after the British had reason to regret "Mr. Honig's" continued freedom.

Unbelievable though it may seem, the sleuths did not take into account that boils come and boils go, and continued to look for a man "with a boil on his nose." There is no doubt that Catling would never have laid hands on Meridor had not the individual traitor Tsorros been succeeded by a collective bureau of informers.

On receiving the list from Tsorros, Catling was in a triumphant mood. He was certain that he had liquidated the Irgun. He wrote a report in this vein to his superiors in Jerusalem, Cairo and London. The brilliant secret police rubbed their hands—they saw in their mind's eye medals and promotions. They did not know that a copy of the list given them was already in our hands. They did not know that we knew what they knew about us. We scanned the list carefully. It contained many names of people who were not in the organisation and of people who for years had played no part in it. There

were some names which would probably and eventually
have reached the British in any case—though it was a
pity that they reached them so soon. Only a few were
actually caught. On the whole it was not so bad. We
adopted new security measures. We had been hard hit,
but we soon recovered. Catling learnt that his joy was
premature, and his superiors in London had cause to be
disappointed.

Meanwhile we considered what to do with Tsorros.
My comrades demanded his execution. By the laws of
the underground their demand was justified. The underground has no prisons in which to keep its enemies and
prevent them from continuing their destructive work:
and the informer is the most terrible of its enemies.
Nevertheless I opposed the execution of Tsorros. I
feared the possibility of error. I demanded full proof. I
could not believe that a Jew could sink so low. I was
mistaken. In the course of time I learnt the truth and
admitted my mistake.

Tsorros informed on me personally. He came to our
house.

Time has passed. I see before me all the boys, the
heroic, the saintly, the pure. And I know that if a man
rises above himself there is no limit to his ascent. And
on the other hand I see Tsorros. He stands by my son's
crib. The child laughs at both of us. Tsorros smiles at
father and son. All the time he is thinking his thoughts.
And again I know, if a man falls there is no limit to
his descent. But, thank God, I saw with my own eyes
that those who are uplifted are many, while those who
fall are few.

2

Routine habits of thinking tripped up the British not
only in their efforts at provocation, but also in pictur-
ing to themselves the way of life of the people of the
underground. To some extent the British fell victim to
their own propaganda against us. They described us as
horrible "terrorists" and applied appropriate identifying marks to us. But as I have already emphasised we

were never terrorists and never had any such special
identifying marks. In our room in Jerusalem the British
found two photographs of me. One was a fairly good
likeness. The second, a street-snapshot, taken for my
soldier's identity card, bore only a slight resemblance.
But when the British sent out their army of detectives
and spies and spent their thousands of pounds in hunting for me, they chose to disseminate the second photograph. Why? Because the first photograph was more
or less "human." Being a photograph of me, it was not
beautiful, but it would not have aroused any negative
feelings in those who saw it. Just an ordinary person.
But the second photograph? It almost confirmed Dar-
win's theory. It showed the kind of face for which we
used to say a man ought to go to gaol. "Physiognomy"
is a science of ignoramuses. In an experiment made in
America, a man who claimed to "read faces" was
shown a variety of photographs. He examined them
carefully and selected the certain "criminal types." It
transpired however that the "criminals" he had chosen
were well-known actors, writers, professors, inventors,
while the real murderers and thieves he had placed
amongst the "sympathetic" photographs. But the British experts, even if they had heard or read of the American experiment, proceeded by the law of ignorance.
The "terrorist" photographs they published were really
horrific. And when the English daily in Cairo, the *Middle East Mail*, published a different photograph, showing me standing by my son's cot holding a toy elephant,
its editor was reprimanded. True, that picture too was
a somewhat peculiar one so far as likeness went, but—
the poor editor was told—how can you show him playing with a child? It may arouse popular sympathy.

And the Government, wanting to harm us, did us a
good turn. The "terrorist" photographs had one good
quality: they did not resemble their owners. Thousands
of copies of my photograph were distributed among the
British police, but had I strolled in the streets of Tel
Aviv by day and every day without disguise, the poor
British sleuths would still not have won the reward

promised for my capture. And it cannot be said, after all, that they did not want it.

One result, however, was that a number of people suffered on my account, or on account of my photograph. Jehoshaphat, one of our devoted officers, was once arrested in Jerusalem in possession of explosives. To my regret there is no resemblance between us. And I doubt whether my unfortunate police photograph could have recalled his rather attractive features. But some of the detectives thought they spotted a resemblance. Their suspicions were aroused while his trial was in progress. At once the courtroom became the scene of frantic activity. The guards were doubled and trebled and then quadrupled. The leading detectives were hastily brought. They came in and went out, looked carefully, had photographs taken. The good news was about to be published to warm the cockles of every official's heart, that "Terrorist No. 1"—as they called me—had been caught. But somebody ultimately gave his final disappointing verdict: "No, that's not the bastard."

Another friend of mine, Aaron, one of our best Information Officers, had a more serious experience. He too resembled neither me nor my photograph. But Aaron suffered from two severe disabilities: he was thin and wore glasses with thick black horn rims. These two clear identifying marks led the Palestine Lawrences to the conclusion that Aaron was I. They arrested him and haled him before the C.I.D. chiefs, who rained questions on him.

Aaron gave as his name that written on his identity-card. I cannot guarantee that it was his real name any more than that the identity card itself was genuine. At any rate the name was not Begin. The detectives were highly indignant. Here they had caught me and I was mocking them, not even admitting my identity. It was not fair.

"What is your real name?" they pressed Aaron. "Do you think we don't know who you are?"

Aaron was very pleased to learn that the British

really did not know who he was and mistook him for
me. As a suspect on his own account his situation was
black; to be accused of being me was not so dangerous.

The interrogation went on for a whole day. The detectives came and went. Aaron grew tired of answering.
They looked at him from in front. They examined his
profile. They made him walk around the room. This
was a rather dangerous experiment. Aaron, too, if I am
not mistaken, has a more or less flat foot. The detectives vacillated between hope (that I was he) and doubt
(that he was I). Finally they lost patience and one of
them shouted at Aaron:

"If so, prove that you are you."

This Aaron was unable to do. Not only was he not
I, but he dare not be himself. His identity card, while
not revealing his identity, did represent him. He was
what was written on it. Aaron, true to underground tradition, is an obstinate fellow. He did not budge until
the British gave up the idea that he was I and began
to believe that he was the man referred to in the identity card. It never occurred to them that he was himself.
Aaron was released, and continued serving in the underground till the end.

After him a number of people were arrested for their
resemblance to the photograph which did not resemble
me. And all because the British were determined to
represent us to the world as men with horns, tails, hoofs
and no conscience.

It never occurred to the British that we lived in the
country as we did: almost openly. They did not understand that we had made a virtue of necessity. How
could we hide in this little country? Partisans of other
peoples operate in impassable mountains or in vast
forests. In Eretz Israel there was neither mountain nor
forest for the rebels to hide in. We were completely exposed to the enemy's eyes. Nevertheless or perhaps as
a result—we saw but were unseen. We naturally had a
variety of names, we used a selection of identity documents, usually home-made—but we were never in
"bunkers." We were not surrounded by bodyguards, we
carried no arms for our own defence. We were teachers

and students, real or imaginary. We were real or imaginary merchants or bookkeepers. We were engineers and mechanics. We were, in short, everyday citizens indistinguishable from other citizens. The police came across our people time out of number. Our members were frequently in their hands. But what could they find on them? They carried no arms. They carried work-tools or documents of the firm employing them. Who would suspect peaceful citizens going to work or coming home? We turned the enemy into men with eyes that could see not, ears that heard not and noses that smelt not.

The matter of bodyguards sometimes caused humorous misunderstandings. Not only our enemies were convinced that I was accompanied everywhere by an armed bodyguard; friends shared that conviction. One of them even expressed his admiration for our excellent security arrangements. He visited me twice at the home of Meir Cahan, called Alex, our "veteran." This house, where many of my underground meetings took place, was surrounded by stately cypress trees. It did not require much imagination to believe that behind these trees lay concealed brave boys with tommy-guns at the ready. How was it they could not be seen and that they did not even cast shadows? Our friend's conclusion was simple. On his second visit he opened the conversation by saying:

"I must congratulate you on your excellent security arrangements. This is my second visit and I still haven't spotted a single one of your guards. . . ."

I was silent. I could not tell my friend the truth. Underground law brooks no exceptions; but I also did not want to lie to him. So I said nothing. And only when we left the underground did he discover that the reason for his not observing the guards was simply that they were not there to be observed.

The question of carrying arms for our own defence was much more serious. From the outset we decided that all our arms would be kept in armouries and would be removed only for carrying out planned attacks. Of quite a different opinion were the F.F.I. (Stern Group) leaders at the time. They made a rule that every member of the underground must carry arms day and night. Should enemy agents come to arrest him, it was his duty to defend himself and, if need be, rather die than go into captivity. F.F.I. commander Isaac Ysernitsky explained this rule to me. After the death of the unarmed Abraham Stern, his followers had decided not to fall into the hands of their would-be captors.

The reason for the rule was tragic, but so were its consequences. In the spring of 1944 there were a number of clashes between the enemy and F.F.I. members who stood and defended their lives and personal freedom. The British forces were of course superior. The initiative, too, was in their hands. And a number of brave F.F.I. members were killed by enemy machine-guns.

At Passover, in 1944, in a small room on the roof of a house in Bnei Brak, I met the F.F.I. commander, Ysernitsky. He was then not yet "Rabbi Shamir" with the long black beard, but some sort of merchant with a curly, fair moustache. We talked mainly about the carrying of arms. Ysernitsky repeated his arguments. I explained our attitude.

"Constant carrying of arms is more harmful than useful. An armed man is liable at any moment to be surrounded by a superior force of police. That means one revolver against many sub-machine-guns. In this case his weapon not only does not ensure his life, but endangers it. On the other hand we have to think of our planning. We shall be unable to retain the initiative in planning—and the initiative is probably our chief source of strength—if at any moment there may be unplanned incidents between one or more underground men and enemy forces."

To drive home my point I told Ysernitsky of what had happened to Yaacov Meridor a few days earlier. He was on his way to visit me together with a comrade when, on the very threshold of my house, they were surrounded by British police armed with sub-machine-guns. The police asked for their identity-cards.

Their identity-cards were of course in perfect order. But the police were not content with checking identities. They searched the men too. And only when they found that their pockets contained no arms did they say "O.K." and allow the two law-abiding citizens to go on and visit their law-abiding friends. But what would have happened if they had found arms in their pockets, ostensibly for self-defence. The chances of a successful defence with revolvers against five or six tommy-guns were obviously very slim indeed. The unequal and unlooked-for contest would have ended in the wounding or arrest of the underground men, or both, or something worse. . . . Whereas, our men being unarmed, the police had been given a wonderful opportunity of making complete fools of themselves.

I do not know whether my arguments convinced the F.F.I. leaders or whether their own experience taught them, but soon after our meeting at Bnei Brak, they effected an "internal disarmament." At first, I was told, there was some dissatisfaction in their ranks. They had imbibed the theory that the principle of personal armament and of "no surrender" was an unchangeable law, distinguishing them from all other underground movements. But the new instructions, which were accompanied by adequate explanation, were obeyed and thenceforth their arms were used only for planned operations.

We thus followed the principle of an "*overt underground.*" Meir Cahan, who likes giving even serious matters a cloak of humour, used to say: "Of course our underground is open. The darkest spot is right under the lamp."

But in order to maintain an open underground you need more than the technique of pseudonyms. What is most necessary is the inner consciousness that makes what is "legal" illegal and the "illegal" legal and justified. We had this consciousness in supreme measure. We were convinced of the absolute legality of our "illegal" actions. That is why we never lost our heads when confronted by British patrols and when having to answer their questions. That is why we never gave a thought to what was in store for us if we fell into enemy hands. We were encompassed by death, but we never saw it. We walked "under the lamp." Not only did we not fear capture; we did not even think about it. We concentrated our thoughts on the revolt itself. This tranquility of spirit has nothing to do with what is called "bravery." It also cannot be communicated by orders. It was the result of complete liberation from spiritual enslavement. It was the result of a consciousness of our ownership of the country crushed by enemy tanks. "Spiritual sovereignty" comes before political sovereignty. Indeed spiritual freedom is the essential condition for the attainment of political freedom.

As an additional condition making possible the "open underground" there was the sympathy of the people from which the underground sprang. We did not at once acquire public sympathy. But our moral status among the people rose daily. In this respect I feel it was the period 1945-46 that was decisive. During that period the Haganah, which was under the control of the official Zionist institutions, joined in our struggle against the British regime. The people suddenly realised that those who had been described by official Zionist propaganda as "crazy" had merely outstripped the official institutions in foreseeing events and in doing what had to be done. The result was that the change of front by the official Zionist leadership after the mass arrests of June 29th was no longer capable of changing public feeling. Thus we found sympathisers in all classes and parties, and this sympathy turned the scales. The "iron wall round the fighting youth," for which we had appealed in our proclamation of the revolt, was in fact built up. The British complained with reason that the Jewish population did not extend active aid in the "fight against terrorism."

In the White Paper of 15th May, 1948 ("Palestine: Termination of the Mandate") which recorded the bankruptcy of the White Paper of 1939, admitted the victory of the revolt, and chronicled the end of British rule, the Government wrote: "84,000 troops who received no co-operation from the Jewish community, had proved insufficient to maintain law and order in the

face of a campaign of terrorism waged by highly organised Jewish forces equipped with all the weapons of
the modern infantryman."

When they spoke of the absence of co-operation
from the "Jewish community" the British were not referring to the heads of the community who, from time
to time though not always, gave them the maximum
help with a view to repelling the "wave of terrorism."
They were referring to the mass of the people. And the
people did not help them. They helped the rebels. They
saw them going out to fight and kept their lips sealed.
They saw them coming back from battle and were silent. Silence was probably the most important, though
not the only aid they gave. The people gave the underground what the country's natural conditions failed to
give: cover. We did not hide behind trees; we were
guarded by living trees. Otherwise we could not have
fought, certainly could not have won. The depth of an
open underground is measured by the sympathy of the
people for its struggle.

3

I must admit that at the beginning our underground
was too "open." It may seem incredible, but it is a fact
that we did not go underground at all. Certainly not
physically. On the contrary we began our fight against
British rule in a little room looking out on the sunny
balcony of a public hotel. That was a hotel which still
adorns the Tel Aviv beach. I "pitched my tent" there
for a very prosaic reason: I could find no other accommodation, and remained there for more than four
months during which we carried out our first operations. Everything was still in its infancy. I did not yet
have identity documents worthy of the name. I did not
yet have a German name to create the impression of a
law-abiding citizen. My pseudonym was "Ben-Zeev,"
a name not calculated to dispel suspicions.[1] And the
British were already hunting for me all over the coun-

[1] After Zeev (Vladimir) Jabotinsky.

try. Our first attacks had brought in their train a ten-day curfew in Jerusalem, Haifa and Tel-Aviv. Later the curfew was to become part of our daily life, but at that time it took us completely aback. Fortune favoured me in the hotel. The British did not look for me there. It could not have occurred to the detective chiefs, Giles and Catling, that I would "hide" in a public hotel. Still, the hotel was subjected to routine searches for suspects, tension was universal and there was a danger that "Mr. Ben-Zeev" would be taken by the police as a routine "suspect."

This danger was averted by the hotel keeper. Mr. Ben-Zvi did not know who exactly "Mr. Ben-Zeev" was, but he understood that he was connected with "those things." Out of his sympathy for "those things" Mr. Ben-Zvi voluntarily endangered his own freedom and livelihood. One curfew night a party of police, civil and military, came to search the Savoy Hotel. They went from room to room, took all the guests into the corridor, and stood them in a line. They examined their papers and ordered "suspects" to one side—for further examination at the police station.

The noise of the search reached Room No. 17. The footsteps and loud voices of the police awakened me. My wife and small son were with me, but fortunately they went on sleeping. They had come from Jerusalem only a few days earlier. At first I had left them at the address which Tsorros had betrayed. I thought it would be best not to drag my wife underground with me. It seemed healthier that she should live openly and not be hounded, that not knowing my whereabouts she should be able to answer police questions with a confident and truthful "I don't know." I soon learnt that this plan was ideal only in theory. Our room in Jerusalem was surrounded day and night by detectives. The authorities waited for father to visit his family. But they were not content with spreading the net, of which they believed in their wisdom we were unaware. They did not stop trying to catch their fish. Night after night a police party visited our room. Their favourite visiting time was between midnight and two a.m. Armoured cars, tommy guns, torches and the eternal question: "Where is your husband?" And the comforting assurance: "It doesn't matter. We'll be back tomorrow. He's got to come sometime."

There was no sense in letting this continue, especially as experience had taught us that the police would not hesitate to arrest my wife and hold her as a hostage. My comrades urged me not to leave her a semi-prisoner in her own house. Eitan went off to Jerusalem, threw the British watchers off the scent and smuggled my family away to Tel-Aviv, to the Savoy Hotel. Thenceforward my wife went with me along the whole way through the underground, anxiously but calmly. She was one of many—mothers, sisters, wives—who displayed remarkable courage. True courage is not expressed in an absence of concern but in overcoming it. One of our friends warned my wife that were I caught I was liable to pay with my life. She smilingly thanked him. She revealed her anxiety neither to me nor to anybody else.

That night in the Savoy Hotel, as I heard the approaching footsteps of the police, I regretted that I had brought her and the child to Tel Aviv. If the British take me as a suspect, I said to myself, their suspicion may fall on her too. And if she is arrested what will happen to the child? Beyond that my thoughts turned on the struggle and its continuation. As to the latter I was quite tranquil. I had not the slightest doubt that once the sword of revolt had been drawn it would not be sheathed before victory was achieved. But I grieved over the interruption that would occur in our work. For we stood at its very beginning. Most of the educational, military and political work was still ahead of us. Was I fated to be present only at the lighting of the spark and not to share in the fanning of the flame?

The heavy footsteps came nearer. There was no way out. I looked through my pockets. I had no documents with me. Everything was in order. They could come. My anxious thoughts evaporated. I felt a peculiar serenity mixed with incomprehensible happiness. I said to myself that I should be thankful for having been enabled to return to my country and to share in raising the flag of revolt. Moreover, whatever happened to me, the banner would now not be lowered. I waited composedly for the knock at the door.

But the voices and footsteps, instead of coming nearer, suddenly began to move away. The police were almost on my threshold, but for some reason did not cross it. What had happened? I preferred not to go out and ask. For another half-hour I heard movements. Then absolute silence reigned. The police left, and the Savoy Hotel went to sleep.

The next morning, Mr. Ben-Zvi asked me whether I had heard any noises during the night.

I answered with a question.

"What happened?"

We both knew and each knew that the other knew. I had to be silent. Mr. Ben-Zvi was discreet:

"We did not want to wake you," he said. "There was a search in the hotel. The police were looking for suspects. Several guests whose papers the policemen didn't like were taken away for further questioning. They've already been released. I thought there was no point in worrying you with all this business. Of course I went with the police from room to room, and when we reached the door to the balcony I said to them, "That's the lot." They saw that we had reached the end of the corridor and believed me, so we went straight up to the third floor."

A brave man. The police had believed him but they might easily have doubted him. Mr. Ben-Zvi risked his own safety in order to enable Mr. Ben-Zeev to continue doing "those things" as a result of which the sons of both were to cease being slaves.

4

Soon afterwards we abandoned the "too open" underground. From the Savoy Hotel I moved to Mahne Yehuda, to a small isolated house on the fringe of the "Yemenite" quarter of Petah Tikva. Conditions there were difficult. The house was neglected. The wind blew day and night through its broken shutters. At night it was cold and dark. There was no electricity and no central heating. But I had one pleasure in those days: I slept on the sheets of the British High Commissioner, Harold McMichael.

In June, 1942, the Irgun had planned to capture Mc-Michael, and to hold him in our underground apartment in the neighbourhood of Petah Tikvah, near the lonely house where I later lived. This plan, a combination of much daring and some political naïveté, was later again broached to the short-lived "Am Lohem"— a group in which a number of young "Haganah" officers co-operated with Irgun officers. For a number of reasons the plan was not then carried out.

In the summer of 1944, after the first curfew period, we considered two alternative "McMichael Plans." The first was to penetrate the High Commissioner's residence and blow up the wing in which lived the man who was instrumental in sending the *Struma* to its doom. The other was to seize the residence, occupy it and, if possible, take McMichael and his staff prisoner, declaring British rule in our country at an end. Both plans were debated at length. Meantime, a number of preparations were made, the terrain was examined, the bases and lines of operation were decided upon and the quarry was shadowed. But reconnaissance revealed that after our first operations the High Commissioner's residence had been provided with substantial defences. We calculated that in the existing circumstances we would have to throw in practically all our available forces. We therefore reconsidered the plan. We came to the conclusion that we were not entitled to risk everything, or almost everything, even for an operation of such striking political significance. We did not give up the plan entirely, but postponed its execution till we should be stronger.

Meanwhile we turned our attention to Ramallah, to the central broadcasting station of the British regime. Our men were to seize the broadcasting station, stop the official "Palestinian" programme and instead send out a call to the Jewish people and the nations of the world to help save the Jews of Europe and liberate our country from the British yoke.

This plan was not simple or easy in those days. In the vicinity was a police fortress. The neighbourhood was Arab, and far from any Jewish centre. As usual, we lacked transport. For three nights we waited vainly at headquarters for the voice of our announcer. Twice our men failed to obtain the necessary transport. On the third night, having secured a number of trucks, our unit reached the radio station and seized it under the very noses of the police in the nearby fortress. The police let loose volleys of fire in all directions and sent up flares for reinforcements.

Our men for the first time operated our "home-made" mortars—and the Ramallah Arabs later reported that we had used heavy guns. The police preferred to remain in their iron-and-concrete fortress. Inside the transmitting station, Avitagar, one of our bravest officers, threw his revolver several times into the air, caught it neatly and pointed it at the astonished British and Arab officials. They were told that no harm would come to them if they helped our men send out the prepared broadcast. But it soon transpired that there was no studio at Ramallah (the studios were in Jeruasalem itself) so it was impossible to broadcast.

After the operation at Ramallah various plans of attack on the High Commissioner's residence were again discussed. But swiftly-moving events prevented their execution. McMichael was removed from his post. (Just before he left the country the F.F.I. made an unsuccessful attempt on his life.) Like so many officials and officers who had failed in Eretz Israel he was transferred to Malaya. And in our stores at Petah Tikva there remained a number of objects carefully prepared for his reception as a prisoner. Among them there were fine linen sheets and as they had been denied the honour of serving McMichael it fell to my lot to lie on them in the house at Mahne Yehuda. I can testify that they were good sheets. The mattress—which had no special history—was, I am afraid, not so good. . . .

Chapter VIII

A Man with Many Names

After some time I forsook McMichael's sheets and moved, this time with my wife and son, to a little house in the Hasidoff Quarter. There I became Israel Halperin.

The Hasidoff Quarter consists of a row of low houses on the road to Kfar Sirkin, near Lydda. It is a worker's suburb, within the municipal boundaries of Petah Tikva, built opposite the well-known Arab village of Fejja. In that period, 1944-45, its houses were frequently without water and had no electricity at all. But it was a verdant neighbourhood, with cultivated fields, blooming gardens, woods and orange groves. An outside observer would no doubt assume that it was because of the abundance of trees that we chose the place as headquarters. This was not so. We found it almost by chance. It was quiet and cheap, and in accordance with our "open underground" tactics we went there to expose ourselves as a means of hiding more effectively. We assumed that it would not occur to the authorities that the "chief terrorist" lived in a place where everybody knew his neighbours. We were not mistaken.

For nearly a year I lived in this small suburb among silent friends of the underground and its vigorous, vociferous opponents. One of the inhabitants knew. He recognised me the first time I went out on to the sandy walk that ran along the length of the row of houses. But he said nothing. My hosts, too, were mercifully silent. The rest of our neighbours had not the least suspicion. They found it all natural and understandable. They were told that the Halperin family was a family of refugees from Poland who had been unable to find accommodation in the town. True, the head of the family did not go out to work every day but for this too a plausible explanation was found. We voluntarily told the neighbours that we lived off an allocation from the refugee aid organisation and that I was preparing for the Palestinian law examinations—hence my working at home. It is characteristic that the landlord, the good Mr. Malkieli, who knew what "business" I was in, assumed that it was connected with law. Malkieli had been a member of the Irgun and knew Meridor, who had been his commanding officer, as well as Eitan and Daniel and Benjamin. He saw all these officers coming on frequent visits to his tenant. But on trying to deduce the object of these visits he came to the conclusion that it was to get legal advice in connection with the trials of underground fighters. It seems that his tenant made the impression of being a bookish lawyer rather than a "commander." Later on he learnt the truth. But, in spite of the danger to himself, he unhesitatingly allowed me to stay on in his house. Malkieli gave me a good deal of help, but I do not believe that he ever changed his opinion about the external appearance of his tenant.

We were soon on friendly terms not only with the landlord, who knew, but with all our neighbours, who did not know. My son used to play or fight with the children. We exchanged visits with the neighbours. Our house was filled with law volumes which were as open as the house itself. It is not surprising, therefore, that it was in the Hasidoff Quarter, at the midst of the underground fight, that I came near to receiving my first fee as a "legal adviser." One of the residents got into a dispute with the Petah Tikva Municipality over a small structure he had put up without a license from the Health Department. He asked me to draft a polite but firm letter to overcome the opposition of the Municipality. I could hardly refuse. I slaved at that letter—not at the contents, but at the handwriting. My handwriting is not very legible. And a Petah Tikva official is, after all, not Ruhama, our all-knowing secretary who knew not only how to keep secrets but even how to decipher my handwriting. Moreover I realised that offi-

cials upon whose good humour the fate of the request
depended should not have hieroglyphics inflicted upon
them. I therefore tried to write in large round letters.
I had to work even harder to explain to the applicant,
a milkman, who saw how much effort I was putting
into his letter, that I was doing it purely out of neigh-
bourliness and expected no payment.

I have many other happy memories of the pleasant
Hasidoff Quarter. In the tiny kitchen, by the light of a
small oil lamp or a candle, we held meetings of the
High Command, took important decisions and planned
operations. The "friends" who visited the "Halperin"
family aroused no suspicions. Occasionally they helped
the Quarter out: they would make up a "minyan"—
the quorum of ten required for Jewish prayers—in the
little synagogue. At times, on Sabbath afternoons or of
an evening, we would go out for a refreshing stroll in
the fields and groves, and while walking, hold a "session" and take decisions on policy. An Arab shepherd
would go by with his flock and greet us, Jewish youngsters played games around us. Nobody could have
imagined that these innocent chatting strollers were being hunted by the British Secret Service and police
throughout the length and breadth of the country.

I remember also the little synagogue which stands
on a rise opposite the houses. In that synagogue where
we all used to attend prayers on Sabbaths and Holy-
days, I was given a new underground name: Israel. On
the first Sabbath after our arrival I was honoured, as
befits a newcomer, by being "called up" to the reading
of the Law. The good warden asked what my name
was. I was afraid to mention my first name lest, in
combination with my father's name, it might recall
something to somebody. I said hesitantly, "Israel the
son of Ze'ev Dov." I picked Israel, I suppose, because
of the deep affection which bound me to my very close
friend Israel Epstein. Thenceforward, until I left the
underground, I was always "called up" by that name. I
must ask forgiveness from the Almighty for dissem-
bling my real name even in Divine Services, but He will
understand that in the circumstances I had no choice.

It was in the Hasidoff Quarter that we experienced the first great search conducted by the Palestine police with the aid of whole regiments of the Occupation Army. On September 5th, 1944, Petah Tikva was surrounded by large forces of soldiers and police. The town had a special attraction for the Mandatory Authorities. They used to say inelegantly: "Bloody Petah Tikva is full of terrorists."

They were not altogether wrong. Petah Tikva, with its free people, attached to the soil, rendered great service to the underground. Our fighters freely used its orange groves without mishap. The soldiers did not even dare look into these orchards. Its fields and woods and trees could tell many a tale of concealed armouries, secret training forces, of rendezvous and exercises. The trees kept their secret as did the youth of Petah Tikva, buoyant and free and fearless who, as often as they suffered blows, recovered and rose again to fight and resist. Twice the military authorities almost succeeded, with the help of Jewish information organised from high up, in liquidating the local detachment of the Irgun Zvai Leumi. But each time our ranks were replenished with young blood and emerged more energetic, more numerous and stronger than before the "liquidation." Petah Tikva was blessedly "full of terrorists."

The Authorities, then, began their search at dawn that day. The town was surrounded on all sides. A curfew was imposed. Soldiers toured the streets on tenders, calling through loudspeakers:

"Curfew, curfew! Stay in your houses! Anybody who leaves risks his life!"

Every house was searched. Every resident was examined. This was indeed the first great search. The soldiers and police wished each other "Good hunting."

At sunrise the neighbour who "knew" woke me up and told me what was happening. He was, naturally, somewhat worried. His tale was not cheerful.

"I have tried to get to Petah Tikva itself," he said, "but the patrols sent me back. They are everywhere. Nobody is going in or out. They will certainly come here too. I think you ought to try to get away through the orange groves."

I rejected his advice. Daniel, who had spent the night in the house, agreed that there was no sense in rushing to the groves. Such a flight would not only "finish" us with the neighbours, but was likely to deliver us to the enemy. It was better to wait for troubles than to meet them half way. The situation was of course serious. But we relied to some extent on the contrariness of the military and police and, having no choice, on our own good fortune. So we stayed where we were, Daniel in his room, I in ours. But we wanted the neighbours to see that we were not concerned by the propinquity of the police. Accordingly, we left our rooms and went out and sat in front of the house. We witnessed an interesting spectacle. On the main road about two hundred yards away, British tanks and armoured cars, filled with soldiers, were on the move. A Jewish policeman, who had previously lived in the Quarter, ran up and down and consoled us by assuring that we would not have to wait long for the searches and would then be done with them for a long time. His promise did nothing to cheer us up. Nobody looked pleased.

Our neighbour, Mrs. Seigel, mother of Rahel and Micky, my favourites in the Quarter (my three year old son was a dangerous rival for the affections of two year old Micky) showed considerable distress. My wife tried to calm her but in vain. Finally, out of confidence in "Mrs. Halperin," with whom she had become very friendly she confessed: "Of course, it's all right for you, Mrs. Halperin, you have nothing to worry about. But I have got a *military blanket* in the house. What am I to do? What am I to do?"

There was no need for her to do anything. We waited in vain for the police and soldiers. They searched Petah Tikva thoroughly, but for some reason, slipped the outlying Hasidoff Quarter. The morning passed. At noon, the curfew was lifted. Daniel, without saying goodbye to Mr. Halperin, whom he "hardly knew," went off to his work. We breathed freely again. The danger had retreated from our threshold.

The search brought a crop of rumours in its train. Our comrades, thoroughly alarmed, racked their brains for a way of saving us, but Petah Tikva was completely sealed off. Afterwards the story went round among the public, which wanted to believe in the Irgun's omnipotence, that a strong unit of our soldiers had penetrated the enemy lines, and borne their besieged comrades to safety. This was one of many legends about us—recalling the story of how I met General Barker and the tale about my Russian origin.

The world's Press published a circumstantial story of a meeting between me and the Commanding Officer of the British Forces in Eretz Israel. It may be that the origin of the story was the suggestion made by an officer on Barker's Staff that we meet and talk as "enemy to enemy." A member of the Haganah Intelligence in Jerusalem, who was in contact with that Staff Officer's representative, conveyed the invitation to Moshe Sneh —the Haganah Commander—who passed it on to me at one of our regular conferences during the brief period of our united struggle in the Resistance Movement. Of course I declined the invitation. I agreed to speak to the Commanding Officer of the Occupation Forces as "enemy to enemy" but I preferred the language of our battle detachments. Nevertheless I learnt from the foreign Press that I had had a secret meeting not merely with Barker's representative but with Barker himself.

The story was highly sympathetic to the underground. It told how I had made a condition that Barker, like me, should come alone and in civilian dress to the café rendezvous. Barker, according to this widely circulated story, accepted the condition, but broke his word and brought a regiment of soldiers who surrounded the café. He went inside but to his chagrin did not find me there. He waited a while, getting more and more restless. Looking round he saw a Catholic priest sitting in the far corner reading a newspaper. Delighted at the opportunity to kill time, he struck up a conversation with him. After some time, seeing that Begin did not appear, he got up, thanked the priest for his company and left the café. The next day he received a letter from me, running roughly as follows:

"You should not break your word of honour. You promised to come alone. Why did you break your promise? You will note that the Irgun always keeps its word. We kept it this time too. I came to the meeting place despite your treachery. The priest with whom you had such a friendly chat was I."

An even more sensational story was published in a Swiss newspaper and from there found its way to every part of the world. Great American newspapers splashed it, and even the Yiddish paper *Bund* treated it seriously. The story was that my real name was not Begin but Freiman, that I had had a special training in the Kremlin, that I had conducted the Communist struggle in Spain and in China and had then been sent by Stalin himself to Eretz Israel in order to make things hot there for the British. . . . An important American journalist was so impressed by this story that on my visit to the United States he telephoned me about it from Chicago to New York.

Another important journalist questioned me about it in a television interview. I replied: "I have read in a Jewish Communist newspaper that I had a secret meeting at the State Department and that I have sold the whole of Palestine to Truman. That paper called me a Fascist."

"What's that to do with our question?"

"Very simple," I said. "I am beginning to find it difficult to decide whether I am Stalin's agent or Truman's agent, or both, whether I'm a Communist Fascist or a Fascist Communist."

These are legends. The truth is that I have never been in Spain or in China, or in the Kremlin or in the State Department. The truth is that I hate all forms of totalitarianism, that I love freedom and free men and believe in their victory everywhere over tyranny and totalitarianism of all kinds. The truth is—to go back to the first story—that I never met nor wanted to meet either Barker or his representative. As for the least important legend of the lot, relating to the search at Petah Tikva, the truth is just as simple: the British authorities searched and did not find.

But there is another, unhappy, truth connected with the search at the Hasidoff Quarter. During the search—and perhaps because of it—I lost my brother-in-law and close friend, Dr. Arnold. It was at his home that I had chanced to meet the seventeen-year-old girl whom I then and there decided to make my wife. I did not err in my choice. I would not like to say as much about hers. The years passed, and we all tasted of the cup of sorrow. Our families were wiped out. Arnold's little son was torn from his mother's arms and murdered in a Nazi gas-chamber. The mother killed herself. All his other relatives were shot or gassed by the Germans and his heart took the blows hardly. He was in Tel Aviv when the news reached him that Petah Tikva was surrounded. He knew where I was living, and was deeply distressed. He died that day. And I was underground, unable even to accompany my old friend to his final resting-place. My friends did him that last kindness for me. But they could not prevent the British, who knew of the relationship, from sending several pairs of spying eyes to the cemetery. My wife, therefore, accepting the laws of the underground, did not go to the funeral of her brother, one of the last survivors of her family. We remained at home, bowed down with grief. I said Kaddish (the Prayer for the Dead) in the little Synagogue. One had to carry on. There was no choice. But the people outside, what did they know, what could they know?

The period of our stay at the Hasidoff Quarter was not barren. The Irgun rallied solidly round the flag of revolt. Many who had left in the days of internal crisis returned to its ranks. Many volunteered. Our numbers grew. Confidence rose. Most important: belief in our strength was awakened. We were loved or hated—but no longer jeered at. Any underground that passes beyond the stage of inevitable initial ridicule has gone half way—perhaps the more difficult half of the way—

to its goal. During that period I wrote the pamphlet "We Believe" in which I expressed our unshakeable belief that "out of our blood will flourish the tree of freedom for our country and the tree of life for our people." And I wrote many other pamphlets, surveys and declarations.

During that period we blew up the British central police headquarters in Jerusalem, forced the police to keep away from the Wailing Wall, stormed the Tegart fortresses, attacked the police stations on the Jaffa—Tel Aviv boundary, and made fun of the Government by confiscating vast quantities of cloth from Government stores under the very noses of the troops. Part of the cloth was distributed among the poor, the rest was sold to buy arms.

But at the end of that period heavy clouds gathered. The storm of internal persecution approached. The "amount of violence" we had given the Mandatory authorities was apparently more than they had expected. The Jewish Agency was subjected to their pressure both in London and Jerusalem. Its leaders were required to extend to the British authorities their "full co-operation in stamping out the terror." Disturbing reports began to reach us. It was rumoured that the Jewish Agency leaders were not refusing to co-operate with the oppressor but indeed were promising that instructions would soon be given to "liquidate the dissidents." The situation became grave. The number of spying eyes increased considerably. Moreover, I learnt that somebody in my neighbourhood was getting suspicious. I could stay no longer in the Hasidoff Quarter. Among the neighbours were members of "Hashomer Hatzair" —extreme left-wing Communist-Socialists who were in favour of co-operation with the British against us. The neighbours were very cordial to "Mr. Halperin." But would they remain so friendly if they discovered who was behind the "lawyer"?

We said goodbye to the Hasidoff Quarter, moved to Tel Aviv, to a little house in Joshua Bin-Nun Street —and I became Israel Sassover.

2

Joshua, the conqueror of Canaan and one of the greatest generals in our history, has been accorded a small side-street in North Tel Aviv, muddy in winter and dusty in summer, and unknown to most of the city's inhabitants. And it is along a street named after another General, the British General Allenby, that Jewish military processions make their way through Tel Aviv . . .

In Joshua Bin-Nun street, there are—or were—two important public institutions: the municipal abattoir and the municipal dogs' home. Neither of them contributed to the amenities of the neighbourhood nor to the musical entertainment of its residents. There was an almost incessant cacophony of chained dogs howling for freedom and doomed animals crying for their lives. As for the smells. . .? No: Joshua Bin-Nun Street was not by any means a salubrious thoroughfare.

There, not far from the greenish Yarkon River, and at the beginning of the period of internal persecution, we found a small, detached house, with a long-neglected garden in front and a rotting orange-grove behind. Yaacov Meridor's sharp eye told him that, despite the proximity of the four-legged canines, it was a good place for anybody hunted by two-legged bloodhounds. I for my part hesitated. The house was not to let, but had to be bought. How could we spend several thousand pounds out of our meagre treasury in order to house me? My comrades, deeply concerned at the lack of security in the Hasidoff Quarter, found a way out. Meir Cahan who, for this special purpose, became "Mr. Goldhammer," a solid citizen of Jerusalem, bought the house, and leased it to me for two years. Mr. Goldhammer then sold "his house" to a Jew from Egypt who, anxious to have it for himself, agreed to take over the lease as well, provided it was only for two years (only two years!). Thus Israel Halperin, the diligent law-student, disappeared from the Hasidoff Quarter

and near the banks of the Yarkon, Israel Sassover came
into the world.

The change was not only one in name and place. I
changed my appearance and my habits. My comrades
decided that a change of hair-style and growing a moustache would not be enough to keep me out of the range
of vision of spying eyes, especially Jewish ones. Consequently they decreed that I must grow a beard. The
law of conspiracy being supreme in the underground,
I let it grow—and added ten or fifteen years to my age.

It was not so simple. You do not grow beards in the
time to takes to move an oil-stove from Petah Tikva to
North Tel Aviv. In the Hasidoff Quarter I was always
seen laden with law books but free from facial hair.
The books could be got rid of. But where was I to
take the beard from? The answer was found. The neighbours of the Hasidoff Quarter were told that, as I was
in mourning, I was obeying Jewish custom in not shav-
ing or cutting my hair for thirty days. At the end of
thirty days I had changed sufficiently to become Israel
Sassover, who might have been a modern Rabbi, or a
politician in one of the religious parties, or merely a
penitent sinner.

My beard and the status it conferred on me also imposed certain obligations in my new surroundings. On
the very first day I was asked by Reb Simcha, the genial beadle of a nearby synagogue, to come along and
make up the quorum at prayers in a house where a
death had taken place. Immediately thereafter I was
invited to become a regular participant at prayers in
the synagogue. And that little synagogue became part
of my daily life at one of the most difficult periods of
our struggle.

The members of this synagogue are a typical cross-
section of what we call the "mass of the people":
craftsmen, artisans, small shopkeepers, workers. They
received their new neighbour with characteristically
benevolent curiosity. They asked me questions which
I had to answer. They gave me my regular place, and
thenceforward I became one of them. I heard later, in
confidence, that if the British had remained in Eretz

Israel ten years longer I might possibly have risen to high eminence and been elected second assistant to the third warden of the synagogue. I was quite popular, even though I never took part in any political discussions—or perhaps that was the reason.

There were of course also pitfalls and dangers. One day, Reb Simcha, the beadle, came to my house and asked me to perform a good deed—to go with him to the Chief Rabbinate and testify that our butcher was an honest, God-fearing man and his meat impeccably *kosher*. "They'll believe you," he coaxed. I do not know whether the Rabbis would have believed me. I know that our butcher was an honest man. But to go through the crowded streets and then undergo cross-examination by rabbinical judges was a little too much for Sassover. Reb Simcha was very persistent and I had to invent a host of excuses before he finally gave me up.

Even greater dangers to my camouflage arose from my occasionally forgetting how extremely orthodox these people were. And several times I was hard put to it to explain my lapses. I used to attend regularly the lessons in Talmud and Biblical commentaries given every Sabbath afternoon by the rabbi. These lessons were attended by most of the members who, hard-worked as they were the whole week, eagerly drank in the learning they could acquire in that weekly twilight hour —proving to me once again how deep was the thirst for knowledge among our people. At one of these lessons the name of Helen, the Hasmonean queen who helped extend and decorate the Temple, cropped up. Somebody asked how a Hebrew queen came by the name Helen. The Rabbi, a learned traveller in all the highways and byways of Jewish lore, was somewhat at a loss when it came to Greek culture. I forgot myself, and blurted out that the name was Greek and that in the Hasmonean era many Jews took Greek names. My neighbours were openly astonished at this sudden display of knowledge. Sassover had already earned the reputation of a know-nothing.

"Sassover," they asked, "where do you know that from?" Their question confused me more than any question I had ever been asked at a University examination. It was with difficulty that I turned aside their curiosity and by resuming my silence, restored my "status" as a passive ignoramus.

It is difficult to say what my neighbours thought of me and my doings. I think they came to the conclusion that I was a good-for-nothing who had had a large dowry from his wife. They could hardly have believed me capable of any work. They pitied my wife deeply, especially the women.

"Poor young thing," they said, "she must have been forced to marry this loafer, this perpetual student." I was certainly not interested in dispelling their illusions.

My first daughter was born in that home. I named her Hasya after my mother who had been murdered by the Nazis in the hospital at Brisk, my birthplace. Hasya's birth was one of our closest kept secrets, known only to half-a-dozen friends. The underground is a hard master. It does not permit mourning for the dead, nor rejoicing for the newly-born. My daughter changed our "status." The Authorities, in their efforts to find me, searched for years for a "woman with a child." Now she was a mother of two children; and the Government lost all trace.

Hasya was born "illegally" many times over. Not only could I not give her my real name, I dared not even lend her my borrowed name. It was impossible to register the existence of "Sassover" or his address. I could also not go to the hospital to welcome her. Israel Epstein took this difficult task on himself. He lent his name to my wife and daughter. This nearly led to a serious misunderstanding. At the same hospital, at the same time, a son was born to a woman whose name was "also" Epstein. When Israel arrived at the hospital, a beaming nurse came out and greeted him: "Good luck to you, Mr. Epstein, your wife's had a son." The behaviour of the "father" must have seemed somewhat strange to the good nurse. Instead of rushing in to see his wife and son, he turned on his heel and fled—to give me the news that I had a son. Only later was the misunderstanding cleared up. We were very pleased to

learn the truth: a circumcision ceremony would have
been a little too complicated.

But a daughter is also entitled to some celebration.
Could Israel Sassover possibly avoid entertaining his
cronies at the synagogue? We decided to do it as prescribed by tradition. On the Sabbath at the synagogue I
was overwhelmed with the warmth of congratulations,
and I was deeply grateful to these good people who
shared my joy in my isolation.

The celebration went off splendidly. Everything had
been prepared—the faithful underground had not forgotten even the sliced salt herring spiked on cocktail-
sticks. And everybody told me there had never been
such a well-managed party in their synagogue.

When the Rabbi, the scholar with his piercing eyes,
came up to me to give me his blessing, I felt like asking him to give a special blessing to the innocent in-
fant who might have to remain "illegal" for many years
to come. But I was silent, and merely mumbled a formal word of thanks.

Twice the Government forces came uncomfortably
near our house. The first was during the period of the
combined Resistance Movement. The Haganah had
lost the semi-legal status it had enjoyed throughout its
existence under British rule, and the British police had
begun to look for its armouries. One of them was directly opposite our house. The whole neighbourhood
knew about it.

One night we were awakened by the rumbling of
heavy vehicles and a voice calling: "One, two, three!"

I peered out through the shutter and saw the police
radio-car, which received and transmitted orders.
Searchlights were playing on the whole neighbourhood,
including our house. The police seemed excited. I
naturally could not tell whether they had come only
for the armoury or whether they meant to search all
the houses. But here, as in the Hasidoff Quarter, there
was nothing to do except wait patiently.

Roxy, however, was impatient. She wanted to chase
the British away at once—and was thus likely to attract
their attention. Roxy was a dog. How came Reb Sass-

over by a dog? Such a man ought, according to popular belief, to be afraid of dogs, not to keep one in his house. And indeed Roxy often introduced an incongruous note. When Sassover took his little son to the synagogue on Friday evenings—there was Roxy trotting after them. That was highly improper. But what could we do? Roxy belonged to the previous tenant who, for some reason, had left her behind. She had wandered away, apparently in search of her master, but finally had found her way back. All the children knew her story. How could we chase her away?

Roxy loved everybody except the police. I have never yet seen such an anti-British creature! It was certainly not my doing. If it had depended on me I would have taught her to be particularly friendly to the British authorities. But it seems she was born anti-British. Otherwise it is impossible to explain why a creature so pacific to every man, woman and child in the neighbourhood, brought the roof down when she scented a British policeman or soldier even at a distance. What went on in the house that night when Roxy discovered a whole unit of the British Army on her very doorstep and, what is more, talking in loud voices in complete disregard of her insistent clamour for their instant departure, is beyond description. Roxy in her desire to drive them away, loudly drew their attention to her master's house. That night I disliked her perhaps more than she disliked the British. But catastrophe passed us by. With the dawn, Roxy had her way: the British departed.

The second occasion was much more dangerous. It happened at the end of the Resistance Movement period but is part of the story of the King David Hotel, which I shall tell in a later chapter.

It was in Joshua Bin-Nun Street that I suffered my only illness in the underground. All at once my body declared a hunger-strike. For several weeks I could retain no food. This was apparently the result of lack of air. For years, after all, my only opportunities for taking the air were in short walks in the immediate neighbourhood. In this sense I was more of a prisoner than many involuntary prisoners. My comrades were very concerned, particularly when I even stopped drinking tea—a decisive proof that I was ill. Avraham proposed calling a specialist, the famous Dr. Zondek. I objected. I was certain the trouble would pass of itself. Moreover his proposal was against the rules of the underground. But Avraham insisted and was supported by Meir and his own doctor. Dr. Zondek came. He gave me a prescription, and some pertinent advice: "Mr. Sassover, why do you sit and study all day? You must go out and get fresh air."

He did not know that that was precisely the advice I could not take. Nevertheless, I recovered.

Our days in Joshua Bin-Nun Street were pregnant with important events. The hounding of the Irgun by our fellow-Jews reached its climax. Yaacov Meridor was handed over to the British. Eliezer was kidnapped. Other important officers were betrayed or kidnapped. We had to hold out, and "deepen" the underground.

During that period the hounding came to an end. The sun of fighting unity rose. The united Resistance Movement was born. During that period, after many operations, came the storming of British Government and military headquarters in the King David Hotel and the storm that followed it. Then followed the evaporation of fighting unity. During that period we saved two of our sentenced fighters from the hands of the hangman. Throughout the period we delivered attack after attack on the oppressor, and the revolt burst into a great flame.

3

Early in 1947 I was obliged to leave Joshua Bin-Nun Street. In the first place my lease with "Mr. Goldhammer" was up. But what was more important, conditions had changed. The landlord had decided to build a hotel on the site of the adjacent garden. It is difficult to live underground next door to a hotel. It would have meant returning to a "too open" underground. Then, our Intelligence Service learnt that the British had begun to pay undue attention to the neighbourhood. We could not be too careful. One might by chance avoid falling into the Government's hands. But one might also accidentally be caught. We could not depend too much on chance. Finally the Haganah leaders now knew of my beard. As long as we were fighting together, it did not matter. But when our paths separated again—the Haganah to their passivity, we to intensified warfare—it was healthier that they should not know what I looked like. So, at any rate, thought our security officers, and I had to take their advice.

Thus another chapter ended, and a new began. The figure of Reb Israel Sassover disappeared from Joshua Bin-Nun Street and in Yosef Eliahu Street, in the heart of Tel Aviv, Dr. Yonah Koenigshoffer came into being.

Quite by chance a passport had been found in one of the public libraries in the name of Dr. Yonah Koenigshoffer. It was rather a long name, but it had the advantage of being purely "Germanic." It was a name reeking of loyalty and the preservation of law and order. So it was decided to suit me to the passport, or rather, to adapt my new photograph to it. My new personality was all ready by the time I had to move. The problem of an apartment was soon solved. Meir Cahan who always inspired confidence as a well-to-do merchant adopted a new name and hired the apartment for his "brother-in-law" whose inability to sign the lease in person was explained by his illness. The apartment was very near the Habimah Theatre. As Meir said —the darkest spot is right under the lamp.

The night before the move, I shaved my beard. Sassover was no more. I looked ten years younger. At first I felt very strange. My son recognized only my voice and said to his mother: "I thought an uncle had come to visit us."

But he did not ask many questions. Strangely enough, though he omitted none of a child's usual questions, he seldom asked about "those things." He knew nothing about his father's special situation, but he used to see him unlike other fathers, at home in the mornings, and with a beard, then without a beard. But he was silent. Perhaps he sensed something instinctively. However that may be, though he knew I was there all the time, he never told anybody who came to the apartment. Sometimes he would ask me, in a whisper and with a mischievous look in his eyes: "You did once have a beard, father, didn't you?"

But that was his secret, or ours. He never mentioned it to anybody else. As for Hasya, she was not yet able to talk. I was safe from that side.

I was unexpectedly secured from another angle. When the landlady saw me for the first time my beard had just been removed and my face looked unusually pale. She concluded that I was suffering from tuberculosis. This was a serious matter to her, and she decided to find out whether her suspicions were justified. She had been told that we came from Petah Tikva. Off she went to Petah Tikva to make inquiries about her new tenant. By a strange coincidence she got on to the track of one Koenigshoffer who had lived in Petah Tikva and was known to have tuberculosis. This proof of her tenant's illness distressed her immensely. My tuberculosis might be contagious, endangering the whole household. She called Meir, my "brother-in-law" and suggested that she would help us find another apartment. At least, she said, I should have myself examined by a doctor. Meir tried to persuade me to do so. But an idea struck me and I said "No." On the contrary, let the word get round that I am tubercular. To be a sick man would be very "healthy" in the underground. The idea worked. In Yosef Eliahu Street we had a wall of isolation round us. And I have to beg pardon of the landlady for the anxiety I caused her. Still—it was not altogether superfluous.

I must ask pardon also of my little son for the troubles he had from his new family name. The children in the neighbourhood and in the Kindergarten called him Koenigsbluffer—and they did not know how serious their cruel joke was. Officials also found difficulty in pronouncing it. One of them, for whom I once opened the door, asked me angrily: "Where do you get such a long name from, Koenigs-something?"

"What can I do?" I replied. "That's what they called my grandfather."

There was one official, however, who did not object to my name. He was the collector for the organisation called "Le'asirenu."

"For the Prisoners." He found me sitting in our front-room, which had a door leading directly on to the garden. He paid no attention to my name. He made an earnest plea for help for the fund which cared for the nation's political prisoners. I agreed, and Koenigshoffer became a registered member. But I must beg pardon of Dr. Yonah Koenigshoffer for signing his name without permission on the "Le 'Asirenu" forms and on other papers. I dare to assume that I did not bring discredit to his good name. And when the moment for which we had all been hoping arrived I "returned" it to him. I hope my comrades returned his passport. Maybe he has taken a Hebrew name by now.

While I was Yonah Koenigshoffer I became the father of a second daughter, Leah. She too was born doubly "illegally." Her family name, like that of Hasya, had to be Epstein. As she came into the world Arab shells from Jaffa were flying overhead. I had to send my greetings to her from afar: she too was a "secret." I could not even make a celebration for her. And Israel Epstein was no more. . . .

The Koenigshoffer apartment was our last station in the underground tunnel. When, after emerging from the underground, I made my first public speech in Jerusalem, our neighbours were thunderstruck to learn from the newspapers that the Commander of the Irgun was "Benny's father." They did not want to believe it at once. "How came it we knew nothing about it?"

Benny first heard about it from the children in the neighbourhood.

"It's your father! It's your father!"

Benny was shocked. His father had never been in the Irgun. What was more, Benny was not an Irgun "supporter." I once overheard a conversation between him and Yefet, a little Yemenite boy, whose family had taken refuge in our building when, at the beginning of the Arab attack, they had been forced to flee from Jaffa. Yefet and Benny were great friends, but differed radically on politics.

"Benny," asked Yefet, "what do you belong to?"

In those days the question was clear to every child. "To belong" meant to one of the armed organisations, Haganah, Irgun or F.F.I. My son answered promptly:

"I belong to Lechi (F.F.I.)."

"Benny, what are you saying? They're no good."

"All right, then. I belong to Haganah."

"Benny, what are you saying? They're no good at all. I tell you. I belong to the Irgun. They're *good*. They beat them all."

After we captured Jaffa, Yefet's parents returned to Jaffa. But Benny remained uncertain of his allegiance. No wonder then that he did not at first believe his father was the Commander of the Irgun. Finally he overcame his hesitancy and came to me, holding the newspaper which had printed my photograph.

"Father, is this you? Tell me the truth, is it you?"

I could no longer conceal the truth from my son. His mother explained everything to him. I took the decisive step out of the underground. The child took it with surprising calmness. Only from time to time he says to me with laughing eyes: "Father, do you remember when we were in the underground?"

I remember. I remember Benny's unhappy and incessant questioning. "Where is Uncle Israel?" And how I used to reply that Uncle Israel had gone to America and would soon return. That was untrue. Uncle Israel went away, but he will never come back.

"Uncle Israel," Benny's best-beloved uncle, was Israel Epstein, my bosom friend. He taught in a school at Petah Tikva, where he was respected by all the teachers and parents, and loved by all the children. I have never met a greater-hearted, more devoted and more honest friend.

Israel was not a member of the High Command of the Irgun. But he was nevertheless one of the few who knew where I lived, and visited me frequently. He handled the publication of *Herut*, our underground newspaper. He knew all the secrets of the underground, and kept them sealed. When our boys fell it was to him I poured out my heart. He was my comforter in days of sorrow and tribulation.

At the end of 1946 we sent him to Europe to engage in the training of the large reserve forces we were building up abroad. He was overjoyed at the mission. But who could foresee the workings of Fate? Several days after his arrival in Rome the Irgun blew up the British Embassy there. Official nervousness was heightened tremendously. Newspapers in various countries published breathless hair-raising stories of an imminent "terrorist invasion of the British Isles." This was very useful. But in Rome it brought tragedy. A number of important Irgun officers were arrested. Among them was Israel Epstein. Others were liberated. He remained in prison. He was under particular suspicion because of his arrival so shortly before the explosion. British Intelligence agents, with whom Italy teemed at the time, demanded that as a Palestinian citizen he be handed over to them. And British agents then had considerable influence with the Italian police. Israel knew this. He determined that he would escape. A plan was made. It miscarried. As he was getting out of the building he was shot by an Italian policeman. The wounds proved fatal.

One morning, as I listened to the first news bulletin from London I heard a report from Rome: "A Polish Jew, Ze'ev Epstein, was seriously wounded in Rome while trying to escape from prison. He was suspected of complicity in the terrorist outrage at the British Embassy."

A Polish Jew? Ze'ev Epstein? A pang in my heart told me who it was. I prayed I might be wrong, but I knew I had lost Israel.

The next day, or that evening, the B.B.C. reported that Ze'ev Epstein had died of his wounds. Ze'ev Epstein? My comrades tried to persuade me that there was another Epstein from Poland named Ze'ev, in Italy. But two days later confirmation arrived. I had lost my boyhood friend—and I was underground. This time I could not even go to the synagogue to say the Prayer for the Dead. And—one had to go on. There was no choice.

The final stage of the revolt, with its gravest events, I passed in the apartment in Yosef Eliahu Street, in the heart of Tel Aviv and the British Secret Service did not know. The apartment near the Habimah Theatre, the house near the Yarkon River, the Hasidoff Quarter were not the only places in which I lived or worked. I had many other "residences"—for short periods at different times. I lived in the Yemenite Hatikvah Quarter of Tel Aviv, at Ramat Gan and in Petah Tikva itself. During the period of martial law I lived with a Jewish police-man who was "helping the British look for terrorists." He helped very well. But in none of these places, the permanent or the temporary, were there any body-guards or alarm-signals. Everything was simple and everyday. An average citizen. A family. An open house. Neighbours that "knew everything." No secrets. The secret was that there was no secret. An open under-ground. And the eyes of the British Intelligence were blinded.

Sir Edward Grigg, formerly British Minister in the Middle East, said in the House of Lords to which he was promoted as Lord Altrincham: "The primary cause of our failure in Palestine was the failure of our Intelligence Service."

That was very true.

Chapter IX

Civil War—Never!

With the end of British rule in our country, no internal fight for power broke out among the Jews. Baldly stated, this may not appear a matter of much moment but in reality it was an historic achievement. History teaches us that on the heels of most wars of liberation, bloody civil strife has invariably broken out. In our own day this rule claimed Gandhi, the apostle of non-violent revolution, as its victim. In some respects the fall of a regime resembles an earthquake, for an earthquake, even after it has apparently spent itself, is often succeeded by a chain of further subterranean upheavals.

It cannot be said that our revolt did not create all the prerequisites for an internal clash. On the contrary, the internal clash seemed much more inevitable here than in many other successful revolts. Our revolution did not come about as a result of orders from above. It did not begin on instructions from the official Jewish leadership; indeed, it arose against the will of that leadership. It continued not only without their consent but in defiance of their prohibitions.

British officials prophesied that on their departure there would be war between Arabs and Jews. They guessed rightly. They also prophesied that when they left the country there would be civil war amongst the Jews themselves, but here they were wrong.

Two factors saved the people from the catastrophe of civil war. In the first place we did not teach the Irgun fighters to hate our political opponents. One sided hatred is obviously a threat to national unity. Mutual hatred brings almost certain civil war. Whenever we saw the manifestations of hatred against us we grieved and were astonished. Was such brother-hatred possible, we asked ourselves.

The second element in the avoidance of civil war was connected with the problem of power. We fought in the underground for the establishment of Jewish rule; we were not concerned with power. Our opponents could never believe this of us. They thought—or at least they said—that the "dissidents'" struggle was nothing but a struggle for power. This was their fundamental historical mistake. The history of religions and nations teaches that dissidence is possible without a revolution, but a revolution is impossible without dissidence. A revolution is not a mere transition. A revolution is not something you put to the vote; it does not come about as the result of a resolution drafted at the end of a general debate. The storming of the Bastille preceded the Declaration of the Rights of Man; the Boston Tea Party preceded the Bill of Rights. A revolution always breaks out spontaneously—or it does not break out at all. It is not subject to discipline. It imposes discipline on those who make it. In essence dissidence and revolution are one, just as revolution and progress are one.

We broke away to revolt because our enslavement demanded it. We dissented in order to fight for our people, not in order to rule them. The striving for power is not in itself illegitimate. On the contrary, it embodies a healthy desire for fulfillment. A fighting underground is also perfectly entitled to strive for power; and this striving may actually fortify its fight against the aggressor. There were indeed some in our underground who believed that the absence of the desire for power was a positive failing. I do not wish here, however, to analyse the facts, but only to establish them. Good or bad, justified or mistaken, the fact is that throughout our underground struggle we did not think of power nor strive for it, and in our hearts we agreed that with the victory of the revolt and the liquidation of foreign rule, the government of our country should be taken over by the official leadership. In this spirit the soldiers of the

Irgun Zvai Leumi were educated. Our struggle was innocent of any secondary motive.

The idea of freedom had captured our hearts completely. The individual identified himself utterly with the idea. If it meant the surrender of his personal liberty —he surrendered it; if it required that he leave his family—he left it; if it involved the endurance of torture—he accepted it; if it called for continuous exposure to danger—he resigned himself to it; if it demanded his life—he gave it. As to who would ultimately rule the State for whose establishment the fighter was prepared for these sacrifices—that was not important. The essential thing was that there should *be* a State, that we should be a nation, a 'free nation in our own country,' that we should open the gates and bring in salvaged exiles, that we should not be downtrodden and humiliated by alien rule, that we should breathe the air of freedom for which our lungs had longed during two thousand weary years of dispersion and ghetto. It is impossible to say whether or not we should have obtained power had we wanted it. One thing is clear: had we aimed at power, we would have fought for it. We aimed however, solely at the liquidation of foreign rule; we fought for it and achieved it.

Had it been otherwise, two hostile camps would have been arrayed against each other in Eretz Israel. Nor can it be urged that it was the supervention of the war with the Arabs that precluded such a development. He who lusts for power exploits any external danger in order to impose his will at home. The truth is that we fought shoulder to shoulder against the Arab aggressor because the camp of the rebels did not aim at power and because we did not hate our brethren in the other camp.

But the danger of civil war was inherent in the historic character of the revolt, just as its elimination was inherent in the moral character of the rebels.

Let us remember that this was a revolt by dissidents and throughout *almost* the whole period the official leaders in the Jewish Agency did not want the revolt. Throughout the *whole* period they certainly did not want the dissidents.

President Truman has said that he would have joined the 'terrorists' had he been in Eretz Israel during the rule of the British. Had he done so, the official leaders would have handed him over to the British for the official leadership did not want the "dissidents" either with or without President Truman—or the street-cleaner in Tel Aviv for that matter. Maybe they had no faith in the prospects of the revolt. Maybe they were afraid of the rebels. Maybe they believed we were very wicked people.

Whatever it was, the fact is that official Zionist leadership wanted us to stop our struggle immediately after we launched it. First they tried to cajole us. When cajolery failed, threats followed. And the "deeds" that came next would have brought about civil war had we not determined that the greatest menace to the future of our people was internal conflict.

2

The efforts at persuasion began in mid-summer, 1944. At that time I was about to meet Mr. Ben Gurion.[1]

It is characteristic that both sides were keen on such a meeting without either knowing of the desire of the other. By 'both sides' I do not mean Mr. Ben Gurion and myself, personally; I mean our respective confidantes and friends.

My friends broached the idea of a meeting with Ben Gurion, and I accepted their proposal. We were then in the throes of our first operations, and were on the point of extending their scope. Mr. Ben Gurion, for his part, was at the apex of his 'extremist' period. 'Biltmore' was in his satchel. This word has been almost com-

---

[1] David Ben Gurion was born in Russian Poland and came to Palestine (then part of the Turkish Empire) in his early youth. A life-long Socialist, he rose to be the leading personality in the Eretz Israel Labour Party (Mapai), was for many years Chairman of the Zionist Executive and, when the British regime withdrew, became first Prime Minister of Israel.

pletely forgotten—and rightly so. It is the name of the
American hotel at which Mr. Ben Gurion defined the
war-aim of our people as a Jewish State in the whole of
Eretz Israel (by which, of course, Mr. Ben Gurion
meant Western Eretz Israel). This foreign name, which
at the time caused a great tumult in the Zionist camp,
was ultimately whittled down into—partition. The Biltmore Hotel continues its solid existence. The teaching
that came out of it—not, of course, a new teaching—
soon disappeared.

But in 1944 is was a 'new' teaching. Not, of course,
as far as its content was concerned. Ben Gurion had
been preceded by Jabotinsky, who had preached the
concept of a Jewish State that included Eastern Eretz
Israel. And Jabotinsky had been preceded by Herzl
whose State idea had been given up by Zionist leaders
a quarter of a century ago.[1] The novelty lay in the
preacher: Mr. Ben Gurion demanding a Jewish State,
the man who only a few years earlier had tried to persuade the Peel Commission that what we needed and
demanded was not a Jewish State but a so-called "national home." He had, it is true, added his own not unsuccessful interpretation of the term, but the trouble was
that the Gentiles before whom he elaborated his thesis
were far greater adepts at the art of interpretation.

In the 'forties' then, Ben Gurion abandoned all his
'historico-philosophical' interpretations and used language that everybody could understand: a Jewish State.
It is said that he was influenced in this direction by Berl
Katznelson. Maybe. It seems to me that Ben Gurion was
deeply influenced, albeit unconsciously, by his meetings
with Jabotinsky in the 'thirties.' And he was certainly
influenced by the Nazi campaign of extermination in
Europe. Ben Gurion was born anew, so to speak. He

[1] Even as late as 1943, Dr. Chaim Weizmann, President of
the World Zionist Organisation, could write of Herzl's book,
The Jewish State, and refer to its "incredibly naive, utterly unnecessary, elaborate plans for the organisation of the emigra-
tion from the Diaspora and the institutions, laws and even
manners of the future state." (Foreword to *The Jewish State*,
Scopus Publishing Co., New York).

not only flung the Biltmore slogan into the arena. He
made a number of speeches, militant of content and
sharp of tone, "against the rulers."

We were delighted at this change, and bore no
grudge against Mr. Ben Gurion. It was Jabotinsky himself who had always taught us to resist "black memories." He used to say: "Any man may make a mistake
or say foolish things. Don't let your memory dwell on
his mistakes or his chatter. And if the good of the people
requires that you stretch out your hand to him, don't
let your memory be 'black.' Forget what must be forgotten and give him your hand."

My friends argued, therefore, that the time had come
to stretch out our hand to Ben Gurion. We intended
saying to Ben Gurion that with the passing of Jabotinsky
it was immaterial to us who would be "at the head" of
the future State. What was essential was the aim, and
the struggle for its achievement. If Mr. Ben Gurion
would lead us in the struggle against British rule and
for Hebrew sovereignty, we would follow him gladly
and enthusiastically. In short, we meant to tell him that
we would place ourselves at his disposal if he was prepared to prove the sincerity of his words with action.

We learnt later that just at that time Mr. Ben Gurion's friends were urging upon him the idea of a meeting between us. They hoped Ben Gurion would get us
to place ourselves at his disposal even if he was not prepared to make good his words with action.

The meeting, however, did not take place. Ben Gurion hesitated. He expressed doubts as to whether he
would "find common political language" with me. His
intention, it transpired, was to stop our military attacks
on the British regime. We were eventually informed that
though he was very interested in the meeting he could
not participate and would like me to meet his personal
representative. We were assured that the man concerned would have full authority.

We met and Ben Gurion's personal representative
opened the conversation in dramatic style.

"You hold in your hands," he said "an instrument
capable of determining the fate of the people. But we

regard ourselves as responsible for the people's fate. It is not desirable that in addition to the force at the disposal of the national institutions, there should exist another armed force in Israel. I hope that the day is not far distant when there will be one unified force in Israel. Until that time it is desirable that we make an arrangement which will prevent harmful actions. . . ."

I replied:

"I do not know if the fighting organisation in which I am active is liable to determine the fate of the people. We have only begun to fight and do not know yet whether we shall win or fail. It may be—and we hope —that what we are doing and shall do will have a historic effect. But it may prove to be only a 'tragic episode.' At any rate, we have decided to fight, for we are certain that if we do not fight we shall achieve nothing. Perhaps it is not we but others who will reap the fruits of our struggle; but that does not matter to us. As for responsibility, we see ourselves also as responsible for the fate of the people. After all, you were all against a Jewish State not long ago. Now you have changed your views—a proof that we were right. We are convinced that to-day again we are right. We have the consciousness of a mission. For better or for worse—that is how it is."

The representative became somewhat agitated.

"You are wrong," he said. "The responsibility is ours and only ours. But that is not what I came to discuss with you. I came to prove to you that it is impossible that you should carry out operations on your own initiative. Consider well: you have no information, certainly not adequate information, about our political situation and prospects. That being so, how can you know whether action is necessary, and when and how to act? You may, by an unconsidered step, easily nullify all we have achieved!"

I replied. "First of all, we have information. Secondly, I don't believe in 'deep secrets.' In this era of radio we know enough."

He would not agree. 'I shall give you some information," he said, "from which you will see for yourself that it is premature to carry out operations against the British regime. We have a good contact with Churchill, who as a friend of Zionism, tells us that the 'old man' has a new plan for Eretz Israel. The details are not yet known, but it is clear that the Jews will get something substantial. The plan has to do with Transjordan. Churchill said: 'I carved up Palestine once. I shall unite it again and carve it up a second time.' "

"Is it true," I asked, "that Churchill has said that he is preparing to put up a strong fight for Zionism as he understands it?"

"No, that's a distortion. Churchill did say something similar, but not quite that. He has explained that he is up against serious opposition to Zionism in his own party. But he trusts to his prestige. He is convinced that his view will prevail, but as long as the war goes on he cannot deal with the matter. He wants a radical solution and that is impossible before the end of the war. That is why he said he prefers one big fight."

"Has Weizmann been in touch with Churchill?"

"Of course. In fact he has free access to Churchill. They had a talk only recently. But Churchill told our British friends afterwards that it was hard for him to talk to Weizmann. After their last talk he did not sleep all night. . . ."

"And what did Churchill tell Weizmann at their last meeting?"

"He didn't tell him anything new. He again emphasized his loyalty to the Zionist idea, but repeated that before the end of the war he could do nothing. During the conversation he came out with these words: 'You may be sure that at the end of the war you will get the biggest plum in the pudding.' "

"What does that mean?"

"That means—a good partition scheme."

"Is there such a thing?"

"Of course. For example, partition without the 'Triangle'[1] is a good partition and we shall accept it."

[1] The 'Triangle' was the term used to denote the area in Central Palestine, north of Jerusalem and reaching almost to

"And what if they propose a 'bad' partition scheme?"

"We won't accept it. There is, in fact, a partition scheme prepared by the British Cairo 'school.' It is connected with the Greater Syria plan. It provides, among other things, that part of Galilee and even some of our settlements in the Emek[2] should be included in the Arab State. To that, of course, we shan't agree. And if they try to impose the scheme on us, we shall revolt. Ben Gurion is prepared for revolt. That is why there must be no action now. On the one hand we have a chance of obtaining from Britain a solution that may not be ideal but will nevertheless ensure independence, large-scale immigration and settlement. On the other hand we must prepare to frustrate a bad plan. Your activities are liable to frustrate the good prospect and at the same time to interfere with our preparations for revolt."

"I don't agree with you," I said. "We, as you know, reject any partition. To us there is no 'good partition' or 'bad partition.' You may call this dogmatism but that is our attitude. The Homeland is a unity and cannot be cut up. In any case, it is clear to us that unless we fight we shall get nothing. I follow the British Press —as much of it as reaches us here. I read *The Economist* for example and I learn there that the White Paper is the fixed policy of the British Government. In general there is no longer any possibility of putting any trust in their promises. Churchill may hint at what he may want to do after the War. Suppose he is no longer in power. And what is to happen in the meantime? You know as well as I do what is happening in Europe. Is it possible for us to wait? And in the final analysis, how can our struggle possibly do any harm to the Jewish national cause? We are lifting the Eretz Israel question into the orbit of public attention—and as for you, if you

the coast, formed by an imaginary line joining the three Arab populated townships of Nablus, Tulkarm and Jenin. The 'Triangle' together with a good deal more of Western Palestine is still cut off from the existing State of Israel.

[2] The Valley of Jezreel, the original kingpin of Jewish agricultural resettlement in Eretz Israel.

find it expedient, you are perfectly entitled to dissociate yourselves from our activities."

"Yes, but there remains the question of discipline,
and that is a very serious matter. We cannot permit you
to take money from a man who contributes to the
Keren Hayesod[1] and thus impose your discipline on
him. A people can have only one army and only one
policy."

"But our people is under foreign rule and there can
be only one policy for an oppressed people: a struggle
for liberation."

The discussion came to an end only at three in the
morning. Ben Gurion's representative finally demanded
that we should submit our plans to the Jewish Agency
or to the Haganah Command. I told him that I had intended telling Mr. Ben Gurion:

"If you fight not only shall we fight with you but we
shall follow you. Until that time comes, however, we
are unable to submit our operational plans. Our struggle requires absolute secrecy in planning and in execution. How can we hand over plans to bodies which
deny our right of existence?"

Finally the man said, with a strange smile: "You
have convinced me of one thing: there must be one
Jewish military force in Eretz Israel." He promised to
give Ben Gurion a full report of our conversation, and
departed.

He did not fear British night-patrols. He was then a
respected law-abiding citizen. I remained with Eliahu
Lankin, who had accompanied me to the meeting
place. I told him of the conversation. We discussed the
future, and dozed off. At dawn, when labourers were
going off to work, we too went off, through side-streets,
to our work. Our comrades were given a full report of
the abortive talk. Mr. Ben Gurion no doubt also received a report. The man who represented him, who ex-

[1] The Palestine Foundation Fund provided by voluntary do-
nations from Jews all over the world and constituting the main
development fund.

pressed his faith in Winston Churchill and who spoke
of Ben Gurion with the enthusiasm of a disciple—was
Moshe Sneh.

3

After the pleading came the threats. They began in
the autumn of 1944. Eliahu Golomb, Chief of the
Haganah, had just returned from London. Apparently
he had been in contact with the British Government
and officials. The influence of Dr. Weizmann in British
Government circles—or what Golomb assumed was his
influence—made a deep impression on the Haganah
chief. At any rate, as soon as he returned from the British capital, Golomb placed himself at the head of the
crusade against the Irgun Zvai Leumi. He called a Press
Conference and there expressed his belief in a change
of attitude by Britain to the Jewish people; he alleged
that many doors (unspecified) in London that were
shut even to the Governments-in-Exile were wide open
to the President of the Zionist Organisation; he claimed
that it was "terrorism" that endangered all the prospects
and demanded that these "childish games" should not
be allowed to continue.

Several weeks later we were asked to meet Mr. Golomb, the so-called "Minister of Security." It was not
easy to agree to go to this meeting. We all doubted
whether in the circumstances prevailing it was desirable
or permissible to meet people who had already declared all-out war on us. The scales were turned, however, by the arguments of Eliahu Lankin. He argued
that direct contact was always desirable. Why should
Golomb's imagination be given a free rein about us, he
asked. We might, of course, not succeed in convincing
him that we had only the one aim of fighting for the liberation of our country. Nevertheless, we might weaken
his belief that our aim was the one he ascribed to us:
"power in the Yishuv." Should we succeed in this—
Eliahu concluded—our objections to a meeting would
be outweighed by its advantages.

These sweetly reasonable arguments did not suc-

ceed in dispelling all our doubts, but we decided to
agree to the meeting and to answer "No" to any demand
for a cessation of our struggle. Golomb was accompanied by Moshe Sneh; the Irgun was represented by
Eliahu Lankin and me. The meeting which took place,
in Tel Aviv's busiest street, Allenby Street, was very
formal. Golomb and Sneh informed us that they spoke
in the name of 'Knesset Israel'[1] and it was in its name
that they demanded the immediate cessation of our activities against the British. Most of their arguments were
not new. Golomb assumed that our military operations,
when they were not aimed at harming the Jewish
Agency, were the consequence of a semi-childish pursuit of heroics. He spoke a good deal about the exploits
of Haganah members in the service of the British Intelligence against Germany, who had been parachuted
into a number of European countries. "That is true
bravery," said the leader of the Haganah, "and your
members could also have been privileged to participate
in these daring operations had you not turned to terrorism."

Golomb's talk was a mixture of light compliments
aimed at capturing our favour and dark threats to intimidate our spirits. "I do not deny," he said, "that there
is a spirit of self-sacrifice among you, but it must now
be directed into another channel. I might possibly admit that your actions may even have had a certain political significance, because you proved that when Jews
start fighting in Eretz Israel they are prepared to go on
to the end and even to die. But if this was your purpose, what you have done is quite enough. You have
proved what you set out to prove. Now you must stop
your activities and"—he added in a more emphatic
tone—"not only stop them but also announce publicly
that you have decided to do so."

Lankin and I replied as we had decided to reply. We
too, did not add much that was new. We dwelt on the
campaign of extermination in Europe. We pointed to
the barred gates of Eretz Israel, and the echo aroused

[1] Official name of the Jewish Community in Eretz Israel.

throughout the world by our operations. We emphasized that we had no desire whatsoever for adventures and heroics, but that we had the rooted consciousness of a mission—the consciousness that if we laid down our arms an endless night of enslavement would descend on our people. But if we fought we should be able, with the help of all the factors set in motion by our struggle, to transform the situation of the country and the people. Consequently we could not accede to the demand to stop the struggle and saw no reason why fellow-Jews should fight us because we fought the British administration.

Allenby Street, teeming with people in the evening, had long gone to sleep, but the four of us continued debating for many hours, bringing forward proofs, recalling past history, prophesying future events. While, as I have said, neither side said anything very new, two of the things Golomb said that night remained indelibly imprinted on my memory. He expressed deep belief not only in a coming Labour victory in Britain but also in the decisive change that that electoral victory would bring about in Britain's attitude to Zionism. We tried to shake this naive belief, but in vain.

Still more surprising—indeed, dumbfounding—was the Haganah chief's view of the effect of our struggle on our own people. He argued that we were teaching the Jews to be cowards, instead of instilling into them courage!

Long after midnight the tense conversation broke up. The parting was not pleasant. Though we said 'Shalom' and even shook hands, the threat and shadow of civil war remained in the air. Before we separated we again emphasized that there was no justification for the Haganah interposing between us and the Mandatory Government. And we expressed the hope that the day would come when we would fight the foreign regime together. Golomb replied: "We shall step in and finish you." And these words, whose full significance we understood only much later, were the last I heard from him. Golomb, who was suffering from advanced heart-disease, died a short while afterwards at a relatively early age.

Chapter X

Have We the Right?

The threats of our own brethren were still echoing in our ears when the British forces delivered a heavy blow against us. Early in the morning of the 21st of October, 1944, the detention camp at Latrun was surrounded by strong forces of the Occupation Army. Some 251 of the detainees were taken out of their beds almost naked, manacled and flown off in a special flight of heavy transport planes to Eritrea in East Africa. Of all the methods adopted, this was one of the severest blows by the oppressor in his efforts to break the backbone of the revolt and to extinguish the fire which inspired it. Mass deportation from the Homeland is no light matter. The explanation which the British authorities gave for the deportation could have been taken as a pleasing compliment to us. They said there was reason to believe the Irgun intended freeing the prisoners in the detention camp by force. We knew, however, that they meant no flattery. They wanted to break our spirit. True, we always had plans to free imprisoned comrades, and when the occasion presented itself we carried them out. But this was merely a typical official excuse designed to conceal the true purpose. That purpose was many-sided. The oppressors wanted to break the spirits and bodies of the prisoners, among whom were some of our best officers and men. They wanted to hurt their families—numbering some thousands of people. They wanted to strike fear into the hearts of Jewish youth and to frighten them away from our ranks. They wanted to test the reactions of the 'organized Yishuv' to the act of deportation—in order to know how far a Government could go not only with 'terrorists' but with Jews in general.

It cannot be denied that our spirits were very low. Again we were subjected to the cruel mental conflict which had begun with our first fatal casualty. The question, I believe, gnaws at every revolutionary: Have we the right to cause, even indirectly, so much suffering and so much sorrow to so many comrades?

I remembered the time when I was a prisoner and an exile. I knew that imprisonment itself is a very heavy punishment for a cultured person. But if you add the burden of strangeness which hangs over the spirit of every exile, if you add the misery of home-sickness you can have some idea of the depths of anguish which must be endured.

This was the double burden of the two hundred and fifty one deportees seized by the British. No wonder, then, that our first reaction was to do everything possible to force the oppressor to bring back our exiled comrades.

We did not of course believe in "intercessions." Had we given "interceders" authority to say that the struggle would be given up completely we could have achieved not only the return of the exiles but their release from restraint as well, and many other things. But our determination to pursue the struggle was unshakeable—and it was necessary only to temper its steel from time to time in the fire of new tribulations. We set about making plans for battle-operations not so much to avenge the exiles, as to prove to the Authorities that their calculations were abysmally wrong.

Night after night our members, and members of the F.F.I., pasted up slogans denouncing the deporters of our comrades. There was also a joint ultimatum of the Irgun and the F.F.I. demanding the return of the exiles. Thereafter we proposed giving the floor to "Comrade Parabellum." But something happened which foiled our plans. On November 1st, 1944, while I waited with Yaacov Meridor for Yitshak Ysernitzky and Nathan Friedman of the F.F.I. Command to meet us to

work out the joint operations, Yaacov casually turned
on the radio. A news-flash from Cairo announced that
Lord Moyne had been assassinated. This immediately
became the signal for an all out crusade by Haganah
and the Jewish Agency for our destruction. The official
leadership made full use of the forebodings occasioned
by the death of Moyne to launch a large-scale attack on
the Irgun. The "open season" began.

2

It was preceded by a secret debate and a public discussion among various "schools of thought" in the official Zionist leadership. Rabbi Fishman (of the *Mizrachi* or religious party in Zionism and Mr. Yitshak
Gruenbaum (of the General Zionists) opposed any
crusade against us on principle. The members of
"Group B" which had broken away from Mapai (Palestine Labour Party) and of the "Left Poalei Zion" favoured "independent action"—that is kidnappings and
allied operations—but opposed direct collaboration of
any kind with the British police and Intelligence. The
Mapai chief, Ben Gurion, gave an interesting opinion
on this at the Conference of the Histadruth[1] called expressly for the purpose of proclaiming the crusade
against us. Mr. Ben Gurion explained that only in the
Diaspora was it wrong to co-operate with alien police;
here in Eretz Israel there was no reason why the
Yishuv should not accept the help of the police in the
"common cause."

Ben Gurion drafted his "four-point plan for the liquidation of the terror." With an enthusiasm worthy of
a better cause, Mr. Ben Gurion said:

"Four steps have so far been projected and I wish to
touch on them in simple and concise language.

[1] Histadruth, the confederation of Trade Unions in Eretz Israel, is relatively far more powerful than the T.U.C. in Great
Britain. Though in electoral terms Mapai is said to control the
Histadruth, it is nearer the fact to say that the Histadruth dominates Mapai.—Ed.

Expulsion from Work

". . . . Anybody connected with these gangs, anybody supporting them, not only those who use the revolver or throw the bomb, but anybody who disseminates their literature or pastes up their proclamations— must be driven out of his job, whether in office, factory or orchard, and must be expelled from the labour exchange. The same applies to pupils at primary or other schools. . . . If he distributes their literature to the youth not only must the profane literature be taken away from him and burnt but he must be expelled from the school. . . .

No Shelter or Refuge

". . . . The second step is not to give them shelter or refuge. I know that here we are up against one of the noblest and most praiseworthy instincts—a humane and particularly Jewish instinct—but if we do not want to be cruel to the Jewish people struggling in the mesh of destruction we cannot now concern ourselves with false pity. It is forbidden to give shelter or refuge to these criminals who endanger our future.

Not to Submit to Threats

". . . . Third: not to submit to their threats . . . and the threats have reached the stage where people far removed from the gangs and vigorously opposed to their wicked behaviour are pleading that there should be no action against them lest we involve ourselves in civil war. . . .

Collaboration (with the British)

". . . . Consequently, insofar as the British authorities and Police are interested in crushing terrorism we co-operate with them. It would be stupid and suicidal if, because of our just grievances in other spheres against the country's existing regime, we should refrain from accepting its help and from helping it in fields where we have, to the extent that we have, a common interest. . . . Without helping the authorities and without being helped by them we shall not succeed in destroying this plague. . . .

"These four demands are for the time being the practical minimum which must be carried out and for which we must mobilize every man and woman, every schoolboy, every factory worker, every townsman and villager . . ."

The opinion represented by Ben Gurion and by his rival Socialists of Hashomer Hatzair was victorious. Rabbi Fishman and Mr. Gruenbaum resigned for a time and remained isolated for a longer time. The "Group B" and "Left Poalei Zion" recorded their "reservation in principle" on the fourth point of Ben Gurion's programme, but accepted its fulfilment. The "season" came down upon us in full force. Thousands of Haganah members were mobilized and concentrated in the big towns. The country was divided into operational regions. Officers were appointed for liaison with the British police. Organized tracking covered every street and alleyway.

The first expulsions from schools and the first dismissals of "suspect" workers from their jobs were carried out. And on the heels of the expulsions, designed to frighten and starve fathers and sons, came the kidnappings and handing over of prisoners to the British. Every day brought its crop of Job's news. Young members were kidnapped; veterans were locked away. The treatment of those kidnapped by the Haganah was grim. Though it was winter the victims were often kept in dark and damp cellars. They were given little food and there were cases of maltreatment at the hands of their fellow-Jewish captors.

Together with the kidnappings by the Haganah, began the implementation of "Point 4": denunciations and deliveries to the British. The police were delighted. Lists of Irgun men they had so long ached to get hold of were now coming in without cessation. Material worth its weight in gold: names, addresses, descriptions, types of duty, rank—all flowed into the files of Giles and Catling.

Richard Crossman, the Labour M.P., stated later in

the British House of Commons that according to his information the Jewish Agency and the Haganah handed over a list of 1500 names of members of the Irgun Zvai Leumi to the British authorities. I think the figure of 1500 is exaggerated—perhaps not by much, but exaggerated nevertheless. There is however no disputing the fact that during that period the names of many hundreds of officers and men of the Irgun Zvai Leumi were handed over to the British police by official Jewish institutions and their 'liaison officers.'

3

How were we to behave in the face of the situation? True, we did not yet know of the use of 'third degree,' but even the 'first degree' was enough to infuriate us. We knew that our comrades were undergoing suffering. The anguish of those kidnapped was carried to us from the depths. How long would we tolerate these cruelties?

Life in the underground enforces seclusion and seclusion makes deep thinking possible. In such conditions you are able to view matters not in their transitory perspective but, as the lovers of classical phrases would say, *sub specie aeternitatis*. We needed such a perspective in those days of severe trial. A deep cellar in certain circumstances becomes an elevated watch-tower. Were it not for the detachment and objectivity which we were able to bring to our deliberations at that time who knows what fratricidal holocaust may have developed among the Jews of Israel. The Mandatory Government would have been satisfied. As it was they laughed, but had it not been for the "watch-tower in the cellar" whence we could see that the morning cometh as well as the night, they would also have laughed last. . . .

We could, of course, have chosen one of several alternatives, the simplest of which would have been to accept the ultimatum of the Agency leaders and surrender. There are two kinds of surrender, just as there are two kinds of war. There is an unjust, aggressive war which brings shame on those who wage it. And there is the just war of liberation which does honour to those who prosecute it. Both are accompanied by bloodshed and suffering, but it is the difference in purpose which establishes the one as profane and the other as sacred. The same applies to acts of surrender. The political and spiritual surrender that came after the 29th of June, 1946,[1] brought dishonour to those who capitulated; but in the surrender of the last defenders (Haganah and Irgun) of the Old City of Jerusalem, in 1948, there was no shame. There is of course a bitter truth in the Latin tag "woe to the vanquished;" and in certain circumstances there is equally ironic truth in its opposite: "woe to the victors." Life is one long chain of revolts and surrenders, which are sometimes so intertwined that one cannot distinguish between them. Man "surrenders" to his convictions, the son to the will of his father, the individual to the laws of society and the State. These "surrenders" frequently cause "revolts" and it is this action and reaction which gives an edge to the savour of life.

We refused to surrender to the *diktat* of the "institutions" not because of any spurious considerations of prestige nor even out of honest self-respect. Had we surrendered we should not have felt any shame. We had, after all, done what we could for our people. We had raised the banner of revolt; we had hit at the oppressor; we had made sacrifices; we had not spared ourselves, our personal liberty, our private lives. And if an internal force many times stronger in numbers and resources threatened to destroy us, where was the shame in surrender? Surely it would have rested upon the "victors."

But we viewed the whole situation in a totally different manner. We examined it from the view point of the whole of Jewry. The extermination of Jews in Europe

[1] During the Haganah's short-lived participation in the revolt, the British Government swooped down on a number of Jewish Agency leaders and officials and threw them into Latrun concentration camp. Ben Gurion took refuge in Paris. But he contrived to patch up peace with the British Government and the Haganah's co-operation in the revolt was subsequently discontinued.

was in full swing. The gates of the Holy Land were barred to any who sought sanctuary. Where then was the political change that could justify the cessation of our struggle? If we were merely to succumb to fear and intimidation, then the revolt as a political factor was finished. For then, to use Wilkin's expression, there would be "nothing to worry about." If the Jewish Agency obeyed the British, and the Irgun obeyed the Agency the rule of the High Commissioner might continue for ever.

No less decisive was the internal implication of the whole matter. I had already told Golomb that we should be prepared at any moment to accept the discipline of Ben Gurion if he would take the lead in the struggle for national liberation. I had then added some heartfelt words. Had Jabotinsky been alive—I said—we should have demanded uncompromisingly that he be given supreme office. But now Jabotinsky was no more. It was immaterial to us who led the people, provided he did lead them in a war of national liberation. The orders of a Ben Gurion sitting in Jerusalem and in effect recognising the White Paper, we would not carry out. But we would gladly carry out the instructions of a Ben Gurion sitting, say in Deganiah[1] calling for revolt against the regime of the oppressor. The declaration had been the subject of jeering comment in the Jewish Agency. These ridiculous dissidents—whispered one official to another—want Ben Gurion to go to Deganiah and play at war. The ridicule did not stand the test of events. Not a year passed and Mr. Ben Gurion began "playing at war" with the British; and we accepted his instructions. However, he did not go to Deganiah but to Paris.

The question had to be decided on its merits. We

[1] Deganiah is one of the oldest and most beautiful of the communal settlements in Israel, situated in Galilee just south of Lake Kinneret. In its picturesque cemetery on the banks of the Jordan the remains of many Zionist pioneers are buried, including the Tolstoyan Socialist, A. D. Gordon, who founded the settlement, and L. J. Greenberg, Herzl's fellow-worker in the Zionist cause.

could not be dishonest with ourselves, nor with the youth of our nation. How would we justify the cessation of our fight? Had the gates been suddenly opened to repatriates? Had we a promise that our brethren were to be rescued from the lands of extermination? There was of course no such justification. In very truth the political situation required an intensification of the struggle, not its cessation. To surrender would be to incur the double shame: of condoning extermination in Europe and enslavement in our homeland. Had we behaved thus, the spiritual revolt—the father of political and military revolt—would have dissolved into thin air. No, we could not accept the Agency's ultimatum.

The second reason for our rejection of the ultimatum was connected with our comrades in revolt, the F.F.I. (Stern Group).

We were very angry with them for not having given us even a hint of the mission to Cairo of Beth-Tzouri and Hakim, the two young men who displayed great courage before the Egyptian Court and went fearlessly to the gallows. While the assassination of Lord Moyne, one of the leading instruments of British policy in the Middle East, was not the cause of the wave of internal persecution it did provide the signal for launching it. The official leadership panicked—and fear drives out reason. A whispering campaign—organized and unorganized—scared people with plans for a general massacre of the Jews of Palestine to avenge the death of the Minister. An atmosphere of fear and terror developed in the country, which, it must be remembered, was still largely isolated from the world at large by war-time conditions. In such an atmosphere it was easy to condemn those who, it was alleged, were trying "to bring down catastrophe on the nation."

As comrades in revolt and partners in danger, we should have been informed by the F.F.I. chiefs of what was going forward. But they had permitted us to be taken completely by surprise. We were very sick at heart. Nevertheless we decided we could not abandon the F.F.I. in the hour of danger. This was one of the two decisive reasons for our refusal to surrender. It soon became clear that our concern for the F.F.I. was unwarranted. Our men were amazed to see active F.F.I. members walking unconcernedly in the streets of Tel Aviv. The riddle was solved later when the united Resistance Movement was formed. I was then told that in November 1944, the F.F.I. promised Golomb that they would suspend operations against the British and consequently Haganah did not touch the F.F.I. during that period. The whole ferocity of the 'season' was directed solely against the Irgun.

There was a second line of action open to us. We could accept the ultimatum with mental reservations—or in plain language—with the intention of breaking our word. We could have taken the course of waiting for the storm to pass. Such cases are not uncommon in the history of underground revolts. But it is characteristic of the moral principle which guided the Irgun that at the decisive meeting of the Command where our attitude to the 'crusade' was thrashed out, this idea did not occur to a single member.

The third possibility was also very simple: to hit back. It cannot be denied that there were among us many who pressed for the adoption of this policy. They adduced legal, moral and practical arguments. A fighting underground has its own laws, one of which is that the informer must pay with his life. Was it moral, argued the comrades, that we, who were prepared to give our lives for our people, should be persecuted by our kinsmen and without any attempt to retaliate on our tormentors? Had we suddenly become "Tolstoyans?"

Moreover if the attackers discover that there is no retaliation they will grow bolder.

It would be wrong to assume that our boys thought that the youth of the Haganah were lacking in courage. On the contrary our 'sabras' knew their own kind, the 'sabras'[1] of the Haganah. Their practical argument referred not to the rank-and-file but to the leaders.

These arguments, all very weighty, were reiterated with every new delivery of a victim to the British. Never-

[1] "Sabra" literally 'cactus,' nickname for Palestine-born Jews.

theless we rejected them. At the meeting of the Command to which I have referred we chose none of the 'simple' alternatives. We decided to strike out along a road which no underground had ever chosen in similar circumstances. We decided not to suspend, nor to promise to suspend, our struggle against British rule; yet at the same time we declined to retaliate for the kidnappings, the denunciations and the handing-over of our men. Neither as individuals nor as an organization. And strange as it may seem—for we are speaking of Irgun fighters—the decision not to retaliate, which ran counter to the very spirit of natural resistance, was honoured by all of them. It was honoured, without a single breach, to the very end, that is until the suspension of the persecution and the beginning of the period of joint struggle agreed upon by the Haganah, the Irgun and the F.F.I.

It must be admitted that those who proposed this "complicated" policy did not and could not produce logical arguments. They were moved by faith, a profound faith that believed the day was not far distant when all the armed camps in Israel would stand and fight shoulder to shoulder against the oppressor. In that hope and with that faith, we said, it was worth while enduring grievous suffering. We dared not destroy our faith by opening a bloody abyss between those who were still brothers and might yet become comrades in arms. We saw our people in Europe in the endless procession of death; we saw the ghettoes going up in flames; we saw the oppressor plotting against us all. And from down the corridors of history, we heard the echo of those other wars, the cursed internecine wars in dying Jerusalem nineteen centuries before. The underground cellar is a high watch-tower. Not logic, but instinct said imperatively: "No; not civil war. Not that at any price." And who knows: perhaps instinct is the very heart of logic.

This dreadful situation continued for many months. We said there would be no civil war but, in fact, throughout the whole country a one sided civil war raged.

When I recall those days, all the love of which the

human heart is capable wells up in me for those young underground fighters, unflinching, fearless, moved by a supreme fighting spirit. They went to concentration camps, were thrown into dark cellars, starved, beaten, and maligned yet not one ever broke his solemn undertaking not to retaliate on his tormentors. I saw them in their anguish and I was tormented with them. But I also saw them in their greatness and I was proud of them. Discipline? What is military discipline, discipline in action, compared with this discipline of inaction, when your whole soul cries out for retaliation and retribution. A human "order" would have been of no avail here. The order came from "somewhere," from the depths of Jewish history; and it was obeyed. We were spared the catastrophe of catastrophes. And before many months went by the revolt embraced the whole people. The persecutors and persecuted of yesterday went out to battle together, to a common battle for our people and our country. . . .

Chapter XI

The "Altalena" Affair

To avoid bloody civil war at all costs—this principle, tempered in the sufferings of the "season," we observed years later in the test of blood and fire of the "Altalena."

It is no longer a secret that this famous arms-ship served as the instrument of a sinister plot. When Mr. Ben Gurion, on the rostrum of the first Israel parliament, modestly boasted "I have some part in that ship lying not far away from here," he was interrupted by a question from a member of *Mapai:* "But who was it who urged you to do it?"

Mr. Ben Gurion was silent. His silence was perhaps even more eloquent than any words. The attack on the "Altalena" was prepared in secret and with intent. The boat was destroyed by fire. Dense smoke rolled out of her and enveloped her. We cannot extinguish that fire; but we will seek to dissipate the screen of smoke.

The tragic fact was that the "Altalena" was late in coming. Had this landing-craft arrived off the shores of Eretz Israel immediately on the liquidation of British rule, that is, in the middle of May, 1948, the whole condition of the nation would have been radically changed. We should then have placed at the disposal of the Government and the Army eight or ten battalions, fully equipped with arms and ammunition—instead of their customary equipment, unlimited readiness for self-sacrifice and short-ranged Sten-guns. At our first attack we should have captured Ramleh. This Arab town, besieged by the Irgun Zvai Leumi at the request of the Haganah in order to draw away enemy forces from the Latrun front, was on the point of falling when we had to withdraw. The morale of the inhabitants had been lowered, mainly by the shelling of our 3 inch mortars. Our boys stormed the approaches to the town and in the opening stages captured large parts of it. But lack of arms and ammunition proved fatal. They needed only a few hundred rifles and additional ammunition, but on the Ramleh front that quantity was not available either to us or to the Haganah Command. Three hundred rifles, or six per cent of the number loaded in the hold of the "Altalena". . . .

Had we been able to capture Ramleh at that time—and its conquest depended solely on these additional arms—the united Jewish forces would have broken the Arab front at Latrun and our strategic situation would have been changed fundamentally, its effects being felt as far as Jerusalem, as far as the Old City. With the fall of Ramleh, the fate of Lydda would have been sealed. Thus we should have smashed the enemy on the central front in the first stage of his invasion, instead of only after the first "truce." And the Jewish forces would have been free in the second stage for a full-scale attack on the 'Triangle.' In a word, we should today have held the Western bank of the Jordan—at least.

Fate decreed otherwise. The "Altalena" with her nine hundred soldiers, five thousand rifles, four million rounds of ammunition, three hundred Bren guns, 150 spandaus, five caterpillar-track armoured vehicles, thousands of air-combat bombs, and the rest of her war equipment, was ready to sail not in the middle of May but only in the second week of June. We received first news of her departure from a French port on the London radio. I was shocked. That very day the "truce" had come into force. Whatever our attitude to the truce might be, I explained to my comrades, we were not entitled to bear the responsibility for the possible consequences of a breach. All the Jewish forces were very tired; the enemy had superior armament. This was no longer an underground partisan-political fight. This was a fight in the open field and the consequences of de-

feat might be destruction for our people. We consequently decided first of all to stop the boat. We did not,
of course, place absolute credence in the B.B.C. report. Perhaps the boat had not yet sailed and the British
Government only wanted to alert the UNO observers?
That day I sent a telegram to our headquarters in
Paris: "Don't send the boat. Await instructions."
Shmuel Katz, in charge in Paris at the time, replied
that my telegram had come the day after the boat's
departure; that he was no longer in contact with her.
He advised us to communicate direct with the "Altalena."

Our first radio message to the "Altalena" was "Keep
away. Await instructions!" We did not know whether
the boat received the message. Later we learnt that
while she was still far from our shores her instruments
worked in only one direction: she received our messages but could not reply. Immediately after sending
this telegram, late at night, we communicated with the
Israel Department of Security and gave them detailed
information about the boat and its cargo of munitions.
Now—we said to the representatives of the Security
Ministry—it is for you to decide whether to permit the
boat to come, or divert her. Official propaganda, hiding behind the smokescreen, pretended that the Irgun
had brought over the "Altalena" in order to prepare
an armed revolt against the Government of Israel.

The decision of the Government—or the Security
Ministry—was that the arms-ship of the Irgun must be
brought in, and as quickly as possible. The decision
was conveyed to me by Israel Galili the day after our
late-night conversation at Irgun Headquarters. Anxiety
gave way to joy. We were all delighted. The burden of
responsibility had been taken off our shoulders. The
Government, after all, knew the situation and its requirements. There was apparently no choice. Arms
were lacking. In particular, there was a shortage of
rifles—yes, ordinary rifles, the basic weapons in the
Eretz Israel battles—and there was a shortage of British .303 ammunition, for lack of which a large part of

the *Haganah* arms was out of action. All these urgent requirements would be brought in the "Altalena."

As for the UNO prohibitions, we would manage somehow. After all, the Government knew. In the circumstances this was no question of morals. Nobody was helping our attacked people; the situation was one of life and death; and we thanked God that the Government understood the situation, weighed what had to be weighed and disregarded what in the circumstances it was forbidden to take into account. At once a code message went out to the "Altalena" where, as we later learnt, it aroused even greater joy. Instead of "Keep Away" it was now "Full steam ahead."

This fact must be re-emphasized, for it is from this point onwards in this sad history that the black smoke-screen has been thrown up. The Provisional Government later published sanctimonious statements that while the Irgun had tried to disregard the UNO truce orders, the Government, in observance of international law, was compelled to destroy the arms brought to Eretz Israel in contravention of the truce.

I must therefore repeat: the Provisional Government knew about the arms ship sailing towards our shores against the instructions which had arrived too late. And it was the Government that decided to bring the "Altalena" in during the truce period. Otherwise she would not have come.

After the Government had ordered the boat to be landed without delay, a conference began between the Security Ministry and our Staff concerning the unloading of the arms and their distribution. The Irgun Zvai Leumi was then an open military force recognised by the official institutions. Before the declaration of the State, the Greater Council of the Zionist Organisation had confirmed the agreement for military co-operation between us and the Haganah. When independence was declared on the 14th May, 1948, there was no immediate formation of a unified army. Haganah continued to exist; and the Irgun, whose soldiers were stationed on various fronts and in some sectors were fighting together with Haganah men, also continued to exist. The well-known journalist, Dr. Azriel Karlibach, at that time published an open letter to me, brimming with enthusiasm and demanding that, now we had beaten the British we should work for establishment of a unified Israel Army. I replied on our radio that several days earlier we had publicly called for the establishment of a unified Army to replace the military organisations. But it depended on the Government, not on us.

When the creation of the Army was announced we continued as a recognised military organisation until the integration of our forces into the Army was completed. In the operational orders of the Front Line and Brigade Commanders, Irgun units appeared as an inseparable part of the Army forces. In liberated Jaffa which, at our request, had been divided into two sectors, one sector was garrisoned by the Irgun. The Prime Minister, Mr. David Ben Gurion, one day visited Jaffa and also inspected Irgun units, who presented arms. I was told that Mr. Ben Gurion, moved at the incident, said to the escort: "I didn't know they had such boys."

Afterwards the Prime Minister sent the following letter to Sergeant Haim, the officer in command of our occupying force in Jaffa:

State of Israel
Provisional Government

22 May, 1948

To the Commander of the Irgun soldiers in Jaffa. Until further instructions you and your men are at the sole orders of the Military Governor of Jaffa, I Chizik.

(*signed*) David Ben Gurion
Head of the Provisional Government and Minister
of Security.

We pointed out to Mr. Ben Gurion's aide-de-camp that it was not customary for a Prime Minister to communicate directly with a local officer. We were gratified at the official recognition of "the Irgun Zvai Leumi sol-

diers in Jaffa," but out of concern for the tender growth
of our State we wished to uphold the status of the
Prime Minister as such.

With his aide and his colleagues we continued to
discuss the creation of a unified army. The details of
the discussion are related elsewhere. Here it is sufficient to mention that we agreed that the Irgun should
bring into the Army complete battalions with their
officers. But as the organisation of battalions required
time, it was agreed between us that we would set up
a temporary Staff of the Irgun Zvai Leumi, approved
by the Prime Minister and Minister of Security. By the
time the "Altalena" arrived we had organized and inte-
grated several battalions into the Army. Other regiments were still in process of organisation, their men
being still dispersed in smaller units on various fronts.
Our Staff was thus an official and recognised body,
when it was called to discuss with the representatives
of the Ministry of Security the unloading of the "Altalena" arms.

We decided jointly on the point on the coast at
which the boat should be brought in. This involved a
change in the instruction we had given the captain in
April. The "Altalena" as she waited for her men, her
arms and her instructions, had been plying for some
months between European ports and the north coast of
Africa. She had been acquired by the Hebrew Committee of National Liberation and the American League
for a Free Palestine, and we had intended bringing her
in while the British forces were still ruling—with men
or arms or both.

At that time we had decided that she should anchor
off Tel Aviv, because by then (the end of 1947) the
British forces had left the Tel Aviv-Petah Tikvah area
as the first instalment of evacuation. The precise spot
we had fixed for landing was Frishman Street. This detail too must be remembered well if the smokescreen
of subsequent distortion is to be dissipated.

A Ministry of Security expert proposed that the boat
should not come in at Tel Aviv but at Givat Olga or
Kfar Vitkin near Nathanya, and so avoid the attention

of U.N.O. observers. Our experts agreed; to them it
made no difference at what point on the coast the boat
arrived. The essential thing was the unloading of the
arms. We, who suspected nothing because we plotted
nothing, never imagined there were other motives than
those affecting the unloading. So that day a further
message went out to the "Altalena": to alter course
and proceed to Kfar Vitkin.

The discussion then proceeded on the distribution
of the arms. We proposed that one-fifth of the arms
should be sent to Jerusalem to the Irgun Zvai Leumi
units there, while the rest should be distributed
throughout the unified army, among battalions consisting of Irgun men as well as among other battalions.
Our proposal was just and justified. There were most
serious reasons for it.

2

Fully to appreciate the affair of the "Altalena" we
must sketch out briefly the military circumstances at
the time of her arrival and immediately before. It also
explains our proposals for the distribution of the "Altalena's" arms.

The period was one of transition. Jerusalem was a
"separate entity." Israel Sovereignty had not been extended to our capital. The official leadership, which had
accepted the U.N.O. decision on partition in its entirety, had resigned itself to the imposition of an international regime in Jerusalem. Mr. Ben Gurion had demanded at a meeting of the Histadruth (T.U.C.) Executive that his movement exert its utmost influence to
prevent even any talk of "conquering Jerusalem" or extending the boundaries of the State. Consequently the
Israel Army was not established in Jerusalem even
after it had been formed and operating elsewhere. In
Jerusalem there remained the Haganah, led by Regional Commander David Shaltiel, the Irgun Zvai Leumi
which fought in co-operation with the Haganah, and
the F.F.I. which had carried out operations without any
formal agreement with the Haganah. But forsaken

Jerusalem, besieged and shelled, cried out for arms—particularly after the catastrophe at Nebi Daniel where, within range of the British guns, a large Haganah unit surrendered to the Arabs and a large quantity of Jewish arms was destroyed or fell into enemy hands.

Our Irgun comrades, too, had no arms for open fight. They cried out to us: Arms! We cried out to our representatives abroad: Arms! But the enemy secret service stood in our way. There were complications. A number of consignments which Yoel had prepared for despatch to us were discovered before they were loaded on to the ships. We sent a quantity of "home-made" arms to Jerusalem. We had in fact nothing to spare. Had we sent them a substantial part of the machine-guns or ammunition we had captured from the British forces we should have strengthened them, but not adequately; and then we should not have been able to capture Jaffa.

Our soldiers in the capital had a small quantity of arms—and they achieved wonders with it, particularly as they had to do most of their own planning. Against the British regime all operational planning had been concentrated in the hands of the High Command. In the war with the Arabs we had to give wide discretion to the regional commanders in Haifa and Jerusalem. This change was the unavoidable consequence of the new conditions, disrupted communications and impassable roads.

Our boys fought a heroic battle in the Old City of Jerusalem. The garrison there was very small: less than a hundred Irgun men, less than 200 Haganah men. Their arms were poor: a few machine-guns, rifles, Sten-guns; very little ammunition. Yet the defenders of the Old City held out with amazing courage against the "irregular" Arab forces and against the regular Arab Legion fighting under British officers and supported by heavy guns and tanks.

The battle went on for weeks. At first there were misunderstandings between the Haganah men and ours. The education in hatred bore fruit even here. Our boys were discriminated against in the matter of food rations. But as time went on relations improved. The common danger brought hearts nearer to one another. The Haganah men came into close contact with the Irgun men and learnt that they bore no resemblance to the descriptions painted in the hate propaganda. There were joint consultations. There were joint preparatory operations. One of our officers gave the Haganah men a course in mine-laying which was of the utmost importance in the defence of the Jewish Quarter and for securing the defence posts.

Before the 14th of May we succeeded in smuggling Gideon, a fine student of mathematics and one of our best officers, into the Old City. (This was "Gideon the Third"; we had a number of Gideons.) With Gideon, who took over the command of our men, a number of other officers and men were brought in, as well as some arms and explosives. On the 14th of May all contact between the Old City and the New was broken. Both were besieged.

Gideon set up a workshop in the Old City for making primitive hand-grenades, which proved of considerable value in repelling enemy attacks. Despite the difficult conditions, he tried to take the offensive. In one clash our men stormed and captured an important strategic position: the Armenian Church, which dominated the Jewish Quarter. The priest thereupon demanded the evacuation of our force from the church area, promising that the Arabs also would not be permitted to use it. Gideon was ordered to withdraw his forces from a position which was vital for the defence of the Jewish Quarter; he did so with a heavy heart. The promise on behalf of the Arabs was not kept. Several hours after our men had withdrawn the Arabs came into the church and opened murderous fire on the Hebrew defenders.

The civilian inhabitants of the Jewish Quarter in the Old City were in despair, particularly after the severe attacks. One of the local rabbis urged surrender. His demand was rejected by both the Irgun and the Haganah. The situation grew worse. A section of the civilian population among whom were many women and children persisted in the demand for the cessation of the hopeless battle. The aid brought to the defenders of the Old City on the one occasion when the Palmach[1] broke through did not improve the situation. The reinforcements brought in consisted of eighty members of *Mishmar Ha'am* (Home Guard). They had very little notion how to handle arms, and certainly did not help to strengthen morale. From the Jericho road the enemy guns continued to shell the Jewish Quarter. The number of dead and wounded steadily grew. Gideon pledged that he and his comrades would fight to their last bullet. But the gallant stand could not, in those circumstances, last very long. There was no food in the Old City. There was scarcely any water. Ammunition was running out. The commander of the Haganah units was wounded; Gideon was wounded. The boys went on fighting. Boys of ten and twelve showed what Jewish children were capable of in the hour of trial. Heedless of enemy fire, they carried ammunition from one post to the other. The position from which resistance continued to the very last moment was the Irgun post at Nissan Bek. But there was nothing left to fight with. Most of the defenders were dead or wounded. The survivors were exhausted. And so the City of David, the Old City, fell into the hands of the enemy. Deep mourning descended on us all.

The attempt to liberate the Old City was renewed after the first truce. But for some reason—some allege that in certain Jewish political quarters the Old City with its Holy Places is regarded as a "headache"— and despite the urgent pressure of the Jerusalem Irgun officers, the attack was delayed until the very last day before the second truce. It was only a few hours before the second truce was due to begin that four companies of the Haganah, three of the Irgun and one of the F.F.I. were ordered into action. The Irgun detachment included the company which had just been engaged in heavy fighting in the capture of Malha, south-east of Jerusalem, where it had lost eighteen men. But their weari-

---

[1] The more thoroughly trained section of the Haganah.

ness and depression disappeared as if by magic when they learnt that the objective was the Old City. It was in fervent spirits they went out. But that operation, too, ended in mourning. The Haganah and F.F.I. failed to breach the wall of the City. The Irgun men forced a breach and established a bridgehead inside the Walls, thus opening the road to conquest. But the hour of the truce—five a.m.—had arrived. Our men while fighting were instructed to withdraw. The truce was, of course, broken by the enemy on a number of fronts. But in Jerusalem we were called on to observe it to the second. And the City of David was left waiting for its liberation without which there can be no security for the rest of Jerusalem—without which there can be no security for the State of Israel.

Before Jerusalem was completely beleaguered in May our men, with the few arms they had, carried out a number of important offensive operations. In Jerusalem, as elsewhere, we were the first to pass over from the defensive to the offensive. At the Jaffa Gate and the Damascus Gate our soldiers penetrated the enemy lines a number of times and inflicted heavy casualties.

The Arab village of Sha'afat, which served as a base for murderous attacks on Jewish convoys, was heavily attacked by an Irgun Assault Unit. And on the 9th of April our men together with an F.F.I. unit, captured the village of Dir Yassin.

Dir Yassin, lying some two thousand feet above sea-level, was an important link in the chain of Arab positions enclosing Jerusalem from the West. Through Dir Yassin Arab forces from Ein Kerem and Bethlehem crossed to the Kastel front, whence they attacked Jewish convoys along the only road from Jerusalem to the coast. After the capture of Dir Yassin—actually the first Arab village to be captured by Jewish forces—the Haganah commander in Jerusalem announced that its capture was of no military value and was, indeed, contrary to the general plan for the defence of Jerusalem. We had, to our regret, to refute Mr. Shaltiel with the aid of a letter from—Mr. Shaltiel. Raanan, the Irgun commander in Jerusalem, radioed to us the following letter he had received from the Haganah Regional Commander:

> "I learn that you plan an attack on Dir Yassin. I wish to point out that the capture of Dir Yassin and holding it is one stage in our general plan. I have no objection to your carrying out the operation provided you are able to hold the village. If you are unable to do so I warn you against blowing up the village which will result in its inhabitants abandoning it and its ruins and deserted houses being occupied by foreign forces. This situation will increase our difficulties in the general struggle. A second conquest of the place will involve us in heavy sacrifices. Furthermore, if foreign forces enter the place this will upset the plan . . .'

When we published this letter we ended with those three points after the word 'plan.' The national interest required that we should not reveal what that plan was. Today those three points are superfluous. It can be revealed that in their place in the original letter there came the highly significant words: 'for establishing an airfield.' That airfield was established at Dir Yassin and, for a time, served as the only means of communication between besieged Jerusalem and the coast. Re-reading that letter we may draw certain conclusions. Its language may not have been in conformity with the requirements of style. Mr. Shaltiel's later verbal declaration was not in conformity with the truth. But the capture of Dir Yassin was not in conflict with the general plan for the defence of Jerusalem. On the contrary: "The capture of Dir Yassin and holding it are one stage in the general plan." Dir Yassin was captured with the knowledge of the Haganah and with the approval of its Commander.

Apart from the military aspect, there is a moral aspect to the story of Dir Yassin. At that village, whose name was publicized throughout the world, both sides suffered heavy casualties. We had four killed and nearly forty wounded. The number of casualties was nearly forty per cent of the total number of the attackers. The Arab troops suffered casualties three times as heavy. The fighting was thus very severe. Yet the hostile propaganda, disseminated throughout the world, deliberately ignored the fact that the civilian population of Dir Yassin was actually given a warning by us before the battle began. One of our tenders carrying a loud speaker was stationed at the entrance to the village and it exhorted in Arabic all women, children and aged to leave their houses and to take shelter on the slope of the hill. By giving this humane warning our fighters threw away the element of complete surprise, and thus increased their own risk in the ensuing battle. A substantial number of the inhabitants obeyed the warning and they were unhurt. A few did not leave their stone houses—perhaps because of the confusion. The fire of the enemy was murderous—to which the number of our casualties bears eloquent testimony. Our men were compelled to fight for every house; to overcome the enemy they used large numbers of hand-grenades. And the civilians who had disregarded our warnings suffered inevitable casualties.

The education which we gave our soldiers throughout the years of revolt was based on the observance of the traditional laws of war. We never broke them unless the enemy first did so and thus forced us, in accordance with the accepted custom of war, to apply reprisals. I am convinced, too, that our officers and men wished to avoid a single unnecessary casualty in the Dir Yassin battle. But those who throw stones of

[1] To counteract the loss of Dir Yassin, a village of strategic importance, Arab headquarters at Ramallah broadcast a crude atrocity story, alleging a massacre by Irgun troops of women and children in the village. Certain Jewish officials, fearing the Irgun men as political rivals, seized upon this Arab *gruel* propaganda to smear the Irgun. An eminent Rabbi was induced to reprimand the Irgun before he had had time to sift the truth. Out of evil, however, good came. This Arab propaganda spread a legend of terror amongst Arabs and Arab

denunciation at the conquerors of Dir Yassin[1] would
do well not to don the cloak of hypocrisy.

In connection with the capture of Dir Yassin the
Jewish Agency found it necessary to send a letter of
apology to Abdullah, whom Mr. Ben Gurion, at a
moment of great political emotion, called "the wise
ruler who seeks the good of his people and this country." The "wise ruler," whose mercenary forces demolished Gush Etzion and flung the bodies of its heroic
defenders to the birds of prey, replied with feudal su-
perciliousness. He rejected the apology and replied that
the Jews were all to blame and that he did not believe
in the existence of "dissidents." Throughout the Arab
world and the world at large a wave of lying propaganda was let loose about "Jewish atrocities."

The enemy propaganda was designed to besmirch
our name. In the result it helped us. Panic overwhelmed
the Arabs of Eretz Israel. Kolonia village, which had
previously repulsed every attack of the Haganah, was
evacuated overnight and fell without further fighting.
Beit-Iksa was also evacuated. These two places over-
looked the main road; and their fall, together with the
capture of Kastel by the Haganah, made it possible to
keep open the road to Jerusalem. In the rest of the
country, too, the Arabs began to flee in terror, even
before they clashed with Jewish forces. Not what happened in Dir Yassin, but what was invented about Dir
Yassin, helped to carve the way to our decisive victories on the battlefield. The legend of Dir Yassin
helped us in particular in the saving of Tiberias and
the conquest of Haifa.

The British Commander at Haifa announced the
evacuation of his forces at the end of April. The Haganah knew the date and mobilized its forces for the decisive clash. At the request of the Haganah North Regional Commander Irgun units, commanded by Amiel,
also went into action, and were ordered to capture a

troops, who were seized with panic at the mention of Irgun
soldiers. The legend was worth half a dozen battalions to the
forces of Israel. The "Dir Yassin Massacre" lie is still propagated by Jew-haters all over the world.

fortified enemy building dominating Hehalutz Street,
the main artery of Hadar Harcarmel. Our men
launched a sudden, surprise attack—and the building
was captured. Our men were loudly cheered by the
inhabitants of Hadar Harcarmel. They then went on
to Wadi Nisnas, captured the whole Quarter and continued to advance towards the purely Arab Quarter.
Meanwhile the Haganah was carrying out successful attacks on the other fronts in Haifa. All the Jewish forces
proceeded to advance through Haifa like a knife
through butter. The Arabs began fleeing in panic,
shouting: "Dir Yassin!"

We must bow our heads to all the Jewish soldiers
irrespective of organisational affiliation, who fought
the Arab invaders with supreme bravery. They all had
great victories. They all had their bitter defeats. They
all suffered from insufficient equipment. We never
taunted others with retreats or defeats. But what fantastic and untrue tales have not been told of our comrades' retreat at Sheikh Jarrah? Everywhere we lacked
arms and ammunition. All this is part of the background to the discussions on the distribution of the
arms of the "Altalena."

Chapter XII

When the Heart Weeps

It can readily be understood why we wanted a part of the good arms we brought in the "Altalena" to be sent to our units in Jerusalem and why we wanted our units in the Army to get their fair share too. It is a natural and accepted tradition in every army, that the commander of every large unit should concern himself with its adequate equipment. Our army was born in the midst of battles. Organisational and spiritual unity was not a matter of tradition, but of goodwill. It was not an easy matter to send our comrades to an army whose officers had hated the underground, persecuted it, besmirched it, kidnapped its members and handed over its officers. Only a few months before the State was established a new wave of organised sadism on the part of the Haganah, acting under the instructions of the official Jewish leaders, had flooded the country. Blood had been spilled. Great nobility of spirit and considerable persuasion were needed in order to forget the past for the sake of our embattled people. Thousands of our boys went into the army, to the front line of fighting. Where were they not to be found? They stood at Negbah and, together with their comrades (their persecutors of yesterday), wrote one of the most brilliant pages in the Jewish war of defence. Led by veteran commander Gil and singing the Irgun song "On the Barricades," they opened the road to Beersheba by capturing from the Egyptians a vital strategic strong-point. They captured Yavneh in the south, and Tarshiha in Galilee, and a huge area of territory in the Mountains of Ephraim. They served on other fronts, fighting and giving their lives for their country's freedom, as befitted its liberators from alien rule, as befitted Irgun fighters. But it cannot be denied that their hearts were filled with pain and anxiety. They loved the Irgun. They had given it their all. And the Irgun had given them everything. They had fought in its ranks for years. They had gone forward, under its victorious banner, to battle and danger, to concentration camp and torture-cell and death. The Irgun was no longer just a military organisation; it had become their life.

I remember our last parade of officers. In the hall there were hundreds of experienced, veteran fighters. In many cases we saw each other for the first time. A time for rejoicing? Certainly. Had we not been privileged to emerge from the underground? Had we not seen the victory with our own eyes? But the occasion was a very sad one. I told my beloved officers that henceforth I was no longer their Commander. Other officers, officers of the unified Jewish Army, would now lead them and to them they owed unqualified allegiance. The Irgun Zvai Leumi had ceased to exist as a military force. There was dead silence in the hall. I saw battle-seasoned veterans, 'men of iron,' who had faced death again and again—with tears in their eyes. "The old order changeth, yielding place to new." A whole world, the world of a glorious and pure ideal, of comradeship and loyalty, a noble and uplifting world, had gone—perhaps never to return. True, it had been worth while. Everything was worth while. We had won. Our nation had arisen again. But the Irgun. . . . And who would lead us now?

There was much anxiety—it cannot be denied. The men who were about to take command of our members had been systematically trained to hate them. No, it was not simple at all. Orders were not of much use here. What we needed was a great deal of persuasion to heal wounds many of which were still open. It was not only our right, therefore, but our duty to see to it that the units we sent into the army should receive adequate and efficient weapons so that they should go into the field with confidence and soldierly self-assurance. As I have

said, even in normal circumstances this concern would
have been natural and justified. All the more so in the
special circumstances, in the *very* special circumstances
in which our Army arose. What we had yearned for in
the days of our Sten-guns, the possibility of giving our
fighters effective arms, was now to be brought about by
the arrival of our arms-ship, the "Altalena." We did not
demand its cargo "for ourselves," as the inventors of the
"armed revolt" myth alleged. There were no longer any
"ourselves" to ask it for. The Irgun had ceased—except in Jerusalem—to be a military force. Our men
were in the army, or were fighting together with army
units on various fronts while awaiting their organised
entry into the Army. All of them were under the command of the Army General Staff. All we demanded was
that out of the cargo of arms which we had brought to
our country after so much effort and toil, adequate
equipment should be given to the former Irgun soldiers
now in the Army.

Israel Galili, previously Commander of the Haganah, and at that time Deputy to the Minister of Security, informed me on the telephone that the Ministry
had agreed to our proposal about Jerusalem. Twenty
per cent of the arms from the "Altalena" were to be al-
lotted to that front. We were overjoyed—and did not
attempt to scrutinise the exact wording of his statement.
Only much later did it become clear precisely what the
real intention behind this "agreement" was. The twenty
per cent was to be sent only to Haganah troops in Jerusalem.

We continued for some time to discuss with Galili the
question of the distribution of the arms. In one of our
many and lengthy conversations I said to him:

"Had the boat come several weeks ago, as we had
planned, we of the Irgun would have had all the arms.
Wouldn't you agree that our boys ought to come into
the Army at least fully-armed and equipped? You yourself demanded that in view of the gravity of the situation all arms and equipment in the possession of the
Irgun should be issued to the Irgun boys who were going into the Army. What, then, is the difference? These

particular arms were merely late in arriving. Our boys
are already in the Army or will be within a matter of
days. It would only mean that they will be mobilised
with the full equipment which we would in any case
have given them. What is wrong with that? Why can't
you agree?"

Our arguments were fruitless. Our proposals were rejected. A day and a night passed. Meanwhile the "Altalena," in accordance with the orders of the Provisional
Government, was ploughing its way towards the Eretz
Israel shore at Kfar Vitkin. We continued to discuss
plans for unloading with the representatives of the Security Ministry.

Galili then informed me that as no agreement had
been reached on the distribution of the arms, they would
not help us to unload them. "We wash our hands of the
unloading of the arms," he declared.

This statement represents the turning-point in the
"Altalena" affair.

The Government negotiated with us about the joint
organisation of the landing of the arms and their distribution. They rejected our just and reasonable proposals. In this they were within their rights, at least
formally. The Government could have said: "We shall
not allow the Irgun to unload the arms." They could
have said to us: "In the circumstances we forbid you to
bring the ship to the shores of the country." For, from
the moment the ship sailed, we had placed it and its
cargo at the disposal of the Government.

This is the whole truth. But in case there should be
some malicious individuals who wish to cast doubts on
the truth of this statement, it is possible to prove it even
against the arguments of the most spiteful and the most
fanatical.

The ship, as had been agreed with the Ministry of
Security, was to anchor off Givat Olga or Kfar Vitkin.
Could we possibly have reached that spot from Tel
Aviv to meet the ship if the Government had said so?
It would, after all, have been enough to block the nar-
row secondary road leading from the main Haifa-Tel
Aviv highway to the Mapai village, and our trucks could

not have got anywhere near the landing point. On the other hand, even if we assume, purely for the sake of argument, that we had by some miracle got through to the ship in such circumstances, would it have occurred to anybody in his senses—in the face of army resistance —to walk into that narrowest of bottlenecks, a completely isolated beach, without equipment, without provisions, without even water! Evilly disposed people may wish to doubt the truth of what we say; but they cannot deny that the Irgun had some acquaintance with strategy and tactics. Yet this is what they asked people to believe of us: that we of the Irgun Zvai Leumi intended to start an "armed revolt" precisely there, at Kfar Vitkin, where our men would have been cut off from the outset, even if they had been able to get there without the consent of the Army.

Our statement is demonstrably unassailable. I repeat, therefore, that had the Government said one word to cause us to think that they were opposed to the unloading of the arms it would never have entered our minds to unload them in defiance of such opposition. But "somebody had urged somebody to do something clever"—and the Government very carefully did *not* say the word. The Government said: "We shall not help you unload the arms." We shall *not help*." Nothing more.

The Government's refusal to co-operate in unloading the arms was a serious blow. We had neither the lighterage, nor the vehicles, nor the required tackle. Even the number of men we could throw into the task after mobilising nearly every one of those who were available, was too small for the purpose. On the spot we were helped by a number of Palmach men in a boat. Today I have no doubt that they were sent not so much to help as to spy on us. At the time we accepted their help gladly and gratefully, without a shadow of suspicion. Why should we have suspected?

Despite the difficulties, we threw ourselves wholeheartedly into the work. True, the Government had said they would not help us, but in view of their dire need of these arms it seemed logically highly probable that

they might change their mind. Moreover, this was not
the only difficult task we had carried out by ourselves.
The work was tackled enthusiastically. The moral
strength and endeavour of the boys seemed to be doubled and trebled. No Salonican stevedore could have
achieved as much as was achieved during those stifling
summer days on the sea-shore, under the burning sun,
without food and with scarcely any water, while the unloading was begun.

And what would have happened if, without assistance
but without interference, we had unloaded all the arms
and all the ammunition from the boat? The evilly-dis-
posed whispered that we intended then to convey the
arms to our underground armouries. But the truth is
that by that time we had no more secret amouries. We
had given the army all our arms and equipment, and
they had full knowledge of where all our concentration-
points had been. How on earth, long after we had
emerged from the underground and after all our people
were known to the Army, could we have hidden arms
enough to equip ten infantry battalions? Yet another
fact worth mentioning: even after Galili had informed
us that no help would be given in unloading the arms,
we still invited the Army Staff to come and supervise
the unloading. One of them twice promised to come,
and once even promised that he would "privately" send
a number of trucks to help us. . . . No less enlightening
is the fact that in all our conversations we emphasised
that the full supervision of the arms, after they were unloaded, would be handed over to the Army. All this was
apparently part of the "secret preparations" for a "revolt against the Government!"

Had we unloaded all the arms from the "Altalena" all
of them would have gone into the hands of the unified
army whose establishment we had called for from the
moment the State was set up. Twenty per cent of the
arms would have been despatched with the Government's consent, to Jerusalem—to Jerusalem as such
and not to any particular force there—and the Old City
might still, in spite of Shaltiel's "dilatoriness" have been
regained from the enemy.

But only part of the arms were unloaded—and went into action only after the killing of numbers of Irgun men. Those arms proved very useful. The "Altalena" was destroyed—but she gave the Jewish people some two thousand modern rifles, about a million rounds of .303 ammunition, and 250 Bren and other machine-guns. At Ramleh and Lydda these much-needed arms —and how they had been needed!—gave decisive service. The ammunition from the "Altalena" brought into action not only the Bren guns that had come with her, but also other Brens which for a long time had lain idle and useless. The "Altalena" arms proved a decisive factor in the fight against the Arab invaders.

And not only her arms. "Altalena" brought over a battalion of fighters. These young people were over-whelmed with joy when they reached the shores of their Homeland. I saw many of them kneeling and kissing the salty, damp sand on the shore. In my ears I still hear the echo of their joyful cries as their boats ran on to the beach.

How their joy was silenced, how they were welcomed is known. Nevertheless they came, and they entered the Army. And in the Army they served faithfully and fought courageously. The boys of the "Altalena" served on many fronts, participated in many victories, from Tarshiha to Eylat. Many of them distinguished them-selves by their outstanding gallantry. Not a few fell in battle. Subjected to the most terrible and most trying of tribulations, they yet knew how to pass the supreme test of love for their country.

These boys must be mentioned also from another point of view. We were engaged, according to our po-litical detractors' story, in an 'armed revolt.' But behold, you experts in armed revolts, how these good-for-noth-ing Irgunists organized their rebellion. Their ship brings a whole battalion of fighters, and carries at the same time a mass of modern weapons. What would be more natural than to place these arms in the hands of the "rebel" fighters? In a twinkling, there on the shore, the organizer of the revolt would have had a complete bat-talion, manned, officered, armed and equipped. But, in

actual fact, what do these "revolt-organizers" do? They
—with the help of a detachment of Palmach, their bit-
terest political persecutors of a short while previously—
first of all land the fighters and send them off—unarmed
—to a distant camp in Nathanya to rest and to sleep,
under the supervision of the Army; while the greased
up arms are unloaded not by soldiery but by experienced stevedores who had been scraped together from
various ports in Eretz Israel. Such was the next stage in
this most peculiar "armed-revolt". . . .

There had been a last-minute delay in the arrival of
the "Altalena." The ship, which by the Government's
instructions, had been ordered to alter its course for
Kfar Vitkin, did not at first anchor there because the
captain could not see the shore-signals which were to
bring him in. He therefore first proceeded to Tel Aviv
and only afterwards sailed up the coast to Kfar Vitkin.
But dawn was approaching, and fearing lest the ship be
spotted by the UNO observers, we decided to postpone
the unloading until the next evening.

After sending the boat off to sea, we returned to Tel
Aviv and at once communicated with the Ministry of
Security. We informed the Security Ministry's liaison
officer that the boat would return that evening. We even
asked whether he thought we were right in not unloading by daylight. He replied "Of course you're right.
I'll tell Israel (Galili) about it." We again invited him
to come and supervise the unloading. He replied that he
might come, and might even send along some lorries to
help in the work. . . .

At dusk the ship returned to Kfar Vitkin. We quickly
landed the men, and began unloading the arms. We
worked all through that night, and were continuing in
the early morning hours. A white UNO aeroplane hovered over us. The ship had been observed. It was essential, now, to speed up the unloading at all costs.

Suddenly we noticed that we were surrounded on all
sides by troops. A few minutes later I received an ultimatum from the local Army Commander, a *ten minute*
ultimatum. I sent word to the officer that this was no

matter that could be settled in ten minutes, and proposed we should meet. Meanwhile, Yaacov Meridor was invited to go to Kfar Vitkin and Nathanya to talk to the heads of the Local Councils who were understandably anxious to avoid undesirable developments. Yaacov explained the situation to them. They promised to communicate with the Government authorities. In the evening UNO observers arrived—an American officer and a French officer. Representatives of the Government, who were standing near by, told us not to permit the observers to enter the shore area. The UNO observers asked to see the ship. We replied to them courteously that in the circumstances we could not allow them to pass. They went away.

We were still surrounded by Government troops on all sides. Somebody proposed that the ship should proceed to Tel Aviv, to the point opposite Frishman Street originally marked on the captain's map. In this way we could extricate ourselves from these siege conditions and I would be able to communicate directly with the Government and put an end to what I still hoped was a perilous misunderstanding somewhere. I was doubtful about leaving the boys, surrounded as they were. But Meridor insisted that I go.

"Here you won't be able to do a thing for us," he said. "I want you to go so that you can straighten out this muddle."

We called the boys together, to take leave of them.

Suddenly, we were attacked from all sides, without warning. With machine-guns, with mortars. I wanted to reverse decisions and remain. Yaacov stood his ground: "You go. This will probably soon blow over. I am responsible here. You have to get us out of this. The boat may blow up if it is hit by a shell. . . ."

This is a very important moment in the dissipation of our detractors' propaganda "smoke-screen." They alleged that we brought the boat deliberately to a point on the foreshore of Tel Aviv opposite the Kaete Dan Hotel because it was at that time the residence of the UNO observers. They said, moreover, that Yaacov

who (in order to avoid bloodshed) signed the agreement of surrender with the Army Commander, undertook to hand the ship over to him. These stories are
demonstrably false. We brought the ship opposite to
Frishman Street, only because this was the destination point marked, in accordance with the original
April plan, on the ship's chart. As for Yaacov, at the
moment when he signed the agreement at Kfar Vitkin
the ship had already arrived at Tel Aviv.

When, on board the "Altalena," we arrived off Tel
Aviv shortly after midnight we were welcomed by a
number of shots from the shore. Binyamin, who was in
command of the men on the ship, insisted that I remain
on deck. We did not return the fire. With daylight we
saw that our point of destination on the beach was surrounded by soldiers. We informed them and repeated
our promise to them that in no circumstances would
we open fire on them. We called upon them also to refrain from firing on us. Our vessel was surrounded not
only from the landwards but from the sea as well. Three
corvettes had closed in upon us and were covering us.
One of them had opened fairly heavy small arms fire on
the little rowing boat in which we went out to the
"Altalena" at Kfar Vitkin. Only skilful manoeuvre by
the ship's captain, Munroe Fine, had saved our little
party in the boat from certain destruction. Fine, one
of the bravest men I ever met, cleverly moved the "Altalena" round so that she shielded us from the corvettes' fire. Those were the conditions in which we had
come aboard at Kfar Vitkin. These same corvettes were
threatening us at Tel Aviv.

The "Altalena" had grounded at the point of destination and was by now wedged on the rocks, helpless
and immobile, some 700 yards from dry land. We
therefore decided to unload the arms from where we
were. As the small boat we sent out reached the shore
we were all subjected to a hail of cross-fire. One of our
volunteers from Cuba was killed on the spot. Shmuel
Merlin was hit in the leg. Avraham Stavsky, the organizer of great contingents of "illegal" immigrants in the

'thirties and the chief driving force in the organization of the "Altalena" personnel, was seriously injured. On board the ship the numbers of wounded soon began to mount. Some of the shooting was directed at specific targets. Thus, each time I went up to the captain's bridge it was subjected to particularly intense fire. When I left the bridge, the shooting was directed elsewhere.

Meanwhile our comrades in the town, with whom we had no contact, had tried to break through the Army lines in order to reach the shore opposite our ship. The Palmach commander then offered to "cease fire" provided we unloaded no more arms. To this we agreed. The fire ceased and the unloading ceased. We informed the commander that we had a number of wounded on board. Our small boat had been damaged and could not be used to land them. We asked for a boat to take them off, as there was now no doctor on board and many of them were in a very serious condition.

The Palmach officer promised to send a boat immediately from Tel Aviv port. We waited. One hour, two hours. But no boat came. The condition of the wounded grew worse.

Suddenly . . . something whistled over our heads. Munroe Fine exclaimed: "That's a shell! They'll set the ship on fire!" We called to the Palmach commander, reminding him that he had promised a complete cessation of fire. He did not reply. A second shell, a third, a fourth. They had bracketed the ship and were creeping up to their target. Munroe was in despair. I proposed that he and his American colleagues who were engaged as navigators and not as soldiers, should leave the ship and that the rest of us should remain. He would not hear of it. He pointed out that the ship would inevitably blow up if the shelling continued, in view of her cargo of explosives and that the only way to save her was to hoist a white flag. This he did. But that symbol of surrender amongst civilized combatants did not help. The shells kept on coming. We called again to the Palmach commander. "You undertook to stop firing. Why are you shelling us?" His answer came after a pause. His actual words deserve to go on record:

"There *is* a general 'cease fire' but the order has not yet reached all the units of the Army."

A few minutes later a shell penetrated the belly of the ship. Fire broke out and smoke poured forth. Our first urgent task was to save the wounded. They behaved with great courage. There was no panic. Nobody jumped into the water. Everybody conducted themselves with perfect discipline and calm. The wounded were taken off first. Fine was magnificent. With his ship enveloped in flames he continued at his post on the bridge giving orders quietly and unexcitedly, adding every now and then "Take it easy." He ordered the flooding of the hold and thereby saved not only the lives of all of us on board but also many in the houses on the Tel Aviv shore. Had the vessel exploded the damage must have been widespread. He directed the building of stages for taking off the wounded. One by one they were lowered. All the time shells were falling around the burning ship, and bullets came whistling past the men as they were getting the wounded away on improvised rafts in the water.

Some of our boys from the town broke through to the sea-shore. They used tiny pleasure-boats and, heedless of the danger, of the flames bursting from the hold of the ship, which might have exploded at any moment, they rowed and paddled their fragile craft through the water. They had come to the rescue of their comrades and were determined to do so in spite of everything.

The "Altalena" went up in flames. The arms that remained in it were destroyed, and the ship became the common grave of a number of the brave men who had come as volunteers to fight for their people.

At the hospital Avraham Stavsky, my good fellow-townsman, who by his energy and labour had helped save thousands of Jews from the Nazi death-ovens and bring them to Eretz Israel, died of his wounds. I had lost him too.

Many more were the fearful deeds that were committed in those days in the execution of the Government's plan to rid itself of what it imagined was a serious political rivalry. It was more than sufficient to create a civil war.

But the alien enemy was at the gates of our Motherland. And we swore an oath: "In no circumstances will we use arms against our fellow Jews."

Several days later, Irgun boys, including boys from the "Altalena," were to be found on all the fronts facing the invader—men like Joe Kohn of Philadelphia and Nathan Cashman of London who gave their lives fighting heroically for Jerusalem, Cashman in the attack on Malha and Joe Kohn in the last attack on the Old City.

On that night in 1948 when the "Altalena" was destroyed, I spoke over the radio about the ship, its arms and its dead. I was moved to tears. And there were mighty heroes of all classes who listened to me from their arm-chairs and jeered at my "soft emotionalism." Let them jeer! There are tears of which no man need be ashamed; there are tears of which a man may be proud. Tears do not come only from the eyes; sometimes they well up, like blood, from the heart. There are tears that spring from sorrow; and there are tears that bring salvation.

Whoever has followed my story knows that fate has not pampered me. From my earliest youth I have known hunger and been acquainted with sorrow. And often death has brooded over me, both in the Homeland and on alien soil. But for such things I have never wept. Only on the night when the State was proclaimed; and on the night of the "Altalena". . . . Truly there are tears of salvation as well as tears of grief. There are times when the choice is between blood and tears. Sometimes, as our revolt against the oppressor taught us, it is essential that blood should take the place of tears. And sometimes, as the "Altalena" taught us, it is essential that tears should take the place of blood. This should be remembered, particularly by those who shelled the "Altalena" and killed its men and shot at those, including wounded men, escaping from its flames.

Let them not boast in their hearts of that act which

"somebody urged them to do" nor excuse themselves on his responsibility. Let them remember everything there is to be remembered, beginning with the secret hatching of the plot and ending with the last shell they fired into the burning and bleeding ship. If they remember this, perhaps they will understand the feeling of the man whose life they tried to take: and possibly they may understand that sometimes it is better that one man should pour tears from his heart over an abomination committed in Israel than that many, many should weep over its consequences. . . .

And so it came to pass that there was no fratricidal war in Israel to destroy the Jewish State before it was properly born. In spite of everything—there was no civil war!

Chapter XIII
United Resistance

Summer of 1945. The summer of the end, of the beginning, of the victory, and the horror; of disillusionment and hope. The Second World War ended. And at once the unity of the victors, who had been held together by a negative interest in the war against the common enemy, began to crumble. The contest between West and East had begun, and with it the preparations for a Third World War which would be more terrible than its predecessor and the most gruesome in the history of man. To the Jewish people that summer brought victory over the Teutonic beast—but with his collapse came terror and horror. There was final and official confirmation at last of the mass extermination of European Jewry. Through the bestiality of our enemies, Europe had become one great graveyard for millions of Jews. What we had foreseen had come to pass. Of seventeen million Jews in the whole world, only eleven millions remained. One third of our people had been destroyed wantonly and almost without resistance.

In Eretz Israel the hounding of the Irgun Zvai Leumi, which would neither surrender nor retaliate, went on. Yet our eyes were turned to the future. With the end of the war, the world had opened to us and we were enabled to draw attention to our small corner in it. Wider horizons had been opened for our military struggle as well. The oppressor had expected we should be drawn into a bloody civil war which would assure him of 'peace' and mastery. But we, the rebels, had determined to disappoint him in this, too. With the turning-point that came at the close of World War II we decided not only to continue our struggle but, despite the internal persecutions, to intensify it.

Meanwhile we endeavoured to bring home to the official Jewish circles the fatefulness of the hour; to persuade them to stop dissipating their energies in fighting us and to direct their prowess against the enemy instead. In May, 1945, we sent a comprehensive memorandum to 250 prominent Jews, heads of institutions, party politicians, scientists and economists. In it we put forward a concrete policy.

We propose, we wrote, that the leading personalities in the Yishuv, both in the Jewish Agency and outside it, both party workers and non-party men, should meet and, as a first revolutionary step, set up two institutions:

1. A Provisional Jewish Government.
2. A Supreme National Council.

"It must be assumed that the members of the Provisional Government who subscribe to the constituent declaration, if they do not go underground, will be arrested immediately by the British authorities. They should gladly accept this risk, or this fate, bearing in mind what millions of ordinary Jews and thousands of their spiritual and religious leaders have given for the Jewish people. They should also bear in mind the political significance of this act, both externally, and more particularly, internally, in rallying the masses to their fighting leadership. But for this reason, the 'conference of representatives' must elect a second and third panel of members for the Provisional Government. The identities of *these* members will not be disclosed and they will conduct the struggle underground if the original members are arrested or incapacitated.

"The Supreme National Council, to which the Provisional Government will be responsible, must be chosen from the representatives of all the Jewish parties which, while maintaining their independent policies, will unite on a minimum programme of political, social and economic aims. There is no doubt that such a basis exists both in the political field (Jewish Government, mass repatriation, a free, democratic regime, equality of right for all inhabitants of the country) and in the social field (raising the standard of living of the workers and of all strata and communities lacking adequate means of existence; social insurance, agrarian reform, distribution of agricultural land among its workers, public ownership of public services, etc.)

"The Government will establish: a General Staff to direct the military uprising; a Social Economic Council to direct a general strike in its various forms and to organise supplies; a Foreign Affairs Council to establish contact with international factors; a Legislative Council which will set up independent courts and draft a constitution for the Hebrew Republic; and other institutions which the war and events will require."

2

The reaction to our proposals was characteristic. We sent representatives to a number of the recipients of our memorandum in order to amplify its contents and to receive their reply.

The late Rabbi Meir Berlin, the President of the *Mizrachi,* said to Amitzur: "If you bring me fifty people who are prepared to sign your proposals, I shall be the first to sign, but you know the situation. . . ." Rabbi Berlin was a brave and dignified man. Once, when British searches were at their height, he proposed to my comrades that I should take refuge in his home. I conveyed my thanks to the learned Rabbi for his kind offer. At that time my security conditions were not at all bad and I saw no reason for endangering Rabbi Berlin by my presence in his home.

But we did think it right and just that the party leaders should endanger themselves and risk their positions in order to break the stranglehold tightening round the whole nation. Rabbi Berlin asked us to bring fifty expressions of approval. We did not succeed in obtaining them. We did not even get five. But we did not despair. Even the ridicule of the 'clever' did not impress us. We knew we were right. That was the main thing; and we were not mistaken. Our fundamental proposals, rejected in May, 1945, were accepted and fulfilled in

May, 1948. Three years is not a long time even in the era of the radio and the airplane.

The ridicule did not endure even three years. In fact it evaporated within a few months of the rejection of our proposals. For the great and bitter disillusionment was not long in coming. The General Election in Britain took place, and of all the illusions fostered during the World War only a bitter taste remained.

Eliahu Golomb had assured me, in the only talk I ever had with him in the underground, that if the Labour Party came to power in Britain we should get "at least a part of our demands." This naive credulity was, it seems, not entertained by Golomb alone. It was shared by many of his colleagues in the various Jewish "institutions." No wonder, then, that these harbourers of illusions jumped for joy at the news that Churchill and Eden had been defeated in the elections and had been replaced by Attlee and Bevin. The celebrants drew their confidence from what they called the "traditional friendship" for Zionism of the British Labour-Socialist Movement. They trusted implicitly in the decision of the Blackpool Conference of the Labour Party which demanded the establishment of a Jewish State in Palestine. Mr. Attlee had even promised the transfer of its Arab population. In the period before the Arab invasion in 1948 it was the British authorities who urged the Arabs to flee the country in order to return later as victors. They may therefore be said to have kept half of the Labour Party's promise: the second half. The first we had to fulfil for them.

Whoever remembers those days in 1945, and what came after, must now find it difficult to understand how the official Jewish leaders could have been so pathetically blind. But facts are facts. Official rejoicing at the victory of the Labour Party was exceeded only by that on the 29th November, 1947, when UNO decided to partition Palestine. *Davar*—the leading organ of the official leadership—wrote in 1945: "The victory of the Labour Party, which raised the banner of undiluted Zionism during the election campaign, is therefore a clear victory for the demands of Zionism within British opinion." The following fulsome greeting was sent to the Secretary of the British Labour Party:

> "Our hearty greetings at your brilliant victory. The workers of Palestine have followed your rise to the highest rung of national and international responsibility with friendship and trust. We are confident that in fulfilling your great plans you will act at once for the salvation of the suffering remnants of our people and for the upbuilding of an independent Homeland."

In addition to the jubilant articles and the enthusiastic telegrams, there were electrically-charged speeches and proclamations brimming over with almost messianic promise. There was even popular dancing in the streets of Tel Aviv. In short: Labour's victory—was our victory; the Attlee-Bevin group had reached "the highest rung of national and international responsibility"—and the Jews must therefore rejoice.

It is interesting to compare in this case, too, the reactions of the official leaders with the political sense of the rebels in their cellars allegedly deficient in "broad political vision." While the illusioned were beating the drum of optimism, the Irgun Zvai Leumi published the following statement:

"In Britain a Labour Party Government has taken office. Before coming to power this Party undertook to restore the Land of Israel to the people of Israel as a free State, to which all the exiles of Zion and those who long for Zion could return.

"This in itself is no guarantee for the attainment of our national aim. The Jewish people, schooled in suffering, has learnt from experience. Men and parties in opposition . . . have for twenty-five years made many promises and undertaken clear obligations. But on coming to power they have gone back on their word and perpetuated the policies of their predecessors. The consequence has been the robbery of our country and the destruction of our people. This experience, which has cost the Jewish people six million lives, teaches us that *only* the war of liberation, independent and purposeful, will set in motion political and international factors and bring salvation to our oppressed and decimated people.

"This historic conclusion remains valid. The struggle in which the youth . . . is engaged, is not being waged in order to obtain 'friendly statements' or the annulment of 'decrees.' It is being waged for the attainment of the fundamental aim: the establishment of Jewish rule in the land of the Jews. And it will go on until this aim is achieved. That is why we have not laid down our arms. And that is why, despite the threats from without and within, we have during the past few days entered a phase of extensive operations.

"But in view of the fact that all the members of the British Government, as members of the Labour Party, subscribed to the programme of mass repatriation to Zion and the establishment of the Jewish State, we consider it our duty, out of a sense of responsibility and of our own free will, to give them an opportunity of proving whether they mean to go the way of all their predecessors—the way of denial and betrayal—or whether they mean to fulfil their solemn public undertakings without delay.

"In view of the known plight of our people, only a very short time—weeks and not months—is required in order to determine whether they mean to translate their words into deeds; or whether to the many tragic illusions of the Jewish people is to be added yet another, perhaps the last illusion, which will be shattered only if we all rally—To War, War to the End, War till Victory."

Only a few weeks went by and the proof was given. Bevin opened his mouth; and the world tumbled about the ears of the credulous. That Midsummer Night's Dream vanished. No Labour promise, no Blackpool resolution, no friendship. All that remained was the traditional British fist, and facing us was Bevin whose dislike for the Jews was already a legend.

With this disillusionment ended the most difficult and most shameful phase in the period of the anti-British revolt. The Agency leaders realised that they

could no longer collaborate with such "authorities."
The order was given to stop the denunciations of the
Irgun, the handing over of prisoners and the kidnappings. The Haganah relaxed its pressure. And the first
feelers were sent out to us for the establishment of a
united front.

We knew that notwithstanding the bitterness of our
experiences we would find the strength of spirit to
stretch out our hand to attain what we had always
longed for: fighting unity, a united Jewish front against
the oppressor. What would we not have endured and
sacrificed for the achievement of this end? Indeed one
of the decisive reasons for our astonishing self-restraint
had been the belief in the inevitability of a united front.
Now the day had come. Our sacrifices had not been in
vain. The very men who had been betrayed and were
languishing behind barbed wire both at home and on
alien soil, at once supported our decision.

And so we accepted without qualification the principle of fighting unity. But we could not agree to immediate negotiations. The Haganah still held one of our men,
Eliezer, a veteran underground fighter. The conditions
in which he had to live were so wretched that they
permanently ruined his health. They could never break
his brave spirit. We informed the Haganah officers that
we would not discuss any agreement so long as the
"state of persecution" continued, or while Eliezer was
still detained. They could not restore the men they had
handed over to the British, but Eliezer was in their own
hands. We refused to compromise on these conditions
and they were finally accepted. One bright day Eliezer
reappeared—to set out on his long, adventurous and
active path in the Diaspora.

Eliezer, together with another of our officers, Hananya, was smuggled into Italy on an oil-ship. Eliezer's
instructions were to organise the Irgun in the Disapora,
and to plan repatriation schemes. Eliezer did his utmost
to carry out these assignments. The Irgun in the Diaspora arose. It served as an auxiliary force in Europe and
cast its fear on our enemies outside the boundaries of
Eretz Israel. It also served as a reserve force for our

units in Eretz Israel. But in the sphere of "illegal immigration" we suffered very heavy disappointments. In Italy Eliezer acquired two ships. The Hebrew Committee of National Liberation in the United States, and the British Government's wages train in Hadera, supplied him with the necessary means. But our agents and the undertaking fell victim to a private vendetta which had nothing to do with us. One of the boats was set on fire, and the other sabotaged. Thus our repatriation work, which had achieved so much before World War II, was seriously crippled. After these failures in Italy it was nearly two years before the Hebrew Committee for National Liberation succeeded in acquiring the *Ben Hecht*. The *Ben Hecht* brought nearly a thousand repatriates who, however, like most repatriates at that time, were at once deported to Cyprus.

But the achievements and failures in the Diaspora were still hidden in futurity in those days in 1945 when Eliezer was released by his kidnappers. Joy was our only feeling at the time. The last obstacle to a meeting between us and the Haganah was eliminated and this meeting, attended by spokesmen of all three armed organizations, duly took place. The Haganah was represented by Moshe Sneh, an old acquaintance, and Israel Galili, whom I then saw for the first time. The F.F.I. was represented by Nathan Friedman, and I spoke for the Irgun Zvai Leumi. This time there was no "ultimatum," nor any talk of "liquidation." We spoke of fighting unity, of the people's hopes.

3

Sneh and Galili proposed a complete merger of all the armed organisations. They urged a number of reasons, but their chief argument was that they were about to form the "Jewish Resistance Movement."

"The Haganah," they said, "has gone to war with the 'White Paper Government.' Why then should you not join its ranks? You used to argue that if we began fighting the British you would be prepared to accept our discipline. Now the time has come. We have begun to fight and we shall certainly continue. And not only is it your duty from the viewpoint of national discipline, but your own principles permit you to join the Haganah, in which your units will be assured, in the transition period, of a certain degree of autonomy."

Nathan Friedman told me later that he might have accepted this proposal. But the Irgun Command had had a preliminary discussion. We were prepared to fight with the Haganah; we were not prepared to dissolve under the cloak of 'unity.' I explained to Sneh and Galili the difference in political and organisational status between the Haganah and the Irgun. The Haganah boasted that they were under the orders of the Jewish Agency. We regarded this connection as a considerable, and possibly a decisive, drawback in the struggle for liberation. There are natural laws which determine the desire of every body to continue to exist and to perpetuate its mode of existence. A legal, recognised, "respectable" body strives to remain legal, recognised and "respectable." An illegal, militant and persecuted body strives to achieve the aim for which it is, indeed, militant and persecuted. Between the natural strivings of these bodies there is an objective conflict. The will of individuals may soften it or heighten it, but cannot dissolve it. This clash of purposes must inevitably end in one of two ways: either the legal body forces the illegal body to stop the struggle which threatens to undermine its legal status, or the militant organisation shakes loose the bonds of its dependence on the legal body. There is no third way.

Even Richard Crossman understood these considerations. In his book *Palestine Mission* he writes of the testimony by Mr. Ben Gurion before the Anglo-American Committee of Inquiry:

"In answer to Manningham-Buller's question whether he agreed with Dr. Weizmann's condemnation of violence, he said that he associated himself with it; but then went on to state that collaboration by the Jewish Agency in suppressing the terrorists had to be given up because it was futile. . . . He seems to want to have it both ways, to remain within the letter of the law as chairman of the Agency, and to tolerate terror as a method of bringing pressure on the Administration. That's a doubtful policy. The Irish leaders made up their minds and went underground. . . . I wonder whether Ben Gurion wouldn't be wiser either to do the same or to accept the lead of Weizmann and the moderates who really and genuinely regard the use of force as a mistake."

I thus explained our attitude to the Haganah representatives. "We cannot give up our independent existence," I said, "certainly not in the first stage of joint action. We are pleased at your change of mind, but we are anxious about the future. Today the national institutions have ordered you to fight in one way or another against the British. Yesterday they told you to fight us. Who can tell what orders they will give tomorrow? The decision is not in your hands. Others decide for you. And if they change their minds what will happen to you, what will happen to us and, most important of all, what will happen to the struggle? I assume you will take orders, but we, as we have repeatedly said, will want to fight the British Government as long as they rule in the country. What will be the result? A new split after the unification? What do we want all these complications for? Let us rather accept the dictates of reality. The Haganah has just entered on the fight. We have been waging it for a long time. Let us therefore, in spite of all that has happened in the past, establish a united front. And if you pursue the struggle consistently it is not impossible that there will be a merger. But if for one reason or another you decide to abandon the struggle, we shall not follow your example. We shall continue to fight. Our agreement will therefore be clear and practical, unaccompanied by any undisclosed 'mental reservations'."

We did not arrive at any practical conclusions at the first meeting. The Haganah representatives had to submit our reply to their superiors, while the underground spokesmen had to consult their comrades. Several days later a second tripartite meeting took place. The F.F.I. leadership had meantime accepted our view, and we agreed together on a common attitude. We decided to pursue our independent existence but, for the sake of fighting unity, agreed to forego independent operations —except for "confiscations." With the approval of the heads of the Jewish Agency, the Haganah representatives accepted our counter-proposals. It was agreed between us that while the underground organisations would retain their organisational independence, the deciding voice on offensive operations against Bevin's Government would be that of the Command of the "Resistance Movement."[1] But proposals could come from either side. The Resistance Movement was authorised to impose on us the execution of operations against the British; we were free to propose operational plans but had to obtain approval for their execution. It was also agreed that there would be no arbitrary decisions. At fixed times there would be discussions among the representatives of the three organisations on the political situation and on military questions. As for operations aimed at seizing arms (or money) from the authorities it was finally agreed that we were to be free to decide on them at will.

This agreement found an echo in the secret telegrams Moshe Sneh sent to his colleagues abroad. These telegrams mysteriously found their way to the British Intelligence, and were seized and decoded by its agents. They were published in a special White Paper by the British Government. I must record that this particular White Paper, on "Violence in Palestine," was one of the few British documents on Palestine that I have read in which there were scarcely any distortions. Maybe there are other such documents, but I have not seen them. The White Paper of 1947 contains facts. Thus for example, it quotes a broadcast of *Kol Israel* (the official broadcasting station of the Jewish Resistance Movement) and adds that this broadcast is of particular importance in view of its having been approved by

---

[1] As far as the Irgun was concerned the "Resistance Movement" and the "Haganah" were synonymous and the two terms are henceforth used interchangeably.

the Head of the Political Department of the Jewish Agency, Mr. Moshe Shertok.

This was true. At one of our meetings I congratulated Sneh on the fine and politically sound broadcast. He acknowledged the congratulations and added:

"Do you think I passed this broadcast on my own responsibility? Moshe Shertok approved the text."

In other telegrams relating to the agreement with the underground organisations Sneh wrote: (Telegram of 23 September 1945.)

"It is suggested that we do not wait for an official announcement but call upon all Jewry to warn the authorities and to raise the morale of the Yishuv. If you agree ask Zeev Sherf for statistical material about the absorptive capacity. . . .

"It has also been suggested that we cause one serious incident. We would then issue a declaration to the effect that it is only a warning and an indication of much more serious incidents that would threaten the safety of all British interests in the country should the Government decide against us. Wire your views with reference as before but referring to statistical material about immigration during the war years. The Stern Group have expressed their willingness to join us completely on the basis of our programme of activity. This time the intentions seem serious. If there is such a union, we may assume that we can prevent independent action even by the I.Z.L. Wire your views on the question of union, referring to statistical material about Jewish recruitment to the Army.—Sneh."

And in a telegram on 1 November 1945:

"We have come to a working arrangement with the dissident organisations according to which we shall assign certain tasks to them under our command. They will act only according to our plan. Sneh, Shaul Meiroff and Bernard Joseph consider such an agreement most desirable but it is not being put into effect because the Party is delaying it. Some of them are opposed to any sort of activity and especially any agreement with the dissidents.

"On Wednesday the following operations were car-

ried out. Two boats were sunk at Haifa port and a
third at Jaffa. They were engaged in hunting immigrants. The railway lines were cut at 186 points. Altogether there were 500 explosions. Railway traffic was
suspended from the Syrian border to Gaza, from Haifa
to Samakh, from Lydda to Jerusalem. In all the operations nobody was wounded or arrested.

"That night the I.Z.L. attacked Lydda station causing
serious damage and a number of casualties. The Stern
Group seriously damaged the oil refineries at Haifa and
one man was killed. The dissidents informed us in advance and we did not oppose Lydda but we opposed
the Refineries operation. Had the agreement been in
force we should have been able to prevent the casualties at Lydda and the operation at the Refineries. I regard the fact that the Party and the Executive are delaying their agreement as a crime. . . ."

The agreement between the groups forming together
the Resistance Movement, that is to say between the
Jewish Agency and Haganah and the underground organisations, was not written in ink but was sealed in
blood. Its fundamental condition was action. It imposed
grave limitations on us, but we observed it not only in
the spirit but even in the unwritten letter. From November 1945 to September 1946, that is until the Haganah stopped fighting, we attacked the British only according to plans approved by the Resistance Movement
leadership, and we did not carry out a single operation
without their prior approval—except for 'confiscation
operations' which we were free, according to the agreement, to carry out on our own.

One of the confiscation operations was effected before the operational agreement had been reached. While
we were still discussing the terms of the agreement, one
of our units penetrated the military camp at Rehovot,
where a British unit consisting of Jewish soldiers was
encamped, and without hurting the soldiers carried off
several hundred rifles, about a dozen Bren guns, a
number of sub-machine guns and a substantial quantity
of ammunition and other military equipment. *Kol Israel*
sharply denounced the operation. Sneh and Galili re-

proached us for carrying it out while engaged in negotiations for an agreement. The F.F.I. members, on the other hand, complained because we had not invited them to participate.

Our position was not pleasant. We did not wish to tell our comrades-in-arms an untruth; but we also could not tell them the truth. The fact was that we ourselves had been taken by surprise. The operation at Rehovot was not carried out on the orders of the Command but on the initiative of the participants themselves. A group of young officers, among the best and most devoted in the Irgun, fearing that they might be forbidden to carry out the plan calculated to enrich our arms store so substantially, had said nothing to anybody—and executed it.

This was a breach of discipline which put us in a difficult position. I therefore severely reprimanded my devoted young comrades. In accordance with the laws of conspiracy I stood behind a curtain and poured out words of rebuke. But in my heart . . . my feelings were mixed. I remembered that in the old Austrian Empire there used to be a special decoration for acts of heroism performed by soldiers in breach of formal military discipline. . . .

Among those who participated in the arms raid at Rehovot were many who played a heroic part in the struggle for liberation. There are not a few whom I shall never see again . . . I hope I have been forgiven the bitter words of reproach, which, in fulfilment of my duty, I addressed to them that night. This was the one and only operation throughout all the years of revolt carried out by Irgun soldiers without instructions or approval or authority from the Supreme Command. If discipline is important in every army how much more so in an army of rebels surrounded by enemies and antagonists? The confiscators of arms at Rehovot realized this and I know they shared my distress. Perhaps they should have been given a medal instead of a reprimand. Or perhaps both together? They received the rebuke; but where are the medals? In our underground army there were no decorations; our fighters were rewarded for the most outstanding acts of heroism only by their own consciousness of duty done. Such was the decoration as given to the undisciplined group at Rehovot. And what a host of useful acts of liberation were performed by those very Bren-guns and rifles!

4

The Haganah's fight against the British lasted nine months, from November 1945 to July 1946. Their co-operation with us lasted ten months, from that same November until the following August. Our joint conferences usually took place once a fortnight. Before every agreed operation there was a meeting between the Operations Officers. The attacks carried out jointly by our Assault Units and the F.F.I. were planned by us. Consequently, Eitan represented us at the operational conferences and, after he was captured, Gideon. Sometimes Uri, the F.F.I. Operations Officer, also attended these conferences. The plans we proposed were dealt with by Yitshak Sadeh on behalf of the Haganah. Sadeh never interested himself in the details of an operation. He would ask for the main lines of the plan, and would generally approve all the proposals of our Operational Officers. His approval was always given to Eitan or Gideon, except in the case of the first agreed operation, against the Lydda Railway Station, when approval was given in writing to the Irgun Command. It was dated 25 October and stated:

"1. The size of the unit, its equipment and disposition, are suitable for the objective (except for the mortar which will not be effective in the circumstances). If the guard is strengthened, the unit must not be increased in personnel but in firepower.

"2. The plan has two parts: (a) the area between the grove and the huts. (b) the hutment area and the tunnels. *Only* the first part is to be carried out (that is: without damaging the tunnels) in accordance with tactical considerations. This part is capable of execution with absolute surprise before the guards recover and are able to offer effective resistance. In the existing circumstances it is almost impossible to carry out the operation in the tunnel in the same way.

"3. The objective itself—the tunnel—is not of great importance and does not justify any deflection from the tactical considerations at this stage.

"4. Successful execution may be greatly helped through a failure of the electric current produced by a short-circuit or by some other means.

"5. Prepare to overcome the guards without using arms.

"Finally: we emphasize that you will receive at least 48 hours advance notice of the time of execution. We shall let you have all information connected with the execution immediately."

There was great satisfaction in our camp at the approaching first joint attack of all the Jewish organisations. A *Herut* article, welcoming the great event invoked "the youth that had carved the way to the struggle for liberation with their bodies":

"What have we not endured throughout the years during which we stood alone on the battlefield, with the banner of freedom in our hands and the fire of faith in our hearts? How many sacrifices have we not made? How many are the fallen, how great the number of captives and exiles? Moreover, do you remember the months of persecution? Do you remember the 'incomprehensible' attitude we adopted when faced by the most terrible threat in our history? Even in those mad days we did not lose our faith that the day would come when we would fight shoulder to shoulder with our erring brothers. That day has come. . . . We should humbly thank the God of Israel for implanting in our hearts the faith, the understanding and the great love which enabled us to avoid the civil war and thus made possible a war of liberation."

But the attack on the Lydda Railway Station, which met with complete success, might easily have ended in failure or in grave consequences for the attackers. Our Assault Unit, together with an F.F.I. unit, went out to Lydda without receiving any information whatsoever of the extensive sabotage operations carried out against the railway-system by the Haganah an hour before midnight. We had not insisted on being supplied with such information and the agreement between us did not contain any detailed clauses to that effect. We had thought that the necessity of such prior notification was too obvious. The consequence was that when our unit arrived at Lydda—after some delay owing to their having made their way on foot by devious paths from Petah Tikvah —the explosions at more than two hundred points throughout the country were already in full progress. Some of them had been heard at Lydda, and the British unit guarding the railway was in a state of alert. A state of alert was also proclaimed in all the police stations and army establishments on the route our men had to take. The danger was great. Nevertheless Eitan —after he had explained the situation to the men and they had expressed their enthusiastic readiness to storm the Lydda Railway Station—decided to go through with the attack. The conditions previously envisaged had changed completely, and the attack could not be carried out according to the original plan. Strong enemy resistance had to be overcome. A number of British soldiers were killed or wounded. We also suffered heavy casualties, one of our best officers being killed. However, important railway installations were damaged. The tactical objective was achieved.

But this was only half the task; our boys still had to be brought back safely to their base. This was no easy matter, for dawn had broken. The roads teemed with powerful British patrols searching for "terrorists." Indeed our men, weary after a night of marching and fighting, encountered several British patrols, but they made no attempt to engage. Eitan ultimately brought the unit safely to base at Petah Tikvah. It was, however, by then afternoon and Eitan who, like all our other officers, knew how great was my anxiety in the agonisingly long hours of waiting, hastened to me to report on the battle, on our casualties and on the difficulties of the withdrawal.

Several days later, at our meeting with the Haganah representatives, we pointed out to them the very seri-

ous consequences which might easily have resulted
from their failure to give us prior notification of their
operations that night. They conceded that we were right
in our complaint and undertook in future to inform us
in advance of all their projected operations.

The military operations carried out by the Haganah
during the existence of the Combined Resistance Movement were not many in number; nor were we able to
secure approval for many operations. On the "night of
the railways" the Haganah also sank three British patrol
boats. Later they twice attacked the radar station at
Haifa. On the first occasion the British forces succeeded
in disposing of the explosives before any damage was
done, but the second time the attack was successful.
One attack was made on the police Observation Post at
Givat Olga, which was blown up.

The Haganah organised "Wingate night" in Tel Aviv.
The aim was to make a demonstrative landing of a repatriates' ship on the beach of the Hebrew city and to
prevent the authorities by force from reaching the
beach. But there was more confusion that night than
action. The British forces got through everywhere.

In February, 1946 the Haganah carried out sabotage
operations against installations of the Mobile Police.
And in June the Haganah brought their armed resistance to a close with the comprehensive and successful
attack on the frontier-bridges.

The attack on the camps of the Mobile Police Force
was preceded by a joint consultation, and caused much
heart-burning. We were supposed to attack one of them
—near Kfar Vitkin. We were particularly interested in
this camp because it contained a large armoury. Our
plan was designed primarily for the confiscation of the
precious arms. For several weeks our boys reconnoitred
and acquired precise information on the camp in general and on the armoury in particular. It was agreed between us and the Haganah that four Mobile Police
camps were to be attacked on the same night, three by
the Haganah, one by us. We had proposed that we
should also attack the camp at Sarona, but the Haganah chiefs decided to allocate only Kfar Vitkin to us.

A few days before the proposed date Galili informed me that special circumstances made it necessary to cancel the attack on Kfar Vitkin. I went to meet him and to explain that the cancellation of the operation would affect the morale of the boys and, what was more, it was a pity to forego the large arms-store which was simply "asking" to be taken away. Galili replied that he sympathised with my view but that the cancellation was simply unavoidable. The reason, he said, was local, but decisive.

I left Galili with a heavy heart. As he had not disclosed details of the "reason" I had not pressed him with questions. Men in the underground have to respect the wishes of those who do not want to give away confidences. From his hints I assumed that the Haganah had an arms-workshop in the neighbourhood of the village and that they were afraid that if our attack was followed by a search the workshop would be found. I told my comrades of my guess; but I had to work hard to appease their anger before they resigned themselves to the cancellation of the operation.

At the appointed time the Haganah went out to attack the Palestine Mobile force. At Sarona they were stalked by tragedy. Part of their force came late. The break-through attempt failed. Four brave fighters were killed before they passed the fence. At a second camp the attack was not carried out at all. At Shafram the Haganah soldiers broke through the barbed wire and succeeded in damaging a few enemy armoured cars. To a lesser extent they succeeded in doing the same—at Kfar Vitkin!

Our boys were justifiably very angry.

"Our operation at Kfar Vitkin was cancelled for 'a special reason.' Why then did the Haganah attack? And why did they not even inform us that they were going to attack at a place where it was ostensibly forbidden to operate? And what did they achieve there after all? One or two enemy vehicles were damaged. Whereas if we had attacked we should not only have inflicted damage but carried off several hundred rifles, machine-guns and ammunition."

I urged all this on Galili and Sneh but I could never extract a satisfactory explanation of their dubious conduct. To this day I do not know what induced the Haganah Command to prevent our carrying out the Kfar Vitkin attack. Maybe they did not want us to operate simultaneously and in the same field.

The Sarona incident was of quite a different kind. There was wide public criticism of the Haganah over the four men killed during the attack. It was unjust criticism. Failures and sacrifices are inseparable concomitants of war. We, whose experience in partisan attacks was so much richer than that of the Haganah, praised the general attack on the Mobile Police Units in spite of the Kfar Vitkin incident. For we remembered the political basis of our struggle. And we paid our respects publicly to the men killed at Sarona.

The Haganah, which as a body had never been seriously persecuted by the British authorities, organised a mass funeral for their four dead. American newspapermen, who did not distinguish between official and unofficial bombs, regarded this funeral as a mark of the Haganah's identification with 'terrorism.' Some of them, describing the participation of Agency leaders in the funeral, reported that the official leaders had joined the Irgun! This was not true, of course; but what is certain is that British Army Intelligence officers took many photographs of the funeral procession and especially of the young people marching in it.

5

The week the Haganah attacked the Mobile Police Units, the soldiers of the underground went out to attack airfields. The plan, worked out in detail by our Operations Section, embraced three military airfields: at Lydda, Kfar Sirkin, and Kastina. Of these the Kfar Sirkin airfield—near the Hasidoff Quarter—was allocated to the F.F.I., who carried out a successful attack. Our Assault Force dealt with the central airfield at Lydda and the big landing field at Kastina. The operation was very difficult. The enemy was by then in a permanent state of alert. The roads leading to the airfields were scoured by mobile patrols. Around the fields were large army camps. In order to reach their objectives our men had to make their way through trackless fields with the mud reaching to their knees. It took them hours to cover short distances through fields which had been turned into vast swamps by the heavy rains. When they reached the approaches to the airfields not only were they soaked to the skin, barefoot and weary, but they had lost completely the most powerful weapon of the underground: the element of surprise. The enemy were ready and waiting. The searchlights swept every inch of the approaches. And they heard an officer shout from a watch-tower at Lydda:

"Keep your eyes on the roads. The bastards are coming."

Nevertheless the Assault Force went into action. Again they split into a 'break-through' group and a 'covering' group. Under a rain of bullets from two directions they advanced towards the barbed-wire fences, broke through them and stormed the airfields. Everything had been prepared for the final act. Our men had even brought little ladders with them—and they proved very useful indeed. In a twinkling the men were up the ladders and inside the great steel bodies of the planes. In went the explosives, the fuses were set—and heavy four-engined Halifax bombers were soon converted into masses of useless metal.

The withdrawal to the base was even more difficult than the approach to the target. Day was breaking. Enemy armour lurked on every road. Feet sank in the mud. But the hearts of the men were singing with joy. They knew that by destroying the planes they had undermined the foundations of the Mandatory's military base. Passing through Arab villages they were greeted with cries of admiration: "Jeddah, jeddah!" In a Jewish village they were welcomed with open arms, joyfully and affectionately. Once it had been: "Terrorists, get out. We don't want you here." Now friendly hearts were opened to them. Seeing their bedraggled condition the residents searched out changes of clothing for them.

Blessings were poured on them in place of the curses of yesterday. After years of persecution and vilification we had won the love of the people.

The Government was thrown into utter confusion. In the House of Commons Lord Winterton angrily demanded a strict inquiry into the incidents in order to establish who was responsible for the negligence which, he said, had enabled the "terrorists" to penetrate the airfields and destroy so many precious planes. The Colonial Secretary made a vague reply and promised to improve the security measures at the airfields.

The Occupation Government in Jerusalem published a communique which aroused universal ridicule. They boasted that "only" a couple of dozen airplanes had been destroyed and that, moreover, attacks on the Ramat David and Akir airfields had been prevented. In our reply we wished the Government such victories every day. We reminded them that when during the World War British forces brought down thirty enemy planes or destroyed as many on the ground, special communiques had been issued announcing the great news. As for the "prevented attacks" on Ramat David and Akir they were purely imaginary attacks dreamed up for the purpose of winning a couple of equally imaginary victories.

The joy of the Jewish people was even greater than the consternation of the British authorities. The announcement that the underground organisations had attacked airfields came as a complete surprise. At first we of the Irgun were silent. The Haganah had asked us not to publish any statement that would identify the attacking organsations. We agreed. The glorification of our arms was far less important than the fact that a united people was now fighting the oppressor. But the Haganah changed its mind, and in an urgent note asked us to accept responsibility for destroying the British planes. So be it. We readily complied. The public was astounded. In the streets of the towns you could see long queues reading every word of our communique. People exclaimed in wonderment: "So the dissidents are capable of such things!" They did not trouble to hide their enthusiasm even from the British authorities. In a Tel

Aviv café a British officer asked for his check. The proprietor replied: "You don't owe us anything. You paid us yesterday—with thirty planes."

The Kastina battle inspired Michael Ashbel, our "Mike," the ascetic soldier and popular poet, to write a song which became one of the favourites of the fighting youth.

Some of the principal places in the Jerusalem area to which reference is made in the narrative are indicated on this map.

Chapter XIV

Parting of the Ways

The following were the operations officially approved by the United forces: the attack on the airfields; a widespread sabotage attack in the south; the blowing up of trains on the three main lines of the country; the F.F.I. attack on the railway workshops at Haifa; and our attack on the King David Hotel. But there were two more operations carried out during that period by the 'dissidents' which were approved only 'unofficially' by the Haganah. One was the attack on the Jerusalem Prison carried out by our Assault Force and the F.F.I. and aimed a freeing captive members of both organisations. The operation caused a stir throughout the world —and echoed as far as Moscow. The *Izvestia* of 22 January, 1946, wrote:

"The London radio announced last night that on the night of the 19th a number of explosions were heard in Jerusalem. Radio transmissions were suspended throughout the country. In the center of Jerusalem gunfire was heard for two minutes. A second statement on the London radio reported that clashes took place with armed Jews in the centre of Jerusalem. A party of Jews attacked the power station. As the result of an explosion part of the wall of the central prison was damaged. In the clashes one Jew was killed and four wounded. One British officer and one police officer were killed; one police officer was wounded."

It was during that period that Moscow radio began publishing news about the sanguinary events in Eretz Israel. As the Jewish underground struggle developed, its operations were reported with increasing frequency in the Soviet Union. After the attack on Acre prison a year later, Moscow radio devoted nearly half an hour to a description of the operation against the Fortress, which it compared to the Petropavlovsk Fortress, notorious from the days of the prolonged struggle against the Tzarist regime. On 1 January 1946, *Pravda* wrote:

"The troubles in Palestine continue. Paris radio quotes a London statement that the British authorities have decided to carry out a comprehensive operation with police and military forces. During the last twenty-four hours, two thousand arrests have been made. The deportation of certain personalities is under consideration. Reinforcements have been sent to Tel Aviv and Jerusalem. Thorough searches are being made in the area in which the chief of the Irgun Zvai Leumi is believed to be hiding."

At that time, early in 1946, we analysed the relations between our people and the Soviet Union. They had as yet undergone no change. The theory of my Lukishki interrogation prevailed in the political articles in the Soviet Press. We wrote:

"We abhor illusions, and we shall not foster them. We view the facts, and reject the feckless practice of adapting them to our assumptions. *Nevertheless we say with absolute confidence that Russia too will help in making Eretz Israel a Jewish State*. How? Though she continues to oppose the concentration of the Jewish people in its Homeland, Russia, which is capable of exploiting the events in Indonesia and the demands of Syria and Lebanon, *wants* the fight of the Jewish people against the British Mandatory. The Jewish State will arise only as a result of our struggle against the British rule in Eretz Israel, and in this struggle we shall be helped by the Soviet Union."

But while the operation in Jerusalem drew attention throughout the world, its practical purpose was not achieved. There was great confusion among the Government authorities. Government office after Government office was evacuated. The British officer referred to in the Russian newspaper had been killed by a British policeman. The British Intelligence Service was again completely at sea. According to the official communique we had tried to blow up the radio station—which adjoined the prison.

Quite different results attended the second operation "unofficially approved" by the Haganah. This was the attack—the third during the revolt—on the C.I.D. Headquarters in Jerusalem and Jaffa. Planned and commanded by our officers, the attack was carried out in combination with F.F.I. members. The buildings were guarded by special military and police units, whose resistance was very fierce. But, covered by a Bren-gun, and in accordance with our tried tactics, the breakthrough party stormed the approaches, blew a hole in the door, withdrew at speed for a moment to wait for the explosion, swiftly advanced with the main load of explosives—and in a few minutes the fortified buildings were heaps of rubble. Many secret files of the Intelligence were destroyed in the attack. In the British House of Commons a member reported in vivid terms: "I saw the police buildings laid flat on the ground."

The police buildings were "laid flat" during days of inactivity of the Resistance Movement. Unhappily such days were not few. We persistently protested against these prolonged pauses. We demanded the intensification of the struggle. It is noteworthy that we called not only for military operations but also for civil disobedience. We wrote:

"A nation fighting for its life and its future has many weapons. Withholding taxes from the regime; disobeying its orders and laws; refraining from the use of its offices, officials and courts; occupying Government lands—that is, lands of which the Government has robbed us—and refusing to leave; setting up a Provisional Jewish Government to lead the national struggle—all these are acts of war. . . ."

We did not, indeed, regard civil disobedience as the final answer. As we said, "all civil resistance, if it has a serious purpose, must inevitably, by the iron laws of events, bring on an armed uprising." But we saw in civil disobedience the embodiment of the people's struggle and its unity. We consequently pressed for it both publicly and in our conversations with Haganah chiefs—

Sneh, Galili, Shaul Meiroff and others. Sneh and Galili promised many times that universal civil disobedience would soon be launched. I am convinced that they were in earnest, just as they sincerely wanted to broaden the military struggle. But their hands were tied. The final decision was in the hands of the "recognised institutions" and the Jewish institutions were divided into two camps: the "activists" and those who, in Crossman's words, "really and genuinely regarded the use of force as a mistake." A vigorous battle of words developed between the two camps.

It was these difficulties the Haganah leaders invoked to explain the prolonged inaction. We argued that it was taking the heart out of our agreement. The agreement was based on the principle of action. It was only after long discussions and many postponements that the Haganah chiefs informed us that we could carry out the attacks on the C.I.D. headquarters—but that their approval was unofficial. They would try, they said, to prevent denunciations of the operations in the Press, but they could not undertake that such denunciations would not appear.

The denunciations appeared right enough—and not only in the general Press. A new propaganda sheet calling itself *Kol Israel Loyalists*, wrote of our attacks as designed to worsen the relations between the British and the Jews. "We regard these operations as not having taken place," it said, with characteristic pomposity.

Nathan Friedman and I protested to Sneh and Galili at this offensive ebullition. They apologised for this publication, claiming that they had been unaware of its contents. But matters were not improved by the publication of some very vinegary comments on the "unofficially approved" attacks of ours in the Haganah journal *Hahomah* (The Wall).

Such were the differences and misunderstandings between us and the Haganah during the period of the United Resistance Movement.

For our internal use we gave each other pseudonyms. Galili was called Jeremiah; Nathan Friedman was Shimon, and I was Yehezkel. Our meetings gener-

ally took place at the home of "Jan" in busy Ben Yehuda Street in Tel Aviv. When I first met our host I
felt I had seen him somewhere before; and, sure
enough, it turned out that we had been at Warsaw University together and near neighbours in the Jewish Academicians' House. The days of youth that were no
more. . . . Now "Jan"—Yanovsky—was a leading
member of the Haganah. Moshe Sneh, another fellow
student of those days, had become the national Commander of the Haganah; Nathan Friedman, also a former neighbour in the Academicians' House and a boyhood friend, had become one of the chiefs of the F.F.I.,
and I had become Reb Sassover. Fate had flung us in
various directions and into different camps, and now
we were sitting round one table, enjoying the hospitality
of our charming hostess and taking counsel together in
the struggle of Israel. . . .

The Haganah chiefs continued to live semi-underground. Until their attack on the police Mobile Force
and our attacks on the airfields they had not been afraid
of arrest. Immediately after these affairs they went under cover. Sneh left home, changed his hairstyle and
finally went off in secret to Paris. Galili cut off his
fine crop of fair hair and, made up with the help of a
professional actor, he might have passed for a merchant, a book-keeper or any eligible bachelor. His disguise was well done, but it did not last long. Several
months later, just before the Zionist Congress in December 1946, I saw Galili again with his thick hair restored. I pointed to his head and remarked: "That is the
symbol of the truce."

2

During the Resistance Movement period the Inquiry
Committee set up jointly by Britain and the United
States arrived in Eretz Israel. On their way, while in
London, all twelve members of the Committee met
Bevin, who promised them that if their conclusions were
unanimous he would implement them. The Committee
worked hard to "hear all sides" and to reach unanimity.

We had the usual spectacle to which the long procession of Commissions had accustomed us. The Arab representatives stated their claims, the spokesmen of the Jewish Agency explained their attitude, the British Government representatives asked to be heard *in camera*. The proceedings were diligently recorded. Some remark or other by a member of the Committee would arouse a storm. Everybody would try to guess who was "for us" and who "against us." Inevitably the inquiry would end, the report be published—and the British would go on doing as they pleased. The Anglo-American Committee was no exception to the usual formula. Jamal Husseini told them that if the British left the country the Arabs would settle matters with the Jews without difficulty. The Jewish Agency representatives hinted broadly that if partition were proposed they would accept it. We all had an embarrassing moment when Mr. Ben Gurion, subjected to cross-examination, claimed that he did not know where the Haganah Command was, or who its Commander was, and that he was not responsible for its activities. . . .

Two American members of the Committee, Mr. Macdonald and Mr. Crum, suggested a meeting with me. Owing to unforeseen security difficulties the meeting could not take place. Before the Committee left for Switzerland Mr. Macdonald sent me a message in which he expressed the belief that there was "a good fighting chance" to secure a radical change in British policy towards Palestine and Zionism. He hoped we would act in such a way as not to spoil this fighting chance.

Mr. Macdonald is undoubtedly a friend of our people. I had heard this already from Vladimir Jabotinsky at the time Macdonald was appointed Commissioner for the Refugees from Nazi Germany. But he was mistaken in thinking that it was possible to secure a change in British policy in Eretz Israel. The report prepared by the twelve members of the mixed Committee was certainly not calculated to achieve such a change. It was a shallow document full of contradictions. It gave nothing tangible either to the Jews or to the Arabs, but afforded complete recognition to British rule. The

Americans indeed did try to secure some concessions to the Jewish Agency viewpoint, but even they subscribed to the dogmatic declaration that "there can be neither a Jewish nor an Arab State in Palestine." The inference was, therefore, self-evident; Palestine must be a . . . British State. The few concessions the Committee did make to the Jews they justified . . . on the grounds of "terrorism." They wrote:

". . . When the war ended and the Labour Government came into power the White Paper still remained in force. The Jews, who had expected an immediate fulfilment by a Labour Government of the Labour Party programme with regard to Zionism, felt a sense of outrage when no change of policy occurred. The bitterness reached a new peak of intensity and the position of the moderates became almost impossible. The Jewish Agency frankly stated in public hearing after V. E. Day it was quite futile for it to attempt to co-operate with the Mandatory in suppressing illegal activity.

"Any decision on the future of Palestine will be futile and unrealistic unless it is made in full cognizance of the political tension among the Jews and the reasons for it. Both in evidence given in public hearings and in numerous private conversations with leading politicians and with ordinary citizens we were repeatedly advised that the maintenance by the Mandatory of its present policy would only lead to a state of war, in which the extremists would have the passive support of almost the whole Jewish population and the moderates would be swept from the key positions which they still hold."

On these grounds the Committee proposed the abolition of the Land Laws of 1940, which prohibited the Jews from buying land in four-fifths of Western Eretz Israel. They also proposed the cancellation of that part of the 1939 White Paper which made further Jewish immigration dependent on Arab consent. Finally they recommended the admission of one hundred thousand Jewish refugees, if possible, within a year. President Truman, who had himself previously recommended that one hundred thousand refugees be admitted to Palestine, expressed his satisfaction at the Committee's acceptance of his proposal. It demanded the dissolution of all "private armies" which, it claimed, endangered "world peace." It also proposed the prohibition of dancing at a certain café on the Sea of Galilee on the grounds of the sacred associations of the place. Of the ten recommendations of the Committee this one alone was implemented by the British. And as a result the British troops stationed in Galilee and deprived of this harmless entertainment cursed both the Committee and Bevin.

When the report was published Sneh proposed that *Kol Israel* should be authorized by all the armed organisations to announce that if the recommendations for the admission of one hundred thousand refugees were implemented no operations liable to impede their entry would be carried out. The implication was clear. We had serious doubts of the desirability of such a "truce" proclamation. But on consideration we agreed to the proposal. We made it quite clear that we did not believe the British Government would voluntarily admit one hundred thousand Jews, but we wanted all possible doubts in the mind of the people to be removed.

We were not mistaken. The Labour Government's ingenuity was equal to the occasion. Attlee announced in the House of Commons that the Committee's recommendations must be treated as a whole. They were interdependent (except, of course, the recommendation against dancing on the shores of the Sea of Galilee). If the Jews wanted 100,000 immigration permits they must disband their illegal armies and hand over all their arms to the legal authorities. . . . Macdonald and Crum reminded Bevin that he had solemnly promised the members of the Commission that if the recommendations were unanimous, they would be implemented. Bevin did not reply. A spokesman, however, stated on his behalf that while the Foreign Secretary did remember that he had said something of the sort, it was self-evident that he had been referring to the recommendations as a whole, and not to some of them or to those which pleased the Jews of New York or President Truman. The recommendations were inseparable.

With this new clarification of the British attitude we pressed the Haganah to resume military action and to launch civil disobedience. We pointed out that there was no sense in further waiting. The British Government must be shown, we said, that they need not expect us to disarm, or, as one of our men put it, that they could expect to get only our bullets. . . . I also sent the Command of the Resistance Movement practical proposals, military and political. On 7 May I received their reply (In the text "chickens" means airfields and "printing press" refers to the Government Printing Press near the Jerusalem Railway Station):

"1. There is no room for difference of opinion on the grounds for resuming operations on a large scale. Nevertheless, decision has been postponed for a week in consideration of information from our people abroad. American friends claim that they are engaged in an effort to secure the annulment of the condition of disbandment and that activity on our part now is likely to frustrate it. This decision of course applied to the operations already approved (more chickens, printing-press). In a week's time a decision will be taken in principle on the resumption of operations and you will then also receive a reply on the detailed plans you have put forward. We therefore propose that our next meeting take place on Tuesday, 14 May at 20 hours at the usual place. Please confirm.

"2. A statement, throwing responsibility on the Government, as proposed by M., will be published by us when the first operation is carried out. . . ."

While we had to wait for more than a week for "the decision in principle on the resumption of operations" the delay was not very long. A number of our plans were approved. One of them was the demolition of trains after taking off passengers—and this opened up a new series of operations. It was followed by the blowing-up of the bridges by the Haganah, and the F.F.I. attack on the railway workshops at Haifa.

It is exceedingly to be regretted that the F.F.I. received no prior notification of the timing of the Haganah attack on the bridges. The F.F.I. claimed that when their men went out to attack the railway workshops the troops were in a state of alert. Moshe Sneh claimed in my presence that he had received a note from Nathan Friedman informing him that the attack on the workshops was being postponed. The grim discussion did not alter the tragic fact that the troops succeeded in ambushing the Jewish fighters on their way back to base and eleven F.F.I. men were killed and twenty captured, among them a number of wounded. Not a single official representative came to pay his respects to the F.F.I. dead. The Haganah member, however, whose body had been recovered after the tragic explosion at the A-Zib bridge was accorded a public funeral.

The attack on the bridges was wide in its scope, and important politically. The men of the Haganah operated in difficult conditions. They had to traverse long distances and withdraw through secondary roads in order not to clash with Army forces. At the bridges which were guarded by a few Arab policemen there were no clashes and the fourteen Haganah men who fell were accidentally killed by the premature explosion of a load of their own explosives. But the difficult task was carried out with thoroughness. Great steel bridges in the north, the south and the east, collapsed under the blows of the Haganah men.

This was the last military operation of the Resistance Movement.

The British forces went over to a large-scale counter-attack. It cannot be said that previously they had failed to react to the Resistance operations. On the contrary, they retaliated in minor operations in various parts of the country, at Rishpun, Givat Haim and at Tel Aviv. At all these places thousands of people assembled, in order to prevent searches for repatriates who had succeeded in landing. The crowds stood unprotected and exposed to enemy bullets. Not only unarmed men, but also women and children were killed—which moved us to ask the Resistance Movement to stop this dangerous "passive resistance" so costly in lives.

The Government forces were out to break the backbone of "Jewish terrorism," and to end all Jewish resistance. Consequently they carefully prepared a monster attack on the Jewish institutions and forces.

It was launched in the early morning hours of 29 June, 1946. Tens of thousands of British soldiers fanned out over the whole country, imposed a curfew, and led thousands of people away to detention. The building of the Jewish Agency was occupied. The heads of the official institutions and active members of the Haganah were arrested in accordance with prepared lists. With the help of these lists searches were also made in the communal villages in which Palmach units were stationed. The lists were amazingly accurate. It is a fact that every communal village in which a Palmach unit was "secretly" stationed, was well known to the British military intelligence. It is not surprising therefore that the consequences were serious. Israel Galili told me the blow to the Palmach was tremendous. Nearly half its members were arrested. The higher ranks of the Haganah were also severely affected.

These events provided us with much food for historicophilosophical thought. Who could have foreseen by what paths our people would be led to liberation. The pioneer colonisation was undoubtedly a mighty factor in the process of rooting our people in the soil of the Homeland. The agricultural settlements could also have served as bases in defensive war against the Arabs. We however encountered many obstacles, as these settlements were closed to us. We had only Nachlat Jabotinsky and Ramat Tiomkin and they helped us considerably in providing training-grounds and in launching various attacks. How much easier would the underground struggle have been if we had had at our disposal a substantial number of villages? What training-courses and field-exercises we could have organised! But Destiny it seems, has its own ways. Before the State was established we did not settle on the land. We fought. Had we settled on the land in those days no real underground would have arisen in the peculiar topographical conditions of Eretz Israel. The British Government would have known exactly where to find us just as they knew where to find the Palmach men. In one surprise search the underground would have been wiped out; and the struggle for liberation would have ended as soon as it began. In our "overt underground" the authorities did not know where to begin to look for us. We were everywhere—and nowhere. True, the lack of rural bases made our task much more difficult. Destiny, however, seemed to prefer our having a difficult task to the Government's laying their hands on us. . . .

But on 29 June there was no time to stand and ponder. The question was: What is to be done? We still had no serious reason to doubt that the Haganah resistance would continue. Throughout the day the Jewish Agency's *Kol Israel* vociferated:

"Britain has declared war on the Jewish people. The Jewish people will fight back. Out with the unclean sons of Titus from our Holy Land! Down with the Nazi-British régime in our country!"

The text of these broadcasts bore a striking resemblance to earlier Irgun proclamations. But, unlike ours, there was a note of nervousness about them. On that day we did not publish slogans. We proposed a programme of action, which we published when we had sent it to the Resistance Movement leadership.

We made the following nine proposals:

1. The establishment of a Jewish Provisional Government, which would fight for the liquidation of the British Occupation Regime;

2. The establishment of a Supreme National Council as the Parliament of the people, to legislate, impose duties and issue orders.

3. The publication of the Declaration of Hebrew Independence and Freedom as the basis for a constitution which should guarantee liberty, equality and social justice for all inhabitants.

4. The establishment of courts of justice and the boycotting of the British courts.

5. The setting-up of a national Exchequer to which all taxes would be paid, and the prohibition of all payment to the Mandatory Government.

6. The creation of a unified Liberation Army which would take an oath not to lay down its arms until our independent State was set up.

7. The establishment of a Supreme Military Command which should proclaim general mobilisation and organise an emergency administration for the daily life of the people, and conduct the struggle.

8. A call for help to the Diaspora.

9. The publication of a call to the peoples of the world—to the United States, the Soviet Union, France and to all the free peoples—to give aid to the Hebrew fighters for freedom.

The positive elements of this programme, which was given wide prominence in the world Press as the 'Freedom Charter of the Irgun Zvai Leumi,' were not implemented in the summer of 1946, but two years later. Again, therefore, we were ahead of history. In historic events there must, apparently, always be somebody who foresees. But is it essential that there should always be somebody who sees too late?

Jewish official circles were falling into confusion and the retreat had begun. At first the many Jewish detainees were ordered not to identify themselves. The stock reply they gave to British interrogrators was "A Jew from Palestine." The British announced that if there were no identifications there would be no releases. The orders of the Resistance Movement were put to the test—and failed. Only a few days passed before the cry arose from the detention camps: "Identify us!" The British identified many—and released a few.

Among the detainees who were not released in spite of their known identities were certain leaders from the Jewish Agency and the Vaad Leumi (Executive of the Eretz Israel Jewish community)—Rabbi Fishman, Yitshak Gruenbaum, Moshe Shertok, David Remez, Dr. Dov Joseph and others. Our men, who had already spent years in concentration camps, gave their new companions a cordial welcome. The two leaders who were best liked by our boys were Gruenbaum and Remez. Remez used to teach them Talmud and preach national unity. Sharett, who kept aloof, contented himself with claiming: "We shall leave here better Jews than when we came in." Gruenbaum evolved an interesting theory in Latrun. For obvious reasons he published at the time only its first part—from which it appeared that the veteran militant had become a defeatist urging the suspension of the struggle and the acceptance of Weizmann's appeasement policy. Many months later we learnt from him what his real intention had been. In view of what happened on 29th June, Mr. Gruenbaum concluded that the Haganah should leave the field of military resistance—so much he had said—but also that the dissidents should continue to fight. I am not certain that this interesting idea was correct. What is certain is that had it been accepted many troubles and stumbling-blocks would have been avoided. However, it was not accepted, and there came a day when honest Mr. Gruenbaum had to cry out at a meeting of the Zionist Gentral Council: "I shall not support a united front of Ben Gurion and Bevin against Begin."

Notwithstanding the friendly relations between the V.I.P.s and the veteran detainees I once received a complaint from the Resistance Movement Command worded as follows: "Yehezkel, your people in Latrun are quarrelling with the imprisoned Zionist personalities. Can you stop this by a direct appeal to them. It is desirable that this should be done without delay. I await your reply—M-I."

I made immediate inquiries through the underground post which we maintained with all our imprisoned men wherever they were. Our officer in charge of the Irgun men at Latrun denied the charge emphatically.

The elements in the leadership whom Sneh and Galili called defeatists eventually defeated the "activists." After long discussions they decided to turn their backs on military resistance and not to launch civil disobedience. They decided to accept the British Government's terms for the release of the Jewish Very Important Persons. "Terrorism" was denounced in a public statement by the official institutions and an undertaking was given that it would be completely crushed. The Jewish V.I.P.s were released, after one hundred days of detention, and travelled to London to an Anglo-Arab-Jewish Conference in order to find a "compromise solution" for the Palestine problem. For them the struggle was suspended, leaving them only the "illegal" immigration.

3

The moral significance of the expansion of repatriation to Eretz Israel, immediately on the suspension of the united Resistance Movement, should not be underestimated. It is true that this campaign, in contrast to the repatriation efforts made before World War II by Joseph Katznelson and Avraham Stavsky, did not bring many Jews into the country. The British authorities seized the refugees in their thousands near the coast of Eretz Israel and deported them to concentration camps in Cyprus. The repatriates from the camps of Germany fought with empty hands against armed soldiers. Although men and women and children were killed in the process, Whitehall produced the old argument against the "unconscionable behaviour of people who press masses of men, women and children into unseaworthy ships." The British Government might hunt immigrant-ships, deport their "illegal" passengers, but they were defending "the law."

On the Jewish side, too, there was a moral aspect to this phase of the repatriation. The Haganah's struggle in Eretz Israel had come to a complete standstill. The leaders were released, and the Palmach men had returned to their bases. The Haganah men went back to their villages and their homes. Israel Galili could let his hair grow. The Haganah again became a semi-legal body. The status quo was restored completely. And it was at this precise moment that the whole burden of resistance to British rule was forced on to the refugees from Germany, on to the defenceless and helpless, on to women and children. They were beaten and deported, some were maimed; others killed. The leaders of the official institutions damaged their throats protesting.

We did not, however, content ourselves with verbal protests. After almost every deportation we delivered a heavy blow at the Government. And F.F.I. fighters succeeded on one occasion in setting oil tanks alight in Haifa harbour, where deportation ships were waiting for their prey.

Maltreatment of the repatriates by the Government reached its climax in the case of the "Exodus, 1947," which Bevin decided to send back to Germany. Protests and appeals met with no response whatsoever. The people themselves, who resisted the British troops, courageously, were dismayed when they were driven out on their new road of suffering from Haifa to Hamburg.

In a letter smuggled out of their prison-ship they wrote:

"The people are depressed. . . . We feel as though we have been sentenced to death. We shall resist at Hamburg, but will it help? The British Government will no doubt employ all the means at their disposal and the world will remain silent, as it has remained silent in the past. But our brothers throughout the world—the Jews of America and England and Eretz Israel—will they too remain silent? We are unhappy under the impression that not everything that could be done is being done for us. . . ."

We published these disillusioned, bitter words, and promised our brothers on the high seas, in the name of "the rebels, the fighters and those who remain true" that "You will not be forsaken in your struggle. We say—Eretz Israel or death."

But we did not possess the immediate means of helping. Just then we were suffering from a double lack. Our treasury was empty and we had no explosives in stock. Retaliation for this sort of thing needed more than a few shots. How could we deliver a big blow? We gritted our teeth. Days and nights passed without action. The people wondered what had happened to the Irgun. Characteristically, even our opponents, many of whom frequently blessed us in their secret hearts while energetically cursing us with their lips, were indignant at our failure to retaliate. But we had no effective reply. No explosives. No money. We ate our hearts out in frustration.

Fortune, however, did not forsake us. Miraculously a sum of money reached us. Miraculously we immediately acquired half a ton of explosives. Giddy completed the miracles. He built the famous "barrel," the barrel on wheels which one morning catapulted from an armoured car (the first of its type in Eretz Israel), shattered the whole Government "security zone" in Haifa and undermined British security in the whole country. The invention had been worked out to the last detail, down to the teeth which stopped the wheels from turning when the barrel hit the wall of the fortress. The Army authorities became very agitated. They had surrounded their security zone with dense barbed wire fences twelve to fifteen feet high—and here came this "catapult" which jumped the fence. A truly impudent barrel. At once they gave new orders—to raise the height of the barbed wire fences to twenty-four feet. And it was done at once. But Giddy also got to work immediately. And it is certain that had the British forces delayed their departure, their fences would have reached a height of sixty feet—and that too would not have sufficed.

But, great as was the effect on the British Government the Jewish defeatists stood their ground. From the 29th of June onwards they dominated the official institutions. They determined to end military resistance. They succeeded only in putting an end to the military resistance of the Haganah.

Dr. Weizmann, President of the Zionist Organisation, demanded there should be no more military operations until the Zionist congress. Sneh refused to give such an undertaking. He was bound by a prior undertaking to the officers of the Haganah that resistance would continue, that "the Jewish people would fight back." Plans had been prepared for the confiscation of arms from a British military camp. This attack was to serve as a reprisal for the confiscation of the great Jewish armoury at Yagur where the British seized several hundred rifles,

hundreds of thousands of rounds of ammunition, thousands of mortar shells, etc. (Incidentally we believed at
the time that the Haganah had dozens of such armouries, and only later found out that we were grievously
mistaken.) Dr. Weizmann demanded Sneh's resignation
as head of the Haganah, otherwise Dr. Weizmann himself would resign his post as President of the Zionist
Organisation. Between the two candidates for resignation a strange misunderstanding arose. Dr. Weizmann
complained that he had received no advance information about the attack on the bridges. Sneh said that he
had. Ultimately it transpired that they were both right:
Sneh *had* sent the information, but Weizmmann had *not*
known. The message did not reach him.

Despite his weak state of health Dr. Weizmann persisted in his ultimatum.

The "activists" amongst the official Jewish leaders
were persuaded that Weizmann's public resignation
would be a severe blow. Hashomer Hatzair (the extreme Communist-Socialist Zionists) had identified
themselves with Weizmann's "anti-violence" policy. A
large section in Mapai (Palestine Labour Party) also
demanded "the cessation of terrorism which threatens
the whole Zionist undertaking with destruction." Dr.
Weizmann emerged victorious. Sneh resigned.

Sneh attended the "decisive" meeting of the Jewish
Agency Executive in Paris, a meeting that discussed for
many weeks the fundamental question: to continue the
struggle or not. Throughout the discussions Ben Gurion
stood firm as a rock for—continuing the struggle. Sneh
supported him consistently, hoping to be able to return
to Eretz Israel with a clear cut decision to "fight back."
Then, suddenly, Ben Gurion changed his mind and
official resistance stopped. And this stoppage was not
interrupted until 30th November 1947, when the UN
decided to partition Eretz Israel and the Arabs started
killing Jews. But although official resistance was suspended, the revolt continued.

In spite of everything that happened I regard the
short period of the United Resistance Movement as the
happiest days of my life. There were always two visions

before my eyes. In the first place we had achieved our
heart's desire: in our wake the whole people had joined
in the struggle for the liberation of our country. The
men and women who had been hounded became the
people's favourites. They too were happy, for they were
vindicated.

My second vision was "introspective." A commander
in war—a real commander who bears the most terrible
of all responsibilities, the responsibility for human lives
—knows how hard is his lot, how many his unseen
torments. But can the responsibility of a "recognised"
commander be compared with the feeling of responsibility in the heart of a "dissident" commander? A dissident commander! His every victory is denounced as a
failure, his failure as catastrophe, as treachery. In his
case, the word "responsibility" is practically meaning-
less. I can only repeat the question I asked in the days
of anguish and disaster: What do the people outside
know, what can they know?

In the days of the Resistance Movement, we were not
publicly recognised, but we were recognised nevertheless. Part of the responsibility—though, indeed only
part—was taken off our shoulders. The whole people
were behind us.

But the days of happiness were brief; the days of sorrow were long. We had no choice, if we were to bring
freedom to our people and ensure life to its sons, but to
continue the revolt. When the Haganah gave up the
struggle, we continued to fight as we had promised to
do. We had once more to load the knapsack filled with
all the troubles of dissident responsibility on to our
backs. There was no alternative, except submission to
oppression. But freedom was in our blood; we could not
submit.

In the Resistance Movement there had not been
much love between the leaders, but the parting was not
without sorrow.

Especially as it was accompanied by the episode of
the King David Hotel.

Chapter XV
The King David Hotel

During World War II the southern wing of the King
David Hotel in Jerusalem was taken over to house the
central institutions of the British regime: Military
G.H.Q., and the Secretariat, the civil Government. As
the revolt against British rule intensified, the great hotel
was developed into a veritable fortress in the heart of
the city. In a neighbouring building, the British Military Police and the famous Special Investigation Bureau
established their headquarters. In the open space between the two buildings a strong military unit was encamped. Machine-gun nests were constructed at a number of points. Soldiers, police and detectives maintained
a close and constant watch on the building which
housed the supreme British rulers in Eretz Israel.

The authorities no longer depended on miracles.
They had learnt from experience. Before our attack on
police headquarters, Catling had boasted: "They won't
come, but if they do, they'll get such a welcome. . . ."

We came; and Catling's welcome evaporated. When
the building went up into the air, he and his chief, Giles,
narrowly escaped with their lives.

The host of watching eyes surrounding the King
David Hotel saw nothing of our reconnaissance—the
messengers of the underground remained unseen, but
saw what they had to see, and found out what they
sought. The plan for an attack on the King David Hotel
began to take shape.

In the Spring of 1946 we submitted our plan for the
first time to the Command of the Resistance Movement. I informed Sneh and Galili that we would undertake to penetrate the Government wing of the King

David Hotel and to carry out an extensive sabotage operation. Without going into details, I emphasized that the employment of explosives would be distinguished by a new device, invented by Giddy. On the one hand our "mines" could not be moved or dismantled as they would blow up on contact. On the other hand we would be able to fix the moment for the explosion of these "mines" by a time mechanism, half-an-hour or even an hour after their introduction into the building. This would allow for evacuation by hotel guests, workers and officials. The rules we had laid down for ourselves made the evacuation of the hotel essential. There were many civilians in the hotel whom we wanted, at all costs, to avoid injuring. We were anxious to ensure that they should leave the danger zone in plenty of time for their safety.

The Haganah Command did not at once approve our plan. They regarded an attack on the headquarters of British rule as too ambitious. They were not against it in principle. They argued that the time had not yet come for such an attack, which was likely to inflame the British excessively. We thought otherwise, but were bound by our agreement and had to bow to their decision. But we did not give up our plan. In our personal talks with the Haganah chiefs, and in our code messages to "Jeremiah" we put forward the plan anew. Our code name for the great King David Hotel was at first "Malonchik" ("little hotel")[1] Later, to improve the camouflage we all called it "Chick". Meantime, the F.F.I. had prepared a plan of attack on another building being used by the Government, the well-known premises of David Brothers. To distinguish between the two, the Haganah leaders named this objective "Your slave-and-redeemer."

Both these plans, which remained pending for several months, were approved by the Haganah Command on

[1] *Malon* is Hebrew for hotel; "chik" is the affectionate diminutive in Russian, hence also in Yiddish and even in colloquial Hebrew.

the 1st July, 1946, two days after General Barker's major attack on the Haganah, the Palmach and the Jewish Agency. The Haganah chiefs did not explain why Operation "Chick" only became feasible after the 29th June. There are grounds for believing that there were two reasons for this change of mind. The Haganah which had adopted the policy of self-restraint in the thirties, was belatedly indoctrinated in the 'forties—with the spirit of "reprisal." The internal literature of the Haganah abounded with articles explaining that operations must always be "reprisals for attacks." Eliahu Golomb even worked up a historico-philosophical justification for this theory. He argued that the wars our people had fought in our country had been essentially defensive. Planned revolts, he claimed, had usually ended in catastrophe. True, the Hasmonean revolt had been crowned with victory, but that was an exception. How could we be sure that the miracle would be repeated? Historical philosophy was reinforced by mathematics. The Haganah writers sought to establish a kind of mathematical relationship between the "attack" and the "reprisal." I remember one of their "equations." "The scope of the reprisal is equal to the magnitude of the attack." A clear criterion, a fixed relationship, war by mathematics—on paper.

Out of the philosophic soil grew the theory, brought to fulfilment in the days of the Resistance Movement, of the "connected struggle." If for example, the Giveat Olga Observation station is interfering with immigration, the Giveat Olga station must be destroyed. If the Haifa Radar Station is interfering with immigration, the Radar Station must be destroyed. The Hashomer Hatzair people, who opposed every form of armed struggle, protested against even these operations which, they said, "weakened our friends and strengthened our enemies." Their anger was unbounded when the members of their party, as members of the Haganah and the Palmach, were sent to blow up railway lines or to sabotage installations of the Palestine Mobile Force. What is the connection, they asked publicly as well as privately, between immigration and railway-tracks? What is the connection, they exclaimed, between our colonisation and the Mobile police units?

Sneh used to explain it to them roughly like this:

"These railway-tracks carry the trains which bring the soldiers who hunt the immigrants. The armoured cars of the P.M.F. carry the police rushing to catch immigrants and to carry out searches in the communal settlements."

Sneh's explanations were not illogical. But the Hashomer Hatzair people regarded them as hairsplitting. They insisted on a "purely connected struggle" and evolved the theory of the "defence of the defence" (defence of the Haganah itself) as the limit of action. This theory, of course, can be extended *ad infinitum*. If you have a defence organisation to defend the defence organisation, you have to evolve means to defend the defence organisation defending the defence organisation. And so on. And, of course, this theory also remained a theory. At Yagur, on the 29th of June, when the British raided the arms stores of the Haganah, there was no defence of the Haganah. And later, after the Arabs had begun their attack in November 1947, Haganah soldiers offered no resistance when British troops disarmed them. In spite of the theory, the Haganah gave orders not to "defend the Haganah."

It was, astonishingly enough, this very piece of doctrinaire reasoning ("the scope of the reprisal is equal to the magnitude of the attack") that led to the approval of our plan to attack the King David Hotel. On the 29th of June 1946 the British occupied the Offices of the Jewish Agency. The Jewish Agency was regarded as "Jewish headquarters." So, according to the doctrinaire argument we must repay them in kind and attack *their* headquarters, in the King David Hotel.

The second reason was a more serious one. The Haganah, which had become accustomed to its convenient "semi-legal" status in the eyes of the British authorities, had never taken efficient steps to observe the rules of caution. The Jewish Agency leaders apparently put their trust in their imagined "international status" which they fondly believed gave them immunity from police action. Consequently there were many secret documents in the Jewish Agency building which a wisely run organisation in such circumstances would never have allowed to be there. The booty which the British forces carried away as a result of their searches in the Jewish Agency building was considerable. The irresponsibility that prevailed in the Jewish Agency reached such a pitch that, as Galili told me, the British were able to take out of a typewriter part of the verbatim report of Mr. Shertok's speech at the Zionist General Council. Mr. Shertok had praised the blowing-up of the bridges, and explained the great political significance of the operation.

The report of Shertok's speech, which corroborated Jewish Agency responsibility for the Haganah's sabotage operations, gave the lie to the emphatic disclaimers Mr. Ben Gurion had made before the Anglo-American Commission only a few months previously. It was not the only document of this kind which the British carried away to the King David Hotel.

Anxiety for the destruction of these documents was plainly indicated at the meeting between Yitshak Sadeh, the Operations Officer of the Haganah, and our Giddy. Yitshak Sadeh asked Giddy how much time he was allowing between the introduction of the explosives into the building and the explosion. Giddy suggested forty-five minutes. Sadeh thought this was "too long, as the British might then manage not only to evacuate their people *but to get the documents out as well*." He consequently proposed that we allow only fifteen minutes for the evacuation of the hotel. Giddy reassured him. Despite his youth Giddy had had far more practical experience in this kind of fighting than had the Haganah Operations officer. He replied that experience had taught him that when the authorities received warning that one of their offices was about to be blown up, they left the building at high speed, and did not waste time on documents. Giddy felt that fifteen minutes might not give a safe margin for evacuating the building. Finally, agreement was reached by a compromise: half-an-hour.

I shall have to return to this meeting between Giddy and Sadeh. In the meantime I go back to the main document connected with the King David Hotel action.

On the 1st July, 1946, two days after Barker's attack on the Jewish Agency, we received a letter from the Haganah Command which ran as follows:

"Shalom!

"(a) You are to carry out as soon as possible the Chick and the house of 'Your-slave-and-redeemer.' Inform us of the date. Preferably simultaneously. Do not publish the identity of the body carrying out the operation—neither directly nor by implication.

"(b) We are also preparing something—shall inform you of details in good time.

"(c) Tel Aviv and neighbourhood must be excluded from all operations. We are all interested in protecting Tel Aviv—as the centre of Yishuv life and our own work. If Tel Aviv should be paralysed by curfew and arrests as the result of an operation, we and our plans will also be paralysed. Incidentally, the important nerves of the other sides are not concentrated here. So —Tel Aviv is 'out of bounds' to Jewish forces."

2

When we received this letter we set about preparing "Operation Chick." We could not do it immediately. The Haganah's request that we attack the Hotel reached us several weeks after they had at first rejected the same plan. In the meantime a number of circumstances had changed. As a result, we had to carry out anew all the reconnaissance operations and reconsider the whole of the operational details. We were well aware that this was the largest of our operations to date and that it might turn out to be unique in the history of partisan wars of liberation. It is no simple matter to penetrate the very heart of the military government, to deliver a blow within the fortified headquarters of a heavily armed regime. I doubt if this operation had any precedent in history.

We dared not fail. After the 29th of June, large sec-

tions of the people had been thrown into confusion.
Barker's blow had been very severe. Defeatism raised
its deathly head. People began to question our ability
to fight the British regime. Many expressed their despair as to the outcome of any "struggle": "Who are
we, what is our strength, that we should be able to
stand up to the British Army?" These questions were
pregnant with danger. They reflected the defeatism that
is fatal to every war of liberation. We realised that
Jewish self-confidence could be restored only by a successful counter-attack in reply to Barker's heavy blows.
We were therefore greatly relieved by the request of
the Haganah, and plunged with enthusiasm into a re-
examination of every detail of the operation. We always planned every undertaking with infinite care.
But to none of our many operations—except, perhaps,
the later attack on Acre Fortress—did we devote so
much preliminary preparation as we did to "Operation
Chick."

Giddy's tremendous inventive and creative powers
were called upon to the full. Innocent milk-cans became the bearers of high explosives. Their action was
doubly assured. One mechanism determined the time of
explosion—half-an-hour after the cans were left in
position; the other secured the cans against any attempt
at removal or dismantling.

A prime consideration was the timing of the attack.
Two proposals were made: one for eleven a.m., the
other for between four and five o'clock in the afternoon. Both plans were based on the same reasoning.
The milk-cans could be brought into the Government
wing of the building only by way of the "Regence
Café" situated in the basement of the wing occupied
by Barker and Shaw. In these morning and afternoon
hours the Café was usually empty. At lunch-time it
was filled with customers, among them civilian men
and women as well as Army officers. It was essential
that the attack be delivered at an hour when there
were no customers in the Café.

Of the proposed hours, which both met this condition, we chose the earlier—11 a.m.—because it was

easier then to coordinate our attack with that planned by the F.F.I. on the David Brothers Building—"Operation Slave and Redeemer." It was clear that these operations must be simultaneous: otherwise the one would interfere with the other.

Next we considered how to give the warnings so as to eliminate casualties. First, to keep passers-by away from the building, we decided to let off a small cracker-bomb, noisy but harmless. Then we chose three offices to receive a telephoned warning, which would be given as soon as our men had got away from the basement of the hotel. These three were: the King David Hotel management; the *Palestine Post*, and the French Consulate-General which is close to the Hotel. Finally, warning placards would be placed next to the milk-cans: "Mines. Do not Touch"—in case British experts should attempt to dismantle the explosives after our telephoned warning had been sent out.

Operation "Chick" was carried out exactly three weeks after we received the Haganah's instructions to execute it. During that time a number of meetings took place between us and the leaders of the Resistance Movement. Once the F.F.I. called for a postponement as they were not yet ready for their task. Twice or thrice we postponed the attack at the request of the Haganah Command. These postponements were very dangerous. Each time the number of people in the know increased. As I have already mentioned, participants in every operation were given a preliminary and detailed briefing on their task. In the case of the Hotel operation, a comparatively large number of men had already been briefed. Every new postponement was therefore liable to endanger not only the plan itself but also its participants. We consequently protested against these postponements, but resigned ourselves to them out of necessity. On July 19th, I received a note from Moshe Sneh:

"Shalom!

"My comrades have told me of the last talk. If you still respect my personal appeal, I ask you most ear-

nestly to postpone the planned operations for a few
more days."

We acceded to this request, and accepted the 22nd
of July as the final date. But the F.F.I. again were unable to complete their preparations; and at the last moment it was decided to go ahead with the attack on the
King David Hotel alone. Because of last-minute consultations, the time of attack was delayed by one hour
and began at twelve o'clock instead of eleven.

The Assault Unit, under the command of the Jerusalem Gideon (dressed in the flowing robes of a hotel
worker), executed the attack with great bravery and
carried out their orders with absolute punctiliousness.
They brought the milk-cans as far as the approach to
the hotel. They then divided into two groups, one for
the "break-through" and the other to "cover" the first.
The first group took the milk-cans into the basement by
way of the Regence Café. They overwhelmed the café
employees and locked them in a side-room. These fifteen Arabs presented no surprise to our men: the
peaceful subjection of the cooks and waiters—the only
persons in the café at the time—was part of the plan.
But our men were surprised by the sudden appearance
of two British soldiers who, their suspicions being
aroused, drew their revolvers. A clash was unavoidable. Both sides suffered casualties. Meanwhile the
covering group outside had clashed with the British
military patrols. In view of the nature of the operation
our men had no machine-guns and had to fight with
sten-guns and revolvers. However, the break-through
party reached its objective. The commander of the operation himself set the time mechanism at thirty minutes and put up the warning placards. The Arab workers were then freed and ordered to run for their lives.
They did not hesitate. The last man out was Gideon,
who shouted, "Get away, the hotel is about to blow up."
At the moment the warning cracker-bomb was exploded
outside the hotel and under cover of its smoke our men
withdrew. The noise caused by the bomb and the unexpected shooting drove away all passers-by in the
streets.

At ten minutes past twelve, Gideon reached the spot at which our "telephonist" was waiting. She immediately telephoned the King David Hotel and warned them that explosives had been placed under the hotel and would go off within a short time. "Evacuate the whole building!"—she cried to the hotel telephone-operator. She then telephoned the office of the *Palestine Post* and announced—as was later testified by the *Palestine Post* telephonist—that "bombs have been placed in the King David Hotel and the people there have been told to evacuate the building." The third and final warning was given to the French Consulate, accompanied by advice to open the Consulate windows so as to prevent the effects of blast. The Consulate officials subsequently confirmed the receipt of the warning. They opened their windows wide, and the French Consulate building suffered no damage.

It was now twelve-fifteen. Gideon was counting the minutes. So far, everything had gone according to plan, except for the casualties we had suffered in the unexpected clash. The milk-cans were lodged in the basement under the Government wing of the hotel. All warnings had been delivered and received. The British had no doubt begun the evacuation and, if things had gone as before in similar circumstances, would very soon complete it. Only one question bothered him: would the explosives go off? Might not some error have been made in the mechanism? Would the building really go up? Would the documents be destroyed?

Each minute seemed like a day. Twelve-thirty-one, thirty-two. Zero hour drew near. Gideon grew restless. The half-hour was almost up. Twelve-thirty-seven . . . . Suddenly, the whole town seemed to shudder. There had been no mistake. The force of the explosion was greater than had been expected. Yitshak Sadeh, of the Haganah, had doubted whether it would reach the third or even the second floor. Giddy had claimed that, though only about 500 lbs. of explosives—a compound of T.N.T. and gelignite—had been put into the milk-cans, the confined space of the basement would heighten the force of the escaping gases, and the explosion would reach the roof. The milk-cans "reached" the whole height of the building, from basement to roof, six storeys of stone, concrete and steel. As the B.B.C. put it—the entire wing of a huge building was cut off as with a knife.

3

But while our Assault Unit in the lion's den had done everything possible to ensure the timely evacuation of the hotel, others had taken a different line. For some reason the hotel was not evacuated even though from the moment when the warnings had been received there was plenty of time for every living soul to saunter out. Instead, the toll of lives was terrible. More than two hundred people were killed or injured. Among the victims were high British officers. We particularly mourned the alien civilians whom we had had no wish to hurt, and the fifteen Jewish civilians, among them good friends, who had so tragically fallen. Our satisfaction at the success of the great operation was bitterly marred. Again we went through days of pain and nights of sorrow for the blood that need not have been shed.

Why was the King David Hotel not evacuated? In this tragic chapter there are certain facts which are beyond all doubt. There is no doubt that the warnings reached their appointed recipients. The *Middle East Mail*, the British Forces newspaper in the Middle East, reported that at several minutes past twelve the telephone operator in the Hotel heard the voice of a woman warning her that bombs had been placed in the hotel which should be evacuated without delay. The telephone operator at the *Palestine Post* testified on oath to a police officer that at twelve-fifteen she received the warning and "at once" passed it on to the duty officer at police headquarters. *Eshnab*, the semi-legal organ of the Haganah, published the statement of a reliable witness who was in the hotel at the time of the explosion. He said:

"When I heard the noise caused by the warning explosion, I decided it was best to get out of the hotel. Many others tried to do so too but the soldiers barred any exit by shooting in the direction of the people trying to get out."

I subsequently learned that when the warning to evacuate the hotel reached a high official he exclaimed: "We are not here to take orders from the Jews. We give *them* orders."

In the twenty-five or twenty-seven minutes which, as testified to by all witnesses, had elapsed from the receipt of the warnings to the moment of the explosion, the authorities had ample time in which to evacuate every person in the hotel. Finally, there is reason to believe that a specific order was given, by someone in authority, that the warning to leave the hotel should be ignored. Why was this stupid order given? Who was responsible for it?

The British Government held no inquiry. Before General Barker left for England he issued his notorious order to the British troops.

"I am determined," he wrote, "that they (the Jews) should be punished and made aware of our feelings of contempt and disgust at their behaviour. We must not let ourselves be misled by hypocritical sympathy expressed by their leaders and representative bodies and by the protestations that they are not responsible and cannot curb the terrorists. I repeat that if the Jewish community really wanted to put an end to the crimes it could do so by co-operating with us. I have accordingly decided that as from the receipt of this letter all Jewish places of entertainment, cafés, restaurants, shops, and private houses are out of bounds. No British soldier will have contact with any Jew, and duty contacts will be made as short as possible and will be limited to the duty concerned. I understand that these measures will create difficulties for the troops, but I am certain that if my reasons are explained to them, they will understand their duty and will punish the Jews in the manner this race dislikes most: by hitting them in the pocket, which will demonstrate our disgust for them."

This order, directed to British officers throughout the

country, fell into the hands of the Irgun Information Service the day it was written. We published it at once. Its hateful contents echoed throughout the world.

With the gathering of the evidence and the revelations of the Haganah Information Service, it was widely suggested that a high official had deliberately prevented the evacuation of the King David Hotel in order, for some reason best known to himself, that a major disaster should occur.

After weighing the matter during the years that have passed I am convinced that *this* theory is contrary to the facts known to us, and is not true. The question of the ancient Roman jurists *Qui prodest*? (whom did it profit?) does not provide the key to the mystery. The question remains open.

At any rate it is clear that we did all we could to ensure the early and complete evacuation of the hotel; that the warnings were given and received in time by the authorities; that they had time enough to evacuate the hotel twice over; that somebody, for some dark purpose, or because he lost his head, or to protect a spurious prestige, ordered that the hotel should not be evacuated.

Immediately after this operation the whole world was flooded with hair-raising lies. At the disposal of the propagandists was a mighty machine. What did we have? The underground *Herut* wrote of "The Battle for the Truth:"

"The battle went on. . . . It will go down as one of the great battles in our history. The antagonists were not tanks, nor armed forces. They were the two ancient antagonists, who have been fighting since the beginning of time: Truth and Lies.

"The contending forces were as usual not evenly-matched. Behind the lie stood the tremendous propaganda machine of a mighty world-wide empire; radio stations whose voice reached the four corners of the earth, hundreds of newspapers, parliaments, governments, embassies. To the aid of the lie there rushed pitiful Jewish newspapers, panic-stricken Jewish institutions, "personalities" shaking at the knees. And they all shouted and screamed, all shut their ears, all competed in the search for stronger words of denunciation, more insulting terms, more humiliating epithets. It seemed that the battle was lost."

Lost? The battle was hard. Our chances of winning seemed infinitesimal. Yet the modest broadsheets beat the mighty engines of propaganda. "Great is truth. . . ."

4

No less difficult was the internal battle for the truth. As the Haganah had requested, we did not publish any statement on the day of the operation identifying the attacking body, "either directly or by implication." But in the Haganah itself confusion reigned. One officer made a series of wildly conflicting statements. At first he advised the Jewish Press not on any account to denounce the operation, hinting broadly that the Haganah had had prior knowledge of the attack. Later in the day when it became known that there had been many casualties, he advised the Press to make no comment at all, positive or negative. His third "guiding directive" was—to denounce the "dissidents" (meaning the Irgun and the F.F.I.) unreservedly.

And the denunciations burst forth! Our little country has never seen such an outburst of journalistic hysteria and self-abasement. *Hamishmar*[1] called for a campaign of extermination. *Haaretz,*[2] as though seeing nightmares, published a poem preaching that no redemption at all was better than redemption proclaimed by a leper. . . . Only after many days did *Haaretz* sober up sufficiently to urge an official inquiry into the reasons why the hotel was not evacuated. Then, and then only, did *Haaretz* write that there had undoubtedly been a warning; that in the pocket of Mr. Jacobs[3]—a senior Jew-

---

[1] *Al Hamishmar*, organ of left-wing Communist-Socialists.

[2] *Haaretz,* organ of middle-class German Jews, or "Yekkies," as they are playfully nicknamed.

[3] A brother of Mr. Norman Jacobs, a well-known Manchester Zionist.

ish official in the Administration who had been killed in
the explosion—there had been found his medals and
decorations, a sign that he was on the point of leaving
the office and that somebody had prevented him from
doing so. The chorus of denunciation was swelled by
Mr. Ben Gurion who, in an interview with the Parisian
France Soir, was alleged to have made this odd comment: "The Irgun is the enemy of the Jewish people—
it has always opposed me."

Strangest of all was the behaviour of the Haganah.
In spite of their earlier demand that we should not
publish the identity of the attacking body, I received a
note from Galili on the evening of the 22nd of July,
asking us to announce that it was the Irgun that had
carried out the attack on the King David Hotel. Galili
added that the Haganah would publish no statement at
all. We complied with his request. We at once drafted
and published a full factual statement on the attack on
the Hotel. We omitted only one fact: that on the 1st
of July the Haganah had asked us to carry out "Operation Chick". . . . But the Haganah, on its side, did not
keep its promise. The next day, the 23rd of July, "Kol
Israel," the Haganah radio station, broadcast a highly
significant statement:

"The Hebrew Resistance Movement denounces the
heavy toll of lives caused in the dissidents' operation at
the King David Hotel."

"Denounces" . . . "dissidents" . . . . This was the
first time for many months that the Haganah spokesman had used the term "dissidents." And we, who had
learnt to understand even the change in the tone of a
phrase, understood the hint. The words were indeed
highly significant. Running away from responsibility is
irresponsibility. It is against all morals, it sins particularly against the morale of fighters.

The same day, Galili sent me a personal letter. Its
tone about what had happened between us was defensive, and it displayed grave anxiety about future developments. Galili, who had succeeded Sneh as Commander-in-Chief of the Haganah wrote:

"To M., Shalom!

"The grave consequences of your action in Jerusalem have brought about unforeseen developments. The newspaper comment disregarded our guidance and was therefore unavoidable in the circumstances.

"The situation is liable to cause tragic and grave complications in the continuance of the struggle. In order to avoid this it is essential that we two meet tonight, 23 July, 1946, at 21 hours.

"Please make an effort to come. I shall wait for you at our last meeting place. Our meeting tonight must precede tomorrow's meeting."

I went to the rendezvous. My heart was very heavy, but Galili did not observe it. When I reproached him for the attitude of the Press, he repeated that the Press had "gone off the rails" and had disregarded the guidance of the Haganah Command. But I complained particularly of the amazing broadcast of "Kol Israel."

"What does this mean?" I asked him. "Don't you know what and who caused the 'heavy toll?' Why do you denounce us? The plan was agreed between us, our men carried out their instructions precisely, the warning was given—why don't you tell the truth?"

It was then that Galili told me of the conversation between a police officer and an official in the Hotel which had come to the knowledge of the Haganah Information Service. This was the conversation in which the official said, "We don't take orders from the Jews." At my demand, Galili promised this information would be broadcast in the next transmission of "Kol Israel." He asked me to ensure that we would not "publish anything likely to complicate the situation," and I gave this promise. We had no wish to increase the panic which had overwhelmed the official institutions.

Then Galili took a note out of his pocket for me to read. It was a note to him from Yitshak Sadeh. I read, and everything seemed to go black. Sadeh claimed, no more, no less, that he had been misled, that Giddy had told him that the attack would be carried out between two and three o'clock in the afternoon—that is, during the luncheon break when the Government offices were empty.

I told Galili at once the relevant facts concerning
the timing of the operation. The Irgun Command had
repeatedly discussed and examined the plan of attack
and never once had we heard of a proposal to carry it
out in the luncheon hour. Giddy had gone to meet
Sadeh after the final decision to attack at midday.
Giddy had later submitted to me a full report of this
meeting with Sadeh, Giddy had never told me an untruth. But even if Galili did not believe in Giddy as I
did—what sense was there in assuming that Giddy had
told Sadeh something different from what had been decided at his own suggestion.

Galili promised to ask his Operations Officer for
further details and asked me to hold an inquiry. I told
him I did not think there were any grounds for an inquiry, but I would ask Giddy, and if Mr. Yitshak Sadeh
insisted on his version we would have the two Operations Officers thrash the matter out in our presence.
Galili acquiesced.

Quite a few days passed before "Kol Israel" broadcast the "Hotel conversation," and then only after we
had sent further pressing letters to Galili. The Press continued to "disregard the guidance of the Haganah;"
and we remained silent—for the sake of the common
struggle.

Meanwhile the conference between Operations Officers took place. The Haganah was represented by
Galili and Sadeh. On our side were Giddy, Avraham
and I. I had had a further talk with Giddy. When he
learnt what Sadeh had written he was astounded. He
explained that Sadeh had never asked him about the
hour of the attack, and that they had not discussed it
at all. They had discussed the explosives and their
likely effect. They had discussed the time to be allowed
for evacuation. They had discussed the operation as a
whole. They had not discussed details. Sadeh never
interested himself in details and had not done so in
this case. And this detail, of the hour of the operation,
was not even mentioned.

During the inquiry I questioned them both impar-
tially. After all, I said to myself, there may have been

some misunderstanding. Question after question was put to Sadeh and Giddy by Galili and me.

This preliminary inquiry came to no formal conclusion. And we—against whom the waves of incitement were beating, or were being driven—demanded a formal court of inquiry to judge between us and the Resistance Movement. We proposed that the presiding judge should be Mr. Isaac Gruenbaum—a member of the Jewish Agency—or Dr. Magnes—President of the Hebrew University—or even Mr. Tobenkin, the leader of Achdut Avodah,[1] Mr. Galili's own political party: all three avowed political opponents of the Irgun. Our proposal was not accepted.

In addition to all the other untruths disseminated about our attack on the British civil and military headquarters, the story was current that as a result of the "King David Hotel outrage" the Haganah broke off relations with us. It seems to me their relations with us were probably never more close than in the period following "Operation Chick." We continued for a long time to prepare co-ordinated plans. In August, 1946, we put forward an operational plan for sinking one of the British deportation ships anchored in Haifa harbour. We called the plan "Operation Launch" and sometimes called it Mr. Launch. On 17 August, 1946 almost a month after "Operation Chick," Galili wrote me:

"I hasten to reply in the Launch matter. I emphasise again that the matter of Mr. Launch is receiving serious attention and I advise caution against interference which may be highly dangerous. As for your claim that this was your concrete proposal—since when is priority given to a *proposal*, particularly when the proposer does not have to know that his proposals were being worked on long before he proposed them?

"I shall reply on other matters without delay."

No, it was not the King David Hotel attack that

[1] Achdut Avodah was then the left-wing of the Labour-Socialists, before it joined up with Hashomer Hatzair in "Mapam."

brought about the severance of relations between the Haganah and the Irgun. It served only to reveal the true character of those relations which were actually severed several months later. They were brought to an end, in accordance with the letter of our agreement, by the "armistice" decided on, one Autumn night, by a certain "prisoner in Paris"[1] against the opinion of the other "Paris prisoner."

5

The attack on the King David Hotel had other consequences. After careful preparation the British Army descended on Tel Aviv in strength in order, as they proclaimed, to track down the terrorists and to destroy them root and branch.

Tel Aviv was occupied by nearly two divisions of infantry and armoured units, accompanied by a swarm of police and Intelligence agents. A day and night curfew was proclaimed. The warning was given: "Anybody leaving his house will be shot at sight." There were house-to-house searches. "Screening" cages were set up. Nobody was to escape the net. Every house was to be examined. Every individual was to be interrogated.

These were the orders of General Cassells, Commander of His Majesty's Forces in the besieged city. The camps at Latrun and Rafiah were swelled by a number of guests who had time to disillusion themselves behind barbed wire.

But it was not these that General Cassells and General Barker and policemen Giles and Catling were particularly seeking. They knew whom they wanted. And they searched. How they searched! But again they did not find.

---

[1] Mr. Ben Gurion was in Paris when his colleagues were seized and interned on 29th June. He remained there until after they were released. The other "prisoner of Paris" was Dr. Sneh who, after a period of hiding, following the 29th June, took refuge in France.

The evening before the curfew was proclaimed we were warned from a reliable source that the British would probably carry out wide-spread searches. As it happened, we had a meeting with the F.F.I. chiefs the same night. We told them of the warning, but it did not seem urgent, and neither they nor we gave it a second thought. After parting from Friedman-Yellin and Yitshak Ysernitzky, I went home to Bin-Nun Street. Avraham, as usual, saw me to my door and we fixed the hour for our meeting on the morrow.

But soon after midnight I was awakened by the deep rumble of tanks and heavy vehicles. My wife woke up too, and Roxy, giving free rein to her anti-British instincts, began barking the roof off.

The warning of searches had been only too speedily confirmed. Had we taken it more seriously we should all have left Tel Aviv at our leisure and waited for the military to finish their house-to-house search. Now we were all caught in Tel Aviv. The situation looked black. What would happen to the boys? As for Israel Sassover, it was clear that his beard would not help him this time. Our Information Service had learnt some time before that the British had become particularly interested in beards and many orthodox Jews had suffered as a result of their suspicions.

What, then, was to be done?

There was a secret compartment in the little house. It had been planned by Yaacov Meridor, before he was denounced to the British. It was admittedly primitive and a sharp eye could have discovered it. For eighteen months it had remained empty. I had never taken cover in it during the many searches in Tel Aviv, not even during the search across the road. But that night I had a feeling I must get out of sight.

For the information of my boy, who was sleeping soundly, and for the Police and Army who were dreaming their dream of captured prizes, I arranged with my wife that I had "gone to Jerusalem," saying which, I climbed into the hiding place.

The British continued to flow past the house. At

dawn they were still coming. From the radio, which my wife had placed as high up as she could so that I could hear it, came the voice of the news announcer. The curfew would continue for several days. Every house would be searched, every resident examined. Several days . . . it was not very cheering.

Now troops were in the garden, and a party settled down to camp there. They came in and made their first search of the house. They were at arm's length from me.

"Where is your husband?" the officer asked.

My wife, claiming that she could not speak English, answered in Hebrew that her husband had gone to Jerusalem.

She was taken away for questioning. There was no choice. She took the two children with her. The "screening-table," set up in the street by the military, was less than a mile away. When she got there, however, they asked her no questions at all. The British policeman on duty took one look at her and said to the Jewish policeman who served as interpreter:

"Tell her to go home!"

She told me afterwards that the policeman's tone was somewhat humiliating. She came home and, by talking loudly to the children, gave me the signal that for the time being everything was in order. So far so good.

But then the troops came back to make a thorough search of the house. They opened cupboards. They looked under beds, and knocked at walls. They knocked at the wall of my compartment. They knocked so hard I could hardly restrain myself from knocking back. Roxy was less restrained.

Nevertheless my hiding place was no Paradise. Involuntarily I recalled the solitary confinement cell at Lukishki. There were certain comparisons between the two. In Lukishki it was hot by day and cold by night. Here it was cool at night—and purgatory by day. There the floor was of stone—here it was of wood. There your bones ached—and they ached no less here. There you could take three and a half steps. Here you dared not move. There you lacked food. Here you lacked water.

That was the worst of it: no water. I had gone without food in Lukishki and elsewhere. Here for the first time I learnt what it meant to go without water. Hunger and thirst—it is best to know neither. But if I had to choose between them, I would unhesitatingly choose hunger. Prolonged thirst is terrifying.

It was August, the place was stifling, and there was not a drop of water. A day went by, and a night. The British continued to camp in our garden. Another day —and another night. No water. A third day and night. My head began to grow dizzy. My body began strangely to dry up. What would happen if, as the radio comfortingly reminded me, this were to go on for days?

The British soldiers kept coming into the house every few minutes. Sometimes they would ask for matches, or for other neighbourly kindnesses; but usually they came to ask for—water. They were drinking our water.

Suddenly I felt something had altered. There was a noise from outside of people moving about and the roar of petrol engines. The troops had stopped coming into the house. What could it mean?

Quiet!—I rebuked myself. Maybe you are mistaken. Don't rejoice too soon at the water you're going to get!

But all my doubts were soon set at rest. My wife was giving me the "All Clear" signal—with a broom, of all things!

And when at last I got to the water I did not drink. I simply thrust my head again and again deep into a bowl of the life-saving liquid. Four days had gone since I had entered my waterless cell.

The curfew was lifted. The first to visit me was Giddy. His astonished question was:

"How on earth did you manage to breathe there?"

That was something I could not answer. I had never worried about the air in my cell; I had thought only of water.

After Giddy came Amitzur and Reuven and Meir, each with his story, a story with the same theme. The

regime, with all their troops and all their detectives and
all their Intelligence agents and all their "terrorists'
photographs" and all their elaborate identifications, had
achieved little.

Avraham, about whom we were anxious, arrived soon
afterwards. He had been gathering news. Yitshak Ysernitzky, the F.F.I. Commander, had been captured in
the guise of "Rabbi Shamir." Of our active members
only one, Zusia, had been captured. All our other officers were safe and sound.

Our joy was so great that we forgot our rules and
talked in loud voices. "Daddy, where have you been all
this time?" came the sudden voice of Benny.

"In Jerusalem."

"In Jerusalem? What did you bring me?"

"Bring you? Well. . . ."

My wife saved the situation.

"He brought you a big wagon, but Uncle Simon (to
Benny Amitzur was Uncle Simon) will have to bring it
home."

I was told later that during the great curfew in Tel
Aviv orthodox Jews in a number of Tel Aviv syn-
agogues gathered to offer prayers to the Almighty to
preserve me from those who were seeking my life.

Nothing I had ever heard moved me more deeply
than this report.

Chapter XVI

The Floggings

Certain elements in the machinery of British government seem to have a special affection for the use of the whip.

In the development of certain British Colonies the whip has been made to serve an educational purpose. It is applied, of course, not to recalcitrant boys but to adults who are treated like disorderly children. When I travelled through Persia on my way from Russia to Eretz Israel, I saw this symbol of British rule. Although Persia was not, at any rate formally, a British Colony, every British officer carried a cane or a little whip and regularly emphasized his orders to the "natives" with a light and pedagogic touch of one of these "sceptres of gentle peace."

While Eretz Israel was ruled as a British Colony, it could not logically be denied the educational privilege of the whip.

It was the early misfortune of two young soldiers of the Irgun Zvai Leumi to be the victims of the whip philosophy. Katz and Kimchi, two lads of seventeen, were sentenced to fifteen years' imprisonment by a Military "Court," for breaking the Emergency Regulations regarding the carrying of arms. But the "sentence" was rounded off by the educational addition of eighteen lashes for each of the boys.

We regarded this degrading addendum to an already severe sentence as a very serious matter with far-reaching moral and political implications. These lashes would wound the soul of Eretz Israel. For seventy generations, in seventy lands we had suffered the lashes of our oppressors. The Polish barons whipped their Jewish "protégés," and the German barons whipped their "protected Jews." Was an oppressor now to whip us in our own country? Would the rebels of our generation, ready and willing to sacrifice their lives for the liberation of their people, tolerate this new humiliation?

What was the purpose of this bestial punishment? Did the regime want to demonstrate that it regarded us as natives; that it would teach these impudent Jews in the orthodox fashion how to behave towards their benevolent masters? Manifestly here was something that affected the whole family of rebels. It affected our whole people, not only in its relations with the Mandatory Power in Palestine, but in its relations with all the peoples of the world. These thirty-six lashes would be felt not only by Jews, but by all oppressed peoples under alien rule. Here the law of the whip must meet its final challenge.

I myself had bitter personal memories of the whip. In 1920, when the Russian Army retreated from Poland, my birthplace, Brisk, was occupied by Polish troops under the command of a Baron General, an arrogant anti-Semite. This General ordered the arrest of a number of prominent Jewish citizens each of whom was to be given twenty-five lashes for alleged "sympathy with the Bolsheviks." The other Jews were herded into the central park of the city and compelled to witness the spectacle. One of the victims of the whipping died several weeks later, more, I am convinced, from shame and humiliation than the physical effects of the flogging. I was seven years old at the time, but the horror of that degrading scene has never faded from my mind.

When the sentence of eighteen lashes for our two young comrades was announced I called a short meeting of the High Command. I found that consultation was superfluous. We had all instinctively seized upon the same idea. If the British Army whipped our boys, we would whip British officers in return. We debated whether a warning ought to be given. Some thought we ought to whip first and explain afterwards, but they were convinced finally that a warning ought first to be

given: that the British authorities should be told that if
they carried out the humiliating sentence on the two
Jewish soldiers every British officer in Eretz Israel
would run the risk of similar punishment. So that the
Authorities, and all others concerned, should be made
fully aware, the warning was published in English as
well as Hebrew. It was a clear, solemn warning. Shmuel
Katz, who was going to take charge of our "English
Department," was not in the country at the time. I
wrote the warning myself. My knowledge of English I
had gleaned mainly from the B.B.C. During my years
in the underground the B.B.C. supplied me with an
abundance of inaccurate information about our operations in Eretz Israel, but also with any amount of accurate information on the English language.

Despite its lack of polish the language and the import
of our warning were unmistakable. Whipping after all is
not an elegant subject, so in phrasing such a warning it
would have been inappropriate to use elegant language.
What had to be said—'if you whip us we shall whip
you'—we said. And we aimed specially at officers. The
order given to our regional commanders was not to
touch private soldiers, but to catch and whip those of
responsible rank. This distinction requires little explanation. The relations between soldiers and their officers
are not profoundly affectionate. Our discrimination was
therefore psychologically sound. Our policy aroused a
certain amount of sympathy among the rank-and-file of
the enormous British Occupation forces. Incidentally,
on one of the posters containing our warning a British
soldier scrawled in big letters: "Please don't forget my
sergeant-major."

Unlike the soldier of the Airborne Division who had
scrawled his threat to "kill sixty million Jews," this particular Tommy thoughtfully added his full name, unit
and regimental number.

Whatever the British rank-and-file may have thought
of the likelihood of their officers' being flogged by the
Irgun—it is clear that the hierarchy refused to believe
that we would dare use the whip in retaliation. That was
probably why, one Friday evening in late December,

1946, they took young Kimche out of his cell in the Jerusalem Jail and demonstrated that the writ of the whip ran in Eretz Israel too. He was given eighteen lashes according to law.

Because of the Sabbath the news reached us only twenty-four hours later. That very Saturday night the boys and girls of the R.P.F. went out to paste up the latest number of *Herut*, which contained a second warning to the government.

"For hundreds of years," we wrote, "you have been whipping 'natives' in your colonies—without retaliation. In your foolish pride you regard the Jews in Eretz Israel as natives too. You are mistaken. Zion is not Exile. Jews are not Zulus. You will not whip Jews in their Homeland. And if British Authorities whip them—British officers will be whipped publicly in return."

The following morning people read two items in the Press. One appeared in the legal newspapers and reported that Kimche had been given eighteen lashes with a heavy cane. The second was the solemn warning of retaliation in our underground paper. Tens of thousands read it, and wondered whether our promise would be kept.

It was. Though we were deeply outraged at what had been done we gave no vent to our feelings and the order went out unchanged to all our regional commanders: to catch British officers and prove to them that if "whip-education" was good for Hebrew soldiers it was good for British officers as well.

In Nathanya, Tel Aviv and Rishon-le-Zion British officers were seized and each received exactly what Kimche had got: eighteen lashes, according to law— the law of just retribution.

The Mandatory's whip still threatened the second boy, Katz. We therefore published immediately a communique on what had happened and what would happen again if the whipping continued. This is what we said:

"In spite of our warning, General Barker confirmed the sentence of lashes imposed by the illegal British court on a Jewish soldier. On Friday, 27 December,

1946 the young soldier was whipped in the Jerusalem Central Prison.

"In accordance with our warning and in retaliation for the oppressors' barbaric act British officers were whipped on Sunday, 29 December, in Nathanya, Tel Aviv and Rishon-le-Zion. One major and three N.C.O.'s were each given eighteen lashes, the exact number of lashes given to the captive Jewish soldier.

"We now warn:

"If the oppressors dare in the future to abuse the bodies and the human and national honour of Jewish youths, we shall no longer reply with the whip. *We shall reply with fire.*"

Katz was not whipped. The authorities, who believed that the whip would teach us a lesson, were themselves taught a salutary lesson.

Why could not these Colonial administrators have been wise on the Friday and so avoided the whole affair? It was a humiliation also for the misguided General Barker. The whip he had so rashly decided to wield broke in his hands.

After we had retaliated, they attempted to induce Katz to say that he was too weak to stand eighteen lashes. Scornfully, he replied:

"Too weak? You're quite wrong. I'm in perfect health. I'm ready to take even thirty-six lashes."

So the "medical manoeuvre" had not worked. Now the Mandatory had no choice but to admit openly that the rule of the whip had failed. In a special communique the British High Commissioner cancelled the sentence of lashes on Katz. A young Arab of sixteen who had also been sentenced to lashes was included in the "amnesty." Respecting the honour of others as we did our own, we rejoiced for him too.

Never again was the British whip used in Eretz Israel. The Mandatory authorities amended their law to restrict whipping. But more important still was the modification of their behaviour. The Military Prosecutor, Major Baxter, in the "trial" of another of our boys uttered these words of wisdom:

"You're too young to be hanged and too old to be flogged."

The echo of the whippings resounded around the world. British prestige had invited and suffered a damaging blow. In his farewell message to the British troops Barker wrote: "Our officers in Palestine were kidnapped, killed and even flogged." Even! Winston Churchill, always deeply concerned about British prestige, accused the Government of not knowing how to "behave like men."

"You whip a Jewish terrorist," he cried, "and the terrorists catch a British major and three non-commissioned officers and whip them the next day. You then cancel the whipping of another terrorist. Do you know what this means?"

Whether the British Government knew what it meant or not, it was clear that the rest of the world did. We received congratulations from Irishmen, from Americans, Canadians, Russians, Frenchmen. Our brother-Jews throughout the world straightened their backs. After generations of humiliation by whipping, they had witnessed an episode which restored their dignity and self-respect. The coloured African and the Chinese coolie, long acquainted with the whip, also raised their heads in joyous acknowledgement. Millions of Russians to whom the knout symbolised tyranny echoed the tribute expressed so succintly in Saslevsky's two words "Good work!" A French newspaper published a cartoon, showing a British soldier holding his tin hat behind him. The caption explained that since the Irgun whipping the British military authorities had decided that to protect the threatened "area," helmets were now to be worn there instead of on the head, and consequently the salute must be similarly transferred. France rumbled with laughter. And ridicule can be more destructive than a high explosive bomb.

We, however, found no cause for merriment in the episode. It was no pleasure for us to whip British officers. But we had to confess to a certain sense of gratification when thousands of officers and men of a proud

and mighty army fled from all the cafes in Eretz Israel
on that Sunday night of December 2, following General Barker's order to all troops to evacuate Jewish
towns, to stay in camp and to keep watch. To keep
watch? We could not help being amused at the implication of this order. Yet for us it was no matter for laughter. We had no desire to humiliate the captured officers. We had no desire to whip British soldiers, nor indeed did we wish to fight them at all. What we did was
forced upon us. We had warned the authorities and
we repeated our warning. The whole unpleasant affair
could have been avoided. The whipping was a British
idea: not ours. There was no whip in our armoury.

One of the whipped officers asked our men:

"Why are you doing this to me?"

The Irgun soldiers told him what had been done to
Kimche. He seemed depressed by what he heard, and
was silent. Afterwards he asked for a certificate which
would confirm, in the name of the Irgun Zvai Leumi,
that he had been whipped.

"What do you want it for?"

"I need it. If the idiots in my Government whip your
people again and you whip us—I want to be in the
clear."

He never had need of a certificate. The British government never again whipped anybody, neither Jew nor
Arab, in Eretz Israel.

But fate decreed that for this service to human self-
respect we should subsequently also have to pay a
heavy price. . . .

Chapter XVII

Ordeal of the Gallows

Sarafand on a spring day in 1946. The central camp of the British Army was a hive of activity. Soldiers were coming and going. The machines in the military workshops were singing their song of toil, the typewriters in the offices were clicking out letters, orders, telegrams, reports. The huge armouries were receiving and issuing war material. Sergeants were yelling orders to their drill squads. Sarafand—the great headquarters of the British Army not only for Eretz Israel but for the whole Middle East—was bursting with military life.

An elaborate system of guards had been stationed in the camp. Double and triple barbed wire fences surrounded it. Entrance was permitted only through the gates, at which every entrant was subjected to a penetrating and exhaustive examination. No security measures were by now regarded as too stringent. "The terrorists"—declared the secret Army orders—"are cunning and bold. They have made daylight raids on a number of camps and got away with quantities of arms and ammunition. Nothing therefore must be left to chance." It was not likely that the "Irgunists" would dare to make an attempt on Sarafand, the camp of camps, where units of the Sixth Airborne Division and of a famous regiment of Hussars were stationed, where there were thousands of troops—yet the many eyes in the Observation Posts must watch sleeplessly the approaches, the fences, the stores and the armouries, just in case. . . . The many eyes were of no avail.

On a spring day in 1946 there arrived at one of the main gates of Sarafand a British Army unit consisting of Jewish soldiers. They came to get their demobilisation orders. Their papers were in order. Their presence was quite normal: demobilisation was in full swing. So Jewish members of the British Army coming to get their demobilisation papers aroused no special suspicion.

These soldiers, however, did not go to the camp offices. They made their way to the armoury. They were not interested in documents; they were there to take arms. But fortune did not smile on these underground fighters. The arms-store specified in their briefing was empty. And so they left the camp empty-handed. Strangely enough nobody had detected their true identity, and to the last day of their Mandatory rule in Eretz Israel, the Army authorities never knew of that particular Irgun visit to their famous military camp.

Some time later, on another day in that same spring of 1946, the day the Anglo-American Committee of Inquiry arrived in Eretz Israel, Sarafand Camp again received a visit. Again our men arrived disguised as a British unit, though this time not as Jewish soldiers awaiting demobilisation. They appeared as armed British soldiers, wearing the red berets of the Sixth Airborne Division whom the Jewish children had nicknamed the *Kaloniyot*—"Anemones"—the name by which they came to be known throughout the Yishuv. The truck that conveyed them was the property of the British Army and had been confiscated on the highway at the last moment. The driver and his companions had been taken prisoner and had handed over the precious papers containing their orders to proceed to Sarafand. The truck did not look any different when it arrived at the gate. The papers were in order, and were perfectly genuine. Only the men were different. The guard at the gate examined the truck, the passengers and their papers. Nothing wrong. The truck went through. Some of the soldiers alighted and remained at the gate to await their comrades. They started chatting with the guards. This was probably against the rules, but what could be more natural than a friendly chat among bored soldiers? Meanwhile the truck continued on its way to one of the armouries stacked with cases of arms and boxes of ammunition. It seemed incongruous that the British forces should have so many arms while our little army of revolt went hungry for a few pieces of lead. Justice demanded a better distribution!

The action in the armoury was brief. The guards were speedily overcome. A group of British officers arriving on the scene were very politely asked to come into the guardroom. Joshua, in command of the operation, placed a guard over them and they remained where they were.

The loading of the arms into "our" lorry then began. Box after box was brought out of the store and put on the truck. Our men worked feverishly. As they toiled at their tasks, numbers of soldiers passed on their way to or from their lunch. Their suspicion might be aroused at any moment. Among our men there was one, included at the last moment, who could by no stretch of the imagination be taken for a British soldier. He was a Yemenite and even a dozen red berets could not change his appearance into that of an average Briton. The men were speaking among themselves while they worked. Joshua had ordered them to do this, or at least to swear occasionally in English, of course—otherwise, not to talk at all. But now and then in the excitement of the operation they forgot themselves and came out with a word in Hebrew.

The heavy truck steadily filled up. A little longer, and it would be possible to move off peacefully with the precious haul. The number of passers-by increased; more and more N.C.O's and men coming from lunch. A small group of our men standing casually on guard a little way away stopped a group of soldiers who had come too close and ordered them to lie down in the ditch. One of them, a sergeant, burst out laughing: "What's the ——— joke?" But the well-victualled sergeant soon discovered that the order was deadly serious, and he and his comrades duly obeyed.

The loading continued. But one of the boys was suddenly overcome with a strong desire for a Vickers gun. He jumped on to a tank standing near the armoury and began dismantling the heavy machine-gun. His zeal was the signal for trouble. At that elevation, he attracted the attention of one of the sentinels at an Observation Post. He fired, and at once the camp was in turmoil. Soldiers ran in all directions. More shots. No one amongst the guard knew who were British troops and who were not. But the laden truck was a clear target. Shots were aimed at it from all angles. Our boys split into two parties. One carried on loading the truck; the remainder returned the fire of the sentries.

Shimshon, who a year later was to lead the great attack on Acre Fortress but was now under Joshua's orders, operated a Bren-gun to silence the enemy fire—and urged that the loading be completed. But Joshua, cool and collected, for all his own eagerness to increase the haul of arms, was responsible for the lives of the men. The disparity of forces was changing to our disadvantage with every second that passed. He therefore ordered his men to get on to the lorry. He himself remained behind. In his hands he carried a small load of explosives. He went into the tent where the British captives were held. He could have blown it up without waiting—but the British had surrendered. And Joshua, who had learnt the ethics of warfare in the Irgun, regarded himself as responsible for the lives of captives. He shouted to the prisoners: "Get out of here. I'm blowing up the store."

The British troops, astonished as they had been at their capture by their own comrades, were now even more dumbfounded. By now they realised that they were at the complete mercy of the Irgun. . . . But they were not given time to recover from their shock. Joshua yelled at them: "Get out." The troops lost no time in obeying. Joshua set the explosives, lit the fuse and raced after the lorry. As he leapt on to the truck it jerked forward. Whether the explosion, coming seconds afterwards, destroyed the armoury or not, it was still of great help to our retiring party, since it increased the confusion and bewilderment in the camp.

At the gate, meanwhile, a minor battle was taking place. Our boys had remained chatting with the guards. But as soon as they heard the shooting from the middle of the camp, they ordered the guards to put their hands up and to get into the guardroom. They then took up stations in the place of the imprisoned guards. The lives of their comrades now depended on them. Had the gate been shut, the fate of all our boys would have been sealed. The British saw this too. An officer rushed towards the gate, shouting: "Shut the gates, shut the gates!" The "Anemones" shouted back "Very good, sir!" but they did not move. When the officer reached them, they disarmed him and put him in the guardroom with the others.

The truck sped towards the gate amid a growing hail of bullets. The gate was reached and passed. Our "guards" flung themselves on to it. Every one was accounted for. Nobody was missing, and nobody killed, but there were some wounded. The truck raced off. The British had recovered from their shock. A convoy of trucks and armoured cars was already giving chase. But outside the camp there was new confusion. There were other soldiers of the Sixth Airborne Division travelling on the road. "Anemones" met "anemones"—who was friend and who enemy? Perhaps these are terrorists? Perhaps those? Our men managed to shake off their pursuers. But it was no longer possible to bring the arms to one of our own stores. The neighbourhood teemed with enemy soldiers. Joshua made a quick decision. He ordered his men to unload the truck and to hide the arms and ammunition in the sand. With nightfall, he decided, another of our units would return and remove the treasure. The task was speedily carried out. A thin layer of sand covered the boxes. The boys threw off the British uniforms and became Irgun soldiers again. The wounded were quickly bandaged. A passing taxi was hailed, the wounded made comfortable inside it. It seemed that all might yet end well.

It did not. Most of the arms and ammunition were removed by the Haganah before our boys arrived to transfer it. Yet their toil and risk were not in vain. True, their own organization did not get the hoped-for accession of strength. But from the political, psychological, and moral viewpoint their achievement was richly re-

warded. The news of the operation at Sarafand was
flashed round the world. The B.B.C. commentator admitted that what had happened at Sarafand was incomprehensible. After previous raids on military camps, he
said sorrowfully, the authorities had taken extraordinary
security measures, yet now the terrorists had made a
successful attack on the largest camp in Palestine and
had carried off arms and ammunition.

The risk and the work were, moreover, worthwhile
in themselves. The arms and ammunition were in the
end used in the service of our people—long after they
were taken from the British stores.

The loss of the spoils was not our only affliction. The
taxi in which the two wounded men, Michael Ashbel
and Joseph Simchon, were travelling was stopped by a
military patrol. Ordered out of the car they were at
once seen to be wounded, and they were both arrested
together with the girl who was looking after them. And
there began a chapter of events whose echoes resounded
to the ends of the world.

The Mandatory government had enacted new Emergency Regulations which made every citizen liable to
arrest, deportation and execution. Legal experts argued
that even in Nazi Germany there had been no law so
arbitrary. And 'Kol Israel' announced in the name of
the Resistance Movement that any attempt to put these
regulations into effect would be regarded as a crime,
and those who implemented them would be treated as
criminals. We rejoiced at the dignified declaration of the
Haganah. To our regret it was never given effect.

In accordance with these regulations Ashbel and
Simchon were tried by a military court. The task of the
three British officers who served as judges was very
simple.

In Bernard Shaw's play on the American War of
Independence "The Devil's Disciple," General Bur-
goyne, angered at the decision of the local officer in
charge, Major Swindon, to hang the rebel Minister
Anderson, says petulantly: ". . . You have committed
us to hanging him; and the sooner he is hanged the
better." Swindon replies, practically: "We have arranged

it for twelve o'clock. Nothing remains to be done except to try him."

For the British officers who tried Ashbel and Simchon, too, the trial was an inconsequential, if necessary, prelude to the inevitable hanging. They were guided by nothing resembling law. They had before them two terrorists, and an unambiguous paragraph in a modest pamphlet entitled "Emergency and Defence Regulations."

The commanding officer who appointed the judges was the same man who had to confirm the sentence. The hearing was brief. Witnesses identified the two as participants in the Sarafand attack. The judges consulted for only a few minutes. They then donned their caps and the president pronounced the sentence in its traditional wording: "to be hanged by the neck until you are dead."

In the Irgun Command we discussed long and earnestly what line Ashbel and Simchon should take in the case. We had to assume that the Mandatory government might enforce their new regulations and hang them—in the assurance that what was called the "organised Yishuv" would not rally round "terrorists" who did not belong to the Haganah. However, the Irgun educated its men, whatever their rank, to be prepared, if needs be, for the ultimate sacrifice, and we had no doubt of the readiness of the two men to make it. But precisely for this reason it was the duty of the Irgun leadership to do everything, as far as the needs of the struggle would allow, to preserve the lives of these men.

Our deliberations led us to the conclusion that a routine defence—engaging a lawyer and constructing a legal argument—would not make the slightest difference to the outcome of the trial. But our decision in favour of a political attack in the court-room was overwhelmingly influenced by a letter we received from Simchon. It contained an appeal which we could not deny or reject. In his letter Simchon wrote:

". . . I have decided to behave as befits a Hebrew fighter, educated by the Irgun, whose only aspiration is to do his duty in the struggle for liberation, even if I am denied the possibility of practical action and the only possibility left to me is to bear the Irgun's message on high. Moreover, I believe I shall not make things easier for myself if I do not make a political declaration, and I should like my trial to be of service to the idea for which I have fought and fallen. Your concern for my life is out of place. I have often faced death and have always felt that I am thus carrying out my duty and my mission as a fighter. There is no room for concern over this individual's fate. The fate of my people is what must always concern us.

"I want my superior officers to know that I am prepared to accept proudly whatever sentence and punishment may be given me. But it will be easier for me to bear the consequences if I know that as a prisoner, too, I have done my duty as an Irgun soldier."

And so, when the two appeared in court it was not as accused but as accusers. Ashbel told the judges:

"If in spite of the lessons of history, your rulers have robbed us of our country and introduced laws of barbarous tyranny, it only means that God has deprived them of their senses, that he has blinded them and has decreed their decline and fall. Come what may, you will not break the spirit of the Jewish people nor destroy the longing for freedom in the hearts of all its sons. And you may take my statement as testimony of the determination of 600,000 Jews united in their struggle to free their country from foreign domination."

And Simchon, who explained at length why he did not recognize the right of that court to try him, declared: "You may imprison and chain us. But you cannot legally judge us. We shall never recognize that you are the judges and we the accused. There can be no justice without law. And the law of the fist is no law. When it operates there are no judges and no accused. There are only cruel oppressors on the one side; and on the other side their resisting victims." And he concluded: "Our people came on to the stage of history long before you and it will remain there long after you have made your exit."

When the sentence was passed, Ashbel and Simchon sang the national anthem, Hatikvah.

Their proud conduct was exemplified not only by this first reaction. In the long days and nights in their cell, sorrowing for their families, waiting, waiting—for the hangman or for news of their reprieve—they demonstrated their spiritual greatness, steeled by the moral training the Irgun had given them.

"I find" (wrote Simchon from his cell) "that during the two days I have spent in the condemned cell I have not once thought about the death that awaits me. You may say that I have lost my sense of balance, that I do not grasp the gravity of my situation. No, my friend. The tranquility in my heart is the result of years of spiritual preparation, of readiness to die for our country. . . . I know what awaits me but I am sure that my death will bring us one step nearer victory. By our death and sacrifice we shall set up a free State for our people which will know how to live and why it lives."

And Ashbel wrote simply:

". . . I have heard that the Resistance Movement has threatened that if the sentences are carried out, there will be bloodshed. If my death can serve as a means of achieving fighting unity in the Yishuv I gladly forego any commutation of sentence that may be granted me; for who knows as well as we what power there is in a fighting Yishuv."

Ashbel's information was mistaken. The Resistance Movement had given no such undertaking. The story that reached him was apparently based on that earlier statement to which I have referred above that the Resistance Movement would regard the implementation of the new Emergency Regulations as a crime and anybody implementing them as a criminal.

In actual fact the reaction of the Haganah and the official institutions was quite different. The Press, guided by them, joined in a chorus of denunciation of the Sarafand operation, and of appeals to the British to remit the death sentence.

The Haganah chiefs did not understand that these two Irgun soldiers had been chosen by the Government in order to make an experiment with the new Regulations, and to see how effective they would prove in intimidating the Jewish youth of the country. The Haganah's threat to retaliate, should the Regulations be implemented, was very well remembered by the British authorities. Now, the first time their brave threat was put to the test, they not only said nothing and did nothing to fulfil it—but they made it clear that, for petty partisan reasons, they had taken up a position "on the fence." This was precisely what the authorities wanted. Had the authorities succeeded in their experiment there is no doubt that following Ashbel and Simchon, many more Jewish fighters would have been sent to the gallows. We had received authentic information that the Government had made up their minds to hang at least one of the two boys.

As for us, it never once occurred to us to leave them to the tender mercies of the authorities. Our decision was clear from the moment the shadow of the gallows began to loom over us. While our fighters were ready to give their lives, we nevertheless had to try to save them. We made no distinction between one fighter and another. When Mattityahu Shmulevitz of the F.F.I. had been sentenced to death we proposed to his organization a plan of attack on the Jerusalem Central Prison in order to free him. The plan was due to be carried out by our combined forces when Shmulevitz's sentence was remitted.

When Ashbel and Simchon were sentenced we warned the British Government for the first time: "Do not hang the captive soldiers. If you do, we shall answer gallows with gallows."

Several days later we captured six British officers. Five of them were taken from the Officers' Club in Tel Aviv. An Irgun unit surrounded the area, and covered the building. A small party went in and took charge of the telephone room. Three or four men with revolvers ordered the scores of officers gathered in the main hall to put up their hands. The officers reluctantly obeyed. The Irgun officer in charge picked out five who seemed to him to be of the highest rank and ordered them to go with him as prisoners of the Irgun Zvai Leumi. They obeyed, and were taken to the cars waiting outside. The remainder were told not to move for fifteen minutes. By the time police and military units arrived there was no trace of either captors or captives.

In Jerusalem, fortune first favoured, then deserted us. Our boys captured a senior Intelligence officer, attached to the General Staff. Captured in the street near the King David Hotel, he showed exemplary discipline. When he felt what seemed to him like a revolver digging into his ribs, he entered the waiting car. Alon, the Jerusalem Commander, reported with unconcealed satisfaction: "We have caught a big fish." But his joy was short-lived. The fish escaped. It was most unfortunate, and should not have happened in the Irgun. The guard let himself be persuaded by the captive to free his hands. The Intelligence Officer found a hole in the ceiling of the room, which had once served as a bakery. When the guard left the room for a moment the prisoner tried his luck and by a stupendous jump—succeeded in escaping. The guard discovered his loss too late. He ran out and chased his captive through the lanes of Jerusalem, but the officer jumped on to a bus and disappeared.

It is significant that nobody at the time believed that the officer had really escaped. I learnt, to my astonishment, that even the Haganah chiefs were convinced that we ourselves had arranged the escape.

No sooner had we captured the other officers than the Haganah Command demanded their release. They and their political superiors had various reasons for their demand. They feared British reprisals. Again they felt that these captures tended to distract the mind of the world—as they certainly did—from the recent Haganah operation against the bridges.

At our first meeting after this operation, I explained to the Haganah people that this was not a military operation in which the decision of the Resistance Movement was final. We could not on any account leave our men to the gallows.

"Gentlemen," I said, "in this we are prepared to go to the end. But there will be no need for it. You will see that by our pressure we shall save the lives of these boys."

Sneh and Galili may have felt sympathetic but they did not accept my view. They continued to press for the release of the British officers. Later Sneh invited me to a further meeting with him. We met a day after the Staff Officer's escape. He began with a word of praise for our behavior.

"I assume," he said, "that you let him escape so that he should report that you do not harm captives. I think this is a wise move which is likely to be helpful . . ."

I struggled with myself. Should I admit our failure? Belief in the release of the officer was so deep and so widespread that it was even unpleasant to tell the truth. But I thought that as we were in fighting co-operation with the Haganah it was my duty to disillusion him. I therefore told him what had happened. He showed no pleasure, but could not conceal his astonishment.

We were convinced that our way was the right one and the only one, and firmly resisted the pressure from all sides to free the remaining five British officers. At a meeting with Haganah and F.F.I. representatives we were told by all of them that if we did not release the prisoners, the fate of our men was sealed. The British Empire, they claimed, would not sacrifice its prestige for the lives of a few officers. The Haganah consequently felt that we should release them and, then there would be hope of saving Ashbel and Simchon. The F.F.I. thought we should hold them to the bitter end and execute them after our two soldiers had been hanged.

We rejected both these views. We admitted that the question of prestige must be a powerful one. One radio station had wildly declared that the kidnapping had shaken the British Empire. But, we felt, there were two threats to prestige between which the British Government would be compelled to choose. The first was the possibility of having to surrender to direct pressure. The second was the possibility that British officers might be publicly hanged. The Government by now knew very well that if our soldiers were hanged we would execute theirs in exactly the same fashion. We therefore argued that the Government would choose the first and lesser blow to prestige in order to avoid the second and far more serious damage. Thus, and only thus, could our boys be saved.

We repeated that we were prepared to carry the matter through to the bitter end, in order not only to save our two soldiers but to prevent any further death sentences on Hebrew fighters.

We kept the five officers in two separate places, three in one and two in the other. But they were all in Tel Aviv. The British army imposed a curfew on Tel Aviv and carried out a house to house search. Several times they nearly stumbled on the prisoners. Finally they began to doubt whether they were in Tel Aviv at all. We took steps to encourage these doubts. A truck containing stretchers was found "abandoned" on the highway outside the town. The authorities became still more confused, and did not know where to begin a new search. They also did not know that the place in which we were holding two of the prisoners was not very secure and might easily be discovered. But this difficulty gave us an idea. A certain Jew had conducted unofficial conversations with the authorities for the purpose of securing the cancellation of the death sentences in exchange for the release of the imprisoned British officers. He informed us that the Government were considering the proposal very seriously indeed, and his impression was that his talks would be successful. Meanwhile, however, internal incitement against us was growing, and various stories were being circulated about the five officers. We therefore came to the conclusion that it would be a good idea to free two of the five. This would make it easier to hold the other three, would silence some of the incitement and might help the negotiations.

We freed the two, who reported that we had treated them well. The military—still searching—were now utterly confused, particularly because of our complete silence. We had made no public statement from the day of the capture of the five. We were averse to any contest for prestige. We did not want to make it more difficult for the Government to retreat from their murderous intentions. We had one purpose only: to save our boys. So we remained silent even when the world Press and radio proclaimed day after day that we would hang the officers if the British hanged the two Jews. We did not deny; but neither did we confirm.

However, our care and indeed all our toil was nearly wrecked—and Ashbel and Simchon nearly sacrificed—by a silly game of prestige initiated by the Haganah. 'Kol Israel,' the Haganah radio station, announced that we had freed the two Britons at the orders of the Resistance Movement. The Haganah chiefs assured us that this mendacious statement had been broadcast without their knowledge. The announcement created so dangerous a situation that we were compelled to break our silence. Had the British Government gained the impression that we were subject to such orders, they would conclude that there was no need to worry about the remaining three prisoners, nor even to consider reprieving Ashbel and Simchon. This simple and logical result of the Haganah's folly was fully confirmed by the man who was in contact with the Government. He told us that were the untruths accepted as fact, there would be nothing left to negotiate about. We consequently published and broadcast a statement that the Resistance Movement had no authority to give us orders and that the statement by the Haganah radio was a complete fabrication.

Within a few days we discovered that our calculations had been well founded. Mr. Rokach, the Mayor of Tel Aviv, informed our liaison officer, Gurion, that the British authorities were inclined to consider a reprieve for the two if we would free the officers. And on 28th June, 1946, Moshe Sneh sent me an urgent note: "I have had information from a responsible member of our Organization in Jerusalem who has talked with the head of the British Army Security Service, under the direct orders of the Commander-in-Chief. This is what he says: 'You may tell your friend that the two will not be hanged. This has been told me definitely, though it must not be stated or announced that such a promise was given officially. But the man told me he is certain that they will not hang. The emphasis on the unofficial nature of the promise shows that it is a promise.'

"That is the end of the message. In our opinion" (Sneh's note went on) "there is no doubt that this is the only way in which the authorities can make a promise or undertaking. You cannot expect more even if they are determined to make a promise.

"We therefore appeal to you to release the three remaining prisoners. And the sooner the better. M."

I replied without delay to this note—which proved how well we had understood the Government. The same day I wrote to the Command of the Resistance Movement:

"Rokach has been negotiating all the time with an official representative of the Government. He has assured us that the matter will be brought to a positive conclusion within the next few days. It will clearly be safer to get a promise from the central government than an anonymous promise, which binds nobody, from a detective. At any rate we shall try to elucidate the seriousness of Rokach's conversations as soon as possible."

Finally I informed Sneh that in any case we would be unable to free the three officers as long as the road curfew was in force, and that we demanded that the period between the release and the cancellation of the death sentence be reduced to a minimum. "We must remember the nerves of the two boys who for a fortnight have been wearing the red uniform of those about to die."

We were given authentic information that the British authorities had promised to reprieve the two men. But we were not satisfied, and asked for a clear undertaking. The next day an official British communiqué announced the annulment of the death sentences in a fashion without precedent in the history of British colonial government. The Commander-in-Chief of the Army had confirmed the death sentences, but the High Commissioner had granted a reprieve—without having been asked to do so. Whatever the calculation which led to the decision to annul the death sentence before we had released their officers, and to the strange way in which it was done—the world as a whole recognized that the Irgun had won this round in the struggle.

Releasing the officers was no simple matter. The Government, indeed, complied with our request for the removal of the road curfew in the Tel Aviv neighborhood—but the captives were in Tel Aviv itself and the army had patrols at almost every street corner in order to receive the released men and—more particularly—to catch their captors. A strange game began. It was not only we who misled the authorities. Jewish youngsters with a sense of fun spontaneously came to our aid. They telephoned all the police-stations in Tel Aviv, telling them that the officers had been seen in the north, in the south, on the beach, in a rowing-boat. The police and military dashed from one place to the other in a series of wild-goose chases.

Meantime, Giddy and Yoel countered all the authorities' moves. The officers, clean, well-shaven and with their uniforms newly-pressed, were put into an enormous box provided with a special ventilator and conveyed on a lorry to the centre of the town, near Rothschild Boulevard. A police patrol followed the truck for a little while but soon gave up, convinced, no doubt, that a truck moving furniture was above suspicion. The box was lowered into the street, the lock was removed, and our men decamped.

A crowd of Tel Avivians gathered round and watched as, first, the box itself opened, and then three smartly turned-out British officers stepped out of it. One of them—a determined fellow—started running after our lorry, but he soon gave it up as a bad job. The universal laughter which the report of this escapade aroused did nothing to enhance the prestige of the Mandatory power.

We ourselves were in no mood for laughter. But our hearts rejoiced that we had saved two comrades from the gallows. In concluding the long account and explanation of the developments in the Ashbel-Simchon chapter which, as was our custom, we circulated throughout the Irgun, we wrote:

"This great little contest has many aspects. Ashbel and Simchon displayed supreme heroism; the detention of the officers is an outstanding manifestation of the sense of Hebrew sovereignty which is the prime essential for the attainment of sovereignty itself; the detention and all that came after it has enhanced the reputation of the Irgun perhaps more than any other operation. Not only Attlee saw it as the 'climax.' Throughout the world the events here have for sixteen days occupied the centre of attention; and the contest itself has ended in the complete attainment of our purpose.

"But above all, there has been in these events one phenomenon which perhaps we alone can understand. It is the quality which has dominated our hearts and mingled with our blood. It is a simple quality, but there is none nobler. It is the quality of *loyalty*."

Chapter XVIII
Dov Gruner

Only a few months later we again faced the ordeal of the gallows. This chapter, too, began on a spring day in 1946.

It was a very ordinary day at the Ramat Gan police fortress. Police came and went, made reports, received instructions. Wireless cars arrived, armoured cars were sent out. The fortress dominates the area and was ringed by fortified defence posts. The machine-gunners stationed at these posts were on the alert, ready to fire at any moment. The sun was high in the heavens—it was noon—but who could foresee the tricks of the terrorists! They had got into Sarafand; why should they not try their luck at Ramat-Gan?

A large military tender drew up outside the building. It created no suspicion. Seated in the tender were a dozen dejected-looking Arab prisoners. The sergeant in charge of the military guard went inside and reported to the duty police-sergeant that the Arabs had been caught in the act of robbing the military camp at Tel Litvinsky. The camp commander had ordered the thieves to be handed over to the Ramat Gan police for preliminary questioning and trial. The duty sergeant accepted the prisoners. The guard sergeant came out to the door and shouted: "Hi, corp—bring the prisoners in here!"

The Arabs were ordered to march into the police-station. The military guards detailed to watch them were obviously taking no chances. Their sub-machine guns were trained on the prisoners who, as they went forward, were kicked or shoved along. The Arabs seemed resigned to the treatment, which they accepted uncomplainingly.

The prisoners and their guards went into the fortress and turned in the direction of the lock-up. An Arab policeman swung open the heavy doors with a look on his face that boded ill for his fellow-Arabs.

Suddenly the Arab prisoners straightened up. Out of their flowing *abbayah's* they drew revolvers and Sten-guns. And, stranger still, the British soldiers turned their arms on the British police. The bewildered police were, however, not given much time to ponder over this strange cooperation between Arab prisoners and His Majesty's troops. The guard-sergeant curtly gave an order: "Put your hands up and get into the cell."

The police-sergeant obeyed and was followed by several policemen. The door was locked behind them. Gad, a young Irgun officer and son of the Mayor of Safed, with his "British" and "Arab" soldiers, took command inside the Ramat Gan fortress.

The second stage of the operation now began. The armoury was locked. A search was made for the keys. They were nowhere to be found. There was no choice; the iron door of the armoury had to be blown open. The danger was great. The guards on the roof of the fortress and round about it were still there, oblivious of the change of personnel that had taken place in the building. True, there was Israel outside the building, with his Bren-gun—Israel, once one of the best Bren-gunners in the British Army, and a machine-gun instructor, Israel who held firmly to the view that no operation was permissible without Bren-gun cover, now waiting for his turn to join the action. But it was not the intention that this operation should be accompanied by a battle. Such operations—taking arms and ammunition for the arms-hungry Irgun—should be carried out peacefully. But because the Irgun so badly needed the arms—there was no alternative. The explosives prepared for the purpose were placed in position. The fuse was lit, and amid the noise of the explosion and the shower of debris, the hole in the wall where the door had been revealed the arms.

The loading began at once. Heavy machine-guns, light machine-guns, rifles, boxes of ammunition, were borne hastily out to the tender by the "Arab prisoners" and "British soldiers." They had to cover a short distance in the open. The officer stationed on the roof was now fully alive to what was going on. He opened a raking fire with his Bren-gun. Almost at once he scored hits. But the work went on. Staggering under their loads, the men ran the gauntlet of the murderous fire, now coming from all sides, which Israel feverishly returned.

For more than half an hour the battle continued. The danger to our boys grew every minute. Through a misunderstanding British reinforcements had been summoned to the police-station. It came about thus. The radio operator in the police-station was a Jewish policeman, whose heart was with the rebels. But the men he saw at the door of his room appeared to him to be "Arabs" and moreover, still acting their part, they spoke to him in Arabic. Bewildered, he leapt to the conclusion that an attack by Arabs was in progress. He jumped up, locked the door and sent out a message of help.

British reinforcements started out from Sarona and Petah-Tikva. The greater danger came from Sarona. But the police-unit that rushed out from there was delayed on the road and prevented from reaching Ramat Gan. Two Irgun soldiers, posted on the road from Sarona, had taken over the direction of the heavy traffic and had succeeded in forming a long zig-zagging line of buses and lorries which barred the progress of the police armoured cars. The troops shouted and cursed but there was no way out of the traffic block. One of the Irgun soldiers dropped the big sun-glasses he was wearing as a disguise. An Arab bus-passenger, smiling broadly, took off his own and handed them to the Irgunist.

The Petah Tikva reinforcements had better luck. They abandoned their vehicle and continued on foot. Had they come close enough our boys would have been cut off. Moreover, the situation at the scene of the encounter had grown desperate. The armoury had been emptied of everything but its dust. But our Bren-gun had been silenced. Israel was lying dead by its side. Two more had been killed carrying their precious loads. Others were wounded—including the driver, who had been hit in the cheek and the arm and was bleeding profusely. But at the order from Gad to withdraw he wriggled into the driver's seat. With bullets still raining down and heedless of the bleeding and pain he started the tender—and brought the load of men and arms to the orange-grove which served as a base.

The underground newspaper *Af-al-pi*[1] in writing of the operation, after paying tribute to the three men who had been killed, went on to cry out against the complacent ones in Israel who could have spared the people the sacrifice of these young lives. "If they would give to the liberation army a tiny percentage of what they involuntarily give to the alien oppressors who, if they are not soon got rid of will take everything from them, we should obtain the arms required for a decisive struggle by means more simple and less painful."

Three of our men lay dead at the scene of the battle. Three? As the men were checked in the peaceful orchard, they discovered that one more was missing. They assumed that he too had been killed. But he was not killed. Covering the loading with a Sten-gun, he had been badly wounded and had fallen at his post. His name was Dov Gruner.

There followed the heroic drama of this wounded prisoner, unique not only in our annals but in human history, the *via dolorosa* of suffering and ultimate sacrifice along which he went despite all our efforts to save him. We wanted to prevent the execution of the men who were sent to the gallows; we had the gravest repugnance to hanging British captives. Not only Joshua at the Sarafand camp ordered his British prisoners to run for their lives before he lit the fuse. Many a time we took British prisoners, scores of them, but once they had raised their hands in surrender they became a sacred trust and safe against all harm. At the Exhibition

[1] Meaning "although."

Grounds in Tel Aviv we raided a British camp for arms. Over forty British soldiers were taken prisoner. They pleaded for mercy, claiming that they had always been pro-Jewish. Our men told them bluntly not to be fools; that they were in the hands of civilised Hebrew soldiers who did not harm prisoners taken in battle.

But it was clear to us, as it should have been clear to the British Government from the day of our declaration in 1944, that we would fight by every means in our power to win recognition as an underground army, and that should the British authorities disregard our incessant warnings and hang any of our men whom they took prisoners—their prisoners in our hands would also hang.

In January, 1947, Dov Gruner was brought before the Military Court. In a scathing, but reasoned and dignified declaration he told the officers of the Court why he refused to recognise their right to try him. Britain, he said, had abandoned the obligation which alone authorised her to be in Eretz Israel. Instead she had determined to transform the country into one of her military bases and to steal it from the Jewish people. He exclaimed:

"Nothing has therefore remained of the legal basis of your rule, which now rests on one principle only: brute force. The bayonet and a reign of terror disguised as so-called 'laws.' These laws are drafted by the bearers of the bayonets; they promulgate them, and they enforce them contrary to the fundamental rights of man, contrary to the wishes of the local population and contrary to international law.

"That is why I cannot recognise your competence to try me. Because as the ancient Romans ruled: no one can transfer to another more right than he himself possesses. And if your whole regime is one of unlawful occupation, how can it confer upon you the power to try me or any other citizen in this occupied country.

"When a regime in any country becomes a regime of oppression it ceases to be lawful. It is the right of its citizens—more, it is their duty—to fight against it and overthrow it. That is what the Jewish youth is doing and will continue to do until you evacuate this country and return it to its lawful owners—the people of Israel. For this you ought to know: there is no force in the world that can break the link between the people of Israel and its one and only country. He who attempts it —his hand will be cut off and the curse of God will fall on him for ever and ever."

And when the three British officers donned their caps and one of them told Dov Gruner that he would be hanged by the neck till he was dead—Dov replied by singing Hatikvah.

Once again we warned the British authorities; this time in the following terms:

"Execution of prisoners of war is premeditated murder. We warn the British regime of blood against the commission of this crime."

We meant to act at once as we had done in the case of Ashbel and Simchon. But we reconsidered our decision. The sentence was subject to confirmation by the British Commander-in-Chief. Important public men told our liaison officers that they were convinced Gruner would be reprieved. They gave several reasons. In the first place he had an excellent record as a frontline soldier in the British Army. Secondly, he had been badly wounded. Finally, the British Government, they argued, would like to avoid the grave consequences of such an execution.

We did not, of course, place complete reliance on these calculations and hints, but they certainly influenced our decision to postpone the execution of our plans. If there were any prospects of saving Dov's life, we did not want to endanger them by premature action which might be interpreted as over-straining British prestige. While that prestige was a clear objective for our blows we had no wish to lower it at the sacrifice of a defenceless comrade who needed our help. Moreover we assumed that if the sentence were confirmed we should have several days to act before the date fixed for execution.

The first assumption was wrong. The General Officer who had been prevented by civilian superiors from

hanging Ashbel and Simchon, confirmed the death sentence passed by his three subordinates. The second
assumption was justified. The death sentence was confirmed—though the confirmation was not published—
on Friday, 25th January, 1947, while the date of execution was fixed for the following Tuesday—the regular
day for executions by the authorities.

Through our regular secret channels of information
we learnt of the confirmation of the sentence on the Friday evening. Orders were given at once for the arrest
of British officers. On the Sunday our Jerusalem detachment captured a British Intelligence Officer, Major Collins. The intensive searches that were at once instituted
were fruitless. But General Barker made no statement.
We consequently acted again the next day. Our men interrupted a court case in progress in Tel-Aviv and arrested the judge, Mr. Justice Windham. Before many
hours had passed, the General broke his silence. That
evening, in an official communiqué published in Jerusalem, it was announced that the Commander-in-Chief
had consented to postpone indefinitely the execution
of the sentence on Dov Gruner, ostensibly in order to
enable him to lodge an appeal with the Privy Council.
We had averted the execution with little more than
twelve hours to spare.

The next day, the British High Commissioner summoned the representatives of the Jewish Agency and delivered an ultimatum. Unless the Irgun Zvai Leumi released its two captives within twenty-four hours martial
law would be declared. The threat struck fear into the
hearts of the official Jewish representatives. When, two
months later, the Government employed the weapon of
martial law, the underground turned it against its wield-
ers and by incessant attacks forced them to relinquish it.
But in January, 1947, the weapon had not descended,
and was only a threat held over our heads. Like many
threats, it sounded far more terrifying than it ultimately
proved to be.

The Jewish institutions subjected us to intense pressure to release the kidnapped men, as they called them.
Cajolery and threats intermingled. The Chief Rabbi

wrote an eloquent letter to "the comforter of Zion" (Menahem means comforter) asking me to do what was necessary to prevent a catastrophe overtaking the Yishuv. Mrs. Goldie Meyerson, then Head of the Political Department of the Jewish Agency, threatened that the Haganah would be fully mobilised in order to trace the two Englishmen.

I cannot say that we were particularly impressed by the fears or the threats of the institutions represented by Mrs. Meyerson. Precisely at such testing times we had learnt to weigh our decisions with complete objective calm. We considered the situation carefully. For the time being we had saved Gruner from death. We concluded that after the announced indefinite postponement of the execution we could gain nothing further by the continued detention of the two prisoners. We were also influenced by a technical consideration, whose importance only we could estimate. Collins was imprisoned in a more or less safe place, and his discovery either by the British or by the Haganah, though possible, was not likely. But Mr. Windham, the more important of the two, who had been detained in haste, was held in a place that was almost open. Had the British imposed martial law and carried out thorough searches they would have found the little house in which we held him. Windham is a member of a fine old English family and it was undoubtedly his detention that had decided the British Labour Government to postpone Dov's execution. Finally, the arrest of the two men had drawn the attention of the whole world to the Gruner case. The British authorities had been placed in a difficult position and conditions had been created which might bring about the complete annulment of the sentence. In the light of these considerations we decided to free Messrs. Windham and Collins.

Mr. Windham behaved like a gentleman—in marked contrast, by the way, to other officers we had captured. They had given us their word of honour as officers not to reveal anything of what they had seen or heard. Yet they had gone straight away with the police to the Rafiah detention camp and there pointed out two of our men as having guarded them while under detention. The two were sentenced by a military court to fifteen years' imprisonment. One of them, Amram Darai, a Yemenite, had taken the opportunity at his trial to deliver a blistering and contemptuous speech, which, coming from a man whom with his dark skin the authorities regarded as doubly a "native," had enraged his judges. He and his companion had laughed outright at the sentence, exclaiming, "Do you really believe you are going to stay here for fifteen years?" Indeed neither the informers nor the judges were to gain much satisfaction from this treachery of the officers. But that they only learnt a year later.

Mr. Windham knew where he had been held. His captors had forgotten to blindfold him. He had seen both the route and the house. But he revealed nothing.

Mr. Windham was a fine man. Our men treated him well, as they treated all their prisoners. And he refused to repay good treatment with betrayal. He was an honourable foe.

After his release a fantastic story gained wide currency in the country. The reason for Windham's arrest, the story went, was that Major Collins had insisted on being brought before a British judge. And as the British law entitles every accused person to be tried by a British judge instead of a "native," the law-abiding Irgun could not refuse his request, and accordingly summoned Judge Windham.

Immediately after the detention of Collins and Windham the British authorities ordered all their officials into special 'security zones' enclosed by barbed wire. The administrators were allowed to leave these "ghettoes" only in convoys of cars, escorted by Bren-gun carriers. So they went out to fear-ridden days in their offices and came back to nightly boredom in their homes. Never in any occupied country had the occupying Power been driven to such straits. As Amram Darai had told the authorities, they had turned the country into a jail and had had to lock themselves up inside it.

But we had little concern about the Government's

"ghettoes." Their fate as rulers of our land, we knew, was sealed. Our hearts were torn with anxiety for Dov Gruner whose life was in the balance while the Government planned their next move. They wanted to hang him but had decided to gain time while the storm his case and his brave bearing at the "trial" had caused throughout the world died down, and while the renewed tension between the Haganah and the Irgun could grow.

Early in February a debate on Palestine took place in the British House of Commons. The Irgun and Dov Gruner served as the central theme. Winston Churchill again demanded the evacuation from Palestine of the British forces whose maintenance, while serving no strategic purpose, was so costly in blood and treasure. Again he urged the handing back of the Palestine Mandate to the United Nations if the United States refused to share in the responsibility of governing the land. But the main burden of his speech was a biting denunciation of the Government's "soft" policy towards terrorists.

"It is quite certain," explained Churchill, "that what is going on now in Palestine is doing us a very great deal of harm all over the world . . . I hate this quarrel with the Jews. I hate their methods of outrage. But if you are engaged in the matter, at least bear yourselves like men." The Government, he said, stated that the sentence on Gruner had been held up pending an appeal to the Privy Council. This was only an excuse. The Jewish Agency had been brought into the matter, but the condemned man refused to sign. The fortitude of this man, criminal though he was, should not escape the notice of the House. In the face of the terrorists' threat, Churchill concluded, the Government had not found the strength to implement the process of law.

His meaning was clear. Gruner must be hanged, and better late than never. This sentiment was echoed by one of Churchill's lieutenants, Oliver Stanley.

"In both recent kidnappings," said Stanley, "the Government has conceded exactly what the terrorists demanded as a result of their reprisals. Rather than that this country should have to suffer further humiliations of this character I would prefer that we clear out of

Palestine and tell the people of the world that we were
unable to carry out our Mandate there."

Pointing to the "most sinister development" which
had culminated in the passing of the death sentence on
Gruner, the kidnapping of Windham and Collins and
their release by the good-will of the terrorists while the
Government had been unable to recover them or to
bring anyone to justice, Stanley remarked: "I do not believe that on these lines it is possible to carry on the
Government of Palestine. No authority can stand up
against such blows." Finally he demanded a strong-
arm policy as the only means of enforcing the Government's authority.

These Conservative attacks reduced the unhappy Colonial Secretary Creech-Jones to helpless bewilderment.
"We share the feeling of humiliation," he pleaded, "and
we are conscious that the prestige of Britain is assailed
by acts of terrorism."

He went on to say, in flagrant contradiction of the
facts, that the Commander-in-Chief had postponed the
execution, not because of the kidnappings, but because
the lawyer who was to obtain Gruner's signature for an
appeal to the Privy Council could not reach him that
day on account of a "riot in the prison." This story was
a fabrication from beginning to end. But after that debate Creech-Jones and Bevin and Barker were spurred
on to prove that they were "men" and that their arm
was no less strong than Churchill's or Stanley's.

In those days I pondered deeply the heroism of men
awaiting death in the condemned cell. Which is nobler,
bravery in battle or fortitude in the death-cell? There
is no answer to that question. But a distinguishing line
can certainly be drawn between these two tests of
fortitude. The volunteer who goes into battle, the soldier
who falls in battle, overcomes his urge for self-preservation by responding to the call of another instinct—
the instinct of loyalty and patriotism. The surrender of
the one for the other by a volunteer is not a "natural"
one. The volunteer, or the rebel who himself decides
his own mobilisation order, has a free choice, and the
choice will not be made except where there is nobility

of spirit, where there is that quality which we call "bravery."

But the soldier goes into battle with arms in his hand—usually with comrades by his side. In the heat of their common action is kindled a flame of fraternity. There is a passion in battle which, albeit unconsciously, profoundly affects the soldier. Comrades to left and to right of him, his weapon ready for action—he advances on the enemy—rather, he is carried towards him on the tempest of battle. And if he falls, he falls with his soul ablaze, and hardly feels the touch of the Angel of Death.

Far otherwise with the man sentenced to death. He has no enemy in front of him. His enemy lurks beyond the locked door, awaiting his prey. . . . There is no glorious battle, no storming assault. There are only thoughts —thoughts of the time that is running out with every tick of the clock. And thoughts beyond time. The days are long, the nights longer. There is too much time to think. There is something and somebody that crops up. The voice of an old mother, the voice of a young betrothed, distant, yet clearly heard. The crimson clothes in which the hangmen have dressed him are an ever present reminder that the number of his days has been set, that the sun rising beyond the dim cell is not driving away the night but is bringing it closer, the infinite night. Here there can be no swift subjugation of the instinct of self-preservation. The sickening struggle with it is continuous; it begins all over again every morning, every hour and every minute when he lies down and when he gets up, and as he paces the locked and lonely call. Not everybody—not even a very brave soldier—is capable of passing this test.

The soldiers of the Irgun endured it calmly.

Chapter XIX

The Choice

Months had passed since Dov Gruner was captured. He had been severely wounded in the jaw. He underwent many operations, suffered much pain. And he astonished enemies no less than friends by his brave cheerfulness and the deep composure of his spirit. At one time, despairing of the results of the treatment he was receiving, we wanted to send a specialist to him, but he refused on the grounds that it was too great an expense for the Irgun to bear. Consigned to the death cell, this front-line soldier gave up all thought of self. He not only never asked for anything from his comrades, but even declined what they wished to give him.

Joshua, the Irgun officer in command of prisoners in the British jail, a seasoned veteran who knew what facing death meant, could not find words to express himself to his superior officers on the greatness of the phenomenon which suddenly revealed itself in Dov Gruner. In a note he sent us at the time Joshua wrote: ". . . And finally he himself. I do not feel entitled to define his bearing in these days. Even the best definition I can think of will not be adequate to convey his firm and unshaken attitude. His courage. His great spirit. A wonderful calmness of spirit. Readiness for everything; and he is so quiet and modest in his ways. In the last few days I have felt that he is completely resigned to his fate and accepts it as a direct consequence of being a fighter in this hard struggle. And I want to emphasize a revealing fact: not once in all this time has he ever asked for anything for himself. He has written nothing, not even to his sister in far-off America. On the other hand he is constantly inquiring about the affairs of the fighting family.

"Today, after confirmation of the sentence, nothing has changed. Kazma, who is attending to him and goes in to see him every day (he is able to) told me today: 'He is calmer today than when he first came, and he is in wonderful spirits.' I take Kazma's word—he understands these things better than we do. Such is the heroic brother of the fighting family. And I hope the family will save him, for the future . . . for the struggle.

"In this grave situation I place all my hope in the family. But should the family be unable to prevent that fate we shall face the test as befits fighters."

The whole world was moved by this revelation of the renewed Hebrew spirit which came from the Jerusalem prison-cell. But Dov himself regarded everything that happened as quite natural, usual, self-understood. When his sentence was confirmed he was pressed to sign an appeal to the British Privy Council. He said curtly and simply: "No." We ourselves knew perfectly well that such an 'appeal' would not save his life; that, on the contrary, it would make it easier for the Government to carry out their designs. Would Dov understand that? Could he understand it? Many were the voices that advised him that an appeal offered a real hope of saving his life. He rejected them all—for the sake of giving hope to his people. He believed in one possibility of saving him which depended on our action. But we repeatedly made it clear to him that the decision to sign or not to sign the appeal was his alone to make. The choice was his—and his alone.

A well-known Jerusalem lawyer came to see him and pleaded with him at length to sign the application for an appeal, explaining that it was not an appeal against the sentence itself, but against the Emergency Regulations as such. The lawyer's intentions were no doubt good, though the method he adopted—not of his own volition, be it noted—was mistaken precisely from the point of view of saving Dov's life. At this interview the lawyer used the Irgun password known to Dov, and only when he told him that the Irgun wanted him to sign, that his signature would save the Yishuv from the great catastrophe of martial law and so on—Dov finally signed. He did not sign an application to appeal but a Power of Attorney to submit an appeal in his name against the Emergency Regulations.

But before returning to his cell he said to his guards: "I feel I have made a mistake."

How few are the parallels in history? Something similar—though only similar—occurred hundreds of years earlier during a struggle by another people against oppression. Joan of Arc signed a declaration recognizing the court that tried her; and at once realized that she had made a mistake. But she did not annul her signature, probably could not. Dov Gruner did not recognize the court of his people's oppressors, and not twenty-four hours later, when he learnt that the decision was again his freely to make, he called the lawyer and tore the Power of Attorney into shreds. . . .

Of course, we all know after the event the juridical procedure was little more than a cloak for political execution. But did Dov know? Could he have known? Would it not have been natural for him even to delude himself that the appeal on "principle" had the possibility of saving him from execution? Nevertheless, with his own hands he cut what might have seemed to him to be his last line of hope. He went on his way, faithful to his idea. He was ready for everything—except a denial of his principles and his creed.

Where is the precedent in history for such a stand in all its aspects?

I received only one letter from him—it was a bundle of little scraps of paper. He wrote:

"Sir,

"I thank you from the bottom of my heart for the great encouragement you have given me in these fateful days. You may rest assured that whatever happens I shall not forget the teachings on which I was weaned, the teachings to be 'proud and generous and strong"[1] and I shall know how to stand up for my honour, the honour of a fighting Hebrew soldier.

"I could use sonorous phrases like the famous Latin saying *'Dulce et decorum est pro patria mori.'* But at this moment it seems to me that such phrases sound cheap; also cynics may add: 'You have no choice.' And they may be right.

"Of course I want to live. Who does not? But if I am sorry that I am about to 'finish,' it is mainly because I did not manage to do enough. I too could have 'let the future fend for itself,' taken the job I was promised, or left the country altogether and lived securely in America. But that would not have given me satisfaction as a Jew and certainly not as a Zionist.

"Many are the theories preached by Jews. One is that of the assimilationists which is a surrender of their nationalism and, little by little, of their religion as well—and that means inevitable suicide for the Jewish people. The second is that of so-called Zionists and it is the way of reliance on negotiation, for all the world as though the affairs of a people were no different from a business transaction. People who accept such a theory are unprepared to make sacrifices, and are invariably ready to make compromises which may put off immediate difficulties but which lead in the end to a ghetto. And let us not forget that even in the Warsaw ghetto there were three hundred thousand Jews.

"The right way, to my mind, is the way of the Irgun, which does not reject political effort but will not give up a yard of our country, because it is ours. And if the political effort does not have the desired result it is prepared to fight for our

[1] From the Betar hymn writen by Vladimir Jabotinsky:
    "With blood and with sweat
    A generation shall be raised
    Proud and generous and strong."

country and our freedom—which alone ensures
the existence of our people—by all means and in
all ways. That should be the way of the Jewish
people in these days; to stand up for what is ours
and be ready for battle even if in some instances
it leads to the gallows. For the world knows that
a land is redeemed by blood.

"I write these lines forty-eight hours before the
time fixed by our oppressors to carry out their
murder, and at such moments one does not lie. I
swear that if I had the choice of starting again I
would choose the same road, regardless of the
possible consequences to me.

                              Your faithful soldier
                              Dov."

In the end two appeals were submitted to the Privy
Council but not by Gruner. The first was submitted by
his uncle, Mr. Frank Gruner of the United States. The
appeal was rejected on technical grounds. But a hint in
this judgment that an "interested Jewish community"
might be entitled to submit an appeal encouraged the
Tel Aviv Municipality to do so. This appeal too was
rejected—though only after Gruner had been executed
and had joined the fellowship of the heroes of history.

It so happened that in the same period the British
Privy Council was dealing with a case of wholesale
murder arising out of superstitious customs on the Gold
Coast of Africa. Several Africans had been sentenced
to death for the murder of members of a rival tribe.
Their lawyer appealed to the Privy Council and the executions were postponed several times. Finally the British
authorities laid down a new ruling: that an appeal to
the Privy Council does not involve the postponement
of an execution in the territories under the British
crown.

More weeks passed after Dov Gruner donned the
crimson uniform of death. At the end of March his
solitude in the condemned cell was broken. He was
joined by three more soldiers of the Irgun, Yechiel

Drezner (who had been arrested and sentenced as Dov Rosenbaum), Mordechai Alkoshi and Eliezer Kashani. They had been arrested on the night of the whippings. The three officers in the military court had donned their caps and one of them had announced: "You will be hanged by the neck till you are dead."

The three had sung Hatikvah.

We issued yet another solemn warning to the British rulers. We reiterated that it was foolish of them to think that murder of prisoners of war would break the spirit of the youth or of the people. "Never in history has there been a liberation movement so steeled as this movement, arisen from the abyss of Hebrew blood and anger." And we told them again that they would bear the consequences of their crime.

Early in February, the removal of Barker from his post had been announced.

We regarded Barker, who tried to crush our people, as our enemy. We sentenced him to death, but were foiled in our efforts to execute the sentence. Several times we almost broke through the elaborate precautions he took for his personal safety, but on each occasion good luck favoured him. On the 13th of February he secretly left the country. The day before his departure he confirmed the death sentences on Drezner, Alkoshi and Kashani.

The new Commander-in-Chief of the British Forces, General McMillan, announced that the execution of the three would not be carried out until Dov Gruner's case before the Privy Council was completed.

The wearers of the crimson gallows-dress grew in number. In March, Moshe Barazani, a member of the F.F.I. was sentenced to "be hanged by the neck till he was dead." Early in April three British officers again donned their caps while one of them uttered the formula to Meir Feinstein, a member of the Irgun. These two wonderful young men greeted the sentence with the singing of Hatikvah.

The British Government announced that these sentences, too, would remain "pending" while Gruner's case was heard and judged by the Privy Council.

We were not disposed to rely on "official" undertakings. So we began by making a plan for the freeing of the condemned men—by force.

The plan we chose was one of a number that were considered. We were not interested in a demonstrative action, nor in a suicide operation. We wanted to rescue our comrades from the hands of the hangman and though the plan bordered on the impossible, there was a chance that it would succeed. We had had gratifying experience of "impossible" operations. Though the plan was daring and hazardous, we confirmed it.

A British armoured car was to enter the yard of the Jerusalem prison—where all the men were being held. In it there would be a number of "British police" carrying official documents addressed to the governor of the prison. One of the "police"—a sergeant—would proceed towards the office while the car was turned to face the gate. At that moment a signal would be given and the six condemned men, who should be in the yard for their regular daily spell of exercise, would jump on to the car and seize arms prepared for them. The "police" would overwhelm the guard at the gate. The heavy machine-gun on the armoured car would provide covering fire while the vehicle in the inevitable confusion among the authorities, forced its way through the gate.

The whole of the Irgun was geared for the operation. Even Giddy had never worked so feverishly. Yoel obtained the necessary "official documents." The Command was inundated with requests from officers to be detailed for the operation. . . .

Shimson and his men watched the highway. They had the most difficult task of all. They had to capture the police-armoured-car. Shimson, our brilliant commando fighter, had performed more complicated feats, but in this case there were two conditions that had to be fulfilled. It was essential to act at the right hour of the day. And it was vital to seize the armoured car without damaging it, hurting its occupants, or enabling them to give the alarm. Otherwise the elements of surprise and deception in the penetration of the prison-yard would be destroyed and the whole plan would be frustrated.

Day after day Shimson and his unit watched the main road to Jerusalem. In vain. Armoured cars went by, but in each case their capture would have involved an armed clash. Shimson might have come out the victor in such a clash but he knew that any encounter would make the vehicle useless for its purpose. We did not despair. Our comrades, who had been informed of the plan, were waiting. They were patient—but who could plumb the depths of their anguish? And who can plumb the depth of the anxiety outside—in the underground? Day after day, the state of alert in the Irgun continued. Night after night we were left only with hope.

On the 14th of April, Gruner, Drezner, Alkoshi and Kashani were transferred from Jerusalem to the Acre Fortress.

It must not be imagined that the British made the transfer because they had learnt of our plans. They knew nothing about it. The chiefs of the Intelligence will learn of our plan to raid the Jerusalem jail only when they read these lines. Had they known, they would unquestionably have kept the prisoners in Jerusalem and laid a trap for their rescuers.

They had their own plan. They were about to make a decisive effort to restore shattered prestige. They were about to demonstrate the firmness of their authority. They found an appropriate moment. The Jewish institutions had again proclaimed war on the fighting underground. Public statements were made prophesying the early liquidation of the 'terrorists.' The British saw the green light.

But the hangman was afraid. He therefore chose to do his work in the dark, and not in Jerusalem but in distant Acre. Even after the transfer of the four to Acre he claimed there was no cause for concern. Stubbs, the Government's Public Information Officer, told a Press Conference that the postponement of the executions till the conclusion of the proceedings of the Privy Council was still in force. The aide-de-camp to High Commissioner General Cunningham told a telephone inquirer:

"Believe me, we don't want to hang that poor boy."

The Attorney General confirmed Stubbs' statement, the Prison Governor confirmed the Attorney-General's statement, and invited Max Kritzman, who acted as attorney for the boys, to come and visit his clients. . . .

Chapter XX

A Tragic Document

I believe there is no precedent in history of a Government carrying out a death sentence in such fear and in such secrecy. The Authorities promised to wait for the decision of the Privy Council; and misled us. They announced that the postponement was still in force; and deceived us.

They issued a permit to Dov Gruner's sister, Helen Friedman, who had come from the United States, to visit her brother—knowing full well what she would find when she got to Acre.

Thirty-six hours after the transfer of the four to Acre jail a strict curfew was imposed throughout the country. Seven hundred thousand people were confined to their houses. Regiments of troops, with tanks and armoured cars, surrounded the ancient fortress at Acre in order to ensure the arrival of four captive Jewish soldiers.

On April 16th, 1947, tens of thousands of people in Eretz Israel turned on their radios to hear the early morning news broadcast. The voice of the announcer came through: Leah Porat reading an official communiqué. But it was not an announcer's voice. It was the voice of a young Jewish woman, choked with tears.

"This morning at Acre Jail Dov Gruner, Dov Rosenbaum, Mordechai Alkoshi and Eliezer Kashani were executed by hanging."

They had not even been permitted the ministrations of a Rabbi in their last moments.

In Dov Gruner, it seems, were fused all the noble qualities of the human spirit. On Passover-eve, pregnant with memories, when all the crimson-clothed prisoners ate together at the Seder-table while the Rabbi, who ministered to them in the Jerusalem prison, related the story of the Exodus, Dov repeatedly offered his seat to the two British police on guard in the death-cell. The cell was very small, there were not enough seats to go round, and Dov at his last Passover Eve, Dov about to die, behaved like the traditional host, giving up his seat to the two aliens, the representatives of the enemy. . . .

But when he faced the enemy himself—we see before us the unflinching rebel. In the death-cell at Acre British officers read out to him the 'sentence' confirmed by their Commander-in-Chief. Regulations require that when the sentence is read out, the condemned man must stand up. But Dov refused to rise. He refused to respect them or their 'laws.' The hangman tried to lift him to his feet. They struck him. But he did not give in; he fought, even in his last moments, and went to the gallows singing.

With him from the cell to the gallows, also singing, went Yechiel Drezner, Mordechai Alkoshi and Eliezer Kashani. What had these fighters endured from the time they, together with a fourth comrade, fell into the hands of the Occupation Army? Here is the report they smuggled out to their officers, and when you read it you may gain some impression of what went on in the hearts of those who read those slips of paper at the time:

"Before Wilhelma, I decided to stop the car and jump into the orange-grove. But the driver had lost control of the car and it ran into a barbed-wire set up on the road by the Army. The barrier was dragged along by the car and it was only the second barrier we hit that stopped us. At that moment a Bren-gun opened fire on us from behind, and then the car was surrounded by 'anemones' with their revolvers aimed at us. We had no choice but to leave the car with our hands up. Eliezer got a bullet in his back and Mordechai (the driver) in the shoulder. The bullet went right through and came out. As we came out I got a blow in the back and rolled into the ditch. As I lay I heard a revolver-shot and I saw a soldier pointing his revolver at

Mordechai. He fired, missed Mordechai and killed his brother-Britisher. He at once hit Mordechai over the head with his revolver and threw him on to me in the ditch. We both got to our feet while, with their revolvers trained on us, they kicked us. We heard more shots. I thought they would finish us all off. When they finally took us into an armoured car we found two others. Eliezer was not there. After that we did not see him. The others had also not seen what had happened to him. He had had some difficulty in getting out of the car and they were under the impression that the soldiers had shot him in the car.

"Then began the chapter of beatings which ended only the next day at seventeen hours—about twenty hours consecutively.

"Amid blows, we were taken into a small armoured car, each of us guarded by a soldier. The guards at once emptied our pockets, ordering us to keep our hands up. They took everything: our watches, about fifty pounds in cash, purses and notebooks, pens and pencils, even a handkerchief and a comb. When they had done with this, they all began to hit us. They aimed particularly at our faces and stomachs. When we doubled up from blows to the stomach they would hit us in the face to straighten us up again. I remember how my nose ran blood like water from a tap and the soldiers called out happily: "I have broken his nose."

"This journey ended in a camp I do not know. They shoved us out and took us to an open field. They stood us in a row, about ten soldiers formed a line in front of us and loaded their rifles. I must mention that we all stood the test, and nobody lowered his head. At that moment an officer came running up and reprimanded the soldiers, who had apparently really meant to finish us off. We were led to a room. They kept us there about half an hour. All the time—from the time we were caught—we had our hands up. After half an hour, when our hands had turned to stone, they put us into a big truck and laid us on the floor. They saw a ring on Mordechai's finger and tried to take it off. When it would not come off they pulled his finger with all their might until they thought it was broken, and then gave up. We came to an anemones' camp and there an officer ordered us to be taken into one of the huts. It was a kitchen which had not been used for some time, about fifteen by forty-five feet. There they undressed us. They took everything off . . . but as we were mancled to each other the clothes remained hanging on our hands. To get them off they pulled with all their strength and injured our hands. What they did not manage to tear off this way they cut off with a razor blade. We were left as naked as on the day we were born.

"They began an organized attack for which they had apparently got an officer's permission or orders. They hit each of us in turn and then all together. Four or five soldiers took part in this. When they got tired, they were relieved by others. They hit us with their fists in the head and the feet, and they kicked us in all parts of the body not even omitting the testicles. Among the beaters were two policemen who had apparently been sent to guard us. One of them moved around with a big baton which he brought down on our backs, or legs or stomachs. One of these blows broke Eliezer's hand and caused a sprain in Haim Golor's back. One blow I got on my neck almost made me faint. This went on until late at night. An officer came in then and ordered them to stop hitting us, to wash us and give us blankets for sleeping. They poured water over our heads and each of us had to wash the other. The wash did not help much as our wounds were bleeding and we immediately became dirty again. The four of us, wet and naked and shivering with cold, lay down in one blanket and covered ourselves with two other blankets. (That was all they gave us). But no sooner had we dozed off than the guard came, kicked us awake and pulled off the blankets. We had such visits about every fifteen minutes.

"Towards morning they ordered us to get up and 'wash' again. The blanket we had lain on was soaked in blood and had changed its colour. After we had washed they gave us clothes so that we should dress.

Three of us were not given our shoes. So, covered in our rags, we were made to run all the way to the 'hospital-room.' On the way every soldier we met hit at us with his fists or his rifle-butt, and our guards did not spare us either. We ran with our hands above our heads. In the dispensary they kept us for about three-quarters of an hour with our hands up until the doctor came.

"A doctor, a short elderly man, looked at our wounds and asked the soldiers if they wanted to go on 'playing' with us. The soldiers replied in the affirmative. 'All right then,' said the doctor, 'I'll bandage their wounds afterwards.' (They did not realize that I understood English).

"They made us run back the same way to the place we had come from. They again undressed us and took us outside, and there poured slop-water over us. Then soldiers standing around were invited to volunteer to hit us, and there was no lack of volunteers. They then took us inside again and ordered us to wash the floor and scratch our blood off the walls. Only then I saw what that kitchen looked like. There were pieces of dried blood on the walls and we had to scratch them off with our nails. They beat us as we did it. Suddenly the policeman pulled us away and ordered us to kneel and kiss the ground. When we refused we were beaten with a cudgel. But we did not do as he asked. They put another pair of handcuffs on me—apparently they had noticed that I was encouraging my comrades in their rebelliousness. When they handcuffed me I did not want to do anything, and they again hit me. Finally they took off the extra handcuffs.

"At about nine o'clock they washed us again . . . and gave each of us a pair of trousers. The same doctor came again and had plasters put on two of us. After that a police officer came, accompanied by the Jewish officer Karlik and several detectives. They hardly questioned us, asked only our names and addresses. All day the police came and went and meantime the soldiers did not stop 'playing' with us. Towards evening only Karlik remained in the next-door room and they took us out to get us to sign the charge-sheet. While Karlik was sitting in the next room a giant corporal came in and ordered us to do all kinds of humiliating things. When we refused he beat us mercilessly. I told the boys not to keep quiet this time so that our cries should reach Karlik. I had told him clearly that he was the only Jew we had met and that he must do everything to get us out of there otherwise they would beat us to death. He promised . . ."

For a long time the Jewish fighters of the Irgun looked for that terror-camp and its inhabitants, the sadists and the 'doctor.' Had we found the camp we should have levelled it to the ground with explosives—but we never discovered where it was. We received reports—of whose authenticity I am not certain—that the unit involved was transferred abroad. It is likely. The British had learned that we did not forgive such episodes. And on the report on the ordeal of our fighters there remained Yoel's observation:

"The British policeman in question was shadowed persistently but it was impossible to lay hands on him, as he left Sarona only in an armoured car. Several weeks after the incident he was transferred and may have left the country. He had been sentenced to death. . . ."

The three Jewish fighters had to endure all this even before they put on their red uniforms. They too held their heads high when they faced their judges. They too tried to comfort their parents and their comrades, instead of being comforted by them. They too fought till the last moment of their lives. And sang. . . .

Their two young comrades, Meir Feinstein and Moshe Barazani, had followed their example in their bearing in the court and during the days of waiting in the condemned cell. But they did not reach the gallows. They too sang on the threshold of death—a song of faith in God: "Lord of the world who reigned before creation." But their song ended with a great explosion which shattered the silence of the prison in occupied Jerusalem.

During our battle for Dov Gruner's life, the idea was mooted of "perishing with the Philistines" in case our efforts failed. Dov was asked whether he would be prepared to choose "Samson's death" when the executioners appeared to lead him to the gallows. Dov at first got the mistaken impression that the idea was simply that he should die by his own hand rather than at the hands of the hangman. And he replied composedly: "If that is the intention, I am prepared to smash my head against the wall of the cell."

Several days later we succeeded in correcting his impression. No, we told him, the idea is not of death at your own hand. A fighter should not take his own life. But where all hope has failed, our ancient hero in the hands of the Philistines showed us the way. Where there is no choice except death, a fighter might try to give his enemy "one last blow."

But Gruner, Drezner, Alkoshi and Kashani were transferred to Acre before preparations could be completed for shattering the pillars of the gallows. In the Jerusalem condemned cell there remained one-armed Meir Feinstein of the Irgun and Moshe Barazani of the F.F.I. They determined, as they wrote in their last moments, to avenge the blood of their four comrades. They now no longer feared for their lives, but were afraid that their execution might come too soon. This sacred fear found expression in the last three notes which Feinstein wrote with his one hand in the name of both of them:

"Comrades, Shalom,
You have not done well in not sending it to us. Who knows whether by morning it will not be too late? Please do not let the time pass. Send it to us without delay. . . . We are determined. Greetings to all. Be strong. We too."

"Shalom, dear comrades: We have received the newspapers, everything is clear to us. And we are glad of this last opportunity to share in avenging our four comrades. As for us, we are sure our organizations will avenge us adequately and in the right way. But it may be that they will surprise us by moving us to Acre. Ask them outside therefore to prepare us something similar in Acre, so that we can be certain that we are

doing it. We are strong. M. Feinstein. M. Barazani."
"Comrades, Shalom: Accept our last greeting and do not
lose heart at our paying with our lives. But we shall
avenge the blood of our four comrades, and no power
on earth will move us from our purpose. My brothers,
carry the banner of revolt with honour and carry on
until we redeem and are redeemed. We march to death
proudly. M.F. M.B."

The night before the execution was due to take place
—a week after the hanging of the four at Acre—the
"it" they were expecting was delivered to them. A
hand-grenade was concealed in an orange. It was constructed in the neighbouring cell by fighters who had not
been condemned to death and who would have given
their lives to save the condemned men. But when the
terrible moment came and all hope of saving their
lives had gone, there was only one thing they could
still do: prepare an instrument of death for them and
their hangmen together. And the two in the condemned cell were waiting: "Who knows whether by
morning it will not be too late?"

Until a late hour the Rabbi sat in the death-cell. He
did not comfort them. They had no need of comfort.
They sang psalms: "The Lord is with me, I shall not
fear." They feared only that they would not be in time.
The Rabbi knew nothing. He promised them that at
dawn he would come to them in their last moments
before the gallows. They, who in their life had overcome death, tried to dissuade him from his second
visit, but the Rabbi insisted. And they would not reveal
the grim secret of their lives. . . .

They did not wait for the executioner to come. They
were afraid that the Rabbi who would be present might
be hurt. So they gave up the idea of dying "with the
Philistines." At the third night watch they clasped
each other in a last brotherly embrace, placed the gre-
nade between their hearts, released the pin, and
squeezed. . . .

Chapter XXI

A Bastille Falls

Immediately after the execution of Dov Gruner and his three comrades, we published a communiqué announcing the setting-up of field courts-martial attached to every unit of the Irgun. Should any enemy troops fall into our hands they would be liable to die—as our four comrades had died. Our units went out on the roads, on the streets in the towns. But the military were literally not to be found. When they left their camps they did so in convoys escorted by tanks. We could, of course, have attacked them too—as we later attacked the troop train from Egypt. But in those angry days that was not the retaliation we aimed at. It was our duty to pay the hangman in precisely his own coin. And we did not succeed.

The army dug in more deeply in their hiding-places. We continued to attack them. But the big debt remained unpaid.

From the "Shuni" hill, that looks down on the Valley of the Crocodile and on which stands an ancient fortress, a convoy of vehicles slowly descended. It was a British military convoy. In the greenish trucks sat soldiers with arms at the ready. In the lead was a jeep carrying the officer commanding the convoy, a captain. The convoy was headed north, to Beirut. That was what appeared on the Movement-order given to the captain.

On reaching the main road it gathered speed. It rushed past fields, villages, settlements. It passed other convoys going in the opposite direction, all carrying men and arms. The soldiers exchanged smiles of greeting, waved.

The British soldiers travelling southward could not hear what their northward-travelling comrades called their commanding officer. Had they heard they would not have exchanged smiles but bullets. The captain's men called him Shimshon—a Biblical name, but not English. That was not his only name. Many of his men did not even know his other name, the one his parents had given him: Dov Cohen. Not an English name at all.

Not all the soldiers travelling north knew that Shimshon was Dov Cohen. None of those travelling south knew that Dov Cohen was Shimshon. But many among the British knew Dov Cohen very well. Dov Cohen had served for years in the commando units of the British Army. His officers and subordinates alike were full of praise for his courage, his exploits in battle, his achievements behind the enemy lines. He had literally conquered the peak. In East Africa he had led an assault on the Italians' chain of mountain positions. He had inspired his men by his example, and Keren had fallen to the British Army. That breach in the Italian lines had opened the way to British victory in East Africa.

Covered with praise and decorations he returned to Eretz Israel from the European front, and the next day he resumed his commando operations. The Assault Unit of the Irgun Zvai Leumi found an experienced battle commander, to whom war and danger had become part of his daily life. Dov Cohen found his place and, perhaps more, he found himself. As he stormed into battle far away at Keren he had shouted "In Zion's name." Now he led his unit for the sake of Zion and on Zion's soil. A pent-up purpose found expression. A dream was realized.

Dov Cohen, in British captain's uniform, took with him Kabtzan and Shmulik, dressed as British privates, and went off, in the jeep loaded with arms, along the road dotted with British road-blocks. At one of these, when the guard came to attention and saluted, Dov was not satisfied. He looked at the soldier sternly.

"Do you call that saluting?" he asked sternly. "Do it again!"

The soldier saluted again.

"That's better," said the captain, briskly, and the jeep went on its way past the saluting soldier.

But on this 4th of May, 1947, Dov Cohen was not transferring arms. This time he was going out to the greatest commando operation of his life, to one of the most daring operations in the history of all commandos. He was not taking his men to Beirut.

He was taking them to Acre.

When the convoy reached Acre it began to shed small groups. They dispersed in all directions. They had many tasks to perform—as many as the roads leading to Acre. For Acre was not just a town inhabited only by Arabs. It was surrounded by a ring of military camps. Our commando unit was not operating behind the enemy lines. It was right in amongst the enemy lines. And the attack could not succeed unless the enemy were prevented from bringing reinforcements, and unless the line of withdrawal for the attackers was kept open.

Giddy had planned the operation in great detail. Shimshon carried it out punctiliously. One unit rained mortar-shells down on the nearby army camp—at once a diversionary and a preventive action. Other units planted mines.

The planning had been thorough, every detail was provided for, not only on the map but on the spot. Giddy and Shimshon had spent hours going over the ground. Many eyes had reconnoitred the terrain before the 4th of May. Sometimes they appeared to be "Arab" eyes, sometimes "British"! But always they were the eyes of Irgun fighters. Thanks to this very thorough reconnaissance a ring was built inside the ring: inside the belt of army camps was fashioned a ring of Irgun security-posts. Thus Acre was surrounded.

Now Shimshon's main force turned towards the fortress. Built by the Crusaders, restored by the Turks, it had withstood in a famous siege the artillery of Napoleon Bonaparte. Acre fortress—the halo of history surrounds it; and the glory of heroism and suffering, from Ze'ev Jabotinsky to Dov Gruner. Now before these unvanquished walls stood Shimshon and his men. They had come to break them open and to bring freedom to their prisoners.

Behind the walls the prisoners waited, impatiently. They knew the signal should already have been given. Why the delay? These candidates for freedom were not ordinary escapees. They were to take an active part in making their way to liberty. The authorities knew nothing. Only a few weeks earlier they had discovered an attempt to build a tunnel out of the Central Prison in Jerusalem. The Government was satisfied that this time the underground had been beaten. The 'terrorists' would not escape. But the 'terrorists' escaped nevertheless; from the Acre fortress which was regarded as impregnable.

Later the High Commissioner, General Cunningham, appointed a special committee of inquiry, headed by the assistant Superintendent of Police, to determine how the fortress had been entered and how the prisoners had escaped. Three years have passed since that Committee ended its work, which served as the basis for a long report sent by Cunningham to London—but only now will the members of that committee and General Cunningham and the British Intelligence Service learn that the prisoners themselves not only knew of the impending attack but took part in it. They had a quantity of explosives, introduced into the prison by the underground in various ways. There was not much of it, but sufficient to blow up, from *within*, the heavy iron bars separating the long dark corridor from the assault group who had pierced the wall *outside*. The burning torches that appeared in the courtyard were designed as an auxiliary operation to facilitate the escape. The important act of the prisoners was the smashing of the great iron gate—an operation that evoked from the General words of generous professional appreciation.

The really decisive explosion, however, was effected outside the fortress. The walls of rock, which had remained unbreached through the centuries, submitted finally to the assault of Shimshon's unit. The assault group approached the southern wall, their advance covered by strategically placed posts. There was plenty of opposition. If we are to believe the official statement, there were more than one hundred and fifty armed police guarding the fortress, apart from the indirect defence provided by the police post close by and the military camps in the neighbourhood. The high towers of the fortress were manned by guards, armed with machine-guns and rifles, to whose fire the attackers were fully exposed. The attack was carried out by daylight, for the liberated prisoners had to be brought to safety before the hour of the night curfew on the roads, when the Occupation Army was holding up all suspicious-looking vehicles.

Supported by ramified cover our men advanced towards the point in the wall chosen for the breach. Giddy had consulted Eitan who, though his hands were chained, and he was 'serving' the fifteen years given him by Colonel Fell, was again 'Chief of Operations.' A small building that served as a bath-house facilitated the approach to the wall. The work was speedily done. The load of explosives was attached to the wall. Our men withdrew. The whole of Acre shuddered with the force of the explosion. Amidst the pall of smoke pieces of debris flew and rolled in all directions. The heart of the attackers beat faster. Had the explosives 'taken' or not? This, after all, was no everyday wall, but the wall of Acre Fortress!

The explosives 'took.' The breach was not large. But it sufficed. There are narrow unobtrusive paths that lead to great highways. There are small furrows that carry mighty streams, there are whispering flickers that grow to towering flames. And there are little breaches that turn into the widest of gates, the gates of emergence from the yoke of oppression, of entry into the anteroom of freedom. A small breach, but adequate, was made at Acre on the 4th of May, 1947. This second

Bastille fell—one hundred and fifty eight years after the fall of the first Bastille.

But before the prisoners could succeed in leaving the darkness of their prison, a battle had developed between their liberators and the British forces. The towers blazed out a barrage of fire; our covering groups went into action. Brens against Brens; rifles against rifles. Breaching the wall was only half the task. The exit of the freed men and their line of approach to the waiting trucks had to be secured. As we used to say: "the withdrawal must be secured in order to complete the victory." The towers were consequently subjected to heavy fire. And under that covering fire tens of prisoners were able to pass through the broken wall.

The bewildered fortress officials sent out a call for reinforcements. The police station, which had had word earlier from an Arab informer of "suspicious movements" in the neighbourhood of the prison, dispatched an armed patrol. From the nearest camp a military party was rushed out. A truck-load of troops came speeding from Haifa thirteen miles away. But, as the British authorities related in their own report, none of these units succeeded in reaching the scene nor in cutting off the Irgun's withdrawal. The police were stopped by a minefield on the road. The troops were stopped by the little threatening canisters. The speeding truck was destroyed. And in the camp attacked by our mortars (they were only two-inch) confusion frustrated the will to send help. The security ring, constructed by us within the Army ring, held firm, particularly as behind it stood fighters who had sworn not to let the enemy pass at any cost.

It seemed that Shimshon was going to fulfil the promise he had made to Avraham. "Don't worry," he had said before setting out, "I'll bring back Eitan and all the other boys hale and hearty."

But blind chance, which operates beyond all human calculations, decreed that Shimshon should keep only part of his promises. Indeed, Eitan and the majority of the Irgun and F.F.I. prisoners were brought safely to an underground base, but Shimshon himself, and with him other fighters who had briefly tasted anew the joys of freedom, never returned.

That Sunday afternoon, a group of British soldiers and police had gone bathing south of Acre and, as usual, carried arms. Alarmed by the noise of the explosion and the echoes of the battle they rushed to the main road and set up a road-block *inside* our security belt. And a second grave incident occurred: the occupants of one of our forward posts were not given the trumpet signal to board their truck, and so they remained within the enemy ring.

Homer Bigart wrote at the time in the *New York Herald-Tribune* that the Acre operation was received enthusiastically by the Jewish population, "but there is no doubt that along with the feeling of triumph, the heart of the Irgun Commander is very bitter at the heavy casualties." Homer Bigart did not err. Or possibly he did. For the feeling of mourning was far deeper than the joy of triumph.

As to what happened during the withdrawal, we were told the details in a letter from one of the prisoners. It was written to Eitan by Mattityahu Shmulewitz of the F.F.I. who told laconically what he himself had seen. The letter needs no comment. I must only decode the pseudonyms: "Shimshon" is Dov Cohen, and "Shimon" is Shimon Amrami, who had been held prisoner by the British since 1944. "Mike" is Michael Ashbel, who had been saved with Shimon from the gallows, only to die "on the barricades." "On the barricades" was the song he had written in the death-cell, leaving his comrades the testament which was to become the favourite song of the underground.

Shmulewitz wrote:

"I have heard how much you were affected by the loss of our dear friends, and something I cannot define drives me to write to you about the tragedy and the last heroic hours of our friends. I know this means reopening of wounds that may be beginning to heal. For it is easier to forget and take comfort when you have work to do. If, nevertheless, I write you about it, it is because I feel that knowledge of their bravery and their

brave deaths may ease somewhat the profound melancholy that follows the loss of friends and comrades.

"As you know we ran into a road-block and into
cross-fire immediately after the railway-station. Several
seconds previously our driver had seen Shimshon running towards us on the road and signalling us with his
hand not to go on to the road. By the time the driver
had grasped the meaning of the signals he had reached
the bend. He swerved round the road-block at speed
and in trying to straighten out he brought the truck
off the road and ran into a cactus fence. The engine
stalled. The machine-gun fire was heavy but we heard
clearly Shimshon's call "After me!" Mike was wounded
while still in the truck, and others were wounded while
they were jumping out at the back. For a few seconds
we ran around looking for a way out of the zone of
fire, but wherever we turned we faced machine-gun
barrels. When we were all wounded and had begun to
run along the ditch by the side of the road we suddenly
saw Shimshon running towards an army vehicle standing in the road. We ran after him and jumped on to it.
There were two unarmed soldiers in it and a driver.
Shimshon forced the driver to start and the more
lightly-wounded among us jumped on to the soldiers
and held them down. There were now only nine of us
left. Haim Brenner had been killed in the ditch by a
bullet in the ncek. Mendel had been wounded in the
back and could run no further. Nitcha too had remained wounded in the ditch and Yitshak Kuzinevsky
remained with him to bind his wounds and did not
succeed in reaching the vehicle.

"It seemed that we were saved. We got out of the
range of fire and began to take stock of the wounded.
We could hold the soldiers no longer as we had no
arms and most of us were wounded.

"We passed Shimshon's jeep and there he ordered
the driver to stop. When he learnt there was a driver
among us (Shemesh) we turned the soldiers out and
transferred the Bren-gun and ammunition from the jeep.
Meanwhile the troops were approaching us again and
we again came under fire. Shemesh took the wheel—and

discovered that the engine would not fire. He started to repair it, when suddenly a truck appeared coming towards us. We jumped out and ran towards it. Shimshon fired a round in the air, and the truck stopped. With Shimshon were Shemesh and Amnon. I dragged Barukh Shmukler and Shimon. They were both wounded in the legs and other parts of the body. Barukh's right elbow was terribly shattered and as we ran under the rain of bullets, he said to me: 'To hell with it. How shall I get used to writing with my left hand. They'll definitely take off my right.'

"The Arabs in the truck jumped out, and between them was a soldier with a rifle. The driver began to argue with Shimshon as he stood with the Bren by the door, with Shemesh at his side. Shimshon fired and the driver fell out of the truck, wounded in the head. At that moment the catastrophe occurred which sealed our fate. Shemesh, as he saw the driver falling out, too hastily jumped into the driver's seat and in his haste got in front of the barrel of the Bren before Shimshon had had time to stop his fire. Shemesh fell dead on the spot. We were left without a driver. Amnon took the wheel and tried to turn the truck round, but he could not. He was wounded in the ribs and the elbow. Shimshon ran back to the jeep, took up a position behind it and held up the advancing soldiers. There he fell. I had never met him before but from the moment I saw him in action he aroused my admiration. His coolness and courage were unsurpassed. Even when he saw that all was lost he made no attempt to save himself but deliberately ran towards the machine gun fire in order to enable us to escape.

"Nissim Kazas flung himself empty-handed on to the soldier who aimed his rifle at him, threw him to the ground and knocked him out with the butt. It's a pity he was wounded. We dispersed in the field on the other side of the road. Mike, Barukh and Shimon did not run far. The three of them lay down together, all seriously wounded, particularly in the hands and legs. Shimon was wounded in the shoulder. Moshe Salamon, Joseph Dahar and I got farther than the others. We reached a cornfield and there lay down to survey the ground. In front of us was corn and we saw soldiers running about in the corn. The road on the other side of the cornfield was steadily filling up with soldiers and police. The cornfield was small and the only way out of it was through an open field beside the road; but there we should have been discovered at once. We decided to lie where we were till dusk.

"After about fifteen minutes soldiers came into the field and found us. They fired at us after we had surrendered and only by a miracle did we come out alive. Joseph was wounded again. We were saved by the intervention of a police officer who told the soldiers not to kill us. Shimon, Mike and Barukh did not have this good fortune, and as they lay wounded on the ground each of them had three shots fired at his stomach. Barukh miraculously was not hit.

"They took us to a truck. The wounded were dragged along the ground and were thrown into it as one throws chattels. We lay in a single heap, the wounded and the dead together. Only Moshe Salamon, who was unhurt, and I, wounded only in the hand, were able to help the others. Of our feelings it is unnecessary to write here.

"After managing to pull the dead away from off the wounded I spent most of the journey talking to Shimon. He knew he was dying. I tried to deny it and to cheer him up. Mike, who also knew his end was near, lay and joked. It was hard to believe that this man was going to die. From time to time he would sigh, but then added at once: "It will still be good. Don't worry." An Egged bus, full of Jews, stood on the road as we pulled up to take on another wounded man, Amnon. Mike, lying on the bench, saw their faces as they looked at the frightful spectacle, and called out to them: "Jews, see, we are dying for your sakes."

"On the way to the hospital they took us to the Acre Police Station. There they threw the wounded on to the pavement. To my shouting, my appeals, and my demands that a doctor should be brought, there was one reply: 'Shut up!'

"The first to die was Shimon. I was with him all the time. He was conscious to the last. I cannot tell you what went on inside me as I saw my good friend dying. His chief anxiety was the sorrow his death would bring to his parents and his friends. 'Give my greetings to all the boys. Tell them not to be sorry,' he said, breathing hard. 'Tell them to carry on. Write to my parents and my sisters and comfort them.' His last words were 'Matty, avenge, a-v-e-n-g-e.'

"Levi died in horrible pain. He was wounded in the lungs and was suffocating. How terrible was my situation, to be at each one's side and see his suffering without being able to help him. Levi threw himself from side to side, sat up and lay down, screaming, until he finally suffocated.

"Mike joked up to the last moment. The same old Mike. I held his hand, felt him growing cold and yet could not believe he was dying. He continued to comfort me to the end. 'Don't worry, it will still be good. We'll pay 'em yet.'

Nichto lay quietly. As he lay on his back I saw the blood oozing from the hole in his back. I turned him over on his side and told him not to move. He was wounded in the leg too and it was hard for him to lie on his side. After a few minutes he said in a submissive voice: 'Matty, may I turn over. It's hard lying this way.'

"When the doctor came at long last he sent me to the others because, he said, I 'felt well.'

"It is certain that most of the boys who died of wounds could have been saved had they been given medical aid. As it was, they were left to bleed for *six hours. . . .*"

Three of the five men taken prisoner during the battle at Acre were brought before the Military Court in Jerusalem. We knew now that if we did not save them, nobody would. We decided to act while their trial was still in progress. We gathered information. We awaited three British officers at the swimming pool at Ramat Gan. They did not come; but two British policemen came. We were disappointed. We

felt that to save Avshalom Haviv, Meir Nakar and
Yaacov Weiss we needed Britons of rank or of 'station.'
Two captured policemen did not seem to be adequate.
But the disappointment did not end there. The Jewish
Agency mobilised the Haganah to find the 'kidnapped'
men. Characteristically they suspected—or claimed that
they suspected—that we were merely anxious to draw
attention to ourselves from the United Nations Committee which was about to arrive. The Haganah issued
an appeal that everything possible should be done "to
rescue the kidnapped men." This time they succeeded.
The British authorities were enabled to find the place
where the policemen were held. Several days later the
British Government accorded a pardon to three members of the Haganah who had been sentenced to various
terms of imprisonment for carrying "illegal arms."

The three Irgun men addressed their "judges" with
vigour and with dignity. Avshalom Haviv drew a
parallel with the Irish rebellion against British rule:
"When the sons of Ireland rose up against you, when
the Irish underground started their fight against you,
you tried to drown the rising in rivers of blood. You
set up gallows, you murdered in the streets, you exiled,
you ran amok and stupidly believed that by dint of
persecution you would break the spirit of resistance
of free Irishmen, the spirit of resistance which is God's
gift to every man worthy of the name. You erred. Irish
resistance only grew in intensity. The blood of the
fighters and the tortured rallied the people to the banner of revolt, until you were forced to withdraw, leaving behind you ineradicable bloodstains and unforget-
table memories. Free Ireland rose in spite of you . . .
"If you were wise, British tyrants, and would learn
from history, the example of Ireland or of America
would be enough to convince you that you ought to
hurry out of our country, which is enveloped in the
flames of holy revolt, flames which are not extinguished
but only flare up the more with every drop of blood
shed by you or in the fight against you. You would
then pay heed to the words of warning uttered by Bernard Shaw in the days of the Irish rising in 1916 after

your hangmen had murdered four Irish prisoners of war.

Mr. Shaw then wrote:

> 'My own view is that the men who were shot in cold blood, after their capture or surrender, were prisoners of war, and that it was, therefore, entirely incorrect to slaughter them. An Irishman resorting to arms to achieve the independence of his country is doing only what Englishmen will do, if it be their misfortune to be invaded and conquered by the Germans. The fact that he knows that his enemies will not respect his rights if they catch him, and that he must, therefore, fight with a rope round his neck, increases his risk, but adds in the same measure to his glory in the eyes of his compatriots and of the disinterested admirers of patriotism throughout the world. The shot Irishmen will now take their place beside Emmet and the Manchester martyrs in Ireland and beside the heroes of Poland and Serbia and Belgium in Europe, and nothing in Heaven or earth can prevent it. . . .'[1]

"These words were historically vindicated up to the hilt. But your rulers are blind and will not learn. Who knows? Perhaps they have been blinded by the Almighty in order to bring down upon them, in the course of time, retribution for all the blood and tears they have caused to flow in our country and outside it. . . .

"You tyrants will never understand the spirit of free men going to death as Dov Gruner and his comrades went—with a song springing from their hearts. And this too you will probably not understand: I, a young Jew, facing the sentence of death, lift my heart to my God, and give praise and thanks for the privilege of suffering for my people and my country, and say with all

---

[1] Letter to the *Daily News,* March 10th, 1916.

my heart: 'Blessed art thou, O Lord, King of the Universe, who has kept us alive and maintained us and enabled us to reach this season.' "[1]

His comrade Meir Nakar delivered a scathing comment on the political situation of the British Mandatory Government:

"British rule in Eretz Israel is bankrupt. . . . A Government whose officials have to sit in barbed-wire ghettoes—is that a Government? A Government which spends about half its budget on police purposes and yet remains helpless in face of the anger of the people in revolt—is that a Government?"

Yaacov Weiss, who in Hungary had saved hundreds of Jews from the Nazis, told of the barbarous treatment of the wounded Irgun prisoners at Acre, and warned the authorities that the law of retaliation would be applied. "And though we shall not compete with you," he declared, "in the maltreatment of wounded men and in sadism, you will, for the rest, be paid in full.

"We hold your threats of murder in contempt," he continued. "We know there will be one outcome of this fight: Our people will attain its freedom and its enslaver will disappear from the land. That is why we are calm. More: we are happy. For there can be no greater happiness than to give our lives for a great ideal and to know, to know absolutely, that we are among those who are directly bringing about its fulfilment."

On the 16th June, 1947, three British officers donned their caps and one of them declared to Haviv, Nakar and Weiss: "You will be hanged by the neck until you are dead."

The three sang *Hatikvah*.

On that very day the United Nations Special Committee on Palestine began its work. There is no doubt that the political superiors of the judges arranged the coincidence of the sentence in order to prove that, in-

---

[1] The *Shehecheyanu* prayer, which the Jew utters on Festivals and the celebration of happy occasions.

quiry committee or no inquiry committee, the British Government was master in the country.

We addressed a memorandum to the committee. We reminded them of the decision of the Special Session of the UNO Assembly calling on all sides in the Palestine dispute to refrain from violence or the threat of violence. We repeated the statement previously made by the underground organisations that we would respect the appeal of UNO if the British Government did likewise. They were a party to the dispute. The UNO appeal applied to them. Death sentences and their executions were acts of hostility and violence, and the Government were obliged to refrain from them. We demanded, finally, the intervention of the Committee on behalf of the sentenced men in accordance with the precedent established in Greece in the same period and in similar circumstances.

In order to facilitate their action a letter was also sent to the Committee by the parents of the boys. The majority of the Committee argued, as I was later told by Dr. Granados, the Guatemalan member, that the UNO appeal applied to Britain as well. The Committee felt that it had been slighted by the very fact that the Government had chosen the day it began its work to pronounce the death sentences. The discussions inside the Committee were very stormy. Dr. Granados, Professor Fabregat of Uruguay and Dr. Brilej of Yugoslavia fought with all their might to persuade their colleagues to demand the annulment of the sentences.

After five special meetings of the Committee the following telegram was sent to the Secretary-General of the United Nations.

"In view of the fact that the majority of the members of the Committee have expressed concern as to the possible unfavourable repercussions that the execution of the death sentences pronounced by the Military Court of Jerusalem on June 16th, the day on which the Committee held

its first meeting in Jerusalem, might have upon
the fulfilment of the task with which the General Assembly of the United Nations has entrusted
the Committee, and considering the opinion of
such members as to the scope of the resolution
on the Palestine question adopted on May 15th
by the General Assembly, the Committee resolved
that the Chairman communicate to the Secretary-
General of the United Nations a copy of this resolution and of the letter received from the relations
of the condemned persons for transmission to the
Mandatory Power."

This telegram was immediately released for publication—and was accorded a rude reply by the Chief
Secretary of the Palestine Government, Gurney.

On the strength of the precedent created in the case
of the Greek guerilla fighters, we pressed our demand
on the Committee to intervene on behalf of the sentenced men, and to call them to testify before the Committee. On 23rd June we wrote this official letter to
the Committee:

"In a memorandum which we shall present to
the Committee during the next few days we shall
deal *inter alia* with the crimes the British Government have committed against our people, both
in our Homeland and in the Diaspora.

"Amongst the long list of crimes you will find
included the torture of prisoners and the deliberate
killing of wounded prisoners. This crime, according to the binding definition of the International Court at Nuremberg, is one of the 'crimes
against humanity,' one of the gravest crimes against
humanity.

"We have no doubt that the Committee, which
has been appointed to express its views on the
methods of the existing regime in our country
as well as on the kind of regime which should take
its place, will not ignore this grave accusation
against the British rulers. We assume on the other

hand, that the Committee will not wish to content itself with hearing the charges but will, in the nature of things, wish to establish the facts which will either confirm or refute the accusation. We therefore propose that the Committee hear competent witnesses who will submit factual material and whom the Committee will be able to interrogate in order to establish the truth of what they say.

"The witnesses who are able to submit to the Committee the most important facts relating to this charge against the British administration are: Yaacov Weiss, Meir Nakar, and Avshalom Haviv, who themselves witnessed and personally experienced the criminal behavior of the British 'security forces' to prisoners and wounded.

"These three prisoners are at present in the condemned cell at the Acre Gaol. They were 'sentenced' to death by a British military 'court' and they stand in imminent danger of being murdered. The Occupation authorities may desire to hasten their execution in order to prevent their appearing before the Committee. The question of their being called to testify, therefore, brooks no delay.

"We respectfully propose to the Committee that it demand of the British Occupation Government the removal of the threat of murder of the three prisoners, and that they bring them as witnesses before the Committee in order to establish the charges of maltreating prisoners and of killing wounded.

"We must point out that this proposal is not intended to replace our earlier appeal to the Committee—which still stands—to take the necessary steps for the annulment of the 'sentences' of the illegal military courts.

  Yours faithfully,

   The Irgun Zvai Leumi in Eretz Israel."

But we could not depend on the Committee, particularly when we saw how the British Government were interested in demonstrating that their authority was superior to that of the Committee, and how they disregarded the Committee's decisions which, as the chairman, Judge Sandstrom, explained, were only non-committal recommendations. We therefore pursued our efforts to capture Britons. We tried to find officers. Several times, in Jerusalem and Herzliah, we almost had within our grasp "Very Important Persons" but were prevented by something or other from consummating the capture. Only in Nathanya did our men finally succeed in capturing two agents of the British Intelligence Service, but their rank was not high. They were sergeants.

The Government immediately imposed martial law on Nathanya and announced categorically that the captives would be found. The Haganah co-operated in the effort to find them. House-to-house searches went on for weeks, and they were thorough and all-embracing. But they were unsuccessful.

On July 23rd Haviv, Nakar and Weiss were led to the gallows.

How they went to the gallows was described on 29th July, 1947, by a witness, Nathan, a prisoner in Acre at the time.

"This morning our three comrades went heroically to the gallows. We knew already last night what was to happen between four and five a.m. As soon as we heard we pressed against the bars and with bated breath watched, helplessly, what was going on around their cell. Major Charlton had left the place in the afternoon and was not seen again. Towards evening a party of hangmen from the police and army arrived. They changed all the condemned mens' things after a thorough search and took Aziz Mizrachi—a fourth man sentenced to death—out of their cell. Afterwards British officers went in and informed them that they were to be executed between four and five in the morning. Their reply was the powerful singing of '*Hatikvah*,' '*On the Barricades*,' and other songs. They then shouted

to us that the hangings would begin at four o'clock in
this order: Haviv, Nakar, Weiss. They added: 'Avenge
our blood.'

"We shouted back: 'Be strong. We are all with you,
and thousands of Jewish youth are with you in spirit.'

"They replied 'Thanks,' and went on singing.

"At two a.m. a Sephardi Rabbi whom we could not
recognise from afar was brought and stayed in the cell
fifteen minutes.

"At four o'clock Avshalom began singing Hatikvah,
and we, pressed against the bars, joined in loudly. At
once armed police patrols came up to the visitors'
fence near our cell. At 4.03 Avshalom was hanged.
At 4.25 we were shaken by the powerful singing of
Meir. Hardly able to breathe we nevertheless joined in.
He was hanged at 4.28. At five o'clock the voice of
Yaacov, this time alone, penetrated our cell, singing
Hatikvah. Again we joined him. Two minutes later
he was hanged. Each of the bodies was left hanging
twenty minutes and was taken out of the cell separately.

"The chief of hangmen were Hackett, Superintendent of Prisons, and Captain Clough, Superintendent
of the Nablus Prison, who hanged Dov and his comrades. At dawn we informed the prison officers,
through the Arab officer, that we would not be responsible for the life of any Englishman who came into the
yard. We declared a fast and prayed. Later in the
morning we found an inscription on the wall of the
condemned cell: 'They will not frighten the Hebrew
youth in the Homeland with hangings. A.H. Thousands will follow in our footsteps.'

"There was also the Irgun insignia and the three
names in the order they were executed.

"We attach part of Avshalom's diary, written in the
cell. At the beginning of the trial he asked that if he
should not live to finish it, it should be finished for
him. His request will be fulfilled."

The next day the two Britons were hanged. We repaid our enemy in kind. We had warned him again
and again and again. He had callously disregarded our

warnings. He forced us to answer gallows with gallows.

But the days were black as starless nights.

Why did the British carry out these senseless executions?—despite our warnings and the pleas of others? Maybe there still echoed in their ears the injunction of Churchill to "act like men" and to "pursue the course of law."

It is certain that the main reason was political, and inherent in the "gallows plan" which the British Government had prepared was the decision to hang and to go on hanging.

It was an official plan and originated in London. The British Government believed that by breaking the spine of prisoners of war they would break the back of Hebrew resistance. Hangings, hangings, and still more hangings! But the question was—as Lenin once put it—who would break whom? There is no doubt that had we not retaliated, avenues of gallows would have been set up in Palestine and a foreign power would be ruling in our country to this day. The grim act of retaliation forced upon us in Nathanya not only saved scores of Jewish young men from the gallows but broke the back of British rule. When gallows are shattered the regime which rests on them must inevitably crash.

This was confirmed in unambiguous terms by none other than the former chief assistant to the Chief Secretary of the British Government in Eretz Israel, Colonel Archer-Cust. In a lecture to the Royal Empire Society, he said: "The hanging of the two British sergeants did more than anything to get us out."[1]

When a nation re-awakens, its finest sons are prepared to give their lives for its liberation. When Empires are threatened with collapse they are prepared to sacrifice their non-commissioned officers.

[1] *United Empire Journal*, November-December, 1949.

Chapter XXII

Meetings in the Underground

Solitude is an unavoidable condition of the underground. Throughout the years of the revolt I had to deny myself almost entirely the pleasure of friendly chats, of meetings with friends, or relatives or acquaintances. The law of the underground forbade "nonessential" meetings. The few people I saw came to discuss the work of the organisation, our relations with other nations, questions affecting the struggle.

One of my most important secret meetings was that with the representatives of the United Nations Committee. The initiative for the meeting was not taken by us, but by members of the Committee. Yet the official Jewish institutions, as I have already mentioned, claimed that everything we did immediately before the Committee's arrival and during their stay was done merely to catch the limelight and to force them to meet and negotiate with us. These bodies alleged this even concerning the operation we planned against Citrus House. It is consequently desirable to tell the true story of the famous tunnel.

Citrus House was in the British Security Zone of Tel Aviv. It housed the military police and civilian headquarters, for the whole area of which the city is the centre. Citrus House, like every such establishment during the revolt, became a heavily defended fortress, guarded by machine-gun nests, surrounded by barbed wire and casting its fear over the population. Not a few innocent passers-by were hit by bullets carelessly fired from this fortress.

Opposite Citrus House stood a small building with a cellar suitable for a store-room. On a summer day in

1947 a prosperous-looking merchant called on the landlord and offered to rent the cellar for the purpose of
storing and packing potatoes. The greying, rather bald-
headed merchant won the landlord's complete confidence as a solid, desirable tenant. The lease was
signed. The merchant arrived with loaded trucks. The
porters who unloaded the first bags were not very
careful, and the street was strewn with potatoes. The
merchant—who was our Alex—loudly berated them,
but willingly agreed to let some of the neighbours
gather up the potatoes and keep them. The contents of
the remaining bags were brought into the house intact.

In the cellar, the work began. Sacks were filled and
carried away in trucks. The potato business flourished
ostentatiously. The sacks taken away contained soil from
under the floor of the cellar, where the "porters" began digging the tunnel to Citrus House. The digging
went on in accordance with an exact plan right under
the noses of the guards of Citrus House. The burrowing
was slow but sure. Not many days had passed before
the diggers reached a point under the middle of the
road. A few days more and they would reach their objectives.

What was the objective? Foreign correspondents
later reported at great length that we had planned the
blowing-up of the Government's fortress as a reprisal
in case they should hang Haviv, Nakar and Weiss.
There was some truth in this assumption but, as I
have already emphasised, our general military policy
was not one of revenge. And as regards the hangings
we had determined from the start to apply strictly and
exactly the law of reprisals.

The Citrus House plan had far-reaching implications and had been worked out in considerable detail.
We proposed introducing into the tunnel which was
to reach the foundations of the fortress an adequate load
of explosives with a time-mechanism set for forty-eight
or seventy-two hours. The tunnel would then be sealed
off to prevent anybody from discovering its source.
The few residents in the neighbourhood would be
warned in time to leave their houses for a short while.

As for the neighbouring buildings, the charge we proposed to employ could not possibly have done more than break some of the windows.

Forty-eight hours before the time set for the explosion we were to publish a special message to the authorities, informing them that at that hour on that day *all* their "Security Zones" would be destroyed, and warning them to evacuate them without delay.

The Mandatory would have the option of heeding our warning or disregarding it. The decision would be their responsibility. Our experience led us to believe that they would obey. Those were the days when buildings and offices of the Occupation regime were evacuated at speed whenever some practical joker telephoned to say "there are bombs in your building." Many government and military offices now had ladders conveniently placed for the easier evacuation of upper floors. The lesson of the King David Hotel had had its effect. Moreover, the warning on this occasion would be published in our name, under our official crest, and the British authorities had learnt that the Irgun did not give empty warnings.

True, at the end of the forty-eight hours only one of the "Security Zones" would be destroyed—that in Tel Aviv. But there was no doubt that the authorities, fearing further explosions elsewhere, would not return to any of their Zones. The Citrus House plan, therefore, was calculated in this way to cause a veritable earthquake beneath the foundations of the regime. They would never know where the next blow was coming.

That, and nothing less, was the scope of the Citrus House operation which the Haganah, having been informed by one of its intelligence agents in the neighbourhood of undue activity in the potato merchant's cellar, succeeded in frustrating. On a night when our men had left the building a Haganah party sealed the tunnel.

Looking back, there seems little point in regretting that Citrus House was not demolished. That fine building now serves the State of Israel. The British regime

left our country and their rule was brought to an end
as a result of a long series of other operations. But
there is every reason to mourn the loss of the young
member of the Haganah who was killed in the mined
tunnel because his superiors, panic-stricken by nightmares, decided to prevent at all costs the delivery of
a blow that might have been quickly decisive.

The claim of the official Jewish institutions that the
operation was not aimed at the British but was designed to draw the attention of the United Nations
Committee to ourselves appears even more strange in
the light of what they themselves said about us to the
Committee. They pictured us as an all but decisive factor in the situation that had been created in the country. Dr. Garcia Granados, in his book of memoirs,
has published the full secret record of a meeting that
took place, at the Haganah's request, between Judge
Sandstrom, chairman of the Committee, and a delegation of five members of the Haganah.

At the close of that meeting, Sandstrom asked: "Have
you anything to add?"

To which the Haganah spokesman replied: "Terror
is a very grave thing and cannot be suppressed by the
British Government. Terroristic activities are an evidence of Jews giving vent to their strong feelings.
Haganah believes that it can cope with terrorist activity only if Jewish immigration and settlement are
freely permitted in Palestine. The feelings of the Jews
of Palestine is that this is the time when the fate of
Palestine must be decided."

But the stupid claim that the Irgun, whose fame
had spread to the four corners of the world, was trying,
in the Citrus House operation, to parade its existence,
is most effectively refuted by a reference to the dates
involved. The Citrus House plan was drawn up long
before the Committee came to Eretz Israel, while the
meeting between representatives of the Committee and
of the Irgun Zvai Leumi took place on 26th June, 1947,
only eight days after the Committee's arrival in Eretz
Israel.

The intermediary was Carter Davidson, the chief

correspondent of the Associated Press. Young and
energetic, Davidson showed no partiality for the British
authorities. I do not know whether he liked Jews. I
was told that later, during the war with the Arabs he
did not display any marked sympathy for the Jews.
In any case, at that time we noticed that the whole
American Press went out of its way to emphasize the
might of the Arabs and their victories, and to overplay
Jewish defeats, real or imaginary. However that may
be, during the revolt, Carter Davidson devoted considerable attention to the operations of the Irgun, re-
porting them with intelligence and understanding. He
repeatedly asked us to allow him to witness one of our
operations. We promised to do so, and at one stage intended to invite him to be present at the attack on
Acre Fortress. But on reconsideration, Fred (that was
Davidson's name for Yoel) told him that we would take
him along on a military operation only if his wife gave
her consent. Davidson protested, but we stood by our
decision, and instead accepted his services in a diplomatic operation—the meeting with Judge Sandstrom.

The chairman of the United Nations Committee,
Judge Sandstrom, informed us that he would be accompanied by Dr. Victor Hoo, the Assistant Secretary-
General of UNO and Chief Secretary of the Committee. We readily agreed. At the last moment, Davidson
asked on Sandstrom's behalf whether he would agree
to the presence also of Dr. Ralphe Bunche, Secretary
of the UNO Trusteeship Council and Dr. Hoo's right-
hand man in the Committee. We agreed to this also.
We on our part, however, asked that Mr. Lisicki, the
Czech member of the Committee, be also invited. The
Judge acquiesced, but, as he later explained, he was
unable to contact Lisicki in time. It was particularly
difficult for him to do so, he told us, because he and
his companions had to "get away" from their party in
order to reach us in secret.

The meeting took place at the home of the poet, Dr.
Yaacov Cohen. Yoel brought the guests who, by gen-
eral consent, were accompanied by Carter Davidson.
We usually avoided spectacular and complicated

arrangements when bringing people to meetings in the underground and our guests were invariably astonished at the simplicity of the technique we employed. But in this case we had to take extraordinary precautions. The members of the Committee were surrounded by British Government agents, ostensibly guarding them. The authorities exerted themselves to convey the impression that we were "terrible terrorists," and that the lives of the Committee members—among whom were several friends of our people—were in danger from us. In actual fact the British security agents were largely occupied in keeping the foreign investigators under observation.

Yoel and his assistants drove our guests round the streets of Tel Aviv in one car while a second car came behind to ensure that they were not being followed. For greater safety, they changed cars en route.

At Yaacov Cohen's home, Avraham, Shmuel and I met them. I introduced myself by my real name. We placed Judge Sandstrom at the head of the table. Our guests had apparently prepared themselves for the meeting. The chairman had his first questions in writing. They were the formal questions one puts to witnesses at an inquiry. There was some amusement when he asked if I bore the rank of general and I had to explain that I bore no formal rank at all.

The three men who faced us were of very different types. A Swedish judge, a Chinese diplomat and an American-negro statesman. They were all interesting personalities. We had had information about Sandstrom which was not calculated to inspire us with confidence in his motives. He had been for many years the President of the Mixed Courts in Egypt and he was allegedly influenced by the British Government. Nevertheless, such facts as we gleaned at first-hand did not confirm our suspicions. Sandstrom showed no particular enthusiasm for our cause—he is altogether a dispassionate kind of man—but he likewise revealed no prejudices against us. Dr. Hoo, the son of a one-time Chinese Ambassador in Moscow, was said to be a man of extraordinary ability. Though not a member of the Committee, to which he had been seconded by the UNO Secretariat, he was regarded as its guiding spirit. Dr. Bunche was later to gain world-wide fame as the Acting Mediator on behalf of UNO. His is undoubtedly a brilliant mind.

The conversation among the six men lasted for more than three hours. It was the first encounter between underground spokesmen and the representatives of an international body. There were moments of deep emotion; and also, naturally, moments of humour and laughter. As I spoke of the historic rights of our people to Eretz Israel I involuntarily recalled another conversation; at Lukishki. And I was profoundly stirred: so few years had passed, and we had reached this advanced stage in our struggle. I believe I raised my voice when I dealt with the British Government's treatment of Irgun captives, of Asher Tratner, of Gruner and his comrades and the three who at that very moment were waiting in the shadow of the gallows. Our guests no doubt sympathized with our feelings, but Judge Sandstrom was somewhat disturbed and expressed the fear that I might be audible outside the house. I apologized and reassured him. He probably concluded that the house and the neighbourhood were surrounded by masses of armed Irgun men. In fact there was nobody outside but a few boys and girls—quite unarmed. We for our part understood our guests' feelings. This was their first meeting with the "terrorists." What gruesome stories had they heard about us? And, after all, if we were captured during our discussions, we had the least reason to fear being taken with representatives of the UNO Committee. But for them to be caught with us . . .

Sandstrom several times put "leading questions." What would happen if the Arabs attacked us after a British evacuation of the country? I knew that the prospect of an Arab-Jewish war was the chief argument the British Government was using against any proposal for their evacuation of the country. I pointed out that the Arabs would not attack us unless a third party encouraged and aided them. But—I emphasized—we were convinced that should they attack us we would smite them hip and thigh. For in modern war it was not num-

bers that decided the issue but brains and morale. As
for brains, it was hardly necessary for me to elaborate.
As to fighting spirit, I said, "You have heard of the
attackers of Acre Fortress. You have read of the men
who went to the gallows. I hope you will see and speak
to the men now condemned to death."

Sandstrom asked: "Was Dov Gruner a high officer in
the Irgun?"

"No," I said, "Dov Gruner was a private." The old
judge could not conceal his astonishment.

During the discussion, Dr. Hoo asked: "Assuming
you get Palestine on both sides of the Jordan as a Jewish
State and you bring in several million people, what will
you do about the increase of population? The country
is small. What is going to happen in three hundred years
time?"

I used the very question he asked to stress the absurdity of the plan to set up a tiny Jewish State in only
a part of the country. But Hoo got his main reply from
Shmuel Katz, who told him: "That is a universal problem. What do you think is going to happen in China in
three hundred years' time?"

Dr. Hoo changed the subject.

Throughout the long meeting, Dr. Bunche took notes.
He wrote longhand but his speed was amazing. As he
wrote he would himself put highly pertinent questions,
and from time to time he whispered to Sandstrom. When
Hoo, who was formally his chief, made some suggestion
about the way to make notes, Bunche retorted promptly:
"I have my own way!"

I wondered whether this reply referred only to Dr.
Hoo or to the State Department as well.

I have to express my thanks to Dr. Bunche for his
diligence and toil in preparing the "Report of the Conference Between Representatives of the United Nations
Special Committee on Palestine and the Commander
and two other Representatives of the Irgun Zvai
Leumi." Within three days he sent it to us for our confirmation.

In that report Dr. Bunche faithfully recorded the
host of questions put to us and our explanation of the

background of our struggle, its aims, and the views of the Irgun on the future of Eretz Israel.

The latter part of his report ran as follows:

"The Commander was asked if he would state the reasons for the opposition to the British by the methods used by the Irgun—was it to force the evacuation of their troops, to release Jewish prisoners, or for what other purposes. He replied that what Irgun might be able to attain would be a matter of action on the basis of proportionate forces. The British, he said, have more than we have, but they also know that we are not easily crushed. What we wish is complete evacuation of the British, the removal of British rule, the setting up of a provisional government and the creation of the Jewish State. The British, he said, had previously told the world that they were here to protect the Jews against the Arabs but General D'Arcy told the Anglo-American Committee that if the British left the country the Jews would control it in twenty-four hours—thus insinuating that the British had to remain in order to protect the Arabs against the Jews.

"In response to a statement, the Commander asked the question: 'How could we resist if we did not have the support of the Jewish people, in the face of the great number of British police and troops here? We are convinced that we must fight, or the Jewish people will be destroyed. We are not professional fighters, we don't take pleasure in shooting or being shot. Remember we have just lost six million people and every Jewish life is correspondingly precious to us. But we fight for a purpose! To avoid subjugation and utter destruction.'

"The Commander pointed out that the fight of his organization did bring troubles to the Jewish people—curfew, restrictions, retaliations, etc. But suffering, as every people that had fought knew, was inseparable from the struggle for independence. He added 'we are not just a handful of fanatics. We exist and gain strength even though we bring troubles to the Jewish people.'

"There was no doubt that the overwhelming majority of the Jewish people were in favour of the struggle.

When the Jews had an opportunity of demonstrating their support—which was not always possible—they did so. For example, he pointed out that, when the Haganah joined the fight for a little while, the Jewish people had utilised the opportunity to applaud the struggle.

"The Commander, raising a legal point, contended that even under the Mandate there is absolutely no right for a British Military Court in Palestine. The mandate, he said, differentiated between forces raised in Palestine, and British forces. The latter are regarded as foreign forces, and it follows that British military courts have no right here at all even on the basis of the Mandate. He emphasized that this point made no difference to the struggle, which would go on in any case, but that it should nevertheless interest the Committee.

"The Commander stated that the Irgun members consider themselves legal fighters, engaged in a legal fight, and that they considered the British to be here illegally. He stated that Irgun has lost many of its men in killed and wounded and that it accepts this as an inevitable result of its operations. The British, he said, have executed four of their members. The Irgun, however, did not cease its activities as a result of this, rather it intensified them. 'It inflicted heavy losses on the enemy and the price is not paid yet.' After the executions, he observed, came Acre. Acre, he said, was no small feat. The fight will go on. The British suggestion that they might be prepared to forego executing Irgun members if the Irgun stopped fighting is ridiculous blackmail.

"Go to Acre and ask the three boys sentenced to death whether they are prepared to buy their lives at the price of our struggle. They sent me letters, just as did Dov Gruner, all saying: 'Whatever happens, fight on!' He added 'we are all prepared to give our lives.' No member of Irgun, he said, ever asks for mercy.

"The Commander was questioned as to the Irgun attitude towards the General Assembly's appeal for a truce during the period of the United Nations inquiry. He replied that in connection with this appeal Irgun had sent to the Committee a reasoned document and had stated publicly that it was prepared to cease operations during this period but only on condition that the British would cease their repressive actions also during this period. To illustrate this condition, he drew our attention to the use of British air and naval forces to intercept ships at sea carrying Jews wishing to come to Palestine, to the promulgation of death sentences, to searches and to the imposition of curfews. These, he said, are acts of repression which the British must cease if Irgun is to observe the truce. Any one-sided cessation of operations, he declared, is impossible.

"The Commander expressed the hope that the Committee would go to Europe and see the men in concentration camps who have been there—first in Nazi Germany and now in the 'Liberated camps'—for seven or eight years. He added that the camps in Europe were not the whole problem, only a part of it, but they reflected the problem in its most dire form.

"The Commander expressed the fear that the General Assembly in September will not have time enough to deal with this problem and that a second committee would be appointed to come to Palestine again and that during all this time men, women and children would be languishing in concentration camps in Europe.

"He stated flatly that if the British execute Irgun men Irgun will execute British men—also by hanging. Irgun men, he said, are rightful fighters. Irgun, he said, is absolutely convinced that it fights not only for the independence of Palestine but for the right of free men.

"In response to a question the Commander replied that the Anglo-American Committee had had no contact with Irgun. He stated that Irgun had sent a memorandum to the American members of the Committee but had not sent it to the British members. He added that some individual American members of the Anglo-American Committee had tried to contact Irgun but that it had not been possible to do so at that time for security reasons.

"The Commander explained that the Stern group had come originally out of the Irgun. They too are fighters, he observed. The Stern group came out as an independent group in 1940 as a result of the splitting of Irgun for various reasons. It was widely believed, he said, that the reason for the split was that Abraham Stern, then a member of the Irgun High Command, had opposed the Irgun proclamation of an armistice during the war against Hitler. This was not true. Stern had subscribed to that proclamation together with the rest of the Irgun Command. The split had come a year later. The relations now between the two groups are good. Irgun is larger but he would not say that Irgun is better.

"In response to a question as to what the effect might be on future Jewish youth of training them to disregard the law, the Commander replied that the Irgun members are trained to oppose what the British Government called law because it was the law of occupation and repression, but that in his view the adjustment to a Jewish state would not be difficult for them. It might be a problem, but a minor problem only, in a Jewish state, because there would be an abundance of constructive work in which the youth would engage.

"The Commander asked if there was any possibility of the Committee taking a positive attitude towards the request of the Irgun in the letter sent to the Committee that some of the Irgun men imprisoned at Acre be called as witnesses before the Committee. Mr. Sandstrom replied frankly: 'There is very little possibility. We have done just about all we can do. We can ask why should these three men be the best men to give evidence of terror in the camps.'

"The Commander replied that the answer to the latter question would be that these men have been before the Military Court and that they had themselves experienced maltreatment and witnessed that of others. He added that he did not think this beyond the terms of reference of the Committee and in fact he felt the Committee was obliged to deal with it, since the Committee can investigate all the problems of Palestine. It is a fact he said, that the existing Occupation Government in Palestine is treating prisoners in a barbarous way. Irgun could supply more witnesses than these three if the Committee would have time to hear them. Irgun, he added, accuses the British Government of maltreating prisoners.

"Mr. Sandstrom observed that the point is that there must be other witnesses who can testify similarly, to which the Commander replied that the case of these three is special. They can tell of men who were shot and wounded after capture in the Acre prison break; of wounded men who were shot dead while lying in agony on the ground; of others who died because they were given no medical treatment, not even water. The three referred to in the Irgun letter had been taken prisoner in that operation.

"The Commander stated that he was not sure that the intervention of the Committee would give any results. Any such intervention, in any case, would be couched in diplomatic terms as was the resolution adopted by the Committee. He added that in his view there was a precedent for granting this request which could be found in the Greek investigation by the UNO Security Council.

"At the close of the meeting the Chairman mentioned the agreement which had been reached at its beginning that there would be no publicity concerning this meeting. The Commander replied, 'Irgun always keeps its word. Ask the British. They will tell you.' He agreed, however, that at some later date when the Committee was gone from Palestine the Chairman could, if he saw fit, release the story of this meeting and the text of the notes taken at the meeting provided he would give a prior opportunity to review such notes before their release. This was agreed upon by the Chairman."

The unofficial conclusion of the meeting was not included in Dr. Bunche's report. Dr. Sandstrom said: "I am sorry that the other members of the Committee would not hear you. We shall report to them, but there is always a difference in effect between what you hear for yourself and what you hear at second-hand."

Dr. Hoo left us with: "Au revoir in an independent Palestine."

Dr. Bunche was the warmest of all. Shaking my hand

he exclaimed feelingly: "I can understand you. I am also a member of a persecuted minority."

Carter Davidson, of the Associated Press, was very happy. In the fierce competition in news-getting he had that evening scooped all his rivals. It was no mean achievement from his point of view. A secret meeting between official representatives of the United Nations Organisation and spokesmen of the fighting Hebrew underground, and he not only the only journalist who knew about the meeting but actually was present at it!

Somebody spoilt his scoop. He conscientiously observed his bargain and cabled not a word. We had promised to publish nothing until the Committee reached Geneva, and naturally we kept our word. Now, the underground knew how to keep secrets; but it was helpless when it had to share them with other people. That very night the secret meeting became public property. One of the UNO representatives—I do not know who it was—told of the meeting to another member of the Committee, or to one of the secretaries, over a drink at the Café Pilz. Diligent journalists overheard the story and at once filed sensational telegrams. The Associated Press Correspondent, instead of getting praise he could have earned had he published his scoop, received an astonished query from his head office.

He rushed to Sandstrom and vigorously demanded that he should now be permitted to send a full report. But Sandstrom decided to publish a denial of the whole story. He had his own reasons. I am sure that they were honourable. As long as he was in Eretz Israel Sandstrom had to come into contact with many British officials, and he had promised us that he would not reveal to a soul any description of me or my comrades. He saw that we had shown him complete confidence. I had told him my name. He consequently did not want to be placed in the awkward position of confirming, even by silence, that there had been a meeting between us. The British would undoubtedly have put questions to him about me. What does he look like? Can you see any signs of a plastic operation? What is the colour of his hair now? What tie was he wearing? I am certain Sandstrom would not have answered these questions, but he preferred to avoid having them put. The next day the Press Officer of the Committee issued a vigorous denial of the newspaper report of a meeting.

We ourselves, a couple of days later, informed our own members, in a circular marked "Strictly secret" that the meeting had taken place. We very seldom marked our documents "secret"; they were all secret. The frequent use by Government offices of the injunctions "Strictly confidential," "Secret," "Top Secret," in my opinion, largely nullifies their value.

We wrote:

"The meeting which took place at the request of the Committee lasted three and a half hours. We do not of course expect the Committee to accept our political demands. The cordial atmosphere that prevailed during the conversation and the impression our words may have made do not blind us to realities. Though the atmosphere was good and the Committee representatives expressed their regrets that we could not address the whole Committee on the credo of the Irgun, there is a great difference between gathering a good impression and taking the correct view.

"At the request of the members of the Committee, the Irgun spokesmen undertook to publish no official communiqué before the Committee itself had issued a statement in Geneva. This information is therefore brought to the notice only of members of the Irgun."

Apart from this brief internal statement we maintained silence. We were in honour bound not to tell the truth about the meeting. We were in no way bound to tell anything other than the truth. We said nothing. Our position was easier than that of the UNO representatives. We were underground; they were in the Kadimah Hotel. Life in the underground is not easy. But it has one saving virtue. In the underground you see only the people you want to see. Outside the underground you see chiefly the people who want to see you. The first type of meeting, though not always interesting, is usually useful. The second type has opposite characteristics. We could be silent to our heart's content. Nobody could ask us embarrassing questions.

But we learnt once again from this incident how much reliance may be placed on emphatic denials. Very often they confirm what it is their object to deny.

Carter Davidson, however, could find some comfort not only in Sandstrom's denial but in the anger of the British authorities. They were beside themselves with rage at the meeting. In Parliament they were subjected to scathing questions.

"We have been looking for him for five years," it was pointed out, "and have not succeeded in getting anywhere near him, yet the Chairman of the UNO Committee appears to have found him with the greatest of ease."

On reading such outbursts I almost felt sorry for the British Intelligence Service. How unhelpful of me not to let myself be caught for five whole years! How could I receive Sandstrom, Hoo and Bunche in the underground and yet refuse to be received by Barker and Gurney and Giles?

                              2

We caused a second international scandal when we met the South American members of the Committee, Dr. Granados of Guatemala and Professor Fabregat of Uruguay. That meeting was very cordial indeed. Fabregat and Granados were in a sense comrades in arms. At the outset of the meeting they told us of their lives in exile and underground while fighting against tyranny in their own countries. Granados is the son of one of Guatemala's national heroes, whose statue is the object of annual popular processions. Yet at one time the son was under sentence of death by the rulers of the people his father had helped to liberate. And he had been compelled to move from one hiding place to another to escape his enemies. After many years of suffering he lived to see a change of regime and became his country's ambassador in the United States and its representative on the United Nations Organisation. Granados was unquestionably influenced by the Hebrew struggle for liberation, both because it was a struggle for liberation and because it was directed against Britain. Britain is not popular on the South American continent which for generations was exploited by British monopolies. Little Guatemala has a special reason for not loving Britain: the British colony which exists to this day in the Western hemisphere is regarded as having occupied Guatemalan territory. God helped us even through Honduras.

Fabregat too was a natural friend of our cause. For many years he was an exile in Brazil before he saw the fruits of his toil and suffering. Uruguay, as I later saw for myself, is one of the freest countries on earth. Its system of social insurance, introduced by the great President Vago, is one of the most progressive in the world. Bigger nations have something to learn from this small people, set down on the shores of the "Silver River," and blessed by God with a heart of gold. The liberator of Uruguay, Artigas, is a member of that great band of South American liberators, San Martin, Bolivar, Terradentas, O'Higgins. But it is characteristic that in English history-books, Artigas is referred to as a "brigand chief." From Montevideo to Tel Aviv the McMillans use the same dictionary.

The South American peoples know how to love and to hate. They are generous and hospitable. Our fight against British rule, which was reported from end to end of the continent, its echoes reaching almost every lonely shepherd's hut, recalled old memories of the revolt against Madrid. The South American peoples regarded our revolt with unconcealed sympathy. I saw that for myself when I visited their spacious, immeasurably rich countries. I heard it from Granados and Fabregat as they told us of their experience and struggles.

Granados impressed us as a political fighter *par excellence*. Fabregat is a humanitarian in the noblest

sense of the word. He moved me deeply when he in-
quired into the condition of the children of Nathanya,
then in the grip of martial law.

"Are not the children in Nathanya going hungry? Are
they getting milk?"

I believe that love of children is the measure of
human affection. In his inquiries in Eretz Israel and
Europe Fabregat first of all saw the children.

The meeting took place in the cosy home of our
friend Israel Waks. Yoel again arranged an excursion
through the streets of Tel Aviv before bringing the
visitors to one of those "secret hideouts" of the underground which in fact were only ordinary rooms placed
at our disposal by courageous friends. The atmosphere
lacked the formality which had characterised at least
the first part of our meeting with Sandstrom, Hoo and
Bunche. Granados spoke for both of them. Fabregat's
knowledge of English is slight, so he spoke ardently
in the language of Cervantes, which Granados translated into excellent English. I had Alex and Shmuel with
me; at times Shmuel had to speak for both of us.

With Granados we had a political debate. I tried to
convince him that he and Fabregat, as friends of our
people, should demand not only the liquidation of the
British Mandate—that was common ground—but that
the whole of the country should become a Jewish State.

"The Arabs and the British," I urged, "have unofficial mouthpieces on the Committee. Our people has
none. You two, who do not hide your feelings, should
counter the demand that Palestine should be Arab or
British, by the demand that Palestine should be Jewish.
If the majority on the Committee decides on a compromise, that is another matter, but let our just demand
at least be voiced by one or two international representatives. Even if you accept the partition plan as just, it
is clear that if it is proposed by you, our devoted friends,
the result may be a 'compromise' between your proposal
and the Arab-British proposal which completely denies
our right to this country."

Granados replied that he could not promise to accede
to our request. He was under the impression, he said,

that the majority on the Committee were inclined to recommend the liquidation of British rule, but they had to take into consideration the presence of Arabs in Palestine. They could not be "one-sided." Morover, he said with a smile, "it would be strange if Fabregat and I were to demand more than Mr. Shertok. And you know as well as we do that the Jewish Agency is proposing partition."

The three of us tried to come back to this point. We urged that while we could not speak for the Jewish Agency, we felt that even they would not regard with disfavour a proposal in the Committee to set up a Jewish State in all Eretz Israel. Our efforts, however, were in vain. While Granados was not enthusiastic about the Jewish official leadership—and had some sarcastic things to say about one of them—he identified himself completely with their attitude on the partition question. And we had to confess to ourselves that his last argument cut the ground from under our feet. No foreigner, however friendly he may be, can claim for a nation more than its own official representatives demand. This unhappy argument was repeated several months later at the session of the UNO General Assembly—this time by Tsarapkin. In this circumstance lies the key to many developments in Eretz Israel in our generation.

The conversation developed into a discussion, at once sad and heartening, about our three boys sentenced to death. Granados told us of the efforts he and Fabregat had made to move the Committee in their favour. I told them how deeply grateful we were. Both disclaimed any right to gratitude. They had only done their human duty. Indeed, they added, we have to thank you for bringing us to Palestine.

"A Jewish citizen told us," went on Granados, "that he is not angry with the underground for all the troubles your actions have caused him because, in the result, it is through those actions that the UNO Committee was set up. We think that he is right."

Fabregat added: "I was invited to a reception by General McMillan, but I replied that I would not come—because of the death sentences."

Honest and worthy Fabregat! Jewish leaders did not show similar dignity in the face of the oppressor's judicial murders. . . .

The reappearance of Yoel signaled the end of the conversation. We shook hands warmly, as members of the same family, of fighters for freedom. As they were turning to go, Granados said to me: "Would you tell me with whom we have been speaking tonight. We should like to be sure that we have met authorized representatives of the Irgun."

He was right. We had said nothing at the beginning of the conversation—for the simple reason that we assumed Yoel had told them I would be present. The names of my companions could in any case not be disclosed.

Apparently, Yoel had observed the rules of the underground to the letter. And throughout the conversation the visitors had not been sure to whom they were talking. Granados had cleverly tried to find out. He seemed to imagine that the "chief" was Alex, the oldest among us. Every time we smoked, Granados would offer a light to Alex, but the latter, who in his youth was a member of a students' "Corporation," would take the cigarette out of his mouth, take the lighter or the matches from Granados, light Granados' cigarette, then give me a light, then Shmuel and finally light his own. All these manoeuvres may well have been simply the accepted politeness of civilized individuals, but Alex got the impression that Granados was testing the ground—without, however, finding out what he sought.

I saw no reason for hiding from Granados and Fabregat what we had revealed to Sandstrom.

I answered Granados: "I cannot tell you the names of my colleagues, and their pseudonyms won't mean anything to you. My name is known, so I shall not hide it from you."

I learnt then to what extent the underground fired the imagination, even though it contained nothing extraordinary except the readiness to suffer and die for a just cause. When I told Granados my name, he stepped back and in a loud voice said: "So you are the man!"

Taken aback by the ringing tone in which the words were uttered and at a loss to find words in reply—I laughed. Fabregat did not laugh. He put his arms round my shoulders and hugged me as one hugs a younger brother and said something in Spanish.

"We are brothers in arms," I said, when I found my voice. "All the world's fighters for freedom are one family."

After more handshakes and expressions of friendship, our guests were whisked away by Yoel.

Chapter XXIII

Meetings in the Dark

During the period of collaboration between the Jewish Agency and the British authorities against the Irgun Zvai Leumi I saw Arthur Koestler. Koestler, who has devoted himself to the special branch of literature which one may call "political psychology," had come to Eretz Israel to study the events at first hand and to gather material for his books. He at once tried to contact the underground, met Friedman-Yellin of the Stern Group, and somewhat pressingly insisted on meeting me.

I was Israel Sassover at the time. We were being hounded by both British and Jews. We were obliged to be circumspect. My colleagues consequently doubted whether in these circumstances I ought to see Koestler. We had been told that he spent a good deal of time in British "society." While nobody cast any doubts on Koestler this information was sufficient to arouse the fear that he might inadvertently let something slip while in that "society." It was therefore decided to inform Koestler politely that to our regret the meeting could not take place. But Koestler did not so easily throw away material for his political psychology—and I came to his assistance.

In the nature of things I was less concerned about my security than were my good colleagues. And I was interested in talking to Koestler as a man who likes looking into the inside of things. I therefore exerted my influence to bring about the meeting. My colleagues hesitantly agreed but made one condition: the meeting must take place in the dark; Israel Sassover's beard must not be seen. I had some doubts about this condition. It is not pleasant to talk in the dark. And why offend Koestler? But my colleagues firmly stood their ground. Alas, my poor beard! I gave in.

Koestler was very cordial. As he was brought into the darkened room I suppose he blinked as he said: "Menachem?"

He did not see me blink as I replied: "Yes. *Shalom* to you. Please take a seat."

It was all very well to be asked to sit down, but how do you find a chair in the darkness? Avraham and Reuven, however, were at home in the darkness they themselves had created, and they seated us both. So we began to talk at each other's voices.

Koestler told me that in the British circles "friendly to Zionism," there was a tendency to favour a transition period of ten years after the end of the war, during which one hundred thousand Jews would be allowed to enter the country. At the end of that period maybe there would be—partition. I replied that we did not believe in the various "transition periods" just as we did not believe in the friendship of the "friendly circles." Koestler rejected my disbelief. He mentioned, as representative of those circles, the younger element in the British Labour Party and cited particularly Michael Foot.

Our talk turned from one theme to another. Koestler asked me if we meant to continue using V-3.

"What is V-3?" I asked wonderingly.

"You know, the electrically-operated mortar that was found near the King David Hotel. The British here call it V-3."

I laughed. Giddy's invention was certainly of great importance, but was there any call for explosive names? The authorities, of course, had their own reasons for calling it V-3, but, intent on cursing us, all they succeeded in doing was to praise the penetrative power of the Irgun.

As our conversation proceeded I gained the impression that Koestler was more interested in what he could not see than in listening. We both smoked heavily. Perhaps we thought the smoke would dissipate the darkness. But lighting a cigarette in the circumstances was no simple matter. My "tormentors" had decided that the darkness must be impenetrable. There must be no glimmer of light from outside, certainly none within. That unhappy beard! Lighting a cigarette involved a special ritual of "light in the darkness." I would grope my way into the next room to light mine. At that moment Avraham or Reuven would go up to Koestler and light his. When both our cigarettes were lit and smoking adequately we again could "see"—each other's voices.

But Koestler did not lightly forego material for his "political psychology."[1] He began smoking his cigarettes with unusual vigour. He all but tore them apart. He would take a long pull, blow out the smoke, then another long pull, until there was nothing left. I watched this rapid consumption of cigarettes with interest. I felt sorry, not for the cigarettes, whose fate it was to go up in smoke, but for Koestler. He mistook the strategic value of the flame. His toil was in vain. The heightened glow of his cigarette did not give him any help in seeing me. On the contrary; the bursts of light that came from his seat enabled me to get a glimpse of the end of his nose. What he should have done was to ask me to pull at my cigarette with all my might, and then he might have seen the end of my nose and perhaps caught a glimpse of my beard! As he made no such request, I did not exert myself. And there was darkness.

We later concluded that the meeting with Koestler

[1] Koestler, who has at times displayed a quaint capriciousness in his pleasure and displeasure with phenomena which have attracted his interest, took the occasion subsequently to deride these security measures of the Irgun, comparing them with the absence of conspiratorial precautions by the Stern Group during their interviews with him. The reader of these Memoirs will understand that Koestler's strictures in this matter probably sprang from honest ignorance of conditions rather than from unworthy pique.

reinforced the rumour that I had undergone a plastic operation, a rumour widely current among the British authorities. I believe they invented it themselves in order to explain why their Intelligence Service, in spite of the searches, the promised prizes and the shadowings, had failed to lay hands on me. Yaacov Meridor had given colour to this theory. When the Intelligence Officer who questioned him in the Cairo prison asked him one day, "Is it true that Begin has had a plastic operation?"—Yaacov replied in unconcealed panic and confusion: "How did you know that? No, no, it's not true!"

The Intelligence Officer was delighted. He was sure he had wrung the secret from Yaacov.

Koestler apparently added another brick to the imaginative structure of the police. He was, of course, under no obligation not to reveal what I did *not* look like. He was very surprised that I received him in the darkness. Several days before meeting me he had met the head of the F.F.I. face-to-face. Why not me? He was not aware that at that time the Irgun had special reasons, which the F.F.I. did not have, for the utmost degree of caution. He also did not know that I was a prospective candidate for the post of second assistant to the third warden of the Synagogue in Joshua Bin Nun Street, and that the beard was an important qualification for the post. In pondering the reason for the riddle, he may have concluded that there was some truth in the reports that I had overlain natural ugliness with artificial beauty. Or that may have been the conclusion drawn by the people whom he told that he had talked to me in an orgy of cigarette consumption.

However that may be, a new spate of stories appeared in the British Press—whence it spread all over the world—about that plastic operation. We were highly pleased at these reports. We were even more pleased when we read in a popular British newspaper that I had had not one plastic operation but four. No less. When I left the underground and was asked by newspapermen—mainly Americans—what truth there was in these stories, I felt I had to reply: "Quite true. I had four plastic operations, but just before the British left I had a fifth to restore my original face."

I must ask Arthur Koestler's pardon, for making him sit in the darkness for two hours and smoke so many cigarettes. I hope he will forgive me as will our very good friend Ivan Greenberg, whom I promised to meet again in the light. And there was light.[1]

That is the paradox in the life of every man who fights in a just cause.

He puts on a heavy, sometimes too heavy, yoke, in order to throw off a yoke. He makes war so that there should be peace. He punishes himself so that there should be no suffering. He employs physical force and believes in moral force. He sheds blood so that there should be no more bloodshed. He accepts enslavement —in prison or concentration camp—for the sake of freedom. He leaves his beloved family—so that families should not be broken up. He sacrifices his life—in order to ensure life. He injects himself with germs—in order to find the cure. He lives in the darkness so that the light should break through.

That is the way of the world. A very tragic way beset with terrors. There is no other.

Late in 1946 there arrived in Eretz Israel Mr. Clark Baldwin, a United States Congressman whose visit to Britain and the Middle East had been approved by President Truman. On his way he had met Mr. Attlee and other British Cabinet Ministers. Mr. Baldwin, who had expressed sympathy for our struggle, asked to meet me. Again there were the usual doubts and the usual suggestions to sit behind a curtain, or in darkness. But this time I rebelled, and it was decided to receive the American politician in "open underground."

The meeting was to take place at Alex's flat. This flat, too, had of course been subjected to British

[1] On that occasion Mr. Greenberg, apologising to me for the precautionary darkness, recalled what Jabotinsky had said when they had once attempted to tell him certain Irgun confidences: "Don't tell me, don't tell me. What I don't know I'm quite sure I can rely upon myself not to reveal, even under torture!"

searches. After the King David Hotel explosion a party of British soldiers arrived at "Mr. Slomnicki's" flat. "Mr. Slomnicki" went out to them wearing a white apron and carrying a big kitchen-knife. Here was a solid, respectable householder employing the enforced leisure of the curfew by doing a little cooking. The interrogation was therefore very brief. Alex himself cut it short. "Excuse me, gentlemen," he said, "but I'm frying chips and they'll get burnt." The soldiers left the cook to get on with his frying and made off. That was obviously no place to look for terrorists. In a room inside a young man was soundly sleeping off the effects of a sleepless night. It was Giddy.

In that same room, saturated with secrets and with the many sorrows and joys of the underground, I met Clark Baldwin. To my misfortune I fell ill on the eve of the meeting, and as he was due to leave the country within a day or two I had to receive him in bed.

Mr. Baldwin was very friendly. He told us of his meetings with the British statesmen, and emphasized his complete understanding of our struggle, even drinking a toast to the independent Jewish State soon to arise. He asked us if we could temporarily suspend our operations in the hope that the American Government would take action to secure the opening of the gates of Eretz Israel. Our reply was clear. But Mr. Baldwin afterwards made his appeal public and in order to avoid misunderstanding we were compelled to publish our reply as well. We summed up as follows:

". . . We regret therefore that we are unable to comply with your request. We can no longer rely on promises, however sincere their purpose. What our tormented people needs is concrete help. And when this is not forthcoming there is no other way left to its sons but to help themselves and to rely on their own fighting spirit and their own spirit of self-sacrifice.

"In this just struggle we shall certainly be accorded the support of freedom-loving men and women in your great country and all over the world."

On his return to the United States, Mr. Baldwin sent a detailed report to President Truman and subsequently published it. We learnt from this report how to behave in the underground. Mr. Baldwin wrote that in order to hide my face I had attached a beard to my chin, and I had lain in bed in order to conceal my height. Such ingenious ideas had never occurred to us. The underground fires the imagination of the people outside it. Even a common-or-garden illness is seen as a trick. As for a beard, it simply must be false. I forgave Mr. Baldwin his doubts about my illness, but it was difficult to forgive his slight to my beard.

I met few journalists in the underground. Only in the latter stages did I see some of the correspondents. Richard Mowrer was very cordial. He had been injured in the King David Hotel explosion and I had sent him a letter in hospital expressing our regrets at his injury and explaining that we had not desired to hurt either him or anybody else. Though he suffered for many months, he nevertheless bore us no grudge. He was not in agreement with everything we did, but was not influenced by the whispering campaign against us. He appreciated our struggle and wrote that we were not terrorists but fighters for freedom who fought with our eyes open.

Turner, the New York Herald-Tribune correspondent showed courage when the *Palestine Post* building was blown up. Disregarding the danger he rushed into the flames and smoke to help rescue the trapped people. When I met him subsequently, he was apparently not certain that I was the person with whom he had been promised the interview. He had no description of me, had only seen the British police photograph. But like many others he had formed a mental picture and when he saw me he exclaimed in mixed surprise and disappointment: "You should be a big man!"

I asked: "With big muscles and horns?"

We both laughed. Imagination has wings. Reality has no horns.

Lorna Lindsey, the writer, displayed warm, even motherly sympathy for our Irgun soldiers. She had herself been struck by tragedy. Her daughter, who had joined the Free French Forces, was killed the day before the end of World War II. She told me much about her daughter. I spoke to her of our men and their love of freedom. Our mutual sense of bereavement brought us closer to each other. The interview became a friendly chat. I was speaking to a mother, who understood.

Twice after the "Altalena" incident, I met author Robert St. John. He had written at length about the "Altalena" and his talks with me in his book "Shalom Means Peace." I shall not discuss his book. These chapters are not the proper place for literary criticism. But I must say this: on reading his description I learnt the meaning of "sensationalism." St. John wrote, for example, that at the entrance to my room he saw two bodyguards who could easily have been—S.S. men. I asked myself: what is the purpose of such an insulting suggestion? I could only explain it by the desire for sensation. Moreover where did the idea of bodyguards at my door come from? St. John, after all, could not have seen them—for the simple reason, as I have already explained, that I never had any bodyguards. Literature which tries to create hair-raising effects achieves its purpose at the expense of valuable thought and often at the expense of truth.

I met Quentin Reynolds after the conquest of Jaffa. He was an old friend of the fighting underground, one of the most active supporters of the American League for a Free Palestine. I remarked that I hoped he did not regret the aid he had given us, particularly his appearance in Ben Hecht's play, "A Flag is Born."

Reynolds shook his fine head: "I'm proud of it," he replied. At his request, we gladly gave him a Sten-gun made in our own Irgun arms factory, as a memento, suitably inscribed on the butt. He took it with him throughout all his wanderings on the way back to America.

In the early days of the revolt I met one of the important officers in the Haganah, Moshe Dayan, who had suggested an exchange of views. Having heard that he was one of the "activists" in the Haganah we agreed. He told me a good deal about his exploits in Syria, which he had penetrated in the days of the Vichy Government, to carry out sabotage operations against important military installations. He did not boast, but from his matter-of-fact descriptions it was plain that he did not lack courage. He had lost an eye in the fighting in Syria. He clearly had lost none of his daring.

I spoke to him of our struggle and its political significance. On many points we found ourselves in agreement, at any rate in the conversation. Moreover he made some encouraging remarks. After our operations, he said, the workers had begun to regard the Irgun with affection. He observed that we did everything possible to avoid hurting Jews, and now it was clear to him and to many others that our operations were directed only against the Mandatory regime. He did not enter into an evaluation of the political consequences of our struggle. About them, he said, there could always be two opinions. But he valued what we were doing particularly for the lessons it taught. We were proving to the whole Jewish youth that it was eminently possible to smite the ruling authorities.

During the Resistance Movement period I had a brief meeting with the famous American Zionist leader, Dr. Abba Hillel Silver. We met in a room near the seashore, rented temporarily by Alex. I spent many days there following disturbing reports on the Joshua Bin Nun neighbourhood. I was the illegal sub-tenant of a sub-tenant who was legal to the landlady but highly illegal to the authorities. Alex had to see to it that the landlady should not see me. Every morning we had to leave the room and go about our business. But where could such illegal tenants go in daylight? We could hardly walk about the crowded streets. There being no choice we went to the nearest "hiding-place"—the seashore. It was certainly very pleasant. They were days of Khamsin (the hot desert wind). The man with the beard and the man with the bald head took an underground bathe. The beard caused difficulties. I had never before been bathing in a beard. I did not know what to do about the skull-cap which invariably covered the head of Israel Sassover. If I took it off, it might arouse comment; a beard and no skull-cap.[1] But if I kept it on it would probably be swept away by the waves. The problem was serious. I solved it the way simple folk solve their social dilemma when faced at a formal table with a variety of knives and forks and don't know which to begin with. They watch their neighbours out of the corner of their eye. Skull-cap on head, and hand on skull-cap I looked around the beach. To my good fortune there were other bearded individuals there, and they not only went into the sea but even sun-bathed without a cap—donning it only when they went off to eat. I did as they did, and drew no special attention to myself. That was the main thing in the underground. If you succeeded in that you could get sunburnt with dignity. The British Intelligence Service might burrow for you under the earth—while you peacefully enjoyed the amenities of the seashore!

In Alex's room I met Dr. Silver. Our talk was very serious. The impression Dr. Silver made on me that day lasted a long time.

Having had the privilege, for a period, of being close to the great Vladimir Jabotinsky, I am not easily carried away by outstanding personalities. I could not tell you —possibly nobody can define—what is meant by "a great man." But I know I felt in my whole being that Jabotinsky was great, that he saw far ahead and combined nobility of spirit with an iron logic. Since that time I simply cannot be impressed by people merely because they are popularly considered "great," certainly not by persons merely because they are the holders of

---

[1] Jewish tradition requires the head to be covered, as a token of respect, when prayer or a blessing is uttered. Strictly orthodox Jews mostly keep the head covered. But there are many degrees of Jewish orthodoxy.

important positions. But I must say that at that first meeting Silver made a great impression on me. "He is a personality," I told my colleagues.

Dr. Silver was the first Zionist leader from whom I heard words of encouragement for our struggle instead of the usual denunciations of the "dissidents." He expressed the hope that the fighting unity achieved in the Resistance Movement would continue. He felt it had to continue. American public opinion was sympathetic to the fighters for, he said, "they too had to fight the British by extra-legal means."

It is said that Dr. Silver was not consistent. I do not know how true this is. I know that in his estimation of the revolt as a liberating factor he remained consistent in spite of pressure from various sides. When I visited the United States he was urged from many quarters to join in a declaration denouncing the "dissidents" on behalf of the Zionist Emergency Council. The same elements pressed the great poet, Zelman Schneour to resign from the Reception Committee. (Schneour published a moving protest.) But Silver emphatically rejected all these proposals for denouncing me and prevented their acceptance by the Zionist body. During the discussion he said to our detractors:

"The Irgun will go down in history as a factor without which the State of Israel would not have come into being."

Chapter XXIV
Pathway to Victory

Within a period of time shorter than was expected even by many of our most sanguine members and supporters, we succeeded in bringing about the collapse of the Occupation regime and what has been described with almost scientific accuracy as the "bankruptcy of British rule in Palestine." The historic turn of events was not the result of any single operation, it was brought about by the cumulative effect of a whole series of underground operations.

In this summing up I will not attempt to engage in analysis, but will leave the documents, especially the British documents to speak for themselves. They eloquently reveal how the British Government, in the final phase of the revolt, tried to save and consolidate their hold on our country and how the Hebrew rebels succeeded, step by step, in foiling their efforts; how we forced them to go to the U.N., and, finally, to go.

After the suggestion of "federation with autonomy" (the Morrison Plan), was rejected by both Arabs and Jews, Bevin proposed a "new plan" for the solution of the Palestine problem. It was put forward on January 10th, 1947, during the Tripartite Conference on Palestine in London. The British called it "cantonisation." Bevin proposed that the country should be divided into a number of Zones which would be granted a wide measure of autonomy in internal affairs under the supervision of a central Government. The transition period would last five years. One hundred thousand Jews would be admitted into the Jewish zone in two years. The monthly quota of immigration certificates would be about 4,000. Thereafter immigration would be subject to the decision of the British High Commissioner.

The Arabs rejected the new plan as they had rejected the "original" Morrison plan—unreservedly. They would not agree to any further Jewish immigration, nor to any partition of Palestine. They demanded an independent Palestine—and at once. The Jewish Agency, too, rejected the plan. The British having failed to obtain the consent of "both sides" to the proposals of the "third side," the Conference collapsed.

We were told that the Agency had not rejected the plan in principle. They could not accept the size of the area to be allocated to the Jews nor the immigration plans. The Agency insisted that the distribution of certificates be handed over to them. With such amendments the Agency would have been prepared to accept "partition" under British supervision. Mr. Shertok on 11th February, 1947 explained to a Press Conference that the Jewish Agency demanded: First, an adequate Jewish area with full authority; second, immigration into this area; and third, the eventual recognition of Jewish independence in at least a part of Eretz Israel. Shertok did not explain what was meant by "an adequate area." On the other hand he made quite clear what he meant by "full Jewish authority." His second condition was that there should be "agreement" on immigration into the Jewish area. But if Jewish authority was to be "full," why was British agreement necessary on immigration?

Morrison had said that his proposed federation might ultimately be converted into a final partition between an "Arab State" and a "Jewish State."

The obstinacy of our enemies rescued us. Bevin would not hear of handing over the four thousand monthly certificates. As for the Arabs, they said simply: "It is all ours; even Tel Aviv. . . ."

But for Arab and British—or Anglo-Arab—stubbornness, we Jews of Palestine would today be living in a "Morrison Ghetto"—unless we, the rebels, had been able to frustrate even that plan, too.

On the 14th February, 1947, the London Conference came to an end. Bevin informed the Arabs that since both sides had shown no inclination to compromise, the Palestine question would be submitted to the United Nations.

Bevin made a long statement in the House of Commons, on the rejection of the British proposals by both Arabs and Jews, and on his decision to submit the Palestine question to the United Nations in September. Bevin made an appeal to "all parties" to keep the peace in Palestine until the U.N. decided. He announced that Jewish immigration would continue to be at the rate of 1,500 a month.

Winston Churchill rose to protest against the "protracted delay." He asked whether it meant that for another year Britain must continue to bear the burden of keeping 100,000 troops in Palestine at a cost of 30-40 million pounds. Richard Crossman said it could be assumed that no decision would be reached in less than two years.

Everybody understood that Bevin wanted to gain time. On the 25th February, the Secretary for the Colonies explained that the approach to the U.N. did not mean that Britain was *surrendering the Mandates*: she was only asking the advice of U.N. as to how the Mandate could be administered.

But on Saturday, the 1st of March, the Irgun Zvai Leumi tore Bevin's calculations to shreds. A new wave of attacks, wide in scope and powerful and deep in penetration was launched. In Jerusalem we broke through the British Army security zone. The Officers' Club, surrounded by barbed wire and machine-gun posts, was blown up. The break through party went in without a hitch. And the covering-party, led by Avshalom Haviv, displayed unusual skill and courage, effectively breaking down enemy resistance before the main attack was developed. A British police patrol in armoured vehicles arrived and joined battle with our men, but our Assault Force emerged from the combat victorious, suffering only a few casualties. The British losses were considerably heavier.

Several hours later, on Saturday evening, units of our Assault Force carried out over ten attacks through-

out the country, including the Navy Camp at Haifa,
Army camps at Beit-Lidd, Pardess Hannah and Reho-
vot, and military transport in the areas of Tulkarm,
Petah Tikvah, Kfar Sirkin, and Kiryat Haim. On the
Sunday morning we continued operations. All were suc-
cessful. The enemy was stunned by these severe blows.

The *Haaretz* correspondent reported from London:
"The attack in Jerusalem came as a shock to London
at the week-end. The evening papers brought out edi-
tions with big headlines on every new report they received. The newspapers emphasize that this is the first
time the terrorists have attacked on the Sabbath, and
they underline that the attack was executed *inside* the
Security Zone. The *Sunday Express* devotes its leading
article to the latest acts of terrorism in Palestine and
says bluntly that 'Britain must get out of Palestine and
stay out.' 'Britain, unlike Nazi Germany,' it goes on,
'cannot repay terror with counter-terror, but we can
apply justice with force and resolution and we should
do so without delay. We must tell the world immediately what we intend doing to give up responsibility
as soon as we can move our troops out of the country
—and we should move them out forthwith."

In spite of the claim of the *Sunday Express*, the
British authorities did answer "terror with counter-ter-
ror." Within twenty-four hours of our attacks Martial
Law, which had been threatened for many months, was
instituted. The plan, which, according to a statement
made in London, had been prepared by Field Marshal
Montgomery, went into force on the 2nd of March.
How many people realise what Martial Law means?
Consider the main provisions of the British plan:

1. Every region affected was placed under the Army,
and the Officer Commanding each region was approved
by the High Commission acting as Military Governor.

2. All Government offices were closed and all their
services to the public were suspended.

3. Civil courts were suspended.

4. A military court was immediately set up by the
Military Governor.

5. The Military Governor was authorized to shut down banks.

6. Postal services were completely suspended.

7. Telephone services were to be limited to a list approved by the Military Governor.

8. Movement into and out of each region was forbidden except for the transport of essential commodities and under special permits approved by the Military Governor.

9. The Military Governor was authorized to confiscate land, houses and transport.

10. The police were brought under the command of the Military Governor.

11. Every soldier was authorized to make arrests as though he were a member of the Police Force.

12. The Military Commanders were authorized to set up courts for speedy trials.

13. Movement of buses and all other mechanically-operated vehicles was forbidden within the zones except under special permit.

On the 3rd of March, the House of Commons heard a new statement by the Colonial Secretary on the "outbreaks" in Palestine. Mr. Creech Jones explained that the British Government had approved the imposition of martial law in certain areas. He added that "the Palestine authorities would receive the full support of the Government in any further action which might prove necessary."

Mr. Churchill rose to ask: "Why is it thought that the measures proposed now are likely to be more effective than others taken at various times during the past twelve months after similar outrages?"

The Colonial Secretary replied that what had now happened was the declaration of statutory Martial Law. Not only had whole areas been cordoned off, but most intensive searches were being conducted. Civil law had been suspended for the moment.

Mr. Seymour Cox asked the Minister to consider the history of a parellel situation in Ireland 27 years earlier. The Minister replied that this was very much in the Government's mind.

But these questions and answers were not as important as the debate in the House of Commons which resulted from our blows on the 1st of March. The "nail" was hit on the head by Winston Churchill at Westminster—and came out at Lake Success, at the United Nations. According to Reuter's account of that historic debate in Parliament:

"Shouting angrily and thumping a despatch-box in front of him, Mr. Winston Churchill demanded in the House of Commons today to know how long this state of 'squalid warfare' in Palestine, with all its bloodshed, would go on before some decision was reached. He said it was costing thirty to forty million sterling a year and keeping 100,000 Englishmen away with the military forces."

Mr. Creech Jones, who had just reported on the outbreak on Saturday in which 18 had been killed and 28 injured, replied that the Government was fully alive to the very serious situation in Palestine and every step would be taken to bring to an end the tragic situation as rapidly as possible. The immediate action, said Mr. Creech Jones, was in the hands of the Military Commander in consultation with the High Commissioner. The Government was not unmindful of the desperate urgency of finding a way out of the difficulty.

Mr. Churchill was not satisfied. "How long is this to go on?" he demanded and repeated the words in a louder voice. "*Is there no means of accelerating the appeal to the United Nations*, or are we just to drift on, month after month, with these horrible outrages and counter-measures, which are necessary but nevertheless objectionable—necessary but painful? How long are we to go on? Can nothing be done to accelerate the appeal?"

Mr. Creech Jones replied that that was a different question. The Government was fully alive to the urgency of the matter. Appropriate steps had already been taken to see *whether it was possible to accelerate the matter, having regard to the procedure of the United Nations*.

But Mr. Churchill was still not satisfied. "When does

he expect to be in a position to announce that the United Nations would be able to give prompt attention to this urgent matter?"

Mr. Creech Jones replied: "I cannot give an answer at this moment, but I can assure him we are pursuing our enquiries at New York with all possible speed. I hope it may be possible within a week to make some announcement on what progress the enquiries have made."

Mr. Churchill: "If I ask the question within a week . . ."

Creech Jones: "I will do my best to answer."

So it is clear that with the blows which they struck on 1st March, 1947, the soldiers of the Irgun Assault Force jogged the painfully slow British and international wheels into movement. The whole of the British Press now demanded that the Government hasten its approach to the U.N., and by 4th of March it was announced from London that Britain had sent an urgent note to Mr. Trygve Lie, proposing the setting-up of a special U.N. Committee to examine the Palestine problem before the autumn session of the General Assembly.

Mr. Churchill gave the Government no rest. Even in the debate on India he referred to the Palestine question and with characteristic stubbornness reiterated the views he had expressed on many previous occasions.

On the 6th of March he said: "In this small Palestine . . . we are to pour out all our treasure and keep 100,000 men marching around in most vexatious and painful circumstances when we have no real interest in the matter." He added that he had for some time past pressed the Government to return their Mandate to the U.N. and invoke its aid if they were unable to maintain order in Palestine.

Meanwhile, however, the British authorities were still trying to save face. Martial Law, imposed on Jerusalem and the Tel Aviv-Petah Tikvah area, continued for fifteen days.

It must be said that in those tense days the mass of the people displayed wonderful civic courage. The official leaders seemed to be bewildered; but the spirit of the people was fine. The British authorities forbade them to travel in buses; so they used carts and bicycles or walked—and jeered at the Government. There was no longer any general fear. You could see men and women, laughing behind the barbed wire fences. The children sang loudly, "Anemones, anemones," the popular satirical song about the Sixth Airborne Division.

And the underground, as I have already related, did its part. In imposing Martial Law the Government had two alternative objectives: a "maximum" and a "minimum." The first was the hope of seeing the underground crushed and dissolved, its commanders on the gallows and its soldiers in Latrun. This dream speedily evaporated. They then hoped to prove that the "new measures" would paralyse the underground. It would have been an achievement if martial law could have prevented the "terrorists" from carrying out any more attacks. We determined to do everything in our power to frustrate Montgomery's "minimum" as well as his "maximum" plan. During those two critical weeks the Assault Force of the Irgun, and the F.F.I., smote the enemy almost incessantly. It was not only Brigadier Davis who spoke of "commandos striking" at the Schneller military camp. The British and American Press described prominently and at length the attack of "the Jewish commandos in Jerusalem."

And in truth the Irgun Assault Force were first-class commandos. Few have ever equalled them. During that period we changed their mode of living. They no longer returned home or to their work after taking part in an attack. They remained, split up in small parties, in the fields, orange-groves and woods, and surprised the enemy in the most unlikely places.

With the lifting of martial law, which had achieved nothing for those who imposed it except further humiliation, we experienced a feeling of real triumph. And when Giddy, exhausted after nights of ceaseless action, but happy, came to see me, I gave vent to my feelings for the first time. Giddy, in accordance with our custom in the underground, stood to attention and waited for me to open the conversation. But for a few moments I threw off the burdensome cloak of the "commander," put my arms around him, and murmured, "You've won, Giddy, you've won. Our boys have won."

The British army copied the German system of giving apposite code names to military operations. The martial law operations in Jerusalem and in the Tel Aviv area were called "Elephant" and "Hippopotamus"—suggesting the crushing of the underground beneath ponderous feet. But martial law was a hopeless failure. The elephant and the hippopotamus had produced a mouse. Churchill's doubts were once again fully vindicated.

Following Britain's request to Mr. Trygve Lie to hasten the discussion in the U.N. Assembly were long diplomatic interchanges between London and Washington, Lake Success, Moscow, Paris and Chungking. Soviet Russia, and apparently also other States, opposed the mechanical appointment of an Inquiry Committee. They wanted a *special session* of the U.N. Assembly in order to discuss the "very urgent question." Early in April Mr. Trygve Lie sent Britain's urgent note to all the members of the U.N. The replies were prompt, and it was announced that the United Nations would discuss the Eretz Israel question not at the regular September session but at a special session on the 28th of April, 1947.

Chapter XXV

The Cross-Roads of History

We must pause here for a moment. We are on the threshold of a fateful turning-point in the history of Eretz Israel. Bevin's obstinate assertion that he did not see how the U.N. could deal with the Palestine problem before September was no mere unpremeditated remark. He was manoeuvering. He wanted to gain time—a year, if possible, during which he might establish contact with the United States and other Governments. He might also reach an agreement with the United States on Eretz Israel, if he had more time. What is certain is that with more time available the Arabs could be strengthened immensely both in arms and in instructors. When then would have been our situation at the onset of the invasion?

It may be argued that the Jews, too, would have exploited the time to intensify their military preparations. I regret to say that there is little foundation for this supposition. The decisive blunders of the Zionist leaders did not arise from ill-will, but from wishful thinking and illusions. The leaders deluded themselves into the belief that partition would be implemented "without undue dislocation." Even in January, 1948, when the country was already in the throes of an Arab invasion, one of the important members of the Jewish Agency told me and my comrades: "We are not yet certain whether the British are with us or against us!" On the 22nd of May, 1947, Mr. Ben Gurion, in a long speech, argued that the demand for a Jewish State in the whole of Western Eretz Israel was now academic and that consequently we should now demand a Jewish State in part of Eretz Israel, leaving *the Mandate* in the rest.

These official leaders also nurtured another illusion: that an international force would be created by the U.N. to enforce partition and to enable the U.N. to keep the peace in Eretz Israel during the transitional period.

In its memoranda to the U.N. Security Council the Jewish Agency supported the proposal of the abortive Implementing Committee of the U.N. that an international force be organised to carry through partition. And in January, 1948, when the local Arab war was in full swing, Mr. Ben Gurion gave the Press a carefully-drafted statement in which he said:

"We demand as of right, and we do so not without good prospects, the aid of the United Nations."

"As of right"—granted. But "prospects?"

These official leaders floundered in a veritable sea of illusions. That is why it cannot be assumed that in the course of an additional year—and a peaceful year at that—with tight British control in Jerusalem, the Jews under blindly deluded leaders would have made military preparations commensurate with those made by Britain in Nablus, Amman, Bagdad, Damascus and Beirut. Posterity will know that on that bright Saturday, March the 1st, 1947, we brought about a turning-point in the history of our country and our people. We deprived the enemy of time for secret preparations; we speeded up events by a full year. And whoever can appreciate what that year might have meant to us, can realise that the Jewish people owe a debt of gratitude to its sons in the Assault Force of the Irgun Zvai Leumi. They opened their attack on the 1st of March at the Goldschmidt House in Jerusalem, concluded it the next day in Petah Tikvah—and so struck a blow that reverberated in London, at Lake Success, in Washington, Moscow and Paris.

2

What sort of brief would the British representatives be armed with when they appeared before the U.N. Assembly special session on Palestine due to open on 28th April? The Government were in a state of *un-*

ambiguous surrender to the "terrorists." Bevin had
wanted a discussion in September; the Irgun had forced
him to start discussing in April. Montgomery and Mc-
Millan had imposed Martial Law; the underground had
beaten both the Field-Marshal and the General. Barker
had raised his whip—and had got his own officers
flogged. The British Government's rule had made itself
the object of universal ridicule, scorn and derision.
"What kind of government is this?" people asked in
many tongues. "How can such a government continue
to manage the affairs of Palestine?" And what did
Creech Jones himself say? On the lifting of Martial
Law he told Parliament, in a sudden burst of candour:
"We never expected martial law to put an end to terrorism."

It was a deplorable background for the case that
was to be submitted to the "judgment of the world."

The British authorities therefore decided to act.
They had been beaten in battle, but at their disposal
was still—the gallows. They decided—not in Jerusalem,
but in London—to lift the shattered prestige of their
regime by means of the hangman's rope. Early in the
morning of 17th April, 1947, Gruner, Drezner, Alkoshi
and Kashani were hanged. The Government carried out
these executions with feverish haste. Today it is clear
why they hurried, and prevaricated, why they dis-
honoured their public undertaking to await the verdict
of the Privy Council. They had no time. On the 28th
April the special session of the U.N. was due to open.
The witness of the gallows must convince the world that
the right arm of the British Government was still strong
and effective. The might of British authority must illum-
ine the set scene as the curtain rose on the Assembly's
proceedings. In any case, it would be bad timing indeed to hold four hangings while the Assembly was
actually discussing Palestine.

Thus when the nations' representatives met to discuss Palestine ten days later, nobody would be able to
say that Bevin's regime had surrendered to the terrorists,
that they were too weak to govern Palestine. And these
four hangings were by no means all. There were more

to come. There were Feinstein and Barazani—whose execution was now fixed for April the 25th. What had Oliver Stanley called for in Palestine? "Firm and resolute authority" as the only means of imposing the Government's policy. The gallows had been erected as a symbol of this "firm and resolute authority."

But on the 4th of May, while the U.N. Assembly was debating whether or not to invite Jewish representatives to appear, we upset Bevin's applecart. Our Assault Force smashed its way into the Acre Fortress . . .

The next day the *Haaretz* correspondent in London wrote:

"The attack on Acre Jail was received here as a serious blow to British prestige *after the hangings on the eve of the U.N. session were to have demonstrated Britain's resolute control of the situation*. Military circles described the attack as 'a military masterpiece . . .' I spoke to a number of 'men in the street' who said: 'It's time we got out.' The news from the U.N. meetings is hardly reported in the Press except for the *Times* and *Manchester Guardian*—yet the Acre incident occupies half the front page in every newspaper, accompanied by pictures and maps. Some of them describe it as 'the greatest jail-break in history,' adding that the authorities regarded Acre Jail as impregnable. Reuter telegrams report that the Palestine authorities are sunk in confusion because 'so many arch-terrorists have escaped.' Months of work, searches, arrests, trials and investigations have been thrown away, and the Irgun has been reinforced by a number of cruel zealots."

On May the 6th, the *Haaretz* special correspondent at the U.N. Assembly's special session reported: "The events at Acre have caused a tremendous sensation here."

Political circles in London were confused. In the House of Commons one Member stormed: "There has never been anything like it in the history of the British Empire," and on May the 13th, Major Rayner drew the Government's attention to the Irgun's threats against British soldiers. (He was referring to our statement that any British soldier falling into our hands would be tried by a field court-martial). A spokesman of the War Ministry replied that the Palestine authorities had informed the War Ministry of these threats, and at once he had appealed to the Jews for help. "I am sure," he said, "that all responsible Jews would wish to dissociate themselves completely from this threat. The most vigorous measures will be taken to bring to justice any terrorists attempting to kidnap or murder British soldiers carrying out their duty."

These threats were still to be put to the test.

It was in the overhanging shadow of the Acre operation—"the greatest jail-break in history"—that the special session of the United Nations Assembly ended and a Special Inquiry Committee was appointed. Before the session ended Mr. Gromyko, the Soviet envoy, made the famous speech which marked the decisive change in the Soviet attitude to Jewish striving for national independence. Speaking of the bankruptcy of British rule in Eretz Israel, Gromyko asserted: "This has now been demonstrated also by the sanguinary events in Palestine which are growing more and more frequent. It has been demonstrated too, by the fact that the British Government has submitted the Palestine question to the U.N."

On the 4th of June, the bankruptcy of the Mandatory regime in Eretz Israel found confirmation from an official British source. That day the report by the High Commissioner on the Acre attack was published. General Cunningham wrote:

"No mere numbers of troops or police can guarantee security against attack on many thousands of buildings, bridges and civil undertakings, such as post-offices, hundreds of miles of roads, railways and oil pipelines . . . Complete defence of all these installations against organized attacks which are liable to be carried out anywhere and at any time of the day or night for years on end, is not a practical proposition.

"The placing of explosives against the walls of a building under cover of fire is a method the Germans successfully employed in 1940 against the most fortified positions in Europe and is capable of execution in all circumstances if done skilfully, with determination and without regard to casualties. The prospects of success of these attacks are even greater in a place like Palestine where the law-abiding community has determined, for purely political reasons, not to dissociate itself from the attackers, who therefore emerge from the civilian population and always have the complete initiative and every operational advantage. . . .

"As I have already emphasized the Special Branch is working under certain disabilities in the present situation in Palestine. I cannot accept the opinion that the Intelligence Service has failed conspicuously, or that it is possible to compare the situation to that which obtained in the Bengal in the thirties, as was recently suggested. It must be borne in mind that the dissidents in Palestine are trained in the underground tactics employed by the underground in Europe during the recent War. . . ."

Once again the Government used the hangman's rope to raise their prestige, which, after the staggering attack at Acre, approached the zero mark. Three of the attackers at Acre were condemned to death. Avshalom Haviv, Meir Nakar and Yaacov Weiss were hanged on the 29th of July, 1947. The Bevin regime was again trying to prove that in spite of the blow at Acre they were maintaining "resolute authority." They would try "by all the means at their disposal"—as the *Daily Telegraph* put it—to crush the illegal activities.

But they were bitterly disappointed. What they saw as their anchor of hope became a deadly trap. They sowed nooses and reaped hangings. On the 30th of July, with the implementation of our warnings of counter-hangings, a tremor went through the whole British Empire. Amidst curses and abuse for the "vile terrorists" a great cry broke forth in Britain. "Out! We must get out of Palestine! Take our soldiers out of Palestine!" A few British hooligans indulged in scattered violence from Tel-Aviv to Glasgow, but this only added to the difficulties of the "civilised Power!"

The policy of "resolute authority" via the hangman's

rope had failed. Legal murder had evoked retribution.

At last the British people realised the folly of opposing the birth of a nation.

Accompanied by the rumblings of this public opinion, the British representatives, six weeks later, went to the United Nations Assembly. A chorus in unison from the British Press escorted Mr. Creech Jones on his departure for New York: "Clear out of Palestine!" And on September the 12th the British Colonial Minister solemnly announced that if the U.N. did not find a solution acceptable to "both sides," the Arabs and the Jews, the British would evacuate their forces and their administration from Palestine. The next day the Press of the world reported that the announcement of evacuation had been received with "relief and unconcealed satisfaction" by the whole British people.

Of course, this too was a tactical manoeuvre. The Government hoped to influence the United States and other countries, as well as the Jews and the Arabs. Why not an agreed solution? Why not try to obtain American participation in "responsibility?" But the manoeuvre was futile. The wonderful word "evacuation" had been uttered; it was impossible to conjure away its magic effects.

Jurists know the inherent "law of life" of legislation. Every law is only the fruit of man's thought and toil. But once it has been promulgated it cuts itself loose from its authors, just as an adult emerges from the control of his parents. The law begins to live its own life, and its consequences are sometimes quite different from those intended by its procreators.

This rule is equally true of historical political declarations. Conceived for certain ends, with their emergence into the world they set in motion forces quite unforeseen by their authors. In deciding to announce their evacuation of Eretz Israel, the British Government had several ends in mind. But the word "evacuation" itself immediately began its independent existence. Nothing now could turn back the tide. The spirit of the British authorities in Eretz Israel was weary, very weary. They were no longer capable of renewing the game: of terror

by day and fear by night, of ghettoes, confinement, surprise attacks, floggings, hangings. Among the tens of
thousands of soldiers in the Occupation Army the *demoralisation of impending evacuation spread overnight*.
For years they had been sitting on scorpions; and they
were overjoyed by the good news of their early departure, which spelt physical and moral relief. How
could the morale of an army so demoralised be restored? The same reaction was reported in the British
Isles. There too, people rejoiced at the good news of
the evacuation of the "boys." It would then have been
impossible to ask millions of Britons directly or indirectly interested in the fate of the boys in the British Army
to reconcile themselves to a renewal of their hopeless
"squalid war."

The Foreign Office continued to manoeuvre. The
United States Government changed their mind several
times. They called for a further session of the U.N.
Assembly, and there they proposed a "trusteeship"
regime in place of partition. They proposed that Britain
should be the trustee. But these manoeuvres could
not save the situation. The Government knew that whatever their rule called itself it would not be tolerated.
The underground would continue to batter them. The
vicious circle would continue to spin dizzily. And there
was no longer any prospect of "strong and resolute
authority."

On the 15th of May, 1948, the British High Commissioner boarded a British warship. A guard of honour
presented arms in his honour, and in honour of the
flag as it was lowered.

The revolt was victorious.

Chapter XXVI
A New Threat

Already during the session of the United Nations in the autumn of 1947, we began warning our people of the secret plan to "influence" an invasion by the Arab States. At that time many people, even outside the official leadership, were inclined to believe that the partition "compromise" would be implemented peacefully or by the "supreme power" of the United Nations. We, however, clearly saw grave dangers in this naïve optimism. We had no illusion about the Government's intentions, nor had we any about the imaginary regiments of Mr. Trygve Lie. But these two illusions, which for a certain period prevailed in official as well as in many non-official Jewish minds, clouded the horizon, undermined resolve, and led to the gravest misfortunes.

At this distance in time, and in the light of subsequent events, these illusions may seem surprising; so surprising, indeed, that it is difficult to understand how they could ever have existed in normally intelligent minds. But natural astonishment does not alter the reality of the fact which evolved. The fact is that the Irgun Zvai Leumi was compelled to mobilise all the means of enlightenment available to the underground in an endeavour to dissipate this cloud of silly optimism. It cannot be said that we laboured in vain; but I cannot, on the other hand, claim that we were entirely successful. Only the bitter events themselves, confirming our warnings, cleared men's vision of the horizon as it grew even redder with fire and with blood.

On October the 1st, 1947, we analysed, in "The Voice of Fighting Zion," the announcement by Mr. Creech Jones of the British Government's intention to evacuate and the possibility of an international force being set up to implement partition. The Underground radio announcer told the people:

"Britain knows that the U.N. has no military force of its own and that at most the General Assembly can recommend the establishment of an international regime and an international police force . . . But one thing is certain, the decision of the General Assembly cannot exclude the Soviet Union from participation in an international force. The Soviet Union was excluded from the U.N. Special Committee on Palestine by a camouflage resolution whereby *none* of the permanent members of the Security Council could participate in it. A similar decision relating to an *international military force* would be absurd. But even should this absurdity be accepted it will not prevent the participation of States like Poland, Yugoslavia or Czechoslovakia. And Britain calculates that this will on no account be permitted by the United States. In other words, it is impossible to decide on the establishment of an international force *without* Russian participation and the United States will not want to establish a force *with* Russian participation. . . ."

On the 12th of October the warning voice was again heard from the underground radio.

"The British Government's plot," it said, "is clear for all to see. . . . Even today the enemy is trying to bring us to accept the Bevin plan. . . . The Occupation Army will evacuate the areas bordering on the Arab States so as to enable their Quisling bands to prepare the armed fist against our people. The sea-blockade will continue. . . ."

On the 16th of November, two weeks before the United Nations decided on the partition of Eretz Israel, we again sounded the alarm through the "Voice of Fighting Zion."

"The public is harbouring three illusions fostered by its leaders. Illusion No. 1: that the partition of the country, if it is accepted by a two-thirds majority in the U.N. Assembly, will be implemented by peaceful means. Illusion No. 2: that if a war breaks out in Eretz

Israel as the result of an attack engineered by British Government agents, the U.N. Committee sitting in Jerusalem will soon restore peace.

Illusion No. 3: that if the U.N. representatives fail in their mission as angels of peace, the Security Council will intervene, issue a command, and stop the war with a wave of the hand.

"These illusions are all very dangerous. 'Official optimism,' which is bound up with the historic tragedy of the partition of the country, has no basis in reality. As it is human to believe that 'everything will be alright,' rather than to face the facts with open eyes, there is a danger that hands will be palsied, and that when the decisive events overtake us we shall be unprepared, morally, in organisation, and in equipment, to meet them.

"It is therefore essential to shatter these illusions. It is essential to tell the people the truth. It is essential that the people be called upon to prepare themselves for war and not for repose, for battles and for sacrifices and not for processions and festivities. Let this be clear: the partition plan is not a plan for peace, despite its inherent renunciation of territory, a renunciation which has no legal validity. The establishment even of this 'ghetto' inside our Homeland will be carried out amidst flames of fire and rivers of blood. . . ."

Two days later, "The Voice of Fighting Zion" warned again:

"Even this caricature of a State will have to be paid for heavily in the lives of our best sons. It is certain that the blood shed in the days to come in order to impose partition will not be less than what we should have to pay for liberating the Homeland in its entirety. . . ."

On the 23rd of November, we again dealt with the British Government's plan. "The Voice of Fighting Zion" said:

"1. The blockade at sea will continue.

2. The entry neither of repatriates nor of war-materials will be permitted.

3. The land frontiers of the country will stand wide

open and Arabs equipped with British arms will stream across them to attack our towns and villages.

4. The Occupation Army will continue to hold strategic key-positions and will restrict the freedom of action of the Jewish forces. . . ."

Several days later we explained in our internal newspaper *Danim* (Leaves):

"Arab resistance, supported by the British, will develop in various ways. The Arabs will not set up any Government in the area to be allocated to them in the U.N. decision, for the setting up of such a Government would mean practical acceptance of the partition plan. It is probable that Abdullah also will not be able to set up such a Government. In the first place, his British patron will not allow him to do so; secondly, he will not wish nor be able to set himself against the whole of the Arab world (most of whom hate him) as an 'ally of the Zionists,' helping them implement the partition plan. If the Arab Legion is sent into action during the coming months, it will be sent to carry out acts of destruction and ruin designed to help Abdullah appear as the 'defender of his Arab brothers.' "

It is appropriate to compare this analysis with the words of Mr. Ben Gurion who even some time later expressed his belief in the peaceful intentions of King Abdullah, the "wise ruler."

On the 29th of November, the General Assembly of the United Nations approved the proposal to set up in Eretz Israel a Jewish State and an Arab State, to unite the two in an economic union and to separate from both the "international city" of Jerusalem. Our people were overjoyed. But the Irgun reminded them that the Homeland had been carved up and warned them that war was knocking at the door. First we asserted the credo of the underground fighters:

"The partition of the Homeland is illegal. It will never be recognized. The signature by institutions and individuals of the partition agreement is invalid. It will not bind the Jewish people. Jerusalem was and will for ever be our capital. Eretz Israel will be restored to the people of Israel. All of it. And for ever."

And we proceeded to explain once again:

"Partition will not ensure peace in our country. From the Arabs' point of view there are two possibilities only: either they will want, and be able, to rise in arms against Jewish rule, or they will not. In the first case they will fight even against a partition state. In the second case they would not fight against Jewish rule even in the *whole* country.

"The dream of an international force being created to impose partition in the name of the U.N. is evaporating, even as we warned months ago it would. In the war that is surely coming, we shall have to stand alone—while the U.N. Assembly issues academic calls for peace, calls whose practical value has already been tested in other places.

"But it is certain that when this war does break out—and the British Government will do their utmost to see that it does—it will be a war for our very existence and future. And in that war all the Jewish forces will be united. Such a war would be capable of changing everything. . . ."

That same day we issued a special Order of the Day to all soldiers of the Irgun Zvai Leumi:

"The conceptions of State, Government, Army, which we have propagated for years in the face of the denial and derision from those very persons who today appear to be intoxicated by the idea of the State, have become the Jewish people's most cherished dreams. And when the people were told that these dreams are really coming true they are naturally overwhelmed with joy. . . .

"We must not blame the people.

"But let us go out with our heads erect and tell them: 'We who have offered our lives for the day of redemption are not rejoicing. For the Homeland has not been liberated but mutilated. The State for which we have striven from our early youth, the State which will give freedom to the people and assure the future of its sons—that State still remains the goal of our generation!"

The U.N. decision of November the 29th raised the temperature of optimism in Eretz Israel. True, on the morrow of the decision murderous attacks were carried out by Arabs in the towns and on the roads. But the public and the official leaders consoled themselves that these were no more than "demonstration outbursts." The general assumption was that there was no cause to fear war on a serious scale. The voice of the Irgun warning of war which would grow in intensity and would end in invasion by the regular Arab armies—remained a voice alone crying in the wilderness.

The Jewish Agency leaders believed with childish faith in the timetable set down in the U.N. decision. The British Government fostered this belief. Their representative at Lake Success, Sir Alexander Cadogan, and their Colonial Secretary, Mr. Creech Jones, spoke with copy-book correctness of "accepting the judgment of the supreme international institution."

Even in December, 1947, the Jewish Agency leaders told us they believed that on the 1st of February, a port would be opened to us in accordance with the recommendations embodied in the decision of the 29th November. The Agency were innocently convinced that through this port, which would be entirely at our disposal, we in Israel would be allowed to bring in huge quantities of arms and equipment. The Irgun strove with all its efforts to convince them of their error. We explained to them at length that if the British opened a port for us it would be equivalent to their giving us direct aid in our struggle with the Arabs, whereas in fact the only help the British Government wanted to give us was to hold us down while we drowned. Our arguments could not shatter the pretty illusions to which they clung.

The consequence was that during December and January the vitally necessary efforts to acquire arms and equipment were not made, though the opportunities of acquiring these munitions were very great. Those were precious months; and the price we paid for wasting them was to be tragically high. One of the representatives of the national institutions who was in a foreign capital at the time declared, in bitter sincerity, to a representative of the Irgun Zvai Leumi: "This was terrible neglect. The people responsible for it should be put on trial."

Early in December we published a call to the people which I regard as one of the most important issued by the Irgun. It was headed "We Warn" and in it we said:

"The greatest danger facing us is that we should not understand in time the magnitude of our immediate peril. The people must know the truth, for only this knowledge can avert the catastrophe.

"The blockade at sea will continue for another five months. The British will permit no reinforcements either of men or of war-material. Jewish blood will be shed . . . And arms will be taken away, and ammunition consumed. Jewish fighters and defenders will be arrested, or will be murdered by incited rioters. Our economy, if it is not destroyed, will be undermined. Communications will be disrupted.

"All this will continue for five whole months. Then, on the night of the 15th of May, 1948, with the end of British rule, the land frontier-posts of our country will fall. The frontiers will not be manned by any Jewish guards, because most of these frontiers are in the areas allocated by the ruinous partition plan to the 'Arab State.' Through these frontiers, which will have ceased to be international frontiers, will come thousands of murderers equipped with British arms.

"We must therefore prepare while there is yet time. First and foremost we must end our defensive situation. We must take up the offensive. We must attack the murderers' bases.

"What we have to prepare is not local defensive plans, but broad strategic plans for repulsing attacks and for preparing the offensive of the liberating Hebrew army. Preparations must be made abroad. New cadres of experienced fighters must be organised.

"All this will be done by united forces. All of us, without exception, will face the same dangers. The situation is terribly grave. The war will be difficult and costly in sacrifices. But there must be no panic. If we all understand what we have to do, we shall smite the enemy hip and thigh."

As usual, we did not content ourselves with an appeal. This call—which was ultimately vindicated by the events—was accompanied by action. After two weeks of Arab attacks the soldiers of the Irgun launched *the first counter-attack by Jewish forces*. For three days, from 11th to 13th December, our units hammered at concentrations of rioters and their offensive bases. We attacked at Haifa and Jaffa; at Tireh and Yazur. We attacked again and again in Jerusalem. We went up to the aggressive village of Sha'afat on the road to the Hebrew University. We penetrated Yehudiyeh and dealt peremptorily with an armed band that had established its base in the village. Enemy casualties in killed and wounded were very heavy.

These attacks were evaluated by *Haaretz* as follows: "A radical change in the situation has taken place with the widespread operations of the Irgun." Of course, it was a radical change. Previously all the Jewish forces—including our units—had been stationed in local defence posts. But you can only "be stationed" in defence posts; you cannot conquer in them. Defensive measures do not prevent casualties. They only permit the aggressor to retain the initiative. They expose you to surprise attacks. They reinforce the morale of the enemy and systematically lower that of the defenders. There is no doubt that attack is the only effective defence. The Maginot Line proved this more than all the text-books on strategy in the world.

Our counter-attack, at once broad in its scope and concentrated in its effect, restored a sense of proportion to the Arabs and confidence to our people. The attack also taught the foreign observers not to be premature in drawing conclusions about "Jewish weakness."

The change was fundamental. On the heels of our counter-attack all the Jewish forces went over to the offensive against the enemy's bases. Even Mr. Ben Gurion found words of praise for our operations—though, of course, when he thus expressed himself he did not know it was we who had carried out these attacks. The day after our successful attack on Tireh, he told journalists: "Do you see how capable our boys are?" He had been under the impression that the attack had been carried out by members of the Haganah.

As we saw the head-on clash with the Arab forces coming ever closer, we set to work to reorganise our fighting body. We began transforming the underground structure of our units. We set up regular battle units. We opened our ranks to volunteers—who began to pour in in thousands. We set up a special Planning Unit headed by Giddy. In the orange-groves at Petah Tikvah and Ramat Gan we set up our first military camps. We altered our training methods: from training for partisan sallies by small units we went over to training for open battle. Overshadowing all these preparations was the concern for the supply of arms. Unlike the official Jewish institutions we could not accuse ourselves of negligence. What little money we had we always converted into arms, and with the small quantity at our disposal we had over a period of years conducted a struggle for liberation against a mighty army of occupation. The official Jewish institutions had enormous sums at their disposal. In August, 1946, the Haganah, after nine months of struggle against the British, had given in. For them the years of revolt had been for the most part years of prolonged quiescence, years of peace-time training and preparation. But when the day of reckoning came, this "preparation" was exposed in all its barrenness. The Haganah, for whose armament the financial resources and efforts of the whole Jewish people had been mobilised, possessed but a few rifles and machine-guns, and a few dozen mortar-shells. Of course, the members of the Haganah, like those of the Irgun and the F.F.I., fought bravely against the Arabs; the whole of the Jewish youth, equipped with only the most meagre arms, stood their ground against tanks and guns. But what a toll in lives could have been saved, and what invaluable parts of the country could have been regained had it not been for the complacency in the days of "preparation"—negligence which sprang directly from a pitiable lack of political vision?

Chapter XXVII

The Spirit of Freedom

Our chief concern was with the provision of arms for our Irgun fighters. We saw their fighting spirit and ground our teeth with vexation at not being able to put the requisite weapons in their hands. The British forces were still in the country. British agents and soldiers were on the look-out for members of the Irgun. We had to beware at every step. Nevertheless, we made a supreme effort to develop our arms manufacturing workshops. The production of munitions of war is quite a complicated manufacturing process. What bitter disappointments we suffered before we were privileged to fire our first Irgun manufactured machine gun! And what terrible disappointments our men suffered when they were sent to the battlefront with nothing more than Sten-guns in their hands. Nevertheless, within a few months we succeeded in producing several thousand sub-machine guns, many thousands of hand-grenades, a quantity of effective two-inch mortars and, in the course of time, some very effective three-inch mortars. But the production of shells was still in its infancy, and the capture of the trainload of shells was still far off.

The production of these arms and the maintenance of camps required far larger sums of money than we ever had at our disposal. After considerable thought we decided to make a direct appeal to the public for contributions to the war effort of the Irgun. It was no simple decision to take. It meant the exposure of many hundreds of underground people. It meant, in effect, the almost complete abandonment of secrecy, and we had to weigh well whether that was not premature.

We had no choice. We preferred taking this considerable risk to closing the Irgun workshops, a step which would have involved an even greater menace to the embattled Jewish people. So, for the first time underground representatives introduced themselves to the public, who had previously seen only the eyes of the bill-posters. We asked the public for their aid for the Irgun's "Iron Fund." The public response was surprising—not to us but to our antagonists.

All the same, the incitement inspired by pettiness bore fruit. At Mograbi Square, in the heart of Tel Aviv, a Haganah officer ordered his men to throw hand-grenades into a large crowd which had gathered to hear the regular loud-speaker broadcast of the Irgun's "Iron Fund" appeal. Numerous people were injured, some slightly, others seriously. The anger of the public was unbounded. Was it for this—they asked—that arms had been given to the Haganah?

That night I went out into Allenby Road. This was the first time for years that I had taken a walk for the sake of walking. It was a distinct breach of the ordinary rules of caution. Nobody came with me. Many might have recognized me. The British were still ruling the country.

That night I came into direct, though one-sided, contact with thousands of Hebrew citizens. I stood among dozens of debating groups. Here and there I caught the surprised, questioning glance of a comrade who had recognized me. But the eyes would turn away as though they had not seen. To the rest, I was just one of the curious bystanders who wanted to hear all the accounts of what had happened at Mograbi Square.

That night I discovered the spirit of freedom that animates our people. The hand-grenades thrown into a huge crowd had not frightened them, it had angered them. Not all the debaters in the street were friends of the Irgun, but almost every one of them denounced the cowardly act of intimidation. Did they think they could shut anybody's mouth in Israel with a hand-grenade? The rhetorical question was put with equal earnestness by stolid Jews from Germany, and by temperamental Jews from Yemen.

And I saw that night that this people will not tolerate oppression from without, neither will they bear for long with tyranny from within. It is a stiff-necked people, and freedom is in its blood.

The grim scene at Mograbi Square took place while we were in the very midst of negotiations with representatives of the Jewish Agency for an operational agreement between the fighting bodies. The negotiations began in mid-December and continued for many months. Its prime initiator was Mr. Yitshak Gruenbaum. Those who took part, apart from Mr. Gruenbaum, were Moshe Shapiro, whose advocacy of the agreement was most energetic, Rabbi Fishman (whom I had met only once previously, when, as a boy of ten, I welcomed him on his visit to my school at Brisk); Mr. David Remez, a leader of the Mapai and Histadruth who, in the face of Mr. Ben Gurion's opposition, stood his ground firmly in favour of the agreement; Mr. Pincus, one of the *Mizrachi* leaders in whose hospitable home the prolonged conversations took place; and Chief Rabbi Dr. Louis Rabinowitz of South Africa, who arrived in the tense days of the "Iron Fund" and Mograbi Square. Avraham, Shmuel and I represented the Irgun.

All the negotiators were imbued with the sense of their heavy responsibility. The Arab attacks were daily increasing. At that stage, it is true, the Agency leaders were not yet certain of the existence of the "British plan." Very soon, however, they too learnt that our political prognosis had been correct, almost to the letter. Of the timetable laid down in the U.N. decision of the 29th November, item after item was abandoned. No port was opened on February 1st, 1948—because the British Government refused to open it. The "Provisional Government Councils" of the two "independent States," due to be set up by the U.N. Implementation Committee before April the 1st were not set up—because the Arabs, on the advice of the British representatives, refused to constitute such a Council, and because the British Government were determined not to have the Implementation Committee in Eretz Israel. The Jewish Agency at long last realized that the Yishuv would not survive unless—as the underground *Herut* had put it—we "tempered our Hebrew steel, consolidated our forces, and staked our future on the prowess of our own right arm."

Though the shadow of the campaign of persecution and vilification by political parties against the Irgun hung over the negotiations we did not hesitate to stretch out our hand once more to our opponents. For it seemed to us absolutely vital that a united fighting front should be established. In mid-January, however, the negotiations threatened to break down and to give place to internecine strife. One of our best officers in Haifa, Yedidiah Segal, was kidnapped by a Haganah unit.

Yedidiah, the son of an old pioneering family which combined spiritual aristocracy with deep religious belief and loyalty to the struggle for freedom, was kidnapped—a fortnight after the chief of the Haganah had personally promised the Jewish Agency members negotiating with us that there would be no more kidnappings. This promise had been made to Mr. Gruenbaum and Mr. Shapiro following the earlier kidnapping of one of our members.

In accordance with our warning, our members took reprisals. They detained one of the Haganah Intelligence chiefs in Haifa. All the Haganah efforts to find him proved fruitless.

On January the 12th, Ammon, the Irgun commander in Haifa, received a letter from the local Haganah commander suggesting an exchange of prisoners. Ammon agreed. The Haganah Intelligence man was freed and reported to his superiors that he had been well-treated. One Irgun member in Haganah hands was released and returned to his post. According to the Haganah the second man still in their hands was also freed. But he did not return either to his post or to his home. Indeed, he never returned. For the man was Yedidiah Segal. His dead body was found in the Arab village of Tireh, a considerable distance from the place where he had been held.

His mother, ignorant of his fate, searched for him. For three days she went from one public worker to another, from one Haganah commander to another. All told her Yedidiah had been freed; but they could not tell her why he had not come home.

Only on January 16th did the Haganah publish a statement "explaining" that Yedidiah had *escaped* from detention and had been killed by Tireh Arabs.

We were again in a dilemma. We did not yet know the details of his murder. The call for reprisal was general. Suddenly we found ourselves—all of us—on the edge of an abyss. The Jewish people were fighting for its very existence. Every day brought a greater toll of victims. And on the horizon—as we knew—was Arab invasion. Was it fated that at such an hour brothers should turn and kill each other?

The bereaved mother came to our aid. She said: "I do not want the shedding of my son's blood to cause a civil war."

Again we halted at the very edge of disaster, the tragic cycle which nineteen centuries ago had sealed the fate of besieged Jerusalem.

But we informed the Jewish Agency leaders that we would not proceed with the negotiations until a public enquiry committee was set up to determine responsibility for the murder. Following our demand such a committee, consisting of Rabbi Fishman, Mr. Gruenbaum and Mr. Shapiro, was set up.

They worked very slowly. Four months later, on May the 15th, 1948, they had not reached any final conclusions. With the invasion, Mr. Gruenbaum remained in Jerusalem, and the committee's work was suspended. Only at the end of June did Gruenbaum tell us that it was his private opinion that the Haganah had not killed Yedidiah Segal.

Chapter XXVIII

The Agreement

With the setting up of the inquiry committee our negotiations with the Jewish Agency were resumed. The practical difficulties were no less serious than the psychological.

We could see two fronts and not one. The primary aim of our revolt—the liquidation of British rule and the evacuation of the Occupation Army—was on the point of being attained. But precisely at that moment the British forces were throwing off restraint. Attacks were not infrequent. We retaliated—as we retaliated for the deliberate mass murder of civilians in the Ben Yehuda Street explosion. We saw grave danger—political as well—in the possible assumption by troops that as they were leaving they could throw off all restraint. Consequently we insisted on the principle of reprisals for all attacks.

We agreed that our soldiers should continue to join in the manning of local stationary defence posts under the immediate command of their own officers and under the overall command of the Regional commanders of the Haganah. But we would on no account agree to the policy of not resisting the British forces when they came to search for and to remove Jewish arms. The Haganah had followed this policy of giving up arms to the British—the official leaders always had an inferiority complex about the British—for nearly six months. From the beginning of the Arab attacks until the British administration was liquidated, hundreds of weapons were taken by the British from Haganah members. British troops disarmed eight Haganah members stationed at the "Hayotsek" factory near Tel Aviv, leaving them defenceless in the face of a large force of Arab attackers, who promptly killed them all. Similar incidents occurred in Jerusalem and at a number of other places.

It was unthinkable to us that our men would voluntarily surrender their arms. In a number of incidents our men had managed to spirit arms away from the posts before the impending search took place. And on one occasion they turned the tables—taking a number of good rifles and machine-guns from the British party which had come to disarm them. We knew from experience that if the British authorities learnt that any attempt to disarm Jews would be met by lead and would have to be paid for in blood, they would forego the unprofitable exchange. We therefore demanded that the Haganah, too, should change its policy and publicly order its members to resist. What had happened—we asked—to the principle of "defence of the Defence?" But there was no response and no change, until the very eve of the Arab invasion. We, however, insisted on its being explicitly agreed that Irgun soldiers should resist any British attempt to disarm them.

Similarly we insisted, as in the days of the Resistance Movement, on the principle of confiscating British arms whenever we could. We knew that even with the agreement signed and the conversion of the Irgun into a "recognized" fighting force, we should not receive from the general fund either arms, or money for buying arms. We demanded, therefore, that we should at least be free to seize arms from the well-supplied Occupation Army.

The question of the joint struggle against the Arab aggressors did not create undue difficulties. The Haganah having also gone over to the princinple of offensive defence, we accepted the Resistance Movement system, whereby we were to submit operational plans and execute them with the approval of the Haganah command.

On these lines and after wearying negotiations, agreement was reached between the Jewish Agency, as the supreme authority over the Haganah, and the Irgun

Zvai Leumi. *Haaretz* reported that when the signature of the agrement became known there was much toasting of fighting unity in the defence posts throughout the country.

These were the terms of the secret agreement between the Haganah and the Irgun Zvai Leumi:

1. The Irgun defence posts will be subject to the sector Commander appointed by the Haganah, who will transmit his orders to their officers through an officer appointed by the Irgun Zvai Leumi.

2. Plans of attack on "A" front (the Arab front) and plans for reprisals on "B" front (the British) will be subject to prior approval (of Haganah). Details relating to the objective and timing will be determined at meetings of the representatives and the technical experts. The Irgun will, in addition, be prepared to carry out plans assigned to it.

3. Irgun members will be bound by the principle of resistance to attempts at disarming them. In certain special circumstances Irgun members at defence posts will take into account the situation of nearby Haganah posts.

4. No operations for confiscating money will be carried out in the area policed by Jews. On the other hand the Irgun will not be disturbed in the free collection of funds, and the national institutions will confirm, both at home and in the Diaspora, that the Irgun receives no allocation from the fund-campaigns conducted for general security requirements.[1]

[1] This clause reflected serious complaints which were coming in from Irgun workers in the Diaspora that officials of the Zionist fund-raising organisations were waging a vicious war against those who were raising money for the Irgun. The most effective weapon which they employed against the Irgun fund-collectors was the untruth, industriously whispered, that the Irgun was receiving support from the Zionist funds and that therefore a separate collection was unnecessary and harmful. In Great Britain, certain patriotic Jews who were honorary workers for the Joint Palestine Appeal (J.P.A.) demanded to know whether in fact the Irgun were receiving a share of the money which was being subscribed by Jews on the general understanding that this was being done. They received the reply from an

5. Plans for the seizure of arms will be worked out in joint consultation and will be carried out by mutual agreement.

6. This agreement in principle is subject to clarification on details before coming into operation. The representatives and experts will clarify these details.

"Very Important Persons" favoured the acceptance of General Marshall's advice not to proclaim a Jewish Government and to accept the "trusteeship plan" instead. Mr. Ben Gurion, who favoured the establishment of a Jewish Government, encountered grave difficulties within his own party, Mapai.

We decided to throw our weight into the balance. We were unconcerned who would head the Government and how it would be composed. Almost every day we proclaimed: "The Hebrew Government will arise; even if the official leadership does not set it up, still it will arise."

It was during these fateful days that Mr. Eliezer Liebenstein, one of Mr. Ben Gurion's lieutenants, came to see me. He told me that Mr. Ben Gurion "appreciated very much" our proclamations demanding the establishment of a Jewish Government; they were helping him overcome the opposition from various quarters. But he asked us to emphasize in our further state-

---

Agency member that he "could not imagine that the Jewish Agency would fail to support the men who were protecting the Yishuv in its hour of danger." The misleading answer was given in good faith, and was probably supplied from Palestine, because similar replies were given in the United States and in South Africa.

The Irgun representatives stood loyally by their undertaking to respect the secrecy of the Agreement quoted in these pages, and it was not until Dr. Israel Lifshitz, on behalf of the Irgun, made the situation clear to Dr. Abba Hillel Silver, in the United States, that the latter, disgusted at what had been done, gave him a letter for publication virtually quoting the relevant passages of Clause 4. But by then grave damage had been inflicted upon the Irgun's fund-raising in the Diaspora; and many a brave boy in the Irgun had to give his life because he was inadequately armed as a direct result of this "clever" political manoeuvre by certain Zionists carrying out their patriotic labours under somewhat less heroic conditions.

ments the *positive* point—that if a Government were established we would support it with all our strength.

I acceded to this request without hesitation. Several days after this talk we published the following statement:

"The Hebrew Government will certainly arise. There is no 'perhaps.' It will arise. If the official leaders set it up, *we shall support it with all our strength*. But if they surrender to threats or allow themselves to be cajoled, our strength and that of the majority of the fighting youth, will be behind the free Government which will arise from the depths of the underground and which will lead the people to victory in the war for freedom."

This statement by the Irgun Zvai Leumi was published *early in May, 1948*.

Chapter XXIX

The Conquest of Jaffa

In the months preceding the Arab invasion, and while the five Arab states (Egypt, Iraq, Syria, Lebanon and Transjordan) were conducting preparations for concerted aggression, we continued to make sallies into the Arab area. In the early days of 1948, we were explaining to our officers and men, however, that this was not enough. Attacks of this nature carried out by any Jewish forces were indeed of great psychological importance; and their military effect, to the extent that they widened the Arab front and forced the enemies on to the defensive, was not without value. But it was clear to us that even most daring sallies carried out by partisan troops would never be able to decide the issue. Our hope lay in gaining control of territory.

At the end of January, 1948, at a meeting of the Command of the Irgun in which the Planning Section participated, we outlined four strategic objectives: (1) Jerusalem; (2) Jaffa; (3) the Lydda-Ramleh plain; and (4) the Triangle.[1]

Setting ourselves these objectives we knew that their achievement would be dependent on many factors but primarily on the strength in men and arms that we would have at our disposal. We consequently decided to treat the plans as "alternatives": we would carry out what we could. As it happened, of the four parts of the strategic plan we executed only the second in full.

---

[1] The generally used name for the Arab-populated area in the centre of Western Eretz Israel lying roughly in a triangle whose points are the towns of Nablus, Jenin and Tulkarm and comprising the bulk of the non-desert area west of Jordan which is now outside the State of Israel.

In the first and third parts we were able to record important achievements on the battlefield—but we did not attain decisive victories.

As for the fourth part, we were never allowed an opportunity even to begin to put the plan into operation. The conquest of Jaffa, however, stands out as an event of first-rate importance in the struggle for Hebrew independence.

At the time we decided on "the strategy of conquest," we had not enough arms for any strategic operation whatsover. But while in February and March we were without an ounce of explosives, in April we succeeded in manufacturing several tons of very powerful material. In March we had only an insignificant number of machine-guns, but in April we carried out two confiscations which transformed the supply situation of our units. We were so enriched that our fire-power in mortar shells was greater, at the time, than that of the Haganah.

On April the 4th, 1948, Giddy led an Assault Unit, under the immediate command of Joshua, to British Military Camp No. 80, near Pardess Hannah, where an anti-tank artillery regiment was stationed. This developed as a frontal attack against a first-rate regiment of British artillery; a few score fought against hundreds, and won.

The advance party overwhelmed the armed guard at the gates of the camp and opened the way for the other units, who were supported by two armoured cars, one seized from the British Army, the other from the British police. With one, the right wing of the camp was held; with the other, the left wing. The surprise attack was brief.

The whole camp was soon in our hands and the anti-tank regiment virtually our prisoners.

The armoury was at once broken open, and the loading began. There were rifles, sub-machine guns, Bren-guns, anti-tank guns and ammunition. But suddenly enemy forces outside the camp opened a counter-attack. Supported by an armoured track vehicle, they bore down on our central holding column. The danger was very grave and the results might have been far-reaching. Destruction of the covering column might have frustrated the whole operation and led to the capture of all its participants. One man, brave Jackson, who had so often used his Scots accent to advantage, saved the situation. He flung himself at the side of the armoured track vehicle, burst the door open with explosives, overwhelmed its occupants—and acquired another armoured vehicle for the Irgun. Meanwhile, however, considerable reinforcements began to pour into our adversaries who were soon pursuing the counter-attack with guns and heavy armour. Their shooting, however, was erratic. Our men disabled a Sherman tank. Our opponents lost a Colonel and seven men killed; besides many who were wounded. Our casualties were one man killed and several wounded. But while the battle raged, the loading of the arms went on. The haul was a substantial one, particularly of rifles, Bren-guns and ammunition. There was also a small quantity of Piat armour-piercing shells—which were, at a later date, to put a number of enemy tanks out of action on the Jaffa front. If only we had had more. . . .

Two weeks later we again visited the Pardess Hannah area. This time Giddy's objective was a British ammunition train on its way from Haifa to the Triangle, carrying tons of precious arms and ammunition to the forces of the Arab guerilla chieftain, Kaukji. It did not reach its destination. It was stopped at Kilometre 41 between Hadera and Binyamina; and we relieved it of a quantity of arms and ammunition which later decided the fate of Jaffa—and more.

But it was not at all a simple operation.

A light mine, calculated to stop but not to destroy the train, exploded as the long train approached the point at which our Assault Unit was waiting. The calculation was exact. The train was shaken but no more. It came to a halt. Our men leapt forward.

But it was easier to stop the train than to seize it. In the first moments a mortar-shell hit our radio-car, wounding several men and disrupting communication with the parties dispersed over a wide area. Our fellows returned the fire but could make no impression on their enemy's armor. The opponent had all the advantages. He was behind an elevated and fortified position, while our men lay completely exposed on flat, even ground.

Repeated attempts to rush the train were beaten off. Meantime we were losing the most precious weapon of all—time. In the vicinity were British military camps. Soon reinforcements might arrive and we would be engaged by superior forces on all sides. All seemed lost.

But Giddy was not the man lightly to forego a train filled with arms and ammunition. How could such an opportunity possibly be thrown away! As he crept round among the men he found to his surprise that one group had captured a British soldier. He had apparently jumped from the train when the mine exploded and fallen straight into their hands. Swift as an arrow the thought went through Giddy's mind: this Tommy could help him seize the train.

"We'll set you free," Giddy told the Tommy. "Go back to your Officer-in-Charge and tell him that a battle unit of the Irgun Zvai Leumi has surrounded the train from all sides. Tell him I give him five minutes to hand over the arms. If he surrenders no harm will come to him or his men. But if he refuses, we shall blow up the train and everybody in it. We have anti-tank weapons. . . ."

The Tommy, who had never dreamt he would be employed on such a "peace" mission, ran back to the train.

Minutes passed. Giddy waited. But no reply came. The worst of it was that he had no means of replying to the silence of the British major: he had no anti-tank weapons and he had no explosives.

Giddy did not wait for his ultimatum to expire. Exposing himself, he approached the armoured coaches. Suddenly, he flung himself down full-length in the sand and gravel. A British soldier had aimed straight for his head; the bullet whistled over him missing by a hair's breadth.

He took up a more convenient position and shouted

with all his might: "Listen to me! This is the commander of a unit of the Irgun Zvai Leumi speaking to you. You are surrounded by my men on all sides. We propose to confiscate the arms in the train, but we have no intention of harming you. Get out of the coaches and raise your hands. If you surrender you will be able to return to your units. But if you continue to resist not a man will remain alive. I shall order the train to be blown up. We shall blow up the train if you do not surrender. This is my last warning."

The psychological weapon proved effective. The officers and men tumbled out of the train. Giddy breathed again.

But three of our men lay dead in the sand. Again we had paid for iron with blood. And among the dead was Avtalyon, who had been captured in 1944 in a partisan operation, horribly tortured, and years later, freed by us from prison.

The men began to load the ammunition on to the trucks which had been recalled to Kilometre 41. The task was a long one, and it was getting late.

Our men, as usual in such circumstances, worked with superhuman energy. But even so they could not load the many tons of precious ammunition quickly enough. Giddy decided to call in the aid of the British prisoners. Giddy called to a sergeant: "Get your men together. I need their help!" The major became more than a little apprehensive.

"Are you going to kill them," he asked?

"Don't be a damn fool," was Gideon's nettled reply. "We are Hebrew soldiers, not barbarians. We don't kill prisoners. We promised not to harm you. Men of the Irgun Zvai Leumi always keep their word. No harm will come to your men. I only need them for work."

The officer was astonished and relieved. True, he had noticed that the "terrorist" Medical Service had bandaged his wounded men and had even taken one who was more seriously wounded to hospital. But he thought that at any moment they might change their attitude.

For four hours British soldiers helped to load arms

on to the Irgun trucks. They worked, moreover, side by side with Irgun soldiers. The task was very hard. Nearly twenty tons of ammunition had to be handled. Every hour Giddy allowed a regulation five-minute break during which he arranged for oranges to be distributed as refreshment among the British soldiers. They worked hard and faithfully. Crate after crate was loaded. Truck after truck was filled—until the work was completed.

The loaded trucks set off. The shells found a temporary home that night in the wine cellars of Zichron Yaacov and in the homes of the Aaronson family.[1] I wonder if the good and noble Baron Rothschild ever dreamt that one day Hebrew soldiers would pour shells instead of wine into his beloved cellars?

The British prisoners were released. Soon afterwards the whole area was surrounded by armoured units which searched energetically for the arms and the confiscators. The search was fruitless. The inhabitants of Binyamina, Zichron Yaacov and Pardess Hannah were somewhat anxious. Would a curfew be proclaimed? Would collective punishment be imposed?

These questions were put to the officer commanding the British pursuing troops. His reply was characteristic of the best British spirit: "There will be no punishment. It was a fair fight."

2

Camp No. 80, the ammunition train and our own production of arms were factors which made it possible for us to launch the attack on Jaffa. During April the plan was completed, the units were selected, and in the intermediate days of Passover, three weeks before the State of Israel was established, we went out to save

[1] Aaron and Sarah Aaronson organised Nili, the Jewish Intelligence Group in World War I which gave invaluable aid to the British Military Forces in planning their campaign against the Turks. Sarah Aaronson was captured by the Turks and killed herself while undergoing torture.

Tel Aviv—and much more—from the threat of destruction.

Our plan was to attack Jaffa at the narrow bottleneck linking the main town with its Manshieh Quarter which thrust northwards, like a peninsula, into Jewish Tel Aviv. The tactical aim was to break the "neck of the bottle" and reach the sea, in order to cut off the bulk of Manshieh from Jaffa. The strategic aim was to subjugate Jaffa and free Tel Aviv once and for all from the loaded pistol pointed at its heart.

Before our attack opened, Tel Aviv had undergone very severe punishment from aggressive Jaffa and particularly from the Manshieh Quarter. During the first few months of Arab disturbances nearly a thousand Jewish men, women and children were killed or wounded in attacks directed from the Hassan Bek Mosque and neighbourhood in the Manshieh Quarter. Arab snipers were able to pick off victims in many of the most important parts of Tel Aviv, and no number of defence posts and sallies could prevent them from adding daily to the death roll of Jewish victims shot in the main streets of the town. The foreign Press wrote of battles in Rothschild Boulevard. Jaffa challenged Tel Aviv. And Tel Aviv remained on the defensive. Thousands of its sons were tied down to the static front defending the city.

On the night of April 25th we set out to put an end to this shameful and perilous situation. In the camp named after Dov Gruner—"Dov Camp" at Ramat Gan —the battle units and auxiliary services were gathered. Throughout the day about one hundred vehicles had been mobilised in the only way available to the underground ever since the beginning of the revolt—by means of temporary confiscation. It was not a pleasant way. But the owners knew from the experience of others that we always did our best to return their vehicles after the operation or, in case of damage, to pay them compensation. They knew, above all, that their vehicles were taken for the purposes of an essential war

and many of them handed over their trucks or cars
with a cheerful willingness. We had no other way.
An underground cannot, and dare not, always use the
same vehicles. Wheels leave tracks. And where were
we to get sufficient money to buy all the vehicles we
needed?

On the night of April 25th, 1948, a long line of
trucks waited on the Tel Aviv-Ramat Gan road, some
of them confiscated from the British authorities, some
confiscated temporarily from their Jewish owners,
some borrowed from friends. And near the main road,
at Dov Camp, hundreds of Irgun soldiers waited for
the signal to go into battle.

But the signal was delayed.

On the roof of the little house in which Camp staff
headquarters had been set up, a conference was in
progress. Runners had brought disturbing news from
the city. The Haganah, they said, had proclaimed a
state of alert and were preparing to prevent us from
carrying out the operation. Somebody proposed that
the attack be postponed for a day or two. The discussion was serious and protracted: but finally the decision
was taken—to attack that night.

Below the courtyard the parade waited—the first open
parade, of six hundred Irgun officers and men. The days
of partisan attacks were over; the time for open battles had begun. The underground was, strictly speaking,
no more.

There they stood, line upon line, the rebels going out
to battle, with their own transport, their own medical
service, their own field communications, their own supply service—and, above all, their perfect faith. The
hour was great.

I went with Giddy into the "square" formed by the
men, to address a few words to them before they went
out to battle. It was eight years since I had given a
public speech. Perhaps for the first time in my life I
suffered from acute "stage fright." Most of the men did
not know me, except as a name and a symbol. I said
to them:

"Men of the Irgun! We are going out to conquer

Jaffa. We are going into one of the decisive battles for
the independence of Israel. Know who is before you,
and remember whom you are leaving behind you. Before you is a cruel enemy who has risen to destroy us.
Behind you are parents, brothers, children. Smite the
enemy hard. Aim true. Save your ammunition. In battle, show no more mercy to the enemy than he shows
mercy to our people. But spare women and children.
Whoever raises his hands in surrender has saved his
life. You will not harm him. You will be led in the attack by Lieutenant Gideon. You have only one direction—forward."

Giddy added his instructions. He emphasized particularly the necessity for saving ammunition, of which
we could never have enough. Line after line, the men
filed out silently to the main road.

The long line of trucks moved off in the direction
of Tel Aviv and threaded its way towards Jaffa. We
entered Tel Aviv at the third night watch. The narrow
streets leading to Jaffa were deserted. In the ruined
buildings of the Alliance School we set up our Staff
Headquarters. In the deserted Freud Hospital we established a field hospital. The men were accommodated
in the neighbouring houses.

Our original plan had been to launch the attack during the night. But the necessary consultations at Dov
Camp had taken time. One delay led to another. It was
impossible to attack as soon as we arrived. There was
still much to be done. The units had to be checked.
Their commanders had to be given a final briefing. The
field telephone system had to be established. And, most
important, the mortars had to be set up.

We had two three-inch mortars: exactly two. They
were British made. We had borrowed them—in a "confiscation" operation more than two years earlier. We
had never used them before because we had no ammunition to fit. And mortars without shells are as useful as
a pen without ink.

For two years these two mortars were the "white
elephants" in our stores. But now it was the 25th of
April. A week earlier we had held up a military train

and had been "disappointed"; shells, shells and more shells. Now we were disappointed no longer. We had mated the mortars with their shells. Only two mortars, it is true, but shells in their thousands.

Mortars and shells may be mated in heaven, but they too need their priest—the gunner who marries them. We had three gunners on the Jaffa front. Hour after hour, day after day, they went on firing and their wonderful hands knew no rest. No wonder, then that the Haganah too wanted to enlist their aid.

On the third day of the battle we were asked by the Haganah Command to divert our mortars to the Tel-Arish area in order to enable a badly battered Haganah unit to withdraw. And after the battle for Jaffa we lent the mortars and their gunners to the Haganah in order to clean up the notorious Salameh village—which then fell into the hands of the Haganah without a further shot and without a further casualty.

From the window of the headquarters building I watched our men going into battle. First the column commanded by Joshua, the silent, next the column led by Eli, experienced instructor and officer, then the platoon of "Kabtzan" ("the pauper") whose name was highly appropriate in the financial sense, but who was rich in unsurpassed bravery and in the love his men bore him. Unit after unit, column after column. The sleepless night had left no trace. They were fresh and buoyant and sang a battle song as they moved up. And as I watched this wonderful youth and heard their singing, I uttered a silent prayer that the Lord of hosts, mighty in battle, should grant them victory and bring them safely back.

The battle for Jaffa had begun.

The fire of the mortars, directed at the enemy rear, began to sow demoralisation behind his line. In the bottleneck itself the battle was mainly a machine-gun duel. Our Brens played well. But their tune was not the only one in the battle symphony. What was that? Giddy knew at once. The enemy was using Spandaus, whose fire-power is much greater than that of any Bren. And the enemy, it seemed, was not short of ammunition.

Burst followed burst. An almost incessant hail of fire poured down on our boys. The enemy had other advantages. In the bottleneck of Manshieh we learnt what all the armies had learnt in the Second World War: there are few better defensive positions than a row of ruined buildings. The buildings in the front area, which during the months of disturbance had been in a "No Man's Land," were nearly all in ruins. Inside and on top of these broken buildings the enemy had established himself with his numerous heavy machine-guns and his apparently limitless quantities of ammunition. Jaffa's defence line was thick and very deep. The Arabs apparently were working under trained and skilful advisers. Their positions were cleverly fortified and they had set up "hedgehog" defences in depth.

And behind the first line, which was of triple or quintuple thickness, there were not only Iraqi and Arab fighters. Behind them stood British troops with tanks and heavy guns, who were positioned to prevent the attackers from reaching the sea.

We began to suffer our first casualties. Among them was Tzadok on the high observation post, who was hit in the head. Many were wounded. The medical service —perhaps the most difficult of war services—had its hands full of work, and blood. There, dashing about and succouring the wounded, ran Moshe Atlet, deeply religious, "equipped" with long side-curls, and armed with a revolver. With him "Topsy," the Yemenite girl who had accompanied the boys in their attack on Lydda airfield. Next to her, Nitzah, of a martyred Hebron family. They and their comrades dashed in and out of the line of fire carrying the stretchers with wounded comrades.

But our men could not break through. In the first frontal clash we were repulsed. We had taken important positions but we had not broken the enemy line and had not made any significant advance. We had not broken the neck of the bottle. Book-strategists, calculators of the average, will wag their heads: of course; why did you get yourselves into the bottleneck, where you could expect fire from both the north and from the south? Any army whose ill-luck has forced it into a bottleneck tries to get out of it. Yet you, partisans that you are, went into one of your own free will. How could you expect to succeed?

Not so fast, my strategists!

With all respect to the books, you do not know the spirit of Irgun soldiers.

3

At an officers' conference we made our first summing-up. We had not succeeded. We had underestimated the enemy's advantages and his fire-power. The area was narrow. Possibilities of movement were very limited. Our armoured cars could not outflank the enemy and attack his rear. And a frontal attack by large numbers apparently could not effect a break-through. We would have to pull out our main body, leaving only the forces necessary for holding the captured positions—and devise another method of attack. The other method was not new. It was the typical Irgun tactic; break-through and covering parties. Lightning advance by a small party with explosives, a speedy temporary withdrawal; blowing-up of the enemy position; seizing it and continuing the advance. Another explosion—withdrawal—advance.

The method would be slow. It had been effective in the partisan fighting against the Government forces. Then all that had been needed was momentary mastery, sufficient to destroy the objective which was the purpose of the attack. Here on this Jaffa front the situation was different. We had not only to attack and destroy, but to capture, and hold what we had captured. Could our tactics succeed in these conditions?

There was no choice. Giddy redisposed his forces, and, after a rest, prepared to renew the battle. Meantime the gunners would continue to shell Jaffa itself. Thank God the British ammunition-train had been a long one. In half a day we gave back to Jaffa what she had given Tel Aviv in months. The shelling, we calculated, would disrupt the enemy's lines of communication and his contact with the front line. Our spirits rose again.

In the afternoon the battle was resumed with greater intensity. Now the sappers went out carrying the shining canisters of explosives. In the bottleneck were a number of projecting positions, heavily fortified, which squarely blocked the way of advance. Should the sappers succeed in destroying them a narrow breach would have been made, and this could be widened.

But the enemy was wide-awake. The British tanks and the Arab Spandaus covered the whole area with raking fire. The British also threw in anti-tank weapons—of which we were so short. The element of surprise was no longer on our side. We were having to pay for every inch of ground.

On the front line we had to use our hands; men instead of guns; courage and self-sacrifice instead of a "softening-up" by shelling; everything cost us blood. Acquiring the arms for the battle had cost blood; the battle itself cost blood; the first breach cost blood; and even the softening-up for which every army paid in sweat alone, cost us blood. The altar of God demanded sacrifices without number. Now we were offering the best of our sons as a Passover-sacrifice in order to ensure that our days should be renewed as of old.

To the thunder of the mortars and the rattle of the machine-guns were now added mighty explosions. Had the sappers done their work? Had the main enemy positions been destroyed? Explosion followed explosion. Had the breach already been made? Was the road clear for the onslaught of the main forces? It soon transpired that only one enemy position had been destroyed, while the main strongpoint, which dominated the whole area, had not been touched. The explosives had gone off too far away for them to damage the big, fortified building. The sappers had done their best in that withering fire; but they could not get beyond a point from which their explosives only "licked" the walls of the position, they could not shake them. Again we had been repulsed.

* * *

Another consultation of officers. We sat on the benches of one of the classrooms at the Alliance School and made our summing-up for the day. The shelling of Jaffa itself had been effective. There was no doubt about that. We had sent in hundreds of shells, and our observers reported direct hits, dislocation of enemy transport, disruption of his communications and confusion among his forces. Our frontal attack had yielded no results commensurate with the effort but we had to carry on. There was no cause for despondency. The battle had only begun. True, our first attack had failed; but we would try again—and succeed. We would re-dispose our forces. A night's rest was sorely needed by the men. On the morrow we would renew the attack—and we would yet capture the enemy positions.

That in essence was the general opinion voiced that night at our conference at Staff headquarters. Giddy explained that it would be necessary to "upholster" our forward positions, to fortify them with sandbags, etc., and, as we advanced, to upholster every new position we captured. This would give the boys at least a minimum of protection against enemy fire, and it would also enable them to advance sufficiently close to that death-dealing enemy key stronghold.

The conference ended. The decision taken, our hearts were filled with new confidence.

The camp went to sleep. The tired soldiers rested, some in the streets and yards, in the half-ruined buildings. The earth or a floor made them a good enough mattress. Our boys had never been pampered. How often had they slept on the heartbreaking stone of prison floors before being privileged to sleep beneath the sky and the stars with their arms by their sides? In truth they were very happy. As for the battle itself, they entertained not a single doubt. Today had been a failure, but tomorrow would bring victory. Retreat was unthinkable. *Abi gezunt!*

The men of the Irgun slept deep and peacefully. Only the senior officers got not a wink of sleep. Every minute of the night was occupied with planning the morrow's battle.

4

With dawn came the newspapers.

As we read them everything went black. One newspaper reported an "abortive" attack by the Irgun at
Jaffa; a second sounded the alarm of an "exhibitionist
attack" of the Irgun at Jaffa; a third announced a
"barren attack" of the Irgun at Jaffa. Exhibitionist,
abortive, barren—the terms were wonderfully similar.
Somebody had obviously given the newspapers official "guidance."

The Haganah command itself published a communiqué couched in exactly similar "abortive," "barren,"
terms. But they went further. They informed the Press
—including the foreign press correspondents—that the
Irgun had drawn forces from all over the country to
launch the attack on Jaffa. This, after all, was giving
information to the enemy.

But this was not all. The authors of the statement
sank low enough to suggest that the Irgun was less concerned with capturing Bustros Road in Jaffa than with
Allenby Road in Tel Aviv.[1]

[1] "Allenby Road" is another name for the votes of the people
of Tel Aviv. During the years prior to the establishment of the
Jewish State, the leaders of the Jewish Labour-Socialist Party in
Palestine (Mapai) developed their political organisation more
and more effectively until they finally established themselves as
the dominating group in the Government of Israel. These men,
in their legitimate pursuit of political office, always regarded
the Irgun as a dangerous threat to their political influence. Thus
while the Irgun dreamed dreams, and pursued and taught ideals,
and "sacrificed regardless on the altar of the Lord," the men
who dominated the Jewish Agency, and therefore the Haganah,
and therefore, subsequently, the Government of Israel, spoke
a very different language—the language of every-day politics.
Unless this "talking and thinking at cross-purposes" is grasped,
the reader may be led in his mind to do less than justice to the
leaders of Mapai (the "official leaders," the "commanders of
the Haganah," the "Jewish Institutions," as they are variously
termed by the author). Moreover, without this prior knowledge
many of the happenings he relates, such as the "official" attitude
to the Irgun in the battle of Jaffa, might appear to the un-
informed reader as fantastic, if not incredible.

We re-read the statement of the Haganah and discovered a transparent threat in its tail: "The Haganah will not tolerate" etc. We read carefully the articles in the newspapers written to explain and justify the words "abortive" and "barren" used in the headlines. And our hearts sank at the appalling thought that *they actually wanted us to be beaten*. There, well to the rear, sat Jewish journalists and Jewish "commanders" waiting hopefully for the defeat of Jewish boys who, after this great Jewish city had suffered six months of sniping, shelling and murder, had gone out to fight the Jewish people's battle against a merciless enemy. Here at the front the blood of our men was being shed for our people, its salvation and its future; here, at the front, we were fighting so that all our people (including our traducers), should be able to live, to work in peace by day and to sleep secure by night.

And yet, there, in the rear, sat members of our own people who, after the first day of our offensive, gloated that "The Irgun has failed." Could there be a more revolting attitude than this? Was this not yet another example of the shameful "self-hatred" that has plagued us Jews ever since we were exiled from our country nearly two thousand years ago?

I spoke to some of the boys who had begun to get ready for the resumed battle. They had read the statement of the Haganah and the newspapers' reports. But strangely enough there were no signs of anger on their part. They, who were marching to the front line, to a high probability of death in action, accepted the abuse as though it was messages of good will.

The only effect of the vilification was to strengthen their will to win.

Deep within me I paid humble tribute to the greatness of this fighting family. They had freely gone into the "bottleneck"—a moral as well as tactical bottleneck. Facing them was the fire of the enemy; behind their backs the denigration by their own people. Where in all history has an army fought and held out in such circumstances?

Perhaps we ought, by then, to have become accustomed to this kind of double attack: of bullets from one direction and abuse from the other. Throughout the years of revolt we had been subjected to insult and opposition from "official" quarters, yet we had continued to fight.

In the fact of this sickening official denigration it would not have been unnatural had these boys asked their commanders: "Why have you led us into this? What are we doing it for? For whom are we giving our lives?" Would they not have been justified if they had said: "This people is not worth our sacrifice. Let those heroes from the rear come up the line and bare their chests to the enemy's bullets. Why should we stand up to Arab bullets and British shells merely to earn Jewish curses?"

Yet, not one man asked any such questions. They read the Tel Aviv newspapers and smiled, or clenched their teeth. Their reaction was unanimous; we will fight on and win, in spite of the enemy and in spite of our Jewish illwishers in the rear.

On that tragic morning of April the 28th, 1948, the little band of Irgun fighters on the Jaffa front displayed a brave and lofty grandeur of spirit, unsurpassed, I venture to claim, in the whole story of human valour.

But let me hasten to record that during that day the band of fighters was compensated for its silent sorrow by the attitude of the mass of the population of Tel Aviv. During that day, and the days that followed, it became clear that the spiteful vituperation of the "inspired" Press and the Haganah were as remote from the true feelings of the people as they were from the truth.

5

While these events were developing in Tel Aviv, Giddy launched the renewed attack on Jaffa. The mortars poured in hundreds of shells, "pin-pointing" by map and by control from the observation posts. The gunners had special orders to avoid hitting hospitals, houses of prayer, and buildings bearing the flags of foreign States. The previous day the French Consul had visited our Headquarters and asked us to refrain from bombarding the various charitable institutions maintained in Jaffa by France. We naturally agreed, insisting only that these buildings should hoist the French flag. Other institutions followed the French example and were similarly spared.

The shelling grew heavier and more effective. Then our units leapt forward and stormed the enemy positions in the bottleneck. The struggle lasted for many hours, almost until nightfall, and was tougher even than that of the first day. Beneath our increasing pressure the enemy troops were driven from a number of positions. At last they began to retreat in disorder.

But once again the British forces came to the rescue. On the first day a British officer in Jaffa had appealed to certain Jewish circles in Tel Aviv to "influence" us not to attack the British forces still stationed in Jaffa—at the railway station and in the security zone. He had promised that if we did not attack them they would "remain neutral." But this promise had been brazenly broken on the very first day. The "neutrality" was of a very special kind: it turned the tracks of the British tanks and pressed the triggers of machine-guns and cannons, sowing "neutral" death among the Jewish forces. On the second day of the battle this very peculiar "neutrality" became even more strange. The British Commissioner of the Lydda district (which included Jaffa) informed the Mayor of Tel Aviv that the British Army was determined to prevent the conquest of Jaffa if necessary by force, and that if the Jewish institutions did not put a stop to the Irgun attack, the Army would go into action against our men.

The truth, of course, was that in fact the British force did not have to go into action—it had never been out of action. The only change was that on the second day the British force increased its activities against us, in order to prevent the impending collapse of the Arab front; and in order to hold on to Jaffa for the overall plan, due to come into effect on May the 15th.

The battle, in consequence, became immeasurably

more difficult for us. But our pressure, exerted by soldiers who were resolved to win, was very great and the enemy was obliged to draw back. Many of his positions were overrun. But before our boys could dig themselves in, the mixed Anglo-Arab forces launched a vigorous counter-attack, supported by heavy artillery, and forced us to withdraw. In this manner positions changed hands again and again. And the battle raged fiercely.

Again we suffered many casualties. But every man who fell was at once replaced. Isolated incidents pierce the smoke of battle and light up the spirit. Nitzah, the girl stretcher bearer, seeing one of our Bren-gunners killed, jumped into his place and fired his gun until she was relieved by another Bren-gunner. Again we attacked and occupied enemy positions; again we advanced. But still we had not broken through.

Then a strange phenomenon was revealed before our eyes: the mass flight from Jaffa. Arab civilians and a variety of Arab "fighters" suddenly began to leave the town in panic.

There appear to have been two causes for this epidemic flight. One was the name of their attackers and the repute which propaganda had bestowed on them. The Beirut correspondent of the United Press cabled that when the first boat-load of refugees arrived there from Jaffa they reported that the information that this attack was being made by the Irgun had thrown the population into a state of abject fear. The second factor was the weight of our bombardment. I do not know exactly how many shells we sent into Jaffa. Yigal Yadin,[1] Operations Officer of the Haganah, told me afterwards that we had not been sufficiently economical with our precious shells. The total load was certainly very heavy. We went all out: the choice was between the subjugation of Jaffa and the destruction of Tel Aviv; and we had resolved to give our lives to avert the latter.

Our shelling made the free movement of enemy

[1] Subsequently Chief of Staff of the Israel Army.

forces impossible and forced them to seek doubtful
shelter in buildings. It disrupted telephone communications, cut the electricity supply, and broke water mains.
Confusion and terror, deepened by the noise of the battle raging at no great distance from the central streets,
reigned in the town. Thus the morale of the enemy was
broken, and the great flight began, by sea and land, on
wheels and on foot. It started with thousands, but very
quickly tens of thousands were sucked into the panic
flood. British sources reported numerous Arab casualties in all parts of the town. A concentration of Iraqi
"volunteers" suffered a direct hit and more than a hundred of them were killed or injured. The enemy was
given no rest and could find no shelter.

The British military authorities tried to calm the panic
stricken Arabs. Jaffa was in utter confusion. The streets
were flooded, the houses gaping and tottering, looting
and murder were rife. There was no authority that could
now prevent the complete evacuation of the town.

The mass flight from Jaffa carried away not only the
civilian population but fighting men as well, not only
in Jaffa but in the surrounding neighbourhood. On the
heels of our attack on Jaffa the Abu-Kebir area fell into
Jewish hands without a shot. I was told later by Haganah officers that Abu-Kebir was so efficiently and
strongly fortified that it could have been held for an
indefinite period.

6

While the second day's battle was in full swing, I went
with Avraham at the invitation of the Jewish Agency
and the Haganah, to meet Galili and Yigal Yadin in
order to clear up the "certain details" on which depended the implementation of our agreement with the
Haganah. As the meeting had been so long delayed, and
the end of British rule was rapidly approaching, there
was not much left to clear up. We suggested that the
clause referring to the seizure of British arms should
not be nullified by automatic disapproval in advance,
but should be implemented in consultation and by mu-

tual agreement. We also discussed plans for operations against the Arabs. This was my first meeting with Yigal Yadin. Several days later, after the fall of Jaffa, I arranged a meeting between him and Giddy. The two young Operations Officers were drawn to each other at once. Giddy praised Yadin to me: "He is young," he said. "He knows what he wants and is full of energy. He is like one of us." Yadin was equally impressed with Giddy. "If Giddy plans an operation," he said, "it will be no whit inferior to any plans I make. I depend on him absolutely."

At that first meeting we also discussed Jaffa. The attack on Jaffa, which had begun in a storm of abuse from "official quarters," now became an operation "approved" by the Haganah.

I returned to our headquarters as the second day's fighting was drawing to a close. It had not been without successes. We had captured a number of bridgeheads preparatory to a breakthrough. Our officers and men had learnt to know the enemy and the terrain. They had also learnt to avoid the mistakes of the previous day. But still the objective had not been attained. Jaffa was not yet "opened." We had not reached the sea. The neck of the bottle had not been smashed.

I called a conference of officers. I gave them an account of the meeting with the Haganah chiefs and how they had agreed to the continuation of the assault if there was a chance of breaking through the enemy lines within 24 hours.

"But," I said, "I do not think we should go on battering our heads against these fortified positions which are in any case covered by British tanks. We have done our best for two days. In these circumstances it is no disgrace—not even for the Irgun—to suspend the direct assault. We shall defend the line we have taken with a strong holding unit. The rest of our troops we shall withdraw."

The atmosphere in the map room became tense. Giddy was silent for a long time. Other officers expressed their opinions on my proposal—some for, many against.

Finally the decision we took was to withdraw most of the units and to leave a limited force at the Alliance School base. It meant the suspension of the direct assault.

That night, however, something strange happened. For the first time in its history the soldiers of the Irgun "mutinied." They point blank refused to carry out the order to withdraw. "Deputations" began arriving in the map room. They spoke in varying styles but to the same effect: "We will not abandon the field. Only let us try once more; we promise to beat them this time. We have not weakened. We will beat them right enough."

Giddy returned from a lengthy tour of the front lines. His face was drawn and wan. He stood before me covered in dirt and dust from crawling on hands and knees, but his fine eyes were burning with refreshed faith.

"I have found some new weak points in the enemy's positions," he said. "I am sure we can break through."

From the front line came the noise of desultory machine-gun fire and shelling—a lull in the storm of battle. I sat in the dim map room and pondered the wondrous phenomenon of this debate between a Commander and his men.

The debate came to an end. The "mutiny" of the men had succeeded. There would be no retreat. The attack would be resumed.

7

It was late at night. The men should have been sleeping, getting a little energy back for the morrow but there was no rest in the camp that night. New strength flowed miraculously into muscles which had been utterly worn out. The officers bent over their maps, working out the details of the plan. Here Joshua would advance, there Eli, here Kabtzan would try to break through. And sappers? Sappers were needed, "living artillery" capable of blowing up building after building, strongpoint after strongpoint. This required not only courage but technical skill and extraordinary agility and perseverance. There were many volunteers. Kabtzan recommended a number of them, headed by Rahamin, a young Yemenite with big black eyes, handsome as a prince, quiet, very polite, reserved, with a good-natured smile that came easily to his lips.

Feverish preparations continued into the morning hours, but the battle did not begin until afternoon. The mortars began to rumble once again, and from their hot jaws leapt hundreds of shells. The decisive battle for Jaffa flared into a mighty blaze.

From the positions already captured and "upholstered" with sandbags our battle units advanced. Their path was hewn out for them by the "living artillery," the sappers. Between two walls of fire—the enemy fire and the covering fire—the sappers crawled and wriggled and dashed along bringing their explosives up to the enemy positions; they lit the fuse, drew back—and then on forward again. The thunder of the explosions was deafening. Step by step, foot by foot, the enemy was pushed back from his positions.

This time the British support and the fire from their tanks were unable to stem the advance. They did indeed subject our line to a gruelling fire, but the line held. And the enemy's main strongpoint, which had blocked our way to the sea for two days and two nights, was at last in our hands.

As though carried along by unseen forces, Rahamin and his comrades went from point to point, from explosion to explosion, and opened the way to victory for their comrades.

But the way through was not opened by explosives alone. A new "weapon" was introduced into the battle: picks. Picks and crow bars were the "weapons" used by the boys to make passages through the ruined buildings.

Giddy obeyed the classic rule of modern strategy: dig in and consolidate every captured position.

Inside the "tunnel" which was created there stretched a number of living "chains." One, for the attack, consisted of the sappers and soldiers; a second of wounded and medical personnel; a third for supply, consisted of bearers of ammunition, equipment, water; a fourth —for entrenchment—of the bearers of sandbags and the "upholsterers." Chain interlocked with chain. Sometimes the "upholsterers" went into battle; sometimes the first-aiders became Bren-gunners, or vice versa. But the chains were not broken. Their living links sprang from opening to opening, from one post blown up to another captured; from building to building, from alley to alley. The links were raked with machine-gun fire. On the Jaffa front there were practically no "dead zones," areas which could be crossed without risk. And if one link fell the breach was filled at once by another. Thus the chains went on, back and forth, back and forth.

Suddenly the supply of sandbags ran out. That night some unusual "robberies" took place in Tel Aviv. Storerooms and shops were broken into. But neither gold nor silver was taken. nothing—except sacks. The "robbers" were even stranger. They were—Jewish policemen, the defenders of law and order. Sacks, sacks, sacks, thousands and thousands of sacks for the Jaffa front!

So the chain of fire and blood and toil and sand, of battle and conquest, stretched itself forward. This phase of the battle began on Tuesday afternoon and ended on Wednesday morning. Fifteen hours without rest. Advance between two walls of fire. A "tunnel" in the midst of the fire; a dark burning tunnel. A new method of street-fighting. A supreme effort of mind, body and spirit. The "hedgehog" defences did not save the enemy. Nor did his strategic advantages. Nor his withering, merciless fire power. The enemy was pressed back to the sea, north and south. His positions were blown into the sky. And over the ruins and smoking piles came the sappers and fighters. They recognised only one direction—forward; only one objective—the sea. Only one aspiration was in their hearts: victory. And thus they conquered.

It was nine o'clock in the morning. With the lines of broken enemy fortifications behind them, the boys at long last reached the sea-shore. Giddy, triumphant, was at their head. The sea was lovely, peaceful and calm, and little waves gently caressed their feet by way of greeting.

When our men reached the sea they were wild with joy. They danced and sang, waved their arms, wasted ammunition by firing into the air. Their rejoicing, after all they had endured and suffered and achieved, was forgiveable. Now Jaffa lay before them, defenceless, on her knees.

Only Giddy was not carried away. He, too, appreciated that we had arrived, and conquered and won. But as a battle commander he knew that though the enemy line was broken and the enemy defeated, the battle was not ended and a counter-attack might be expected at any moment.

The counter-attack came sure enough and lasted for two whole days. The British forces now did not content themselves with helping the Arabs. They began to play "first fiddle." Tanks, heavy machine-guns, two-inch and heavier mortars, guns and even planes were thrown into the battle, in order to wrest the fruits of victory from us and to prevent the capture of Jaffa—as the Lydda District Commissioner had warned the Jews and promised the Arabs.

The counter-attack was also a "defensive attack." On Thursday, the fifth day of the battle for Jaffa, the British forces opened a very heavy shelling of our positions. Many of our men were killed; many were injured. Among those blown to pieces by British shells—we could only collect his scattered limbs—was Lieutenant Joshua, one of our best battle commanders. And among those who were killed by British fire was Lieutenant Uri, the Tel Aviv Regional Commander, a gallant officer who, dashing forward to blow up a building so as to close the path to an armoured car, fell dead from its bullets.

After the shelling and the attack the British authorities announced officially that it was not their intention to attack Tel Aviv, but "to prevent the further advance of the Irgun Zvai Leumi into Jaffa." *From a military point of view Arab Jaffa had fallen to the Irgun Zvai Leumi on the morning of Tuesday, 27th April.* Its immediate

capture was prevented only by "British Jaffa" with its
tanks and guns and mortars and *'planes and its threat
to destroy Tel Aviv*. But the ultimate Jewish conquest
of Jaffa could no longer be prevented.

It is true, therefore, that British forces prevented by
force of arms our further advance into the now almost
dead city. But the British authorities wanted more;
they wanted Manshieh back under their control. We
clung for two days to our new line and repulsed wave
after wave of enemy counter-attacks. Our line never
broke.

While the counter-attack was still in progress, our
units began mopping up Manshieh itself. The Manshieh
Police Station fell without a shot. A pocket of resistance
was encountered at the Hassan Bek Mosque, but it
easily yielded. The Mosque was not damaged. On its
high tower we hoisted our flag. The whole of Tel Aviv
saw it that Wednesday morning. Tremendous crowds
stood and feasted their eyes on the spectacle. For six
months that tower had sniped death into the streets of
the city—and now at last redemption had come.

During the mopping-up operation a grave incident
occurred. A group of Arabs put up their hands in surrender. As our unit approached, however, one of the
Arabs drew a revolver and shot our unit commander
dead. The Arab was killed on the spot. But our men
were boiling with anger, and it was no easy matter re-
straining them from wreaking vengeance.

8

While the prisoners were being taken, while the en-
circled area was being mopped up and the British
counter-attack was developing, we called a Press Conference in the map-room: the first Press Conference
after years of revolt and war. The newspapermen, both
local and foreign, had bombarded us incessantly
throughout the days of battle: they wanted information.
A mortar shell fell in the courtyard, a few dozen yards
from the map-room. The counter-attack was in full

swing. Some of our guests asked us to shorten the explanations.

In opening the meeting I could not resist the temptation to "counter-attack" myself.

"Gentlemen," I said, "we have invited you to see the results of the futile, showy, abortive attack of the Irgun Zvai Leumi."

And they saw and wondered.

Tel Aviv was in transports of joy. Huge crowds filled the streets cheering the victors. A feeling of tremendous relief, of a mortal danger overcome—a danger to every man, woman and child—pervaded them. Jaffa would no longer be able to attack Tel Aviv. Thousands of refugees, who had been living in passage ways and under staircases, would be able to return to their homes.

The British G.H.Q. for the Middle East announced that the Irgun Zvai Leumi attack on Jaffa, which was outside the area allocated to the Jews in the U.N. decision, had brought about a radical change in the situation and necessitated a redisposition of the British forces in the area. The B.B.C. added that British forces hastily flown in from Cyprus and Malta had landed at Jaffa in order to prevent the town from falling into the hands of the Jews. These statements were designed to frighten the Jews and hearten the Arabs; but they, too, were of no avail.

We replied to the implied threats of the British authorities with a hint of our own: "The Irgun still has thousands of three-inch mortal shells and there are still British camps in Eretz Israel. We understood the British were anxious to effect the evacuation of their troops undisturbed and without further casualties. Let the British think it over."

The Jewish institutions were not inclined to take our advice. But we helped them by other means. Using a substantial load of explosives, we turned the Manshieh Police Station, which the British had demanded for themselves, into a heap of ruins. And by blowing up house after house on both sides of the main street we effectively blocked it to all possible traffic to Tel Aviv.

The British, their sense of realism restored, agreed to a "new line," the line fixed by the Irgun soldiers. This line, in due course, safe and sound, we handed over to the Haganah.

The fate of Jaffa was sealed. A few days later the "Emergency Committee" representing the remnants of the population asked for "terms." Early in May—on the eve of the invasion by the five Arab states—the Emergency Committee signed the surrender of the town. It was received by the Haganah Tel Aviv Regional Commander. The town was occupied jointly by Haganah and Irgun units.

9

It might seem that the capture of Jaffa is unconnected with the Jewish rising against British rule. But in political and historical perspective it is in fact part of it. For it was not by chance that the British Government wanted to hold on to Jaffa at any price. As a wedge sticking into the heart of Tel Aviv it was designed to serve the Mandatory's plan of "exit and re-entry." Jaffa was intended to threaten Tel Aviv *after* the 15th of May, especially after the 15th of May. Jaffa was designed to paralyze Tel Aviv and to tie down Jewish forces. Jaffa was an instrument—perhaps the chief instrument—in the attempt to subjugate the Jews and to reduce them to asking for British "mediation" and "guardianship." This plan was foiled; and we foiled it just in time, at the end of April.

During the three weeks that remained before the invasion by the armies of the five Arab States, the Arabs, under British military direction, would have poured into Jaffa more forces, more arms and more heavy guns for the bombardment of Tel Aviv. There is no certainty that the British forces would have left Jaffa on the 15th of May. In other parts of the country they stayed on until the middle of July.

But let us assume that the British Government kept their promise and evacuated Jaffa on the 15th of May. By then we should have operated not only against strengthened enemy forces, but in entirely different conditions. Beginning with the morning of the 15th of May came the Egyptian bombing of Tel Aviv from the air, which repeatedly paralyzed all traffic in the city. These were the conditions in which we should have had to move forces, bring up reinforcements, supplies, food and ammunition to the many fronts hemming in Tel Aviv no less than they hemmed in Jaffa.

That is not all. Gaza is not far from Jaffa by sea. The Egyptian forces that landed in Gaza could have landed even more conveniently in Jaffa. On the 15th of May we had neither a Jewish Navy nor a Jewish Air Force.

The miracle of dissidence again saved our people. Our attack on Jaffa at the eleventh hour not only saved Tel Aviv from certain destruction. Our "premature" attack, which brought obstreperous Jaffa to its knees before it could rise to destroy us, saved the whole Jewish front from breaking. The conquest of Jaffa was one of the fateful events in the Hebrew war of independence.

Chapter XXX

Dawn

On the 10th or 11th of May, 1948, the chief of the Haganah informed me that the majority of the official institutions had at last succeeded in overcoming their many doubts and had agreed to the proclamation of a Provisional Hebrew Government immediately on the withdrawal of the Mandatory regime. I told my informant that we would recognise the Provisional Government and give it our support without regard to its composition. But I added this grave warning: "If the Jewish Government is proclaimed on Friday, May the 14th, the first enemy planes will be over Tel Aviv on Saturday morning."

Our thoughts were concentrated on the development of the battle for our independence, for our existence, on the many fronts that were about to be opened, in the north, the south and the east, in the air and on the sea. Nevertheless it was impossible not to dwell on the great and wondrous event occurring before our very eyes. A regime resting on a hundred thousand bayonets had collapsed; and in its place and on its ruins a new regime was about to arise; a nation was coming to life; a very old nation which had gone down into the pit of destruction was being re-born.

There is no doubt that revival of Hebrew national independence in our generation has no precedent in human history. A nation had been driven out of its country after the loss of its liberty and the utter failure of its uprisings. It had wandered about the face of the earth for nearly two thousand years. Its wanderings had been drenched in blood. And now, in the seventy-first generation of its exile this wandering people had returned to its Homeland. The secular tour was ended. The circle of wanderings was closed and the nation had returned to the Motherland that bore it.

The miracle of Return was accompanied by the miracle of Revival. Within a generation there developed within the Jewish people the strength to take up arms, to rise against alien rule, to throw off the yoke of oppression. How long, how endless were the years of exile, of humiliation and destruction. And how short, in comparison, were the years of revival, reinvigoration, and armed uprising. History has no parallel in its records.

On Saturday night, May the 15th, I went to the secret radio station of the Irgun Zvai Leumi opposite Meir Park, in the centre of Tel Aviv. I felt no stage-fright. I was among my friends, in "my house," in the radio station from which the voice of Revolt and Freedom had for years gone forth to every town and village in our land. But the solemnity of the hour overawed me:

"After many years of underground warfare" (I told my listeners) "years of persecution and moral and physical suffering, the rebels against the oppressor stand before you, with a blessing of thanks on their lips and a prayer in their hearts. The blessing is the age-old blessing with which our fathers and our forefathers have always greeted Holy Days. It was with this blessing that they used to taste any fruit for the first time in the season. Today is truly a holiday, a Holy Day, and a new fruit is visible before our very eyes. The Hebrew revolt of 1944-48 has been blessed with success—the first Hebrew revolt since the Hasmonean insurrection that has ended in victory. The rule of oppression in our country has been beaten, uprooted; it has crumbled and been dispersed. The State of Israel has arisen in bloody battle. The high way for the mass return to Zion has been cast up.

"The foundation has been laid—but only the foundation—for true independence. One phase of the battle for freedom, for the return of the whole People of Israel to its homeland, for the restoration of the whole Land of Israel to its God-covenanted owners, has ended. But only one phase. . . .

"The State of Israel has arisen. And it has arisen 'Only Thus:'[1] Through blood, through fire, with an outstretched hand and a mighty arm, with sufferings and with sacrifices. It could not have been otherwise. And yet, even before our State is able to set up its normal national institutions, it is compelled to fight—or to continue to fight satanic enemies and blood-thirsty mercenaries, on land, in the air and on the sea. In these circumstances, the warning sounded by the Philosopher-President Thomas Masaryk to the Czechoslovak nation when it attained its freedom after three hundred years of slavery, has a special significance for us.

"In 1918 when Masaryk stepped out on to the Wilson railway station in Prague, he warned his cheering countrymen: 'It is difficult to set up a State; it is even more difficult to keep it going.' In truth, it has been difficult for us to set up our State. Tens of generations and millions of wanderers, from one land of massacre to another, were needed; it was necessary that there be exile, burning at the stake and torture in the dungeons; we had to suffer agonising disillusionments; we needed the warnings—though they often went unheeded—of prophets and of seers; we needed the sweat and toil of generations of pioneers and builders; we had to have an uprising of rebels to crush the enemy; we had to have the gallows, the banishments beyond seas, the prisons, and the cages in the deserts—all this was necessary that we might reach the present stage where six hundred thousand Jews are in the Homeland, where the direct rule of oppression has been driven out, and Hebrew independence declared in part at least of the country, the whole of which is ours.

"It has been difficult to create our state. But it will be still more difficult to keep it going. We are surrounded

---

[1] "Only Thus" was the legend beneath the emblem of the Irgun Zvai Leumi, a raised right arm grasping a bayonetted rifle. This device was bestowed upon the Irgun by its founder, Vladimir Jabotinsky, who, in the teeth of bitter opposition from "official" Zionist quarters, taught the Jewish people that they would have to fight for their national freedom which they would achieve "only thus." His prophesy was amply vindicated.

by enemies who long for our destruction. And that same oppressor, who has been defeated by us directly, is trying indirectly to make us surrender with the aid of mercenaries from the south, the north and the east. Our one-day-old state is set up in the midst of the flames of battle. And the first pillar of our state must therefore be victory, total victory, in the war which is raging all over the country. For this victory, without which we shall have neither freedom nor life, we need arms; weapons of all sorts, in order to strike the enemies, in order to disperse the invaders, in order to free the entire length and breadth of the country from its would-be destroyers.

"But in addition to these arms, each and everyone of us has need of another weapon, a spiritual weapon, the weapon of unflinching endurance in face of attacks from the air; in face of grievous casualties; in face of local disasters and temporary defeats; unflinching resistance to threats and cajolery. If, within the coming days and weeks we can put on this whole armour of an undying nation in resurrection, we shall in the meantime receive the blessed arms with which to drive off the enemy and bring freedom and peace to our nation and country.

"But, even after emerging victorious from this campaign—and victorious we shall be—we shall still have to exert superhuman efforts in order to remain independent, in order to free our country. First of all it will be necessary to increase and strengthen the fighting arm of Israel, without which there can be no freedom and no survival for our Homeland. . . .

"We shall need a wise foreign policy in order to free our country and maintain our State. We must turn our declaration of independence into a reality. And we must grasp this fact: that so long as even one British or any other foreign soldier treads the soil of our country, our sovereign independence remains nothing but an aspiration, an aspiration for whose fulfilment we must be ready to fight not only on the battlefront but also in the international arena. Secondly, we must establish and maintain the principle of reciprocity in our relations with the nations of the world. There must be no self-denigration. There must be no surrender, no favouritism. There must be reciprocity. Enmity for enmity. Aid for aid. Friendship must be repaid with friendship. . . .

"We must foster friendship and understanding between us and every nation, great or small, strong or weak, near or far, which recognises our independence, which aids our national regeneration, and which is interested, even as we are, in international justice and peace among nations.

"Of no less importance is our internal policy. The first pillar of this policy is the return to Zion. Ships! For heaven's sake, let us have ships! Let us not be poisoned with inertia. Let us not talk empty words about absorptive capacity. Let us not make restrictions for the sake of so-called order. Quickly! Quickly! Our nation has no time! Bring in hundreds of thousands. . . . We are now in the midst of a war for survival; and our tomorrow and theirs depend on the quickest concentration of our nation's exiles.

"And within our Homeland: justice must be the supreme ruler, the ruler over all rulers. There must be no tyranny. The Ministers and officials must be the servants of the nation and not their masters. There must be no exploitation. There must be no man within our country—be he citizen or foreigner—compelled to go hungry, to want for a roof over his head, or to lack elementary education. 'Remember ye were strangers in the land of Egypt'—this supreme rule must continually light our way in our relations with the strangers within our gates. 'Righteousness, Righteousness shalt thou pursue!' Righteousness must be the guiding principle in our relations amongst ourselves. . . .

"The Irgun Zvai Leumi is leaving the underground inside the boundaries of the Hebrew independent state. We went underground, we *arose* in the underground under the rule of oppression, in order to strike at oppression and to overthrow it. And right well have we struck. Now, for the time being we have Hebrew rule in part of our homeland. And as in this part there will be Hebrew Law—and that is the only rightful law in this country—there is no need for a Hebrew underground.

In the State of Israel we shall be soldiers and builders. And we shall respect its government, for it is our government. . . .

"The State of Israel has arisen, but we must remember that our country is not yet liberated. The battle continues, and you see now that the words of your Irgun fighters were not vain words: it is Hebrew arms which decide the boundaries of the Hebrew State. So it is now in this battle; so it will be in the future. Our God-given country is a unity. The attempt to dissect it is not only a crime but a blasphemy and an abortion. Whoever does not recognise our natural right to our entire homeland, does not recognise our right to any part of it. And we shall never forego this natural right. We shall continue to foster the aspiration of full independence.

"Citizens of the Hebrew State, soldiers of Israel, we are in the midst of battles. Difficult days lie ahead of us. . . . We cannot buy peace from our enemies with appeasement. There is only one kind of 'peace' that can be bought—the peace of the graveyard, the peace of Treblinki. Be brave of spirit and ready for more trials. We shall withstand them. The Lord of Hosts will help us; he will sustain the bravery of the Hebrew youth, the bravery of the Hebrew mothers who, like Hannah, offer their sons on the altar of God.

"And you, brothers of our fighting family, do you remember how we started? With what we started? You were alone and persecuted, rejected, despised and numbered with the transgressors. But you fought on with deep faith and did not retreat; you were tortured but you did not surrender; you were cast into prison but you did not yield; you were exiled from your country but your spirit was not crushed; you were driven to the gallows but went forth with a song. You have written a glorious page in history. . . . You will not recall past grievances; you will ask for no reward.

"But for the time being let us think of the battle, for only the outcome of the battle will decide our fate and future. We shall go on our way into battle, soldiers of the Lord of Hosts, inspired by the spirit of our ancient heroes, from the conquerors of Canaan to the Rebels of Judah. We shall be accompanied by the spirit of those who revived our nation, Zeev Benjamin Herzl, Max Nordau, Joseph Trumpeldor and the father of resurrected Hebrew Heroism, Zeev Jabotinsky. We shall be accompanied by the spirit of David Raziel, greatest of the Hebrew commanders of our day; and by Dov Gruner, one of the greatest of Hebrew soldiers. We shall be accompanied into batle by the spirit of the heroes of the gallows, the conquerors of death. And we shall be accompanied into battle by the spirit of the martyrs, our ancestors tortured and burned for their faith, our murdered fathers and butchered mothers, our murdered brothers and strangled children. And in this battle we shall break the enemy and bring salvation to our people, tried in the furnace of persecution, thirsting only for freedom, for righteousness and for justice. . . ."

*   *   *

I went out into the night. The streets of Tel Aviv were deserted. That morning the city had had a taste of aerial bombardment.

My comrades told me that almost every Jewish home with a radio had listened in to my address, and I was thankful to learn that my words had helped to hearten the people.

Darkness was all about us. Black-out. Not a glimmer of light. The darkness would continue. Blood would still be shed. But beyond the sorrow and the darkness the rosy dawn was breaking through. We had come forth from slavery to freedom. On the morrow the sun would shine.

And Jewish children once more would laugh.

Chapter XXXI

We Bow Our Heads

This is not a history of the Jewish revolt against the Mandatory rule in Eretz Israel. The revolt—not the direct armed uprising, but the political and spiritual revolt—did not begin in 1944. In historic perspective the revolt will be seen to have begun in 1920, when Jabotinsky fired the first shot in the defence of the Old City of Jerusalem. Though the immediate target of that shot was the Arab rioter, it struck indirectly at the regime and its plans, to which the savage sentence inflicted on Jabotinsky and his followers bears testimony. During the quarter of a century that followed, there were numerous rebellious phenomena, in Eretz Israel and abroad, in song and deed, in thought and demonstration, with plough and rifle—until the revolt broke out in all its ferocity. In the years between 1944 and 1947 it developed into a military uprising against British rule.

This is not a history of the Irgun Zvai Leumi. The underground organisation for liberation called Irgun Zvai Leumi in Eretz Israel arose years before the outbreak of the direct armed revolt. The beginning of the I.Z.L. may be found in the Jewish Legion formed by Jabotinsky and Joseph Trumpeldor during the First World War. The spring from which the Irgun was nurtured was Betar—in both senses.

In 1938 when certain Arabs, with the encouragement of the authorities, organised attacks on the Jews, the Irgun Zvai Leumi, under the supreme leadership of Vladimir Jabotinsky and under the direct command of David Raziel, performed the decisive act: they revolted against the heritage of the Diaspora, they broke with the policy of "self-restraint" and went out to attack. Heroism and self-sacrifice characterised those earlier fighters, who paved the way for the rebels of later years.

I have written neither the history of the revolt, nor of the Irgun. Nor have I written the history of the military uprising itself, nor even dealt with all the factors which made the revolt or with all those who shared in it. Many are the names I have not mentioned—yet they are names that should be engraved in the memory of our people. Even of those I have mentioned—often under their underground pseudonyms—I have written only a fraction of the wonderful things there are to tell about them and what they did. I have not written history, nor do I pretend even to have painted a general picture. I have merely presented a few chapters on the most important events of the period as they are reflected in personal memories.

The full history of the revolt, the history of the Irgun and of the armed uprising against the Mandatory rule, has yet to be written. It is right that every act performed for the liberation of our people should be recorded and remembered. It is right that everybody who worked in one way or another for the creation of reborn Hebrew strength and for its application in the struggle for liberation should be singled out and remembered. In what we call history there is considerable injustice. History, especially the chronicles of war and revolt, records the names of a few who stood at the head. But the truth is that often the main work is done by the "craftsmen," the rank-and-file, the unknown soldiers. Let us not reconcile ourselves to this historic injustice. The chronicles of the Jewish struggle for liberation should be written in their entirety. Let not those who carried out the undertaking, the unknown soldiers, be left to the fate of Kohelet's "poor wise man."[1]

I am certain that the complete account of the revolt will yet be written. It is important for our people that it should be, not only in order to do justice and to set an example in doing justice. It is important also for the

---

[1] A reference to Ecclesiastes IX 14 and 15.

future, for the education of people in the lore of living as free men. We dwell in a world of violence, in an era of cruelty, when even great nations do not feel secure in their independence. How much so must small nations be watchful in guarding theirs?

We are a small nation which has laid the foundations for its freedom. Our enemies are many; our friends are very few. Who knows what the morrow holds for us, whether there will not be new attempts to subjugate us?

The history of the revolt and the fact of its victory will guide us in the unknown future. They will teach us never to despair even in conditions of enslavement. For a nation, enslaved, dispersed, beaten, decimated, on the brink of utter destruction, can yet arise to rebel against its fate, and so come to life again. Few against many. The weak against the strong. Hounded, isolated, forsaken, abandoned. What of it? No arms? They can be acquired—if needs be from the enemy. No forces? They can be raised. No preparations? The struggle itself will teach and train. Only, man's whole spirit must be utterly devoted to his ideal, and he must be prepared to give his life for it. Perhaps this is the only condition. All the rest will come of itself. If you have the anvil— (love of your country)—and the hammer—(the ideal of freedom)—you will undubitably find the iron from which to fashion the weapons for the struggle.

This is the lore of revolt. All peoples have read of it. It is needed above all by our people. If we learn and remember, we shall overcome all our enemies. They will never succeed in enslaving us again. Never. Even if they overwhelm us we shall throw off their yoke. If we have no arms, we shall make them. If we have no force, we shall create it. They will not break us. The lore of revolt and the spirit of freedom will sustain us and our children.

If these chapters serve in any way to invoke that spirit, and to deepen man's faith in his ability to smash his fetters—the author will be amply rewarded.

But the author knows that it is not he who will have earned this achievement. It is his duty therefore, to pay humble tribute to those whose achievement it is, to all who gave their lives for our people and for the renewal of our days as of old.

I hope, however, that I may be permitted, at the close of these chapters, to pay my last and special tribute to the heroes and martyrs of the Irgun Zvai Leumi.

Their life was struggle; their death heroism; their sacrifice sacred; their memory eternal.

INDEX

A

Aaron, I.Z.L. information officer, 155
Aaronson, Aaron, 454 and n
Aaronson, Sarah, 454 and n
Abdullah, King of Transjordan, 227, 433
Abu Kebir, 131, 468
Achdut Avodah Party, 302 and n
Acre Fortress, 140, 351ff, 377, 392; storming of, 93f, 106f, 115, 142, 318, 363ff, 388, 390, 425
Agronsky, Gershon, 143
Akir camp, 111f, 264
Alex, see under Cahan, Meir
Alkoshi, Mordechai, 124, 349ff, 353ff, 359, 424
Allenby, General, 176
Alon, I.Z.L. officer, 117
Altalena, affair of the, 107, 215ff, 219ff, 228f, 232, 234, 409
American League for a Free Palestine, 219, 409
Amitzur, Bezalel, I.Z.L. officer, 110, 116, 245, 306
"Am Lohem," 165
Amman, 423
Amnon, I.Z.L. officer, 117, 369
Amrani, Shimon, 106, 367ff
Amritsar, 94f
Anglo-American Committee of Inquiry, 251, 270ff, 289, 316, 389, 391
Anglo-Arab-Jewish Conference, London, 280
Anglo-Iraqi oil pipeline, 141
"Arab Bureau" (Cairo), 74
Arab Legion, 221

Arab States, 449, 476
Archer-Cust, Col., 380
Arieh, I.Z.L. Commander, 117
Arnold, Dr., 174
Artigas, J. G., 397
Ashbel, Michael, 265, 320ff, 330f, 338, 367, 370f
Attlee, C. R., 246, 247, 331, 406
Austin, Warren, 99
Auschwitz, 64
Avraham, I.Z.L. Commander, 110, 116, 182, 301, 304, 307, 366, 386, 403f, 441, 468

B

Bagdad, 423
Baldwin, Clark, 406ff
Barazani, Moshe, 349, 358f, 425
Barker, General, 100, 172, 287, 291f, 296, 303, 312f, 338, 342, 349, 424
Bar Kochba, 54 and n
Beersheba, 229
Begin, Benny, 186f
Beirut, 423
Beit-Dajan, 139
Beit-Iksa, 227
Beit-Lidd, 142, 416
Ben-Eliezer, Arieh, 103ff, 109
Bergson, Peter, see under Kook, Hillel
Ben Hecht, the, 250
Ben Yehuda Street explosion, 444
Ben-Zvi, Mr., 162ff
Berlin, Rabbi Meir, 245
Betar, 32, 54 and n, 485
Bethlehem, 128
Beth-Tzouri, 210